Romanian pocket dictionary

English-Romanian & Romanian-English

John Shapiro

Romanian pocket dictionary
by John Shapiro

Edited and published by Fluo!Languages.

First edition: March 2017

This dictionary includes processed information, partly based on data which forms part of the English Wiktionary project.

ENGLISH-ROMANIAN

A

aardvark • *n* porcul termitelor *(m)*
aardwolf • *n* lupul de pmânt *(m)*
abaca • *n* abaca *(f)*
abacus • *n* abac *(n)*, abac *(f)*
abandon • *v* abandona, prsi, lepda, renuna
abandoned • *adj* vicios *(m)*, desfrânat *(n)*, imoral *(n)*, neruinat *(n)*, abandonat *(m)*, prsit *(n)*
abandonment • *n* abandonare *(f)*, abandon *(n)*, renunare *(f)*
abasement • *n* înjosire *(f)*, degradare *(f)*, umilire *(f)*
abashment • *n* jen *(f)*, ruine *(f)*, ruinare *(f)*
abatis • *n* abatiz *(f)*
abattoir • *n* abator *(n)*, mcelrie *(f)*
abbatial • *adj* abaial
abbey • *n* abaie *(f)*
abbreviate • *v* scurta, abrevia, simplifica
abbreviated • *adj* prescurtat *(n)*, abreviat *(n)*
abbreviation • *n* abreviere *(f)*, prescurtare *(f)*, abreviaie *(f)*
abdomen • *n* abdomen *(n)*, burt *(f)*
abdominal • *adj* abdominal *(n)*
abduct • *v* rpi, abduce
abductive • *adj* abductor
abductor • *n* rpitor *(m)*, muchi abductor
abecedary • *n* alfabet *(n)*
aberrance • *n* aberan *(f)*
aberrant • *adj* aberant *(m)*
aberration • *n* deviere *(f)*, deviaie *(f)*, aberaie *(f)*
abhor • *v* abhora, detesta
abhorrence • *n* abhorare *(f)*, aversiune *(f)*, repugnan *(f)*
ability • *n* putin *(f)*, capacitate *(f)*, iscusin, abilitate *(f)*, iscusin *(f)*, îndemânare *(f)*, dibcie *(f)*
abiogenesis • *n* abiogenez *(f)*
abject • *adj* abject
ablactation • *n* ablactaie *(f)*
ablation • *n* ablaiune *(f)*
ablative • *adj* ablativ
ablaut • *n* apofonie *(f)*, ablaut *(n)*
ablaze • *adv* în flcri • *adj* strlucind, scânteind, lucitor
able • *adj* abil, capabil, abilitat *(m)*, competent *(m)*
ablution • *n* splare *(f)*, abluiune *(f)*
abnegation • *n* abnegaie *(f)*
abnormal • *adj* anormal *(n)*, nenormal *(n)*
abnormality • *n* anormalitate *(f)*
abnormity • *n* nenormalitate *(f)*, abnormalitate *(f)*
abolish • *v* aboli, distruge
abolition • *n* abolire, abolirea sclaviei *(f)*, abolirea sclaviei
abolitionism • *n* aboliionism
abolitionist • *n* aboliionist
abominable • *adj* abominabil, detestabil *(m)*
abomination • *n* aversiune *(f)*, abominaiune *(f)*
abort • *n* avort *(n)*, întrerupere de sarcin *(f)*
abortion • *n* avort *(n)*, avort, embrion *(m)*, germen *(m)*, abandon *(n)*
abortive • *n* abortiv *(n)*
abound • *v* abunda
about • *adv* cam • *prep* în jurul, despre, lâng
above • *adv* deasupra • *prep* deasupra
abrade • *v* abraza
abrogate • *v* abroga, anula
abrupt • *adj* abrupt
abruptly • *adv* abrupt, deodat
abscess • *n* abces *(n)*
abscissa • *n* abscis *(f)*
abscission • *n* absciziune *(f)*
absence • *n* absen *(f)*, neatenie *(f)*
absent • *adj* absent *(n)*, absent *(f)*, neprezent *(n)*, inexistent, inexistent *(f)*, neexistent *(n)*, neatent *(m)*, distrat *(m)*, absent
absinthe • *n* absint, pelin *(m)*
absolutism • *n* absolutism *(n)*
absorb • *v* absorbi
absorbable • *adj* absorbibil *(n)*
absorbed • *adj* absorbit *(n)*, captivat *(n)*, îngândurat *(n)*, absorbit *(f)*
absorbency • *n* absorban *(f)*, capacitate de absorbie
absorbent • *n* absorbant *(m)*
absorption • *n* absorbire *(f)*, absorbie *(f)*
abstain • *v* abine
abstention • *n* abinere *(f)*
abstract • *n* rezumat *(n)*, conspect *(n)*, extras *(n)*, concentrat *(n)*, esen *(f)*, abstracie *(f)*, extract *(n)*
abstraction • *n* abstracie *(f)*
abstractionism • *n* abstracionism *(n)*
absurd • *n* absurd • *adj* absurd, iraional
absurdity • *n* absurditate, absurd
abundance • *n* abunden *(f)*
abundant • *adj* abundent
abuse • *n* abuz *(n)*, abuz verbal, jignire verbal, ofens verbal, violen *(f)*, abuz fizic,

violen sexual, abuz sexual
abyss • *n* abis *(n)*, adânc *(n)*, adâncime *(f)*, prpastie *(f)*, hu *(n)*
abyssal • *adj* abisal
acacia • *n* acacia *(f)*
academic • *adj* universitar *(n)*, universitar *(f)*, academic *(n)*, academic *(f)*
academy • *n* academie *(f)*, universitate *(f)*, seminar *(n)*
acanthus • *n* acant *(f)*
accelerate • *v* accelera
acceleration • *n* acceleraie *(f)*, accelerare *(f)*
accelerator • *n* accelerator *(m)*, iuitor *(m)*, repezitor *(m)*, accelerator *(n)*, pedal de accelerare *(f)*
accelerometer • *n* accelerometru *(n)*
accent • *n* accent *(n)*, intonaie *(f)*
accept • *v* accepta
acceptability • *n* acceptabilitate *(f)*
acceptable • *adj* acceptabil
acceptance • *n* acceptare *(f)*, acceptan *(f)*, primire *(f)*, acceptare, accepie
access • *n* acces *(n)*, apropiere *(f)*
accessible • *adj* accesibil *(n)*
accessory • *adj* accesoriu • *n* accesoriu *(n)*
accident • *n* accident *(n)*
accidental • *adj* accidental *(n)*, întâmpltor *(n)*, accidental *(f)*
acclamation • *n* aclamare, aclamaie
accompaniment • *n* acompaniament *(n)*
accompany • *v* acompania, însoi, a însoi
accord • *n* acord *(n)*, înelegere *(f)*
accordion • *n* acordeon *(n)*
account • *n* cont *(n)*
accountability • *n* responsabilitate *(f)*, responsabilitate angajat *(f)*
accountancy • *n* contabilitate *(f)*
accountant • *n* contabil *(m)*
accounting • *n* contabilitate *(f)*
accumulation • *n* acumulare *(f)*
accuracy • *n* precizie *(f)*, acuratee *(f)*, exactitate *(f)*
accurately • *adv* exact, precis
accusative • *n* acuzativ *(n)*, caz acuzativ *(n)* • *adj* acuzator, acuzativ
accusatory • *adj* acuzatoriu *(m)*, acuzatorie *(f)*, acuzatorii
ace • *n* as *(m)*, iot *(f)*
acerola • *n* acerola *(f)*
acetabulum • *n* acetabul *(n)*
acetamide • *n* acetamid, etanamid
acetone • *n* aceton *(f)*
acetylene • *n* acetilen *(f)*
acetylenic • *adj* acetilenic
ache • *v* durea • *n* durere *(f)*
achene • *n* achen *(f)*
achylia • *n* achilie *(f)*
acid • *n* acid *(m)*, acidul lisergic dietilamida-25 *(m)* • *adj* acru, acid
acidification • *n* acidificare *(f)*
acinus • *n* acin *(n)*
acknowledge • *v* recunoate
acknowledged • *adj* recunoscut *(m)*, recunoscut *(f)*, acceptat *(m)*
acknowledgement • *n* recunoatere *(f)*, recunotin *(f)*, apreciere *(f)*, chitan *(f)*, recipis *(f)*, adeverire *(f)*
acne • *n* acnee *(f)*
aconite • *n* aconit *(m)*, omag *(m)*
acorn • *n* ghind *(f)*
acoustics • *n* acustic *(f)*
acquaintance • *n* cunoscut *(m)*, cunoscut *(f)*, cunotin
acquisition • *n* achiziie *(f)*, achiziionare *(f)*
acquit • *v* achita
acrid • *adj* acru, caustic
acrimonious • *adj* acrimonios
acrimony • *n* acrimonie *(f)*
acrobat • *n* acrobat *(m)*
acrobatics • *n* acrobatic, acrobaie *(f)*
acrocyanosis • *n* acrocianoz
acromion • *n* acromion *(n)*
acronym • *n* acronim *(n)*
acropolis • *n* acropol *(f)*
across • *adv* dincolo, trans-, pe cealalt parte, de-a curmeziul, în curmezi, transversal, orizontal • *prep* dincolo de, peste, prin
acrostic • *n* acrostih *(n)*
acrylic • *adj* acrilic
actinium • *n* actiniu *(n)*
actinometer • *n* actinometru *(n)*
actinomycosis • *n* actinomicoz *(f)*
action • *n* fapt, aciune
active • *adj* activ
activist • *n* activist *(m)*, activist *(f)*
activity • *n* activitate *(f)*
actor • *n* actor *(m)*, actri *(f)*, personaj
actress • *n* actri *(f)*
actuality • *n* actualitate *(f)*
acuity • *n* acuitate *(f)*
acupuncture • *n* acupunctur *(f)*
acute • *adj* ascuit
adapt • *v* adapta • *adj* adaptat *(m)*
adaptability • *n* adaptabilitate *(f)*
adaptable • *adj* adaptabil, adaptabil *(f)*
adaptation • *n* adaptare *(f)*
adapter • *n* adaptor *(n)*
add • *v* aduga, aduna
addax • *n* addax *(n)*, adax *(n)*
addictive • *adj* dependent
addition • *n* adaos *(f)*, adugire *(f)*,

adunare
additional • *adj* adiional *(m)*
address • *v* pregti, îndrepta, prepara, îmbrca, adresa, face curte, încredina • *n* adres *(f)*, adresare *(f)*, discurs *(n)*, comportare *(f)*, inut *(f)*, îdemânare *(f)*, dexteritate *(f)*, abilitate *(f)*
adenine • *n* adenin *(f)*
adenoid • *n* adenoid *(n)*
adequate • *adj* adecvat
adherent • *n* aderent *(m)* • *adj* aderent *(m)*
adieu • *interj* adio
adipose • *adj* adipos
adjacent • *adj* adiacent *(m)*
adjectival • *adj* adjectival
adjective • *n* adjectiv *(n)* • *adj* adjectiv *(m)*, adjectiv *(f)*
adjourn • *v* amâna
adjust • *v* ajusta, potrivi, regla
adjustable • *adj* ajustabil *(n)*
adjustment • *n* ajustare *(f)*, acomodare *(f)*
adjutant • *n* adjutant *(m)*
administration • *n* administrare *(f)*, administraie, administrare
administrative • *adj* administrativ
administrator • *n* administrator *(m)*
admirable • *adj* admirabil
admiral • *n* amiral *(m)*
admiration • *n* admiraie *(f)*, admirare *(f)*
admissible • *adj* admisibil
adobe • *n* chirpici *(n)*
adolescence • *n* adolescen *(f)*
adolescent • *n* adolescent *(m)*, adolescent *(f)* • *adj* adolescent *(m)*
adopt • *v* adopta
adoption • *n* adoptare, adopie
adoptive • *adj* adoptiv
adorable • *adj* adorabil, vrednic de adorare *(m)*
adorably • *adv* în mod adorabil
adoration • *n* adoraie *(f)*, adorare *(f)*, apreciere *(f)*, stim *(f)*
adorn • *v* decora, ornamenta, înfrumusea, împodobi, orna
adrenaline • *n* adrenalin *(f)*
adrift • *adj* în deriv • *adv* în deriv
adroitness • *n* abilitate *(f)*, dexteritate *(f)*
adult • *n* adult *(m)*, adult *(f)* • *adj* adult
advance • *v* avansa
advantage • *v* avantaja • *n* avantaj *(n)*
advantageous • *adj* avantajos *(n)*
adverb • *n* adverb *(n)*
adverbial • *adj* adverbial *(n)*
adversary • *n* adversar
adverse • *adj* nefavorabil *(n)*, advers, ostil, opus *(n)*, opus *(f)*
adversity • *n* adversitate *(f)*
advertisement • *n* anun *(n)*, reclam *(f)*
advertising • *n* publicitate *(f)*, reclam
advice • *n* sfat *(n)*
advise • *v* sftui, recomanda
adze • *n* tesl *(f)*
aeration • *n* aerare *(f)*
aerial • *n* anten *(f)* • *adj* aerian
aerobic • *adj* aerobic
aerobics • *n* gimnastic aerobic *(f)*
aerodrome • *n* aerodrom *(n)*
aerodynamics • *n* aerodinamic *(f)*
aerometer • *n* aerometru *(n)*
aeronautics • *n* aeronautic *(f)*
aeroscopy • *n* aeroscopie *(f)*
aerospace • *n* aerospaiu *(n)* • *adj* aerospaial
aesthetics • *n* estetic
affability • *n* afabilitate *(f)*, cordialitate
affable • *adj* cordial, afabil
affair • *n* afacere
affiliation • *n* afiliaie *(f)*, afiliere *(f)*, uniune *(f)*
affinity • *n* afinitate *(f)*
affirmation • *n* afirmaie *(f)*
affix • *n* afix *(n)*
affront • *n* afront *(n)*, afront
after • *adv* dup • *prep* dup, peste, în urm, în cutarea, pe urmele, în urma, ca urmare a
afterdeck • *n* punte posterioar *(f)*, puntea din spate
afterlife • *n* viaa de dincolo *(f)*, viaa de mai târziu *(f)*
afternoon • *n* dup-amiaz *(f)*
afterwards • *adv* apoi, târziu
again • *adv* iari, din nou
against • *prep* contra
agave • *n* agav *(f)*
age • *v* îmbtrâni • *n* via *(f)*, vârst *(f)*, etate *(f)*, perioad, majorat, epoc *(f)*, ev, er, er *(f)*, generaie *(f)*, venicie
agency • *n* agenie *(f)*, agentur *(f)*
agglomeration • *n* aglomeraie *(f)*
agglutination • *n* aglutinare *(f)*
aggregate • *n* mas, tot
aggression • *n* agresiune *(f)*
aggressive • *adj* agresiv
aggressiveness • *n* agresivitate *(f)*
aghast • *adj* îngrozit
agitate • *v* agita
agitation • *n* agitare *(f)*, agitaie *(f)*
agitator • *n* agitator *(m)*, agitator *(n)*
agnostic • *n* agnostic *(m)*, agnostic *(f)*
agnosticism • *n* agnosticism
agony • *n* agonie *(f)*, suferin *(f)*
agouti • *n* aguti *(m)*
agreeable • *adj* plcut *(n)*, agreabil *(n)*,

potrivit *(n)*, conform *(n)*
agreeably • *adv* agreabil, în mod agreabil
agreed • *interj* de acord
agricultural • *adj* agricol
agriculture • *n* agricultur *(f)*
agrobiologic • *adj* agrobiologic
agrobiology • *n* agrobiologie *(f)*
ahead • *adv* înainte, în faa
aid • *n* ajutor *(n)*, ajutor *(f)*, ajutor • *v* ajuta
aileron • *n* eleron *(n)*
ailment • *n* indispoziie
aim • *n* ctare *(f)*, int *(f)*, el, obiectiv *(n)*, scop *(n)*, intenie *(f)*
aimless • *adj* fr scop, fr plan
aimlessly • *adv* fr int, la întâmplare
air • *v* aera, aerisi, ventila, zvânta, transmite • *n* aer, vzduh, aer *(n)*, eter, atmosfer, arie *(f)*
aircraft • *n* aeronav *(f)*, aparat de zbor *(n)*, aparat zburtor *(n)*
airing • *n* aerisire *(f)*, ventilare *(f)*
airline • *n* companie aerian *(f)*
airplane • *n* aeroplan *(m)*, avion *(m)*
airport • *n* aeroport *(n)*
alabaster • *n* alabastru *(n)*
alanine • *n* alanin *(f)*
alas • *interj* vai
albatross • *n* albatros *(m)*
albedo • *n* albedo
albeit • *conj* totui, dar
albinism • *n* albinism *(n)*
albumen • *n* albu *(n)*
albumin • *n* albumin *(f)*
alcazar • *n* alcazar *(n)*
alchemist • *n* alchimist *(m)*
alcohol • *n* alcool *(m)*, alcool *(n)*
alcoholic • *n* alcoolic *(m)*, alcoolic *(f)* • *adj* alcoolic
alcoholism • *n* alcoolism *(n)*
alder • *n* arin *(m)*, anin *(m)*
aleatory • *adj* aleatoriu
alembic • *n* alambic *(n)*
alfalfa • *n* lucern *(f)*
alga • *n* alg
algebra • *n* algebr *(f)*
algebraic • *adj* algebric *(n)*, algebric
algorithm • *n* algoritm *(m)*, algoritmi
algorithmic • *adj* algoritmic *(n)*, algoritmic *(f)*
alien • *n* strin *(m)*, alien *(m)*, strin *(f)*, alien *(f)*, strin, extraterestru
aliphatic • *adj* alifatic
alive • *adj* viu
alkaline • *adj* alcalin *(n)*
alkaloid • *n* alcaloid *(m)*
alkene • *n* alchen *(f)*
all • *n* tot • *adv* tot *(m)*, toata *(f)*, toi, toate
all-knowing • *adj* atottiutor, omniscient
allay • *v* astâmpra, alina
allegretto • *n* allegretto *(m)* • *adv* allegretto
allergy • *n* alergie *(f)*
alleviate • *v* uura, alina, calma
alley • *n* alee *(f)*
alliance • *n* alian *(f)*
alligator • *n* aligator *(m)*
allot • *v* aloca, repartiza
allotropic • *adj* alotropic
allow • *v* lsa, acorda, permite, admite, îngdui
alloy • *n* aliaj *(n)*
allspice • *n* ienibahar *(n)*
allude • *v* face aluzie, referi
allusive • *adj* aluziv
ally • *n* aliat *(n)*
allylic • *adj* alilic
almighty • *adj* atotputernic, omnipotent
almond • *n* migdal *(f)*, migdal *(m)*
almost • *adv* aproape
aloe • *n* aloe *(f)*
alone • *adv* singur
aloneness • *n* singurtate
along • *adv* împreun, înainte • *prep* de-a lungul, în lungul
aloof • *adv* distant
aloofness • *n* rezerv *(f)*, distan *(f)*, rceal *(f)*
alpaca • *n* alpaca *(f)*
alpha • *n* alfa *(m)*
alphabet • *n* alfabet *(n)*
alphabetic • *adj* alfabetic *(n)*, alfabetic *(f)*
alphabetical • *adj* alfabetic *(m)*
alphanumeric • *adj* alfanumeric *(n)*, alfanumeric *(f)*, alfanumerici
already • *adv* deja
also • *adv* i, de asemenea, înc
altar • *n* altar
alteration • *n* alterare *(f)*, schimbare *(f)*, alteraie *(f)*
alternation • *n* alternare *(f)*
alternator • *n* alternator *(n)*, generator de curent alternativ *(n)*
although • *conj* dei, cu toate c, insa
altitude • *n* altitudine *(f)*, înlime *(f)*, înlime
altruism • *n* altruism, generozitate *(f)*
altruistic • *adj* altruist, generos, binefctpr *(m)*
alveolar • *n* alveolar *(f)*, consoan alveolar *(f)* • *adj* alveolar
always • *adv* totdeauna, mereu, întotdeauna
amaranth • *n* amarant *(m)*
amaryllis • *n* amarilis *(m)*

amateur • *n* amator *(m)* • *adj* amator *(n)*, neprofesional *(n)*
amateurism • *n* amatorism
amaze • *v* uimi, minuna
amazement • *n* surprindere *(f)*, uimire *(f)*, uluire *(f)*
amazing • *adj* uimitor, extraordinar
ambassador • *n* ambasador *(m)*
amber • *n* chihlimbar *(n)*, ambr *(f)*
ambergris • *n* ambr *(f)*
ambidextrous • *adj* ambidextru
ambiguity • *n* ambiguitate *(f)*
ambiguous • *adj* ambiguu, cu multe sensuri
ambulance • *n* ambulan *(f)*
amelioration • *n* ameliorare *(f)*, îmbuntire *(f)*
amen • *adv* amin
americium • *n* americiu *(n)*
amethyst • *n* ametist *(n)* • *adj* purpuriu
amiability • *n* amabilitate *(f)*, afabilitate *(f)*
amide • *n* amid *(f)*
amine • *n* amin *(f)*
ammonia • *n* amoniac *(n)*
ammunition • *n* muniie, muniie *(f)*
amnesia • *n* amnezie *(f)*
among • *prep* între, printre
amorous • *adj* amoros *(m)*, de amor, amorezat *(m)*, înamorat *(m)*
amount • *v* evalua • *n* sum *(f)*, valoare *(f)*, cantitate *(f)*, msur *(f)*
ampere • *n* amper
ampere-hour • *n* amper-or *(m)*
amplification • *n* amplificare *(f)*
amplitude • *n* amplitudine *(f)*, amplitudini
amulet • *n* amulet *(f)*
an • *art* un *(m)*, o *(f)*
analgesic • *n* substan analgezic *(f)* • *adj* analgezic *(n)*
analog • *adj* analog, analogic
analogous • *adj* analog, analogic *(m)*
analogy • *n* analogie *(f)*
analysis • *n* analiz *(f)*
analyzable • *adj* analizabil *(m)*
analyze • *v* analiza
anarchic • *adj* anarhic *(m)*
anarchism • *n* anarhism
anarchist • *n* anarhist *(m)*, anarhisr *(f)*, nihilist *(m)*
anarchy • *n* anarhie
anathema • *n* anatem *(f)*
anatomical • *adj* anatomic
anatomy • *n* anatomie *(f)*
ancestor • *n* strmo *(m)*
ancestral • *adj* ancestral *(n)*
anchor • *v* ancora • *n* ancor *(f)*
anchovy • *n* sardele *(f)*, hamsie *(f)*, anoa *(f)*
and • *conj* i
androgynous • *adj* androgin
anecdotal • *adj* anecdotic
anemia • *n* anemie *(f)*
anemone • *n* anemon *(f)*
angel • *n* înger *(m)*
angelic • *adj* îngeresc, angelic
angelica • *n* angelic *(f)*
anger • *n* furie *(f)*, mânie *(f)*, enervare *(f)*
angiography • *n* angiografie *(f)*
angiopathy • *n* angiopatie *(f)*
angiosperm • *n* angiosperm *(f)*
angle • *n* unghi *(n)*, col *(n)*, ungher *(n)*, cotire *(f)*, cotitur *(n)*, punct de vedere *(n)* • *v* pescui
angry • *adj* mânios *(m)*
anguish • *v* suferi, chinui • *n* agonie *(f)*, chin *(n)*
angular • *adj* unghiular *(n)*
anhydride • *n* anhidrid *(f)*
animal • *n* animal *(n)*, fiar *(f)*, jivin *(f)* • *adj* animal, animalic, slbatic, sufletesc
animate • *v* anima, însuflei
animation • *n* animare *(f)*, însufleire *(f)*
anime • *n* anime *(n)*
animism • *n* animism *(n)*
animosity • *n* animozitate *(f)*
anise • *n* anison *(m)*, anason *(m)*
ankle • *n* glezn *(f)*
annals • *n* anale *(n)*
annexation • *n* anexare *(f)*
annihilate • *v* anihila
annihilator • *n* anulator *(m)*
anniversary • *n* aniversare
announce • *v* anuna, vesti
annoyance • *n* enervare *(f)*
annual • *n* anuar *(n)* • *adj* anual
annually • *adv* în mod anual
annul • *v* anula, revoca
annulment • *n* anulare, invalidare
annulus • *n* inel *(n)*, coroan de cerc *(f)*, coroan circular *(f)*, coroan solar *(f)*
anoa • *n* anoa *(m)*
anomaly • *n* anomalie *(f)*
anonymity • *n* anonimitate *(f)*, anonim *(m)*
anonymous • *adj* anonim
anonymously • *adv* anonim
anorexic • *n* anorexic *(m)*, anorexica *(f)*
answer • *n* rspuns *(n)*, rezolvare *(f)*, soluie *(f)*, soluionare *(f)* • *v* rspunde, soluiona
ant • *n* furnic *(f)*
antagonism • *n* antagonism
antagonist • *n* antagonist *(m)*, oponent

(m)
antagonistic • *adj* antagonic, antagonist
antaphrodisiac • *n* antiafrodisiac *(m)* • *adj* antafrodisiac *(m)*
ante • *n* miz *(f)*
anteater • *n* furnicar *(m)*
antecedent • *adj* antecedent
antelope • *n* antilop *(f)*
antenna • *n* anten *(f)*
antepenultimate • *adj* antepenultim *(m)*
anterior • *adj* anterior
anthem • *n* imn naional *(n)*, imn *(n)*
anther • *n* anter *(f)*
anthill • *n* furnicar *(n)*, muuroi *(n)*
anthrax • *n* antrax *(m)*
anthropocentrism • *n* antropocentrism *(n)*
anthropoid • *n* antropoid *(f)*, antropoide • *adj* antropoid, antropomorf
anthropology • *n* antropologie *(f)*
anthroposophy • *n* antropozofie
anti-inflammatory • *n* antiinflamator
antibacterial • *adj* antibacterial
antibody • *n* anticorp *(m)*, anticorpi
antic • *adj* neadecvat *(n)*, demodat *(n)*, învechit *(n)*
antichrist • *n* antihrist *(m)*, anticrist *(m)*
anticipate • *v* anticipa, prevedea
anticipation • *n* anticipare *(f)*, anticipaie *(f)*
antigen • *n* antigen
antihero • *n* antierou *(m)*
antimony • *n* antimoniu *(n)*, stibiu
antiparticle • *n* antiparticul
antipathy • *n* antipatie *(f)*
antiproton • *n* antiproton *(m)*
antiquity • *n* antichitate *(f)*
antithetical • *adj* antitetic
antler • *n* corn, coarne
antonym • *n* antonim *(n)*
anus • *n* anus *(n)*
anvil • *n* nicoval, ilu, nicoval *(f)*
anxiety • *n* anxietate *(f)*, team *(f)*
anxious • *adj* anxios *(n)*, nelinitit *(n)*, îngrijorat *(n)*, nerbdtor *(n)*, doritor *(n)*
any • *pron* oricare
anything • *n* cineva, ceva • *pron* orice, nimic
anywhere • *adv* oriunde
aorist • *n* aorist *(n)*
apartment • *n* apartament *(n)*
apathy • *n* apatie *(f)*
apatite • *n* apatit
ape • *v* imita, maimuri • *n* maimu *(f)*
aperiodic • *adj* aperiodic *(m)*
aperture • *n* deschiztur *(f)*
apex • *n* culme
apheresis • *n* aferez *(f)*
aphid • *n* afid *(f)*, afide
aphorism • *n* aforism, aforisme
aphrodisiac • *n* afrodiziac *(n)* • *adj* afrodisiac
apocalyptic • *adj* apocaliptic
apogee • *n* apogeu *(n)*
apostasy • *n* apostazie *(f)*
apostrophe • *n* apostrof *(n)*
apparatus • *n* aparat *(n)*, aparatur *(f)*, echipament *(n)*
apparent • *adj* vdit *(n)*, evident *(n)*, clar *(n)*, manifest *(n)*
apparition • *n* apariie *(f)*, ivire *(f)*
appeal • *v* apela, a face recurs, atrage • *n* recurs *(n)*, apel *(n)*, atragere *(f)*
appear • *v* aprea, prea, da impresia
appearance • *n* apariie *(f)*, ivire *(f)*, viziune *(f)*, înfiare *(f)*, aspect *(n)*, aparen *(f)*, prezentare *(f)*
appease • *v* astâmpra
appendage • *n* membru *(n)*, extremitate *(f)*, anex *(f)*
appendix • *n* apendice *(n)*, anex *(f)*
appetite • *n* poft *(f)*, apetit *(n)*, râvn *(f)*, ardoare *(f)*, sârguin *(f)*
applaud • *v* aplauda
apple • *n* mr *(n)*, lemn de mr
applicability • *n* aplicabilitate *(f)*
applicable • *adj* aplicabil *(m)*, adecvat *(m)*, potrivit *(m)*
application • *n* aplicare *(f)*, aplicaie *(f)*, aplicaie computeric *(f)*
apportion • *v* distribui, aloca, repartiza
apposition • *n* apoziie
appraisal • *n* evaluare *(f)*, apreciere *(f)*
appreciate • *v* recunosctor, îi da seama
appreciation • *n* apreciere *(f)*
apprehension • *n* arestare *(f)*, arest *(n)*, înelegere *(f)*, concepie *(f)*, pricepere *(f)*, opinie *(f)*, idee *(f)*, prere *(f)*, aprehensiune *(f)*
apprentice • *n* ucenic *(m)*
approach • *v* apropia
approachable • *adj* accesibil *(m)*, abordabil *(m)*
approbation • *n* aprobare *(f)*
approximately • *adv* aproximativ
approximation • *n* aproximare, aproximaie *(f)*
apricot • *n* cais *(f)*, cais *(m)*
apron • *n* sort
apropos • *adv* apropo • *prep* apropo de
apse • *n* absid *(f)*
apt • *adj* potrivit *(n)*, apt *(n)*
aquamarine • *n* acvamarin, acvamarin *(n)*

aquarium • *n* acvariu *(n)*
aquatic • *adj* acvatic
aqueduct • *n* apeduct *(n)*
aqueous • *adj* aptos
arable • *adj* arabil *(n)*
arachnid • *n* arahnid *(f)*
arbiter • *n* arbitru *(m)*, arbitri
arbitrary • *adj* arbitrar
arbitration • *n* arbitrare, arbitraj *(n)*
arbitrator • *n* arbitru *(m)*
arboretum • *n* arboret *(n)*
arc • *n* arc *(n)*
arcade • *n* arcad *(f)*, pasaj *(n)*
arch • *n* arc *(n)*
archaeologist • *n* arheolog *(m)*, arheolog *(f)*
archaeology • *n* arheologie *(f)*
archaic • *adj* arhaic *(n)*, învechit *(n)*
archaism • *n* arhaism *(n)*, arhaisme, cuvânt învechit *(n)*
archangel • *n* arhanghel *(m)*
archbishop • *n* arhiepiscop *(m)*, mitropolit *(m)*
archdiocese • *n* arhidiocez
archer • *n* arca, sgettor, sagitar
archipelago • *n* arhipelag *(n)*
architect • *n* arhitect *(m)*, arhitect *(f)*
architectural • *adj* arhitectonic *(n)*, arhitectural *(n)*
architecture • *n* arhitectur *(f)*
archive • *v* arhiva • *n* arhiv *(f)*
ardor • *n* ardoare *(f)*, înflcrare *(f)*, pasiune *(f)*, arden *(f)*, ari *(f)*, ferbineal *(f)*
are • *n* ar *(n)*
area • *n* arie *(f)*, arii, suprafa *(f)*, areal *(n)*, zon *(f)*
arena • *n* aren *(f)*
argent • *n* argint *(n)* • *adj* argintiu *(m)*, argintiu
arginine • *n* arginin *(f)*
argon • *n* argon *(n)*
arguable • *adj* argumentabil *(m)*
argue • *v* discuta, pleda, certa, a aduce argumente
argument • *n* argument *(n)*, ceart *(f)*, disput *(f)*, contraargumentare *(f)*
argumentative • *adj* cu argumente, argumentativ, plin de argumente
argus-eyed • *adj* vigilent, cu ochii în patru
aria • *n* arie
arise • *v* ridica, scula
aristocracy • *n* aristocraie
aristocratic • *adj* aristocratic
arithmetic • *n* aritmetic *(f)* • *adj* aritmetic
ark • *n* arca *(f)*
arm • *n* bra *(n)*, arm *(f)* • *v* arma
armadillo • *n* tatu *(m)*
armchair • *n* fotoliu *(n)*
armed • *adj* armat
armistice • *n* armistiiu *(n)*
armor • *n* armur *(f)*
armpit • *n* subsuoar *(f)*
army • *n* armat *(f)*, oaste *(f)*, mulime *(f)*, multitudine *(f)*, puzderie *(f)*
arnica • *n* arnic *(f)*
aromatic • *adj* aromat *(m)*, aromatic *(m)*, aromatic
around • *adv* peste tot, ici-colo • *prep* în jurul, împrejurul, aproape de
arrange • *v* aranja, ordona, pune în ordine
arrangement • *n* aranjare, aranjament
arrest • *v* opri, aresta, deine • *n* arestare *(f)*, arest *(n)*, arestare, deinere *(f)*
arrival • *n* venire *(f)*, sosire *(f)*
arrive • *v* ajunge, sosi
arrogance • *n* trufie, mândrie, arogan *(f)*
arrogant • *adj* arogant
arrow • *n* sgeat *(f)*
arrowhead • *n* sgeata-apei *(f)*, sgeata-apelor *(f)*
arrowroot • *n* maranta *(f)*
arsenic • *n* arsen *(n)*
art • *n* art *(f)*, art, oper de art, lucrare de art
arteriosclerosis • *n* arterioscleroz *(f)*
artery • *n* arter *(f)*
arthritis • *n* artrit *(f)*, artroz *(f)*
arthromere • *n* artromer
arthropod • *n* artropod *(n)*
artichoke • *n* anghinare *(f)*
article • *n* articol *(n)*
articulate • *v* articula
articulation • *n* articulaie *(f)*
artifice • *n* artificial *(m)*
artificial • *adj* artificial *(n)*, fals *(n)*, nenatural *(n)*
artillery • *n* artilerie *(f)*, artilerie *(f)*
artiodactyl • *n* artiodactil *(n)*
artist • *n* artist *(m)*, artist *(f)*
artistic • *adj* artistic
as • *adv* la fel de • *conj* ca, cum, aa cum, precum, când, pe când, în timp ce, pe msur ce, deoarece, pentru c, fiindc • *prep* ca, ca i, în calitate de
asbestosis • *n* asbestoz *(f)*
ascend • *v* înla, urca, sui
ascendancy • *n* superioritate *(f)*, supremaie *(f)*, ascenden *(f)*
ascendant • *n* strmo *(m)*, predecesor *(m)*
ascomycete • *n* ascomicet *(f)*
ascus • *n* asc *(f)*
asexual • *adj* asexual

ash • *n* cenu *(f)*, scrum *(m)*
ashamed • *adj* ruinat *(m)*
ashen • *adj* cenuiu
ashore • *adv* pe mal, la rm
ashtray • *n* scrumier *(f)*
ask • *v* întreba, cere, invita, ruga
asleep • *adj* adormit
asparagine • *n* asparagin *(f)*
asparagus • *n* sparanghel, sparanghel *(m)*
aspect • *n* aspect *(n)*, aspect
asphodel • *n* asfodel *(n)*
aspic • *n* piftie *(f)*
aspiration • *n* aspiraie, aspirare, inspiraie
aspirin • *n* aspirin *(f)*, aspirin
ass • *n* mgar *(m)*, asin *(m)*, idiot *(m)*, fund *(n)*, popou *(n)*, cur *(n)*, futai *(n)*
assassinate • *v* asasina
assessment • *n* evaluare *(f)*
assets • *n* avere *(f)*
asshole • *n* cur *(n)*, goaz *(f)*
assiduous • *adj* asiduu, struitor *(n)*, harnic *(n)*
assign • *v* atribui, destina, împri, categoriza
assimilation • *n* asimilare *(f)*, asimilaie *(f)*
assist • *v* asista, ajuta
assistance • *n* asisten *(f)*, ajutor *(n)*
assistant • *n* asistent *(m)*
associate • *n* partener, asociat, coleg, tovar *(m)*, camarad *(m)* • *adj* asociat
association • *n* asociere *(f)*, asociaie *(f)*
associational • *adj* asociaial *(n)*, asociaional *(n)*
assuage • *v* alina
assume • *v* presupune, prepune
astatine • *n* astatin *(n)*
aster • *n* aster *(m)*
asterisk • *n* asterisc *(n)*, stelu *(f)*
asteroid • *n* asteroid *(m)*, asteroizi
asthma • *n* astm *(f)*
astigmatism • *n* astigmatism *(n)*
astonishment • *n* uimire *(f)*, surprindere *(f)*
astound • *v* uimi, ului
astral • *adj* astral *(n)*, stelar *(n)*
astrology • *n* astrologie *(f)*
astronaut • *n* astronaut *(m)*
astronomer • *n* astronom *(m)*, astronom *(f)*
astronomy • *n* astronomie *(f)*
astrophysics • *n* astrofizic *(f)*
asylum • *n* azil *(n)*, adpost *(n)*, sanctuar *(n)*
asymmetrical • *adj* asimetric *(n)*, nesimetric *(n)*
asymptote • *n* asimptot *(f)*
asymptotic • *adj* asimptotic *(n)*
asynchronous • *adj* asincron *(m)*
at • *prep* la, înspre, spre
ataraxia • *n* ataraxie *(f)*
atavism • *n* atavism *(n)*
atheism • *n* ateism
atheist • *n* ateist *(m)*, ateist *(f)*, ateu *(m)*
atheistic • *adj* ateist *(n)*
athlete • *n* atlet *(m)*, atlet *(f)*, atlei, atlete, persoan atletic *(f)*
athletic • *adj* atletic *(m)*, atletic
athletics • *n* atletism
atlas • *n* atlas *(n)*
atmosphere • *n* atmosfer *(f)*, ambient *(m)*, ambian *(f)*
atmospheric • *adj* atmosferic
atoll • *n* atol
atonement • *n* rscumprare *(f)*, reconciliere *(f)*, remucare *(f)*, expiere *(f)*, ispire *(f)*, expiaie *(f)*, cin *(f)*
atrium • *n* atrium *(n)*, atriu *(n)*
atrocious • *adj* atroce
atrocity • *n* atrocitate *(f)*
atrophy • *n* atrofie *(f)*, atrofiere *(f)*
atropine • *n* atropin *(f)*
attach • *v* atasat, anexat
attachment • *n* ataament *(n)*, ataare *(f)*
attack • *v* ataca • *n* atac *(n)*
attacker • *n* atacant *(m)*, atacant *(f)*
attention • *n* atenie *(f)*, drepi
attentiveness • *n* atenie *(f)*, consideraie *(f)*
attenuate • *v* atenua
attenuation • *n* atenuare, diminuare
attest • *v* atesta, confirma, adeveri
attestation • *n* atestare *(f)*, adeverire *(f)*, confirmare *(f)*, autentificare, atestare
attic • *n* pod, mansard
attitude • *n* atitudine *(f)*, poziie *(f)*, postur *(f)*
attract • *v* atrage
attraction • *n* atracie *(f)*, atragere *(f)*
attractive • *adj* atractiv
attributive • *adj* atributiv *(n)*
atypical • *adj* atipic *(n)*, netipic *(n)*, neconform *(n)*
auburn • *adj* rocat-cafeniu
auctioneer • *n* conductor de licitaie *(m)*
audacity • *n* îndrzneal *(f)*
audible • *adj* auzibil
audio • *adj* audio
audiovisual • *adj* audio-vizual *(m)*
augmentative • *n* augmentativ *(m)* • *adj* augmentativ *(n)*, augmentativ *(f)*, mritor *(n)*
augury • *n* augur *(n)*, auspiciu *(n)*, semn *(n)*, piaz *(f)*
auk • *n* alc *(f)*, pinguin nordic *(m)*
aunt • *n* mtu *(f)*

aureole • *n* nimb *(n)*, aureol *(f)*
aurochs • *n* bour *(m)*
austere • *adj* auster *(n)*
austerity • *n* austeritate *(f)*
authentic • *adj* autentic, adevrat
authentication • *n* autentificare *(f)*
author • *v* crea, scrie • *n* autor *(m)*, autoare *(f)*
authoritarian • *adj* autoritar *(n)*
authority • *n* autoritate *(f)*, autoriti
authorization • *n* autorizare *(f)*, autorizaie *(f)*, împuternicire *(f)*
autism • *n* autism
autobiographical • *adj* autobiografic
autobiography • *n* autobiografie
autochthonous • *adj* autohton *(m)*
autodidact • *n* autodidact *(m)*
autograph • *n* autograf
automatic • *adj* automat *(n)*, automat *(f)*
automatically • *adv* automat, în mod automat
automation • *n* automatizare *(f)*
automaton • *n* automat *(n)*
automobile • *n* automobil *(n)*, main *(f)*
autonomous • *adj* autonom *(n)*, autonom *(f)*
autumn • *n* toamn *(f)*
available • *adj* disponibil, procurabil
avalanche • *v* coplei • *n* avalan, alunecare de teren *(f)*, ebulment *(n)*, alunecare *(f)*
avant-garde • *n* avangard *(f)*
avarice • *n* avariie *(f)*, aviditate *(f)*
avaricious • *adj* avar *(m)*
avenge • *v* rzbuna
avens • *n* cerenel *(m)*, clunul-doamnei *(m)*
avenue • *n* cale *(f)*, avenue *(f)*
average • *n* medie • *adj* mediu
aversion • *n* aversiune *(f)*
aviation • *n* aviaie *(f)*
avidity • *n* lcomie *(f)*, aviditate *(f)*
avocado • *n* avocado *(n)*
avocet • *n* cioc-întors *(n)*
avoid • *v* evita, ocoli
avow • *v* mrturisi
await • *v* atepta, servi masa
awake • *v* detepta, scula, trezi • *adj* treaz
awaken • *v* scula, detepta, trezi
award • *n* trofeu, medalie, decizie
away • *adj* absent, indisponibil • *adv* de aici, departe, încolo, în continuare
awestruck • *adj* copleit *(m)*, cuprins de uimire *(m)*
awful • *adj* oribil, teribil, atroce, îngrozitor, înfiortor *(m)*, impresionant *(m)*
awkward • *adj* neîndemânatic, stângaci
awl • *n* sul *(f)*
axial • *adj* axial *(m)*, axial *(f)*
axiological • *adj* axiologic *(m)*
axiology • *n* axiologie *(f)*, teoria valorii *(f)*
axiomatic • *adj* axiomatic *(m)*
axis • *n* ax *(f)*
axle • *n* ax *(n)*, osie *(f)*
aye-aye • *n* aye-aye *(n)*, ai *(m)*
azalea • *n* azalee *(f)*
azure • *n* azur • *adj* azuriu

B

baboon • *n* babuin *(m)*
baby • *n* bebe *(m)*, bebelu *(m)*, pui *(m)*, copil *(m)*, imatur, iubire *(f)*, iubito *(f)*, iubitule *(m)*, drgu *(f)*, frumoaso, mezin *(m)*, mezina *(f)* • *adj* mic, copilului
babyhood • *n* pruncie *(f)*
babysitter • *n* doic *(f)*
baccalaureate • *n* bacalaureat
bacchanal • *n* bahic *(m)*, dionisiac *(m)*, de bacanal
bachelor • *n* flcu *(m)*
bacillus • *n* bacil *(m)*
back • *n* spate, dos, spinare, sfârit *(n)* • *adj* în spatele, anterior • *adv* înapoi
backbone • *n* coloan vertebral *(f)*, ira spinrii *(f)*
backdrop • *n* decor *(n)*, fundal *(n)*
backpack • *n* rucsac *(n)*
backside • *n* partea posterioar *(f)*, partea dorsal *(f)*, fund
backward • *adj* înapoi, spre-napoi, ctre spate, regresiv *(m)*, îndrt
bacon • *n* bacon *(n)*, slnin *(f)*, lard
bacteria • *n* bacterii
bacteriology • *n* bacteriologie *(f)*
bad • *adj* ru
badge • *n* distincie *(f)*, insign *(f)*, carte de identificare *(f)*
badger • *n* viezure *(m)*, bursuc *(m)*
badly • *adv* ru
badness • *n* rutate *(f)*
baffled • *adj* confuz
bag • *n* pung *(f)*, sac
bagel • *n* covrig
bagpipes • *n* cimpoi *(n)*, cimpoaie *(f)*, gaid *(f)*

bait • *n* momeal *(f)*, nad *(f)*
bake • *v* coace
baker • *n* brutar, pâinar
bakery • *n* brutarie
baklava • *n* baclava
balance • *n* echilibru, cumpt, balans *(n)*, balan *(f)*, bilan
balanced • *adj* echilibrat *(m)*
balcony • *n* balcon *(n)*
bald • *adj* chel, pleuv
balk • *n* hat *(n)*, hotar *(n)*, grind *(f)*, lonjeron *(n)*, obstacol *(n)*, piedic *(f)*, fent *(f)*
ball • *n* minge, bil, bil *(f)*, ghem *(n)*, coi *(m)*
ballad • *n* balad *(f)*
ballast • *n* balast, lest
ballerina • *n* balerin *(f)*, baletist *(f)*
ballet • *n* balet *(n)*
ballistic • *adj* balistic
balloon • *n* balon *(n)*, balon
ballroom • *n* salon de bal *(n)*, sal de dans *(f)*
balls • *n* boae, coaie, ou
balsa • *n* balsa *(m)*
balsam • *n* balsam *(n)*
baluster • *n* balustru *(m)*
balustrade • *n* balustrad *(f)*
bamboo • *n* bambus *(m)*, bambu *(m)*
ban • *v* interzice • *n* ban *(m)*
banana • *n* banan *(f)*, bananier *(m)*, banan *(m)*, banan
band • *n* fa, formaie *(f)*
bandage • *n* bandaj, fa, pansament
bandicoot • *n* peramel *(m)*
bandy • *adj* crcnat
bang • *n* breton *(n)*
banish • *v* alunga
bank • *n* banc *(f)*
banker • *n* bancher *(m)*
bankruptcy • *n* faliment
banner • *n* steag *(n)*, drapel *(n)*, stindard *(n)*, flamur *(f)*
banquet • *n* banchet *(n)*, osp *(n)*, chef *(n)*, mas *(f)*, festin *(n)*, praznic *(n)*
banyan • *n* banian *(m)*
baobab • *n* baobab *(m)*
baptism • *n* botez *(n)*
baptist • *n* baptist *(m)*, baptist *(f)*
baptize • *v* boteza
bar • *v* bara
barbarism • *n* barbarism *(n)*
barbel • *n* mrean *(f)*
barber • *n* brbier *(m)*, frizer
barberry • *n* dracil *(f)*
barefoot • *adv* descul
barely • *adv* de abia
bargain • *n* afacere *(f)*
barge • *n* mahon *(f)*
barium • *n* bariu *(n)*
bark • *v* ltra • *n* ltrat, scoar
barley • *n* orz *(n)*
barn • *n* hambar
barometer • *n* barometru *(m)*
barracuda • *n* baracud *(f)*
barrage • *n* baraj *(n)*
barrel • *n* butoi, bute
barren • *adj* nefertil *(n)*, steril *(f)*
basal • *adj* de baz, bazal, fundamental
basalt • *n* bazalt
base • *n* baz *(f)*, fundament, baz, cazarm
baseball • *n* baseball
basement • *n* subsol *(m)*
basidium • *n* basidie *(f)*
basil • *n* busuioc *(m)*
basilica • *n* bazilic *(f)*
basilisk • *n* vasilisc *(m)*
basin • *n* chiuvet *(f)*
basis • *n* baz *(f)*
basket • *n* co *(m)*, baschet
basketball • *n* baschet, minge de baschet *(f)*
bass • *n* biban *(m)*
bassoon • *n* fagot *(n)*
basswood • *n* tei *(m)*
bastard • *n* bastard *(m)*, bastarzi, bastarde, hibrid *(m)*, hibrizi, corcituri, haimana *(f)*, haimanale
bastion • *n* bastion *(n)*
bat • *n* liliac *(m)*, bât *(f)*, baston *(n)*, ciomag *(n)*, mciuc *(f)* • *v* bate
batch • *n* arj *(f)*
bath • *n* cad *(f)*, baie
bathroom • *n* baie *(f)*, toalet *(f)*, closet *(n)*
bathtub • *n* cad *(f)*
batik • *n* batic, baticul
batiste • *n* batist
battalion • *n* batalion *(n)*
battery • *n* baterie *(f)*, pil electric *(f)*
battle • *n* btlie *(f)*
bay • *n* golf *(m)*
bayonet • *n* baionet *(f)*
bazaar • *n* târg *(n)*
be • *v* fi, exista, egala
beach • *n* plaj *(f)*
beak • *n* cioc *(m)*
beam • *n* grind *(f)*
bean • *n* fasole *(f)*, bob *(m)*, pstaie *(f)*, teac *(f)*
bear • *n* urs *(m)*, juctor de burs *(m)*, speculant *(m)* • *v* cra, duce, purta, aduce, declara, suporta, tolera, da rod, se îndrepta
beard • *v* înfrunta, sfida • *n* barb *(f)*
bearded • *adj* brbos

beast • *n* bestie, fiar
beat • *v* bate
beatitude • *n* beatitudine *(f)*
beau • *n* iubitul
beautiful • *adj* frumos *(n)*, frumoas *(f)*
beauty • *n* frumusee *(f)*, frumusee
beaver • *n* castor *(m)*, biber *(m)*, psric *(f)*
because • *adv* din cauz c, din cauza • *conj* pentru c, din cauz c, datorit, deoarece
become • *v* deveni
bed • *n* pat *(n)*
bedbug • *n* ploni *(f)*, pduche de pat
bedlam • *n* balamuc *(n)*, haos *(n)*, zpceal *(f)*
bedouin • *n* beduin *(m)*, beduini
bedroom • *n* dormitor *(n)*, dormitoare
bedtime • *n* timpul de culcare
bee • *n* albin *(f)*
beech • *n* fag *(m)*
beef • *n* vit *(f)*
beehive • *n* stup
beekeeper • *n* albinar *(m)*, albinar *(f)*, apicultor *(m)*, apicultoare *(f)*
beer • *n* bere *(f)*
beery • *adj* mirosind a bere, ameit de bere *(m)*, mirosind a bere *(f)*
beeswax • *n* cear de albine *(f)*
beet • *n* nap *(m)*, sfecl *(f)*
beetle • *n* gândac *(m)*
beetroot • *n* sfecl roie *(f)*
before • *adv* înainte • *prep* înainte, dinainte
beg • *v* ceri, ruga
beggar • *n* ceretor *(m)*
begin • *v* începe
beginner • *n* începtor *(m)*, începtoare *(f)*
beginning • *n* începere *(f)*, început *(n)*, iniiere *(f)*, debut *(n)*, start *(n)*
begonia • *n* begonie *(f)*
beguile • *v* înela, ademeni, amgi, încânta, captiva, fermeca
behave • *v* purta, comporta
behavior • *n* comportament *(n)*
behaviorism • *n* behaviorism *(n)*
behead • *v* decapita
behind • *n* spate, urm • *adv* în urm, în spate, spre spate, îndrt, spre-napoi • *prep* dup
behold • *v* vedea
beige • *n* bej *(n)* • *adj* bej
being • *n* fiin, creatur, fptur, existen, natere
belch • *v* râgâi
beleaguer • *v* împresura
belief • *n* credin, convingere *(f)*, convici-une *(f)*
believe • *v* crede
bell • *n* clopot *(n)*
belles-lettres • *n* beletristic *(f)*
belligerent • *adj* beligerant *(m)*, de rzboi *(f)*, belicos *(m)*, certre
bellow • *v* mugi, rage
bellows • *n* foale *(f)*
belly • *n* burt, abdomen, pântece, vintre
beloved • *n* iubit *(m)*, iubit *(f)*, drag *(m)*, drag *(f)* • *adj* iubit *(m)*, iubit *(f)*
below • *prep* sub, dedesubt
belt • *n* curea *(f)*, centur *(f)*, cordon *(n)*, brâu *(n)*
beluga • *n* beluga *(f)*
bemoan • *v* boci, deplânge, jelui
bench • *n* banc *(f)*
bend • *v* îndoi, curba
beneath • *prep* sub, dedesubt
benefit • *n* avantaj *(n)*, beneficiu *(n)*, beneficii
benevolence • *n* bunvoin *(f)*
benevolent • *adj* binevoitor *(m)*, binevoitoare *(f)*
benign • *adj* blând, benign
bent • *adj* gârbov, îndoit
benzene • *n* benzen *(m)*
berate • *v* admonestare, certare
beret • *n* beret *(f)*
berkelium • *n* berkeliu *(n)*
berry • *n* bac
beryl • *n* beril *(m)*
beryllium • *n* beriliu *(n)*
beseech • *v* implora
beset • *v* împresura
beside • *prep* lâng, alturi
besiege • *v* împresura
bestial • *adj* bestial *(n)*, bestial *(f)*, animalic *(n)*, animalic
bestiality • *n* bestialitate *(f)*
betray • *v* trda, descoperi, afla, a induce în eroare, a îndruma greit
betrayer • *n* delator, denuntor, informator, iud, trdtor, turntor, vânztor
betroth • *v* logodi
betrothal • *n* logodn *(f)*
better • *v* îmbunti • *adj* mai bun, mai bine • *adv* mai bine
between • *prep* între
betwixt • *prep* între
beverage • *n* butur *(f)*
bewail • *v* boci, deplânge, jelui
bewilder • *v* a dezorienta
bewilderment • *n* uluire *(f)*, consternare *(f)*, stupoare *(f)*
bewitch • *v* vrji, fermeca, fascina
bible • *n* Biblie *(f)*
bicameral • *adj* bicameral
biceps • *n* biceps *(m)*

biconvex • *adj* biconvex *(n)*, biconvex *(f)*
bicycle • *n* biciclet *(f)*
bifurcate • *v* bifurca
bifurcation • *n* divizare, bifurcare
bigamy • *n* bigamie
bike • *n* biciclet *(f)*
bikini • *n* bikini
bilberry • *n* afin
bile • *n* bil, fiere, irascibilitate *(f)*
bilingual • *adj* bilingv *(n)*, bilingv *(f)*
bill • *n* halebard *(f)*, cosor *(n)*, halebardier *(m)*, cioc *(n)*, plisc *(n)*, inventar *(n)*, not *(f)*, act *(n)*, proiect de lege *(n)*, plângere *(f)*, factur *(f)*, not de plat *(f)*, afi *(n)*, poster *(n)*, placard *(f)*, bilet de banc *(n)* • *v* anuna
billiards • *n* biliard
binary • *adj* binar
bind • *v* cupla, conecta, lega
binding • *n* legare *(f)*
bindweed • *n* volbur *(f)*
binoculars • *n* binoclu *(m)*
binturong • *n* binturong *(m)*
biochemistry • *n* biochimie *(f)*
biographer • *n* biograf *(m)*
biography • *n* biografie *(f)*
biological • *adj* biologic
biology • *n* biologie *(f)*
biomass • *n* biomas *(f)*
biophysics • *n* biofizic *(f)*
biotite • *n* biotit *(n)*
birch • *n* mesteacn
bird • *n* pasre *(f)*
birth • *n* natere *(f)*, origine *(f)*, început *(n)*
birthday • *n* aniversare, zi de natere
birthmark • *n* semn de natere *(n)*, aluni *(f)*
biscuit • *n* biscuit *(m)*
bisexuality • *n* bisexualitate *(f)*
bishop • *n* episcop *(m)*, nebun *(m)*
bismuth • *n* bismut *(n)*
bison • *n* zimbru *(m)*, bizon *(m)*
bit • *n* frâu, burghiu *(n)*, bucat
bitch • *n* cea *(f)*, lupoaic *(f)*, vulpoaic *(f)*
bite • *v* muca, înepa • *n* muctur *(f)*, înghi-itur *(f)*
biting • *adj* pictor *(n)*, tios *(n)*
bitter • *adj* amar
bittern • *n* bâtlan-de-stuf *(m)*, buhai-de-balt *(m)*
bitterness • *n* amrciune *(f)*, amreal *(f)*, fiere
bittersweet • *n* lsnicior
bitumen • *n* bitum
black • *n* negru, negru *(n)*, negres *(f)*, neagr *(f)* • *adj* negru
blackamoor • *n* cioroi *(m)*
blackberry • *n* mur *(m)*, mur *(f)*
blackbird • *n* mierla-neagr *(f)*, mierl *(f)*
blackboard • *n* tabl *(f)*
blackbuck • *n* antilop cu coarne spiralate *(f)*
blacken • *v* înnegri
blackmail • *v* antaja • *n* antaj *(n)*
blacksmith • *n* fierar *(m)*, potcovar *(m)*
bladder • *n* vezic *(f)*, bic *(f)*
blade • *n* lam *(f)*
blame • *v* inculpa, învinui, învinovi, blama
blameless • *adj* inocent *(m)*, inocent *(f)*, neprihnit *(m)*, nevinovat *(m)*
blameworthy • *adj* condamnabil *(m)*, de condamnat
bland • *adj* prevenitor *(m)*, afabil, gentil, pritenos, prietenos *(m)*, blând, linititor *(m)*
blank • *n* cartu orb *(n)*, loc gol *(n)* • *adj* inexpresiv *(n)*, neexpresiv *(n)*, nescris *(n)*, curat *(n)*, necompletat *(n)*
blanket • *n* ptur *(f)*, valtrap
blaspheme • *v* blestema
blast • *n* rafal (de vânt), vijelie, suflare, suflu, explozie *(f)*
blasted • *adj* distrus *(n)*, blestemat *(n)*, afurisit *(n)*, sterp *(n)*, mort *(n)*
blearedness • *n* urdoare
bleed • *v* sângera
blender • *n* malaxor *(m)*
bless • *v* binecuvânta, blagoslovi
blessed • *adj* binecuvântat *(n)*, blagoslovit *(n)*, binecuvântat *(f)*
blessing • *n* binecuvântare *(f)*, benedici-une *(f)*
blind • *adj* orb
blink • *v* clipi • *n* clipire *(f)*, clipit *(n)*, clip *(f)*, clipit *(f)*
bliss • *n* beatitudine *(f)*, euforie *(f)*, extaz *(n)*
blister • *n* bic
bloke • *n* tip *(m)*
blond • *n* blond
blood • *v* însângera • *n* sânge *(n)*
bloody • *adj* sângeros, crunt
blossom • *v* înflori
blot • *v* pta
blouse • *n* bluz *(f)*
blow • *v* sufla, fi purtat, umfla, cânta la un instrument, fluiera, uiera • *n* furtun *(f)*, suflare *(f)*, rsuflare, lovitur *(f)*
blue • *n* albastru • *adj* albastru, azuriu, deprimat *(m)*, trist *(m)*
blueberry • *n* afin *(f)*, coacze negre *(n)*, afin *(m)*, coacz negru *(m)*
blueprint • *n* copie de plan, schi *(f)*, plan *(n)*

bluethroat • *n* gu-albastr *(f)*
bluish • *adj* albstriu, albstrui
blunt • *adj* tocit, neascutit
blush • *v* împurpura, înroi, îmbujora, roi • *n* împurpurare *(f)*, înroire *(f)*, îmbujorare *(f)*, roea *(f)*, fard *(n)*, dres *(n)*
boa • *n* boa
boar • *n* vier, mascur
board • *n* scândur *(f)*
boarding • *n* îmbarcare
boat • *n* barc *(f)*, luntre *(f)*, vapor *(n)*
bodily • *adj* trupesc, corporal
body • *n* corp *(n)*, trup *(n)*, trunchi *(n)*, tors *(n)*
bodyguard • *n* gard de corp *(f)*
bohemian • *n* boem *(m)* • *adj* boem
boil • *n* abces *(n)*, furuncul *(n)*, buboi *(n)* • *v* fierbe
bolt • *n* bol
bomb • *n* bomb *(f)*
bombardment • *n* bombardament, bombardare *(f)*
bomber • *n* bombardier *(n)*, avion de bombardament *(n)*
bond • *n* legtur *(f)*, alian *(f)*
bone • *n* os
boner • *n* erecie *(f)*
bonfire • *n* rug *(n)*
bonhomie • *n* bonomie *(f)*, bun dispoziie *(f)*
bonito • *n* bonit *(f)*, plmid *(f)*
bony • *adj* osos
boo • *interj* bau, huo
booger • *n* muc
book • *v* rezerva • *n* carte *(f)*
bookbinder • *n* legtor de cri *(m)*
bookbinding • *n* legare de cri
bookkeeper • *n* contabil *(m)*
booklet • *n* crticic *(f)*, brour *(f)*, plachet *(f)*
bookseller • *n* librar *(m)*
bookshop • *n* librrie *(f)*
bookworm • *n* molie de cri *(f)*, oarece de bibliotec *(f)*
boom • *n* bubuit *(n)*, detuntur *(f)*, avânt *(n)*, prosperitate *(f)* • *interj* bum
boomerang • *n* bumerang
boor • *n* ran *(m)*, bdran *(m)*, mojic *(m)*, necioplit *(m)*, incult *(m)*
boot • *n* cizm
bootstrap • *v* pornire • *n* limb de ghete *(f)*, amorsare *(f)*, bootstrap *(n)*
booty • *n* prad
booze • *n* pileal
borage • *n* limba-mielului *(f)*
border • *n* bordur *(f)*, margine *(f)*, grani *(f)*, frontier *(f)*, cant *(n)*
bore • *v* gaurii, plictisi
boreal • *adj* boreal
bored • *adj* plictisit
boredom • *n* plictiseal *(f)*
borer • *n* main de gurit, bormain *(f)*
boring • *adj* plictisitor, plicticos, anost, fastidios
born • *adj* nscut
boron • *n* bor *(n)*
borough • *n* târg
borrow • *v* împrumuta
borscht • *n* bor
boss • *n* ef *(m)*
bot • *n* bot
botanical • *adj* botanic
botanist • *n* botanist *(m)*
botanize • *v* botaniza
botany • *n* botanic *(f)*
botfly • *n* streche *(f)*
both • *conj* atât ... cât i ...
bother • *v* deranja, incomoda, necji, supra • *n* agitaie *(f)*, îngrijorare *(f)*, deranj *(n)*, incomodare *(f)*
bottle • *n* sticl *(f)*
bottom • *n* fund, cur *(n)*, ezut, dos, pasiv, zân *(f)*, fund *(n)*
botulism • *n* botulism *(n)*
bougainvillea • *n* bougainvillea *(f)*
bough • *n* creang *(f)*
boulder • *n* bolovan *(m)*
bouncing • *adj* viguros, robust *(m)*, plin de via *(m)*
bound • *adj* obligat *(m)*
boundary • *n* frontier *(f)*, grani *(f)*, limit *(f)*
bouquet • *n* buchet *(n)*, arom *(f)*
bourgeoisie • *n* burghezie
bovid • *n* bovideu *(n)*, bovid *(n)*
bovine • *n* bovin *(f)* • *adj* viel
bow • *n* arc *(f)* • *v* apleca, închina
bowel • *n* intestin gros *(n)*, pântec *(n)*, pântece *(n)*, sân *(m)*
bowl • *n* castron *(n)*
bowler • *n* popicar *(m)*
bowling • *n* bowling, popice
bowsprit • *n* bompres *(n)*
box • *n* cutie *(f)*, loj *(f)*, caban *(f)*, barac *(f)*, cimiir *(m)*
boxing • *n* box *(n)*
boy • *n* biat, fiu, biat *(m)*, tip *(m)*
boyar • *n* boier *(m)*
boyfriend • *n* prieten *(m)*
bra • *n* sutien *(n)*
bracelet • *n* brar *(f)*, curea *(f)*
brachial • *adj* brahial
bract • *n* bractee *(f)*
braid • *n* împletitur *(m)*
brain • *n* creier *(m)*, erudit *(m)*, intelect

(n)
brake • *v* frâna • *n* frân
bramble • *n* mur *(m)*, rug *(m)*
bran • *n* trâe
branch • *v* ramifica, sri • *n* ram *(n)*, ramur *(f)*, creang *(f)*, ramificare, filial *(f)*, sucursal *(f)*, bran *(f)*
branched • *adj* ramificat *(n)*, ramificat *(f)*
branchy • *adj* rmuros *(m)*
brand • *v* stigmatiza, marca, însemna, întipri, grava, înfiera • *n* marc *(f)*, efigie *(f)*
brandish • *v* flutura, învârti
brandy • *n* rachiu, vinars
brashness • *n* tupeu *(n)*
brass • *n* alam *(f)*, almuri
brat • *n* plod, odrasl, vlstar, copil, puti *(m)*
brave • *adj* curajos, brav
bravery • *n* bravur *(f)*, curaj *(n)*, brbie *(f)*
bravo • *n* bravo • *interj* bravo
brawl • *n* încierare *(f)*, ceart *(f)*
brazier • *n* vas pentru jeratic, armar *(m)*
brazilwood • *n* fernambuc *(m)*, pernambuc *(m)*
bread • *n* pâine *(f)*
breadfruit • *n* arbore de pâine *(m)*
breadwinner • *n* câtigtor de pâine *(m)*, salariat
breaker • *n* concasor *(n)*
breakfast • *v* lua micul dejun • *n* mic dejun *(n)*
bream • *n* pltic *(f)*
breast • *n* piept *(f)*, sân *(m)*, piept
breastplate • *n* pieptar *(n)*
breaststroke • *n* bras *(n)*
breath • *n* respiraie, suflu *(m)*, halen *(f)*, alen *(f)*
breathe • *v* respira
breed • *n* ras *(f)*
breeze • *n* adiere, boare, briz
breviary • *n* breviar *(n)*
brewer • *n* berar *(m)*, fabricant de bere *(m)*
brewery • *n* fabric de bere *(f)*
briar • *n* mrcine
bribe • *n* mit *(f)*
brick • *n* crmid
bridal • *n* nunt *(f)*
bride • *n* nevast *(f)*, mireas *(f)*
bridegroom • *n* mire *(m)*
bridge • *n* pod *(n)*, punte *(f)*, bridge
bridle • *v* înfrâna • *n* frâu
brie • *n* brie *(n)*
brief • *adj* scurt
bright • *adj* luminos, clar, strlucitor, detept
brilliance • *n* strlucire *(f)*, genialitate *(f)*, suprainteligen *(f)*, inteligen genial *(f)*, splendoare *(f)*, mreie *(f)*, grandoare *(f)*, magnificen
brilliancy • *n* strlucire *(f)*, brilian
brimstone • *n* pucioas *(f)*
brine • *n* saramur *(f)*
bring • *v* aduce
broadcast • *v* difuza, emite, prezenta • *n* difuzare *(f)*, transmisiune *(f)*, emisiune *(f)*
broccoli • *n* broccoli
broken • *adj* rupt, frânt
broker • *n* agent *(m)*
bromide • *n* bromur *(f)*
bromine • *n* brom *(n)*
bronchitis • *n* bronit *(f)*
bronze • *v* bronza • *n* bronz *(n)* • *adj* bronzat
brood • *v* cloci
brook • *n* pârâu *(n)*
broom • *n* mtur *(f)*, drob *(m)*
broth • *n* sup
brothel • *n* bordel, lupanar
brother • *v* înfri, fraterniza • *n* frate *(m)*
brother-in-law • *n* cumnat *(m)*
brotherhood • *n* fraternitate *(f)*, frie *(f)*
brotherly • *adj* fresc, fratern
brown • *n* brun, maro *(n)* • *adj* maro, brun
bruise • *v* zgâria • *n* julitur *(f)*
brunch • *n* brunch *(n)*
brunette • *adj* brunet
brush • *v* peria, vopsi, picta, mtura, terge • *n* perie *(f)*, pensul *(f)*, periat *(n)*
brutal • *adj* brutal *(n)*, brutal *(f)*
bryophyte • *n* briofit *(f)*
bubble • *n* balon *(n)*, bic *(f)*, bul *(f)*
bubo • *n* bubon *(n)*
bucket • *n* gleat *(f)*, cldare *(f)*, gleat
buckthorn • *n* verigar *(m)*
buckwheat • *n* hric *(f)*
bud • *n* boboc *(m)*, mugure *(m)*, mugur *(m)*
buffalo • *n* bivol *(m)*, bizon *(m)*
buffer • *n* memorie tampon *(f)*, memorie intermediar *(f)*
bug • *n* gândac, gânganie, microfon *(n)*
build • *v* cldi
building • *n* cldire *(f)*, construire *(f)*, edificare *(f)*, edificiu *(m)*
built • *v* construi, construit, cldit
bulb • *n* bulb *(m)*
bulk • *n* masa, vrac • *adj* masiv, voluminos
bulky • *adj* mare, voluminos, mthlos
bull • *n* taur *(m)*
bulldozer • *n* buldozer *(n)*
bullet • *n* glon *(n)*, glonte *(n)*, halíce *(n)*
bullfighting • *n* corid *(f)*

bullfinch • *n* botro
bullock • *n* junc
bullshit • *n* rahat, ccat *(n)*, vrjeal *(f)*, trombon *(n)*
bully • *v* intimida • *n* tiran *(m)*
bulrush • *n* papur
bumblebee • *n* bondar *(m)*
bumper • *n* bar de protecie *(f)*
bun • *n* chifl *(f)*
bunch • *n* mnunchi
bund • *n* legatura *(f)*, uniune *(f)*
bundle • *v* a lega (la un loc), a matisa, înfofoli, încotomna • *n* snop *(m)*, mnunchi, fascicul *(n)*, legtur *(f)*, colet *(m)*, pachet *(n)*, fascicul de fibre nervoase
bunny • *n* iepura
bunting • *n* presur *(f)*
buoy • *n* geamandur *(f)*
burden • *n* sarcin
burdock • *n* brusture
bureau • *n* birou *(n)*
bureaucracy • *n* birocraie *(f)*
bureaucrat • *n* birocrat *(m)*
bureaucratic • *adj* birocratic *(m)*
burgeon • *v* înmuguri, înflori
burglar • *n* sprgtor *(m)*
burgundy • *adj* bordo
burial • *n* înmormântare *(f)*, îngropare *(f)*, înhumare *(f)*
burn • *v* arde • *n* arsur *(f)*
burning • *n* ardere *(f)* • *adj* arztor *(n)*, ardent *(n)*, ferbinte
burp • *v* râgâi
burrow • *n* vizuin *(f)*
bury • *v* îngropa
bus • *n* autobuz *(n)*, magistral *(f)*
busboy • *n* picolo *(m)*
bush • *n* arbust *(m)*, tuf, tufi de arbuti
bushbuck • *n* antilop-de-pdure *(f)*
business • *n* întreprindere *(f)*, afacere *(f)*, afacere
businessman • *n* om de afaceri *(m)*, businessman *(m)*
bustard • *n* dropie *(f)*
bustle • *n* freamt, turnur *(f)*
busy • *adj* harnic
but • *conj* dar
butane • *n* butan
butcher • *v* mcelri, omorî, tia • *n* mcelar
butt • *n* cur *(n)*, fund *(n)*, patul pustii *(n)*, izbitura *(f)*, lovitura puternica cu capul • *v* lovi puternic, izbi cu capul
butter • *n* unt *(n)*
buttercup • *n* piciorul-cocoului *(n)*, glbenea *(f)*
butterfly • *n* fluture *(m)*
buttermilk • *n* zar *(f)*
butterwort • *n* foaie-gras *(f)*, îngrtoare *(f)*
buttock • *n* buc *(f)*, buci
button • *n* buton *(n)*, nasture *(m)*
butyl • *n* butil *(m)*
buxom • *adj* durdliu
buy • *v* cumpra
buyer • *n* cumprtor *(m)*, cumprtoare *(f)*, client *(m)*
buzzard • *n* oricar *(m)*
by • *prep* lâng, de, cu
bye • *interj* pa
bypass • *n* deviaie *(f)*, ocolire *(f)*

C

cabbage • *n* varz *(f)*, legum *(f)*
cable • *v* cablare *(f)* • *n* cablu, frânghie *(f)*, cablu *(n)*, cabluri, conductor *(m)*, cablu optic *(n)*, televiziune prin cablu, telegram *(f)*, telegrame
cacao • *n* arbore-de-cacao *(m)*, cacao *(f)*
cache • *n* cache
cacophony • *n* cacofonia *(f)*
cactus • *n* cactus *(m)*
cadaver • *n* cadavru *(n)*
cadence • *n* caden, ritm, tact
cadmium • *n* cadmiu *(n)*
caecum • *n* cec *(n)*, cecum *(n)*
cafeteria • *n* cofetrie *(f)*
caffeine • *n* cafein *(f)*, cofein *(f)*
cage • *n* cuc
cake • *n* tort, prjitur *(f)*, turt *(f)*, bucat *(f)*
calamity • *n* flagel, calamitate *(f)*, calamiti
calamus • *n* obligean *(f)*
calciferous • *adj* calcaros
calcium • *n* calciu *(n)*
calculable • *adj* calculabil *(n)*
calculate • *v* calcula, socoti
calculation • *n* calculare *(f)*, calcul *(n)*
calculator • *n* calculator, computer *(n)*, computere, main de calculat, calculator *(m)*, calculatoare *(f)*, tabele
calculus • *n* calcul *(n)*, calcul diferenial *(n)*, piatr, calcul *(m)*
calendar • *n* calendar, agend *(f)*, program *(n)*, calendar *(n)*
calf • *n* viel *(m)*, viea *(f)*, pui *(m)*, pulp *(f)*, gamb *(f)*
californium • *n* californiu *(n)*

call • *v* chema, striga, telefona, suna, vizita, numi • *n* chemare, vizit *(f)*
calligraphic • *adj* caligrafic
callus • *n* bttur
calm • *v* liniti, calma • *n* linite *(f)* • *adj* linitit, calm *(m)*
calmly • *adv* calm
calmness • *n* calm *(n)*, linite *(f)*
calorie • *n* calorie *(f)*
calorimetry • *n* calorimetrie *(f)*
caltrop • *n* colii-babei *(m)*
calyx • *n* caliciu *(n)*
cam • *n* cam *(f)*
camel • *n* cmil *(f)*
camellia • *n* camelie *(f)*
camera • *n* camera photographica *(f)*, machina photographica *(f)*, aparat foto
camphor • *n* camfor *(n)*
campus • *n* campus, teren universitar
camshaft • *n* arbore cu came *(m)*, ax cu came *(n)*
can • *v* putea
canal • *n* canal *(m)*, canal *(n)*
canary • *n* canar *(m)*
cancel • *v* anula
cancer • *n* cancer
cancerous • *adj* canceros
candle • *n* lumânare
candlestick • *n* sfenic
cane • *n* tij *(f)*, baston *(n)*
canister • *n* canistr *(f)*
cannabis • *n* cânep *(f)*
cannibal • *n* canibal *(m)*, canibal *(f)*
cannibalism • *n* canibalism *(n)*
cannibalistic • *adj* canibalistic *(n)*, antropofag, canibalic *(n)*
cannon • *n* tun *(n)*
canoe • *n* canoe *(f)*
canonize • *v* a institui ca regul (sacr), canoniza, a declara ca sfânt
canonized • *adj* canonizat *(n)*, canonizat *(f)*
cantaloupe • *n* cantalup *(m)*
cantankerous • *adj* suprcios, susceptibil, iritabil
cantata • *n* cantat *(f)*
canteen • *n* cantin *(f)*
canthus • *n* cantusul *(m)*
canto • *n* cânt *(n)*
canvas • *n* canava *(f)*
canyon • *n* defileu, canion *(n)*
caoutchouc • *n* cauciuc *(n)*
capability • *n* capabilitate *(f)*
capable • *adj* capabil
capacitance • *n* capacitate electric *(f)*
capacity • *n* capacitate *(f)*, capacitate
cape • *n* cap *(n)*, promontoriu *(n)*, cap *(f)*
caper • *v* sri, zburda, opi • *n* salt *(n)*, souritur *(f)*, tumb *(f)*, opit *(n)*, caper *(f)*, caper *(m)*
capercaillie • *n* cocoul de munte
capillarity • *n* capilaritate
capillary • *n* vas capilar
capital • *n* capital
capitalism • *n* capitalism *(n)*
capitalist • *n* capitalist *(n)*
capitate • *adj* capitat
capitulate • *v* capitula
capon • *n* clapon
caprice • *n* capriciu *(n)*, impulsivitate
capricious • *adj* capricios
capybara • *n* capibara *(f)*
car • *n* main *(f)*, automobil *(n)*, vagon, cabin *(f)*
caracara • *n* caracara *(m)*
caramel • *n* caramel, caramel
carapace • *n* carapace
caraway • *n* chimen
carbine • *n* carabin *(f)*
carbohydrate • *n* carbohidrat *(m)*
carbon • *n* carbon *(n)*, crbune
carbonate • *n* carbonat *(m)*
carbonic • *adj* carbonic *(n)*
carburetor • *n* carburator *(n)*
carcass • *n* cadavru *(n)*, corp mort *(n)*, hoit *(n)*, stârv *(n)*, carcas *(f)*
carcinogenic • *adj* cancerigen, carcinogen
card • *n* card *(m)*, carte *(f)* • *v* carda, scrmna, drci
cardamom • *n* cardamom *(m)*
cardboard • *n* carton *(n)*, mucava *(f)*
cardiac • *adj* cardiac *(m)*
cardinal • *n* numr cardinal *(n)*, cardinal *(m)* • *adj* cardinal *(m)*, fundamental *(m)*, cardinal, rou purpuriu *(m)*, rou cardinal
cardiologist • *n* cardiolog *(m)*
cardiology • *n* cardiologie *(f)*
cardoon • *n* cardon *(m)*
care • *n* grij, ps • *v* îngriji
carefree • *adj* fr, lipsit de griji
careful • *adj* precaut, prudent, precaut *(m)*, prudent *(m)*
careless • *adj* nepstor, neglijent
caress • *v* dezmierda, alinta, mângâia
caribou • *n* caribu *(n)*, karibu *(n)*
carillon • *n* carilon *(n)*
carmine • *n* carmin *(n)*, cârmâz *(n)*, coenil *(f)*, carmin • *adj* carmin, stacojiu, cârmâziu
carnation • *n* garoaf *(f)* • *adj* roz
carnivorous • *adj* carnivor *(n)*, carnivor *(f)*
carob • *n* rocov *(m)*, rocov *(f)*
carp • *n* crap *(m)*
carpel • *n* carpel *(f)*

carpenter • *n* dulgher *(m)*, tâmplar *(m)*, lemnar *(m)*
carpet • *n* covor *(m)*
carriage • *n* vagon *(n)*
carriageway • *n* osea *(f)*
carrier • *n* semnal purttor *(n)*
carrot • *n* morcov *(m)*, carot *(f)*
carry • *v* duce, purta, cra
cart • *n* car *(n)*, cru *(f)*, aret
cartilage • *n* cartilaj *(n)*
cartilaginous • *adj* cartilaginos *(m)*, cartilaginos
cartography • *n* cartografie
cartoon • *n* caricatur *(f)*, desen *(n)*, desen animat *(n)*
cartridge • *n* cartu
cascade • *n* cascad *(f)*, circuit-cascad *(n)*
case • *n* caz *(n)*, cazuri, lad
cash • *n* numerar *(n)*, bani lichizi *(m)*, bani ghea *(m)*, bani, numerar în cas *(n)*
cashew • *n* acaju, anacardier *(m)*
cask • *n* bute *(f)*, butoi *(n)*
castanet • *n* castaniete
castaway • *n* vas naufragiat
castle • *v* face rocad • *n* castel *(n)*
castrate • *v* castra
casuistry • *n* cazuistic *(f)*
cat • *n* pisic *(f)*, motan *(m)*, cotoi *(m)*, mâ *(f)*, felin *(f)*
cataclysm • *n* cataclism *(n)*
catacomb • *n* catacomb *(f)*
catalysis • *n* cataliz *(f)*
catalyst • *n* catalizator *(m)*
catalytic • *adj* catalitic *(n)*
cataract • *n* cataract *(f)*
catastrophe • *n* catastrof *(f)*, dezastru *(n)*, deznodmânt *(n)*
catastrophic • *adj* catastrofic, catastrofal *(n)*, catastrofic *(f)*, dezastruos *(n)*, dezastruoas *(f)*
catch • *v* prinde
catchment • *n* domeniu de precipitaii *(n)*
catechism • *n* catehism *(n)*
categorization • *n* categorisire
category • *n* categorie *(f)*, categorii, categorie
catenary • *n* linie aerian de contact
caterpillar • *n* omid *(f)*, enil *(f)*
catfish • *n* somn *(m)*, silur *(m)*
catgut • *n* catgut *(n)*
cathedral • *n* catedral *(f)*
cation • *n* cation *(m)*
catkin • *n* ament *(m)*, mâior *(m)*
catnip • *n* iarba-mâei *(f)*, ctunic *(f)*
cattail • *n* papur *(f)*
cattle • *n* bovine, vite
caudal • *adj* caudal
cauliflower • *n* conopid *(f)*
cause • *v* cauza, pricinui • *n* cauz *(f)*
caustic • *n* caustic
cautiously • *adv* prudent, cu pruden, prevztor, cu prevedere, precaut, cu precauie
cavalry • *n* cavalerie *(f)*
cave • *n* peter *(f)*, cavern *(f)*, grot *(f)*
caviar • *n* caviar *(n)*
cedar • *n* cedru
cedilla • *n* sedil *(f)*
ceiling • *n* plafon *(n)*, tavan *(n)*
celebrate • *v* celebra, srbtori
celebration • *n* srbtorire *(f)*, celebrare *(f)*, festivitate *(f)*, srbtoare *(f)*, petrecere *(f)*, serbare *(f)*
celebratory • *adj* celebrant *(m)*
celeriac • *n* elin-de-rdcin *(f)*
celery • *n* elin *(f)*
celesta • *n* celest
celestial • *adj* ceresc *(n)*, cereasc *(f)*
cell • *n* celul *(f)*, chilie *(f)*, celular *(n)*, mobil *(n)*
cellar • *n* pivni *(f)*, beci *(n)*
cello • *n* violoncel *(n)*
cellular • *adj* celular *(m)*
celtuce • *n* salat chinezeasc *(f)*
cement • *n* ciment
censor • *v* cenzura • *n* cenzor *(m)*
centaury • *n* fierea-pmântului *(f)*, intaur *(f)*
centennial • *n* centenar
center • *v* centra, concentra • *n* mijloc, centru
centime • *n* cent
centipede • *n* centiped
central • *adj* central
centralization • *n* centralizare
century • *n* secol *(n)*, veac *(n)*, centurie *(f)*
ceramic • *n* ceramic *(f)* • *adj* ceramic *(n)*
cereal • *n* cereal *(f)*
cerebellum • *n* cerebel, creiera
cerebral • *adj* cerebral
ceremonially • *adv* ceremonios *(n)*
ceremony • *n* ceremonie *(f)*
cerium • *n* ceriu *(n)*
certain • *adj* cert, anume, sigur
certainly • *adv* bineîneles, desigur
certainty • *n* certitudine *(f)*, siguran *(f)*
certify • *v* certifica
certitude • *n* certitudine *(f)*, convingere *(f)*, siguran *(f)*
cerulean • *n* albastru
cetacean • *n* cetaceu *(n)*
chaff • *n* pleav *(f)*
chaffinch • *n* cintez *(f)*
chain • *n* lan
chair • *n* scaun *(n)*, scaune, preedinte *(m)*,

preedini, preedint *(f)*, preedinte
chairman • *n* director
chalice • *n* caliciu *(n)*
chalk • *n* cret *(f)*
challenge • *v* provoca • *n* provocare *(f)*
chameleon • *n* cameleon *(m)*
chamois • *n* amoa *(m)*, capr-neagr *(f)*, capr-de-munte *(f)*
champagne • *n* ampanie *(f)*
champion • *n* campion *(m)*, campioan *(f)*
championship • *n* campionat *(m)*, campion *(m)*, campioan *(f)*
chance • *v* risca • *n* ans *(f)*, anse, ocazie *(f)*, întâmplare *(f)*, accident *(n)*, probabilitate *(f)*
chancellor • *n* cancelar *(m)*, cancelar *(f)*
chandelier • *n* candelabru *(n)*
change • *v* schimba, transforma, modifica, înlocui • *n* schimb *(n)*, schimbare *(f)*, modificare *(f)*, schimb (de bani) *(n)*
changeable • *adj* schimbabil *(m)*, modificabil *(m)*
channel • *n* canal, canal *(n)*, canal *(m)*
chaos • *n* haos *(n)*
chaotic • *adj* haotic
chapel • *n* capel *(f)*
chapter • *n* capitol
character • *n* personaj *(n)*
characteristic • *n* caracteristic • *adj* caracteristic
characterize • *v* caracteriza
charcoal • *n* crbune *(m)*, crbune de lemn *(m)*
chard • *n* mangold *(m)*, sfecl furajer *(f)*
charge • *v* încrca • *n* sarcin *(f)*, acuzare *(f)*, inculpare *(f)*, încrctur *(f)*
chariot • *n* big *(f)*, car de lupt *(n)*
charisma • *n* carism, charism *(f)*
charismatic • *adj* carismatic *(m)*
charm • *v* fermeca, încânta, fascina, descânta, vrji • *n* amulet *(f)*, talisman *(n)*, farmec, arm *(n)*, graie *(f)*, breloc *(n)*
charming • *adj* armant, fermector, încânttor, carismatic *(m)*
chart • *n* hart maritim *(f)*
chase • *n* urmrire
chaste • *adj* cast
chauffeur • *n* ofer *(m)*
chauvinism • *n* ovinism *(n)*
check • *n* ah, not de plat *(f)*, socoteal *(f)*, factur *(f)*, control *(n)*, verificare *(f)*, supraveghere *(f)*, inspecie *(f)*, verificare
checkmate • *n* ah-mat *(n)* • *interj* ah mat
cheek • *n* obraz, buc *(f)*, buc
cheerfulness • *n* veselie *(f)*
cheerleader • *n* majoreta *(f)*
cheers • *interj* sntate!, pa, mersi
cheese • *n* brânz *(f)*, ca *(n)*, cacaval *(n)*
cheetah • *n* ghepard *(m)*
chemical • *adj* chimic
chemist • *n* chimist *(m)*, chimist *(f)*
chemistry • *n* chimie *(f)*
cheque • *n* cec
cherry • *n* cirea *(f)*, viin *(f)*, cire *(m)*, viin *(m)*
chervil • *n* hasmauchi *(m)*
chess • *n* ah *(n)*
chest • *n* torace *(n)*, piept
chestnut • *n* castan • *adj* roib
chew • *v* mesteca • *n* caramea *(f)*
chick • *n* pui, tip *(f)*
chickadee • *n* piigoi *(m)*
chicken • *n* pui, gin *(f)*
chickpea • *n* nut *(m)*
chicory • *n* cicoare
chide • *v* mustra, certa
chief • *n* cpetenie *(f)*, ef *(m)*
chiefly • *adv* mai ales, mai cu seam, îndeosebi, în principal
chilblain • *n* degertur *(f)*
child • *n* fiu *(m)*, fiic *(f)*, copil *(m)*, copil *(f)*
childhood • *n* copilrie *(f)*
chimney • *n* co *(n)*, cos *(m)*, horn, cmin *(n)*, fumar *(n)*
chimpanzee • *n* cimpanzeu *(m)*
chin • *n* brbie *(f)*
chinchilla • *n* inil *(f)*, cincila *(f)*
chip • *n* surcea, achie, fragment *(n)*, cip *(n)*
chipmunk • *n* veveri dungat *(f)*
chiropractor • *n* chiropractician *(m)*
chisel • *n* dalt *(f)*
chivalry • *n* cavalerie *(f)*, cavalerism *(n)*, galanterie *(f)*
chlorine • *n* clor *(n)*
chocolate • *n* ciocolat *(f)*, pralin *(f)*, bomboan *(f)* • *adj* ciocolatiu *(n)*, de ciocolat
choir • *n* cor
choke • *n* oc *(n)*
choler • *n* furie *(f)*, mânie *(f)*
choose • *v* alege, vrea, prefera
choral • *adj* coral
chorale • *n* coral *(n)*, cor *(n)*
chord • *n* acord, coard *(f)*
chromium • *n* crom *(n)*
chromosome • *n* cromozom *(m)*
chronicle • *n* cronic *(f)*
chronological • *adj* cronologic *(m)*
chronology • *n* cronologie *(f)*
chrysanthemum • *n* crizantem
chuck • *n* mandrin *(f)*
chufa • *n* migdal-de-pmânt *(f)*
church • *n* biseric *(f)*, biserici, biseric, serviciu religios *(n)*, slujb *(f)*, ceremonie reli-

gioas *(f)*
churlish • *adj* ursuz
cicada • *n* cicad *(f)*, cicoare *(f)*
cigar • *n* trabuc *(n)*
cigarette • *n* igar *(f)*, igaret *(f)*
cinch • *n* ching *(f)*
cinema • *n* cinematografie *(f)*
cinereous • *adj* cenuiu, plin de cenu
cinnabar • *n* cinabru *(n)*, chinovar *(n)*, vermillon *(n)*, cinabru
cinnamon • *n* scorior *(m)*, scorioar *(f)*
circle • *n* cerc
circuit • *n* ciclu *(n)*, circuit *(n)*, circuit
circular • *adj* circular, de cerc
circulate • *v* cercui, a face cercuri
circumcise • *v* circumcide
circumcision • *n* circumcizie *(f)*
circumference • *n* circumferin
circumscribe • *v* circumscrie
circumstance • *n* circumstan *(f)*, împrejurare *(f)*
circumvent • *v* înconjura, ocoli, conturna
circus • *n* circ *(n)*
cistern • *n* cistern *(f)*
citadel • *n* citadel *(f)*, cetate, fortificaie *(f)*
citation • *n* citare *(f)*, citat *(n)*
citizen • *n* cetean
citizenship • *n* cetenie *(f)*
citron • *n* chitru *(m)*, chitr *(f)*
citrus • *n* citrice, agrume
city • *n* ora *(n)*, cetate *(f)*, urbe *(f)*
civet • *n* zibet *(f)*
civility • *n* civilitate *(f)*, politee *(f)*, curtenie *(f)*
civilization • *n* civilizaie *(f)*, cultur *(f)*, civilizare *(f)*, civilitate *(f)*
civilized • *adj* civilizat *(m)*, civilizat *(f)*
claim • *v* revendica *(f)* • *n* pretenie *(f)*, revendicare *(f)*, petiie *(f)*, reclamaie *(f)*
clairvoyance • *n* clarviziune
clam • *n* molusc comestibil *(f)*
clandestine • *adj* clandestin
clapper • *n* limb *(f)*
claret • *n* vin de Bordeaux *(n)*
clarification • *n* clarificare *(f)*
clarify • *v* clarifica
clarinet • *n* clarinet *(n)*, clarinet *(f)*
clarinetist • *n* clarinetist *(m)*
clarity • *n* claritate
clasp • *v* apuca
class • *n* clas *(f)*
classical • *adj* clasic *(n)*, clasici, clasic *(f)*
classifiable • *adj* clasificabil *(m)*
classification • *n* clasificare *(f)*, clasificaie *(f)*
classify • *v* clasifica
classroom • *n* clas *(f)*
clavicle • *n* clavicul *(f)*
claw • *n* ghear *(f)*, clete *(m)* • *v* zgâria
clay • *n* argil *(f)*, lut *(n)*, hlei *(n)*
clean • *v* cura, terge • *adj* curat
clear • *adj* clar, limpede, senin, liber *(m)*, curat *(m)*
clear-sighted • *adj* vz ascuit *(n)*
cleat • *n* crampon *(n)*
clef • *n* cheie *(f)*
clematis • *n* clematit *(f)*
clemency • *n* clemen *(f)*, îndurare *(f)*, buntate *(f)*, blândee *(f)*
clergyman • *n* cleric
clerk • *n* secretar *(m)*, birocrat *(m)*, funcionar *(m)*
clever • *adj* detept
click • *v* clica • *n* clic *(n)*, clicare
client • *n* client
cliff • *n* stânc *(f)*, falez *(f)*, pant *(f)*
climate • *n* clim *(f)*
climatology • *n* climatologie *(f)*
climax • *n* culme
climb • *v* urca, sui
clinic • *n* clinic *(f)*
clip • *n* agraf *(f)*
clitoris • *n* clitoris *(n)*, lindic
cloakroom • *n* garderoba
clock • *n* ceas *(n)*, contor de parcurs *(n)*
clod • *n* bulgre *(m)*
clog • *v* înfunda
cloister • *v* claustra • *n* claustru *(n)*, arcad *(f)*, mnstire *(f)*, clugrie *(f)*, sihstrie *(f)*
close • *v* închide, termina, finisa • *adj* aproape
closed • *adj* închis, privat *(m)*
closeness • *n* prietenie *(f)*
closure • *n* închidere *(f)*
clot • *v* închega • *n* cheag
cloth • *n* pânz *(f)*, stof *(f)*, cârp *(f)*
clothe • *v* îmbrca
clothes • *n* haine, îmbrcminte, rufe
clothing • *n* îmbrcminte *(f)*, hain
cloud • *v* înnora, înnegura, întuneca • *n* nor *(m)*, negur *(f)*
cloudiness • *n* stare noroas *(f)*
cloudless • *adj* senin, clar, limpede
cloudy • *adj* înnorat
clove • *n* cuioare, cel *(m)*
clover • *n* trifoi *(n)*
clown • *n* clovn *(m)*, claun *(m)*, bufon *(m)*, imbecil *(m)*, cretin *(m)*, neghiob *(m)*, paia *(f)*
cloy • *v* stura
club • *n* bât *(f)*
clubfoot • *n* varus
clumsy • *adj* stângaci, neîndemânatic, greoi, grosolan, butucnos

clutch • *v* aga, apuca • *n* ambreiaj *(n)*, pedal de ambreiaj *(f)*
coach • *n* antrenor *(m)*
coagulable • *adj* coagulabil
coagulation • *n* coagulare *(f)*
coal • *n* crbune *(m)*, tciune *(m)*
coarse • *adj* grosier, aspru
coast • *n* coast, rm de mare, coborâre la vale, liman, mal, limit, hotar
coati • *n* coati *(m)*
coating • *n* strat
cobalt • *n* cobalt *(n)*
coca • *n* coca *(m)*
cocaine • *n* cocain *(f)*
cock • *n* brbtu *(m)*, coco *(n)*
cock-a-doodle-doo • *interj* cucurigu
cockatoo • *n* cacadu *(m)*
cockchafer • *n* crbu *(m)*
cockerel • *n* cocoel *(m)*
cockpit • *n* carling *(f)*, cabin de pilotaj
cockroach • *n* gândac *(m)*, libarc *(f)*
cocksucker • *n* muist *(m)*, muist *(f)*, sugator de pula *(m)*, sugatoare de pul *(f)*, muist
cocktail • *n* cocteil *(n)*, cocktail *(n)*
cocoa • *n* cacao *(f)*, pulbere de cacao *(f)*, cacao
coconut • *n* nuc de cocos *(f)*
cod • *n* cod
code • *n* cod *(n)*
codification • *n* codificare *(f)*
coding • *n* codare-decodare, codificare-decodificare
coefficient • *n* coeficient *(m)*
coercion • *n* coerciie *(f)*, coercitare *(f)*
coffee • *n* cafea *(f)*, arbore-de-cafea *(m)*, cafeniu
coffin • *n* sicriu *(n)*, cociug *(n)*
cognitive • *adj* cognitiv
cohesive • *adj* coerent, coeziv
coin • *n* moned *(f)*
coke • *n* cocs *(n)*
cola • *n* cola *(f)*
colander • *n* strecurtoare *(f)*
cold • *n* frig, grip *(f)*, rceal *(f)* • *adj* rece, înfrigurat
cold-blooded • *adj* cu sânge rece
coldness • *n* frig *(n)*, rceal *(f)*
collaboration • *n* colaborare *(f)*, colaborri
collage • *n* colaj *(m)*, colaj *(n)*
collapse • *v* prbui, prbuire *(f)* • *n* colaps *(n)*, cdere *(f)*
colleague • *n* coleg *(m)*, coleg *(f)*
collect • *v* culege
collection • *n* colectare *(f)*, colecie *(f)*
collectivism • *n* colectivism *(n)*
collectivization • *n* colectivizare *(f)*
collector • *n* colecionar *(m)*
college • *n* facultate *(f)*, institut *(n)*, colegiu *(n)*, coal secundar *(f)*
collision • *n* ciocnire *(f)*, coliziune *(f)*
colloid • *n* coloid *(m)*, suspensie coloidal *(f)*
colloquial • *adj* colocvial, familiar
colloquy • *n* colocviul *(n)*
cologne • *n* ap de Colonia *(f)*
colon • *n* dou puncte
colonel • *n* colonel *(m)*
colonial • *adj* colonial
colonialism • *n* colonialism *(m)*
colonist • *n* colonist *(m)*, colonist *(f)*
colony • *n* colonie *(f)*
color • *v* colora • *n* culoare *(f)*, culoare de piele *(f)*
colored • *adj* colorat *(n)*, plin de culoare *(n)*
colossal • *adj* colosal
colostrum • *n* corasl, colastr
colt • *n* mânz *(m)*, novice *(f)*, începtor *(m)*
coltsfoot • *n* podbeal *(m)*
columbine • *n* cldru *(f)*
column • *n* coloan, pilar, column, stâlp, coloan *(f)*
coma • *n* com *(f)*
comb • *v* pieptna
combat • *v* combate • *n* lupt, btaie *(f)*
combative • *adj* combativ *(n)*
combination • *n* combinare *(f)*, combinaie *(f)*
combine • *v* îmbina, combina • *n* combinat *(n)*
combustion • *n* combustie *(f)*, combustii, ardere *(f)*, arderi, oxidare *(f)*
come • *v* veni
comedy • *n* comedie *(f)*
comfort • *n* confort, consolare *(f)*
comfortable • *adj* confortabil, comod
comma • *n* virgul *(f)*
command • *v* comanda, ordona, porunci, controla, stpâni
commandment • *n* comandament *(n)*
commence • *v* începe
commendable • *adj* ludabil, elogiabil, recomandabil
commendation • *n* ludare *(f)*, elogiere *(f)*, recomandare *(f)*
commercial • *adj* comercial *(n)*, comercial *(f)*
commiseration • *n* comptimire *(f)*, compasiune *(f)*, comizeraie *(f)*
commiserative • *adj* comptimitor
commission • *n* misiune *(f)*
commit • *v* comite
commodity • *n* marf, articol de consum,

obiect de uz, bun de consum
common • *adj* comun, obinuit, uzual
commotion • *n* freamt
communal • *adj* comunitar *(n)*, public *(n)*
communicate • *v* cumineca
communication • *n* comunicare *(f)*, comunicaie *(f)*, comunicare, veste *(n)*, tire *(f)*, mesaj *(n)*, legtur *(f)*
communism • *n* comunism *(n)*
communist • *n* comunist *(m)*, comunist *(f)* • *adj* comunist
community • *n* comunitate *(f)*
commutable • *adj* comutabil *(m)*
commutator • *n* colector de comutaie *(n)*, colector *(n)*
compact • *adj* compact *(n)*
companion • *n* tovar *(m)*
company • *n* societate *(f)*, firm *(f)*, companie *(f)*, întreprindere *(f)*
comparable • *adj* comparabil
comparative • *adj* comparativ, comparativ *(m)*
compare • *v* compara
compartment • *n* compartiment *(n)*, compartimente
compass • *n* busol *(f)*, compas *(m)*, diapazon *(n)*
compassion • *n* compasiune *(f)*
compatriot • *n* compatriot *(m)*
compendium • *n* compendiu
compensable • *adj* compensabil *(n)*
compensate • *v* compensa
compensation • *n* compensare *(f)*, compensaie *(f)*
competition • *n* competiie, concuren *(f)*, concurs *(n)*, competiie *(f)*
competitive • *adj* competitiv *(n)*
competitiveness • *n* competitivitate *(f)*
compile • *v* alctui, compila
compiler • *n* compilator
complacency • *n* automulumire *(f)*, autoîncântare *(f)*
complain • *v* plânge
complaint • *n* plângere *(f)*, nemulumire *(f)*, reclamaie *(f)*, indispoziie *(f)*, tulburare *(f)*, dereglare *(f)*, deranjament *(n)*
complementarity • *n* complementaritate *(f)*
complementary • *adj* complementar *(n)*
complete • *v* completa, termina • *adj* complet
completed • *adj* complet
completely • *adv* complet *(n)*, complet
completion • *n* final
complex • *adj* complex
complexion • *n* trstura *(f)*, ten *(f)*
complexity • *n* complexitate *(f)*
compliant • *adj* cooperant, maleabil *(m)*
complicate • *v* complica
complicated • *adj* complicat *(n)*, alambicat *(n)*
compliment • *n* compliment *(n)*
complimentary • *adj* laudativ *(m)*, mgulitor *(m)*, gratuit *(m)*, de favoare, de felicitare
comply • *v* se supune
component • *n* component *(f)*
compose • *v* compune
composed • *adj* calm, linitit, netulburat
composer • *n* compozitor *(m)*
composite • *n* amestec *(f)*, compoziie *(f)*, compus *(m)* • *adj* compus *(n)*, alctuit *(n)*, multiplu *(m)*
composition • *n* compunere *(f)*, compoziie *(f)*, alctuire *(f)*
composure • *n* calm, autocontrol
compote • *n* kompot
compound • *n* compus chimic *(m)*
comprehend • *v* cuprinde, înelege
comprehensibility • *n* comprehensibilitate *(f)*
comprehensive • *adj* cuprinztor, multilateral *(m)*
compressed • *adj* comprimat *(m)*
compromise • *n* compromis *(n)*
compulsion • *n* constrângere *(f)*
compulsive • *adj* coercitiv *(m)*, constrângtor *(m)*
compulsory • *adj* obligator *(m)*, care se cere
compunction • *n* compunciune *(f)*, remucare *(f)*, regret *(n)*
computer • *n* computer *(n)*, calculator *(n)*
comrade • *n* tovar *(m)*, camarad *(m)*
concavity • *n* concavitate *(f)*
conceal • *v* ascunde
conceit • *n* trufie *(f)*, vanitate *(f)*
conceited • *adj* înfumurat *(m)*
concentrated • *adj* concentrat *(n)*, nediluat *(n)*
concentration • *n* concentraie *(f)*, concentrare *(f)*
concept • *n* concept *(n)*
conception • *n* concepere *(f)*, zmislire *(f)*, concepie *(f)*, concepere, concept *(n)*, imagine *(f)*, idee *(f)*, concepii
concern • *v* preocupa, îngrijora • *n* preocupare *(f)*, îngrijorare *(f)*, frmântare *(f)*, concern *(n)*, întreprindere *(f)*
concerned • *adj* preocupat, îngrijorat
concert • *n* concert *(n)*
concession • *n* concesiere *(f)*, încuviinare *(f)*, concesie *(f)*, concesiune *(f)*, teren concesionat *(n)*, concesie profesional *(f)*

conciliate • *v* concilia, îmbuna
conclude • *v* conchide, încheia, concluziona
concord • *n* acord, consens *(n)*
concordance • *n* concordan *(f)*, acord *(n)*, potrivire *(n)*
concrete • *n* beton *(n)* • *adj* concret *(n)*, beton
condemnation • *n* condamnare *(f)*
condensation • *n* condensare *(f)*
condescension • *n* bunvoin *(f)*, amabilitate *(f)*, condescenden *(f)*
condition • *v* condiiona • *n* condiie *(f)*, stare, condiie
conditional • *adj* condiional
condolence • *n* comptimire *(f)*, consolare *(f)*, condoleane
condom • *n* prezervativ *(n)*
conduct • *n* conducere *(f)*, dirijare *(f)*, comandare *(f)*, comportament
conductance • *n* conductan *(f)*
conductor • *n* dirijor *(m)*, dirijoare *(f)*, ef de orchestr, conductor *(m)*
cone • *n* con *(m)*, con
coneflower • *n* mrit-m-mam *(f)*, ruji galbene
confederacy • *n* confederaie
confederation • *n* confederaie *(f)*
confer • *v* conferi
confess • *v* mrturisi, spovedi
confession • *n* confesiune *(f)*, mrturisire *(f)*, recunoatere *(f)*, spovedire *(f)*
confidence • *n* siguran *(f)*, confiden *(f)*
confidential • *adj* confidenial *(n)*, confidenial *(f)*
confidently • *adv* sigur
configuration • *n* configuraie *(f)*, dispunere *(f)*
confirm • *v* confirma
confirmation • *n* confirmare *(f)*
confiscate • *v* confisca
conflagration • *n* conflagraie *(f)*, incendiu *(n)*
conflict • *n* conflict *(n)*, ceart, conflict
confluence • *n* confluen *(f)*
conform • *v* acorda, concorda, conforma, alinia
conformable • *adj* conform
conformist • *n* conformist, conformist *(f)*
conformity • *n* conformitate *(f)*
confound • *v* încurca
confuse • *v* încurca
confused • *adj* confuz *(n)*, haotic *(n)*, încurcat *(n)*
confusing • *adj* confuz *(n)*, încurctor *(n)*, zpcitor *(n)*, haotic *(n)*
confusion • *n* confuzie *(f)*
congratulate • *v* ferici, ura, felicita
congratulations • *interj* felicitri
congregation • *n* congregaie *(f)*, adunare de fideli, organzaie fondat religios *(f)*
congress • *n* congres *(n)*, partid *(n)*
conical • *adj* conic
conidium • *n* conidie *(f)*
conifer • *n* conifer *(n)*, conifere
conjecture • *n* ipotez, presupunere *(f)*, supoziie, teorem
conjugate • *v* conjuga
conjugation • *n* conjugare *(f)*
conjunction • *n* unire *(f)*, legare *(f)*, conjuncionalizare, conjunctare, conjuncie *(f)*
connect • *v* lega, îmbina, conecta
connected • *adj* conectat *(n)*, legat *(n)*, unit *(n)*
connection • *n* conectare *(f)*, legare *(f)*, unire *(f)*, îmbinare *(f)*, legtur *(f)*, conexiune *(f)*, jonciune, relaie *(f)*, coresponden *(f)*, înrudire *(f)*
connective • *n* conectiv *(n)*
connotation • *n* conotaie *(f)*
connotative • *adj* conotativ
connote • *v* sugera, implica
conquer • *v* cuceri, învinge
conscience • *n* contiin *(f)*
conscientiousness • *n* contiinciozitate *(f)*
conscious • *adj* contient
consciousness • *n* contiin *(f)*
consecutive • *adj* consecutiv *(n)*, succesiv *(n)*
consequence • *n* consecven
conservation • *n* conservare
conservative • *n* conservator *(m)*, conservatoare *(f)*
consideration • *n* considerare *(f)*, motiv *(n)*, considerent *(f)*, consideraie *(f)*, respect *(n)*, recompens *(f)*
consist • *v* consta, consista
consistent • *adj* consistent *(m)*
consolation • *n* consolare *(f)*
consolidated • *adj* consolidat
consolidation • *n* consolidare *(f)*
consonant • *n* consoan *(f)*
constant • *adj* constant *(n)*, constant *(f)*, neschimbat *(n)*, stabil *(m)*
constantly • *adv* constant
constellation • *n* constelaie *(f)*
consternation • *n* consternaie *(f)*, consternare *(f)*
constipate • *v* constipa
constipation • *n* constipaie *(f)*
constituency • *n* circumscripie electoral *(f)*
constituent • *n* constituent *(m)*, component *(m)*

constitutionality • *n* constituionalitate *(f)*
constraint • *n* constrângere *(f)*, obligaie *(f)*
construct • *v* construi *(f)*, construi
construction • *n* construire *(f)*, cldire *(f)*, construcie, structur, oper *(f)*, construcie *(f)*
constructive • *adj* de construcie *(n)*, construcional *(n)*, constructiv *(n)*
constructivism • *n* constructivism *(n)*
consul • *n* consul *(m)*
consulate • *n* consulat *(n)*
consultation • *n* consultare *(f)*, consultaie *(f)*
consumable • *n* consumabil *(n)* • *adj* consumabil *(m)*, comestibil *(m)*, mâncabil *(m)*
consume • *v* consuma, se consuma
consumption • *n* consum *(n)*
contact • *v* contacta • *n* contact, atingere, legtur *(f)*
contagion • *n* contagiune *(f)*
contagious • *adj* contagios, molipsitor
contain • *v* conine
container • *n* container *(n)*, recipient *(m)*, cutie *(f)*, butelie *(f)*
contamination • *n* contaminare *(f)*
contemplate • *v* cugeta, contempla, chibzui
contemporary • *adj* contemporan *(n)*, contemporani, contemporan *(f)*
contemptible • *adj* dispreuibil *(m)*, nedemn *(m)*
content • *n* coninut *(n)* • *adj* mulumit • *v* mulumi
contentment • *n* satisfacie *(f)*, mulumire *(f)*
contest • *n* controvers *(f)*, disput *(f)*, dezbatere, competiie *(f)*, întrecere *(f)*
contestable • *adj* contestabil
contestation • *n* contestare *(f)*, tgduire
contiguity • *n* contiguitate *(f)*
contingence • *n* contact *(n)*, atingere *(f)*, tangen *(f)*
continuation • *n* continuare *(f)*, continuri
continuity • *n* continuitate *(f)*
continuous • *adj* continuu *(n)*, neîntrerupt *(n)*
continuously • *adv* încontinuu, perpetuu, continuu, neîntrerupt
continuousness • *n* continuitate
contraceptive • *adj* contraceptiv *(n)*, anticoncepional *(n)*
contract • *n* contract • *v* a incheia un contract cu
contracture • *n* contracie *(f)*, cotractare
contradiction • *n* contradicie *(f)*, contrazicere
contradictory • *n* contradicie *(f)*, contrazicere *(f)* • *adj* contradictoriu, contrar
contrarily • *adv* în mod contrar, în mod invers
contrarious • *adj* contrar, potrivnic
contrary • *adj* contrar *(n)*, opus *(n)*, contrar
contrast • *n* contrast *(n)*
contravene • *v* contraveni
contribution • *n* contribuie *(f)*, donaie *(f)*, contribuire, contribuie
contrive • *v* inventa, improviza
contrived • *adj* forat, artificial
control • *v* comanda, controla • *n* control *(n)*, autoritate *(f)*, grup de control *(n)*, grup de comparaie *(n)*, comand *(f)*, mecanism de siguran *(n)*, element de control *(n)*, element de comand *(n)*
controllable • *adj* controlabil
controlled • *adj* controlat *(n)*
controlling • *adj* controlor *(n)*
controversial • *adj* controversabil *(n)*, controversat *(n)*, discutabil *(n)*, polemizat *(n)*
controversy • *n* controvers *(f)*, disput (principial) *(f)*, discuie *(f)*
controvert • *v* contrazice, tgdui, nega
controvertible • *adj* discutabil *(n)*, polemizabil *(n)*, controversabil *(n)*
convention • *n* convenie *(f)*, întrunire *(f)*, tratat *(n)*
conventional • *adj* convenional *(n)*
convergence • *n* convergen *(f)*, convergen
convergent • *adj* convergent
conversation • *n* conversaie *(f)*, convorbire *(f)*
conversational • *adj* conversaional *(n)*
conversion • *n* transformare, conversiune, conversie, prefacere, conversie *(m)*
convert • *v* converti, transforma • *n* convertit *(m)*, convertit *(f)*
convertible • *adj* convertibil *(n)*
convey • *v* transporta, cra, transmite, transfera
conviction • *n* convingere, credin
convince • *v* convinge
convincing • *adj* convingtor
convoy • *n* convoi *(n)*
cook • *v* gti • *n* buctar
cooked • *adj* copt
cooker • *n* aragaz *(n)*
cool • *adj* friguros
coolness • *n* coolitate *(f)*
cooper • *n* dogar *(m)*
cooperate • *v* coopera
cooperation • *n* cooperare *(f)*
coordinate • *v* coordona • *n* coordonat *(f)*, coordonate

coordination • *n* coordonare *(f)*
coot • *n* lii *(f)*
copacetic • *adj* grozav
cope • *v* înfrunta, împca, confrunta
copper • *n* cupru *(m)*, aram *(f)* • *adj* armiu
copse • *n* crâng *(n)*, dumbrav *(f)*, pdure mrunt *(f)*, subarboret *(n)*, tufi de arbuti
copy • *v* copia, imita • *n* copie *(f)*, duplicat *(n)*
coral • *n* coral *(m)*, corai, coraliu • *adj* corai, coraliu
cord • *n* cordon, coard *(f)*, cordon *(n)*, cablu *(n)*
cordon • *n* cordon *(n)*
core • *n* miez *(n)*, esen *(f)*
coriander • *n* coriandru *(m)*
corkscrew • *n* tirbuon *(n)*
cormorant • *n* cormoran *(m)*
corn • *n* cereal *(f)*
corncob • *n* tiulete
corncrake • *n* cristei *(m)*
cornea • *n* cornee *(f)*
cornflower • *n* albstrea *(f)*
corollary • *n* corolar *(n)*
corporation • *n* corporaie *(f)*, societate pe aciuni *(f)*
corporeal • *adj* corporal *(m)*
corpse • *n* cadavru *(n)*, corp mort *(m)*
corpuscle • *n* corpuscul, particul
corpuscular • *adj* corpuscular
correct • *v* corecta • *adj* corect
correctable • *adj* corigibil
correctly • *adv* corect, în mod corect
correctness • *n* corectitudine
correlation • *n* corelaie *(f)*
corresponding • *adj* corespunztor *(n)*, corespondent *(n)*
corridor • *n* culoar *(f)*, coridor *(m)*, coridor *(n)*, coridor aerian *(n)*
corroborate • *v* susine, corobora, adeveri
corrupt • *v* corupe • *adj* corupt *(m)*, corupt *(f)*
corruption • *n* corupie *(f)*
corymb • *n* corimb *(n)*
cosecant • *n* cosecant *(f)*
cosine • *n* cosinus *(n)*
cosmetician • *n* cosmetician *(f)*, cosmetician *(m)*
cosmic • *adj* cosmic
cosmogony • *n* cosmogonie *(f)*
cosmology • *n* cosmologie *(f)*
cosmos • *n* cosmos *(m)*
cost • *n* cost, pre • *v* costa, preui
cotangent • *n* cotangent *(f)*
cotton • *n* bumbac *(m)*, bumbac *(n)* • *adj* de bumbac
cotyledon • *n* cotiledon *(n)*
cougar • *n* pum *(f)*
cough • *v* tui • *n* tuse
coulisse • *n* culis *(f)*
coulomb • *n* coulomb *(m)*
council • *n* consiliu *(m)*
counsel • *v* consilia, sftui, povui, recomanda • *n* consultan *(f)*, sfat, pova, sftuire, consultaie *(f)*, expertiz *(f)*, consultan
count • *v* numra • *n* socoti, numrare *(f)*, numrtoare *(f)*, conte *(m)*
countable • *adj* numrabil *(n)*
countdown • *n* denumrare *(f)*, numrare regresiv, numrare invers *(f)*
counter • *n* contor, numrtoare *(f)*, numrtor
countercurrent • *n* contracurent *(m)*
counterexample • *n* contraexemplu *(n)*
countersign • *v* contrasemna
countess • *n* contes *(f)*
countless • *adj* nenumrabil, de nenumrat
country • *n* ar *(f)*, pmânt, naiune, stat *(n)*, patrie *(f)*, ar, sat *(n)* • *adj* rural, ara
countryside • *n* sat *(n)*
county • *n* jude
couple • *v* cupla, împerechea, împreuna • *n* pereche, cuplu *(n)*
courage • *n* curaj *(n)*
courageous • *adj* curajos
course • *n* curs
court • *n* curte
courthouse • *n* tribunal
courtliness • *n* curtoazie *(f)*, curtenie *(f)*
courtship • *n* curte
courtyard • *n* curte *(f)*
cousin • *n* vr *(m)*, var *(f)*
cove • *n* golf
covenant • *n* legmânt
cover • *v* acoperi
covered • *adj* acoperit
covetousness • *n* poft nemsurat *(f)*, râvnire excesiv *(f)*
cow • *n* vac *(f)*, femel
coward • *n* la *(m)*, la *(f)*
cowardice • *n* poltronerie *(f)*, laitate *(f)*
cowardly • *adj* la, fricos, miel • *adv* la *(n)*
cowbell • *n* talang *(f)*
cowboy • *n* vcar *(m)*
cowgirl • *n* vcri *(f)*
cowherd • *n* vcar, boar
cowslip • *n* ciuboica-cucului *(f)*, limba-cucului *(f)*, calcea calului *(f)*
coyote • *n* coiot *(m)*
crab • *n* crab *(m)*
crack • *v* crpa • *n* crptur *(f)*, fisur *(f)*
cradle • *n* leagn *(n)*, furc *(f)*
craft • *v* a face de mân, construi
craftsman • *n* meteugar *(m)*, artizan

crake • *n* ralid *(n)*, cristei *(m)*
cram • *v* înghesui, îndesa
cranberry • *n* merior
crane • *n* cocor *(m)*, macara *(f)*
cranesbill • *n* geraniu *(m)*
cranial • *adj* cranian *(n)*, cranial *(n)*, de craniu
crank • *n* manivel, rotire, învârtire, maniac
crankshaft • *n* arbore cotit *(m)*, vilbrochen *(n)*
cranny • *n* fisur *(f)*
crap • *n* porcrie, ccat *(m)*, rahat *(m)*
crass • *adj* cras, grosolan, grosier
craving • *n* poft *(f)*, sete *(f)*, râvn *(f)*, ardoare *(f)*
crawl • *v* târî
crayfish • *n* rac
crazy • *n* nebun *(m)*, nebun *(f)*, sonat *(m)*, sonat *(f)* • *adj* nebun *(m)*, înnebunit, tulburat, nebun, necontrolat
cream • *n* smântân *(f)*, crem *(f)*
create • *v* crea
creation • *n* creaie *(f)*, creare *(f)*
creationism • *n* creaionism *(n)*
creative • *adj* creativ *(n)*, creator *(n)*, inventiv *(n)*
creativity • *n* creativitate *(f)*
creature • *n* creatur, fiin, fptur *(f)*
credibility • *n* credibilitate, credibilitate *(f)*
credible • *adj* credibil, plauzibil, demn de încredere
credit • *n* credit
creed • *v* crede • *n* credin
crematorium • *n* crematoriu
crescent • *n* semilun *(f)*
crest • *n* creast
cretin • *n* cretin *(m)*, cretin *(f)*
cretinism • *n* cretinism *(n)*
crevasse • *n* crevas *(f)*, crptur *(f)*
crevice • *n* sprtur *(f)*, fisur *(f)*
cricket • *n* greier *(m)*, crichet *(n)*
crime • *n* infraciune, crim *(f)*, criminalitate *(f)*, delicven *(f)*
criminal • *n* infractor *(m)*, infractoare *(f)* • *adj* infracional
crimson • *n* carmin • *adj* carmin
crippled • *adj* schilod, infirm
crisis • *n* moment crucial *(n)*, toi *(n)*, criz *(f)*
criterion • *n* criteriu *(n)*
critic • *n* critic *(m)*, critic
critically • *adv* critic, în mod critic
criticise • *v* critica
criticism • *n* critic *(f)*
crocodile • *n* crocodil
crocus • *n* brându *(f)*
crone • *n* bab *(f)*
crooked • *adj* strâmb
crop • *n* cultur *(f)*, recolt *(f)*, crava *(f)*, pr scurt, gu • *v* recolta, culege, cultiva, tunde, decupa, tia
crosier • *n* pateri
cross • *v* cruci, închina • *n* cruce
cross-legged • *adj* picior peste picior
crossbill • *n* forfecu *(f)*, forfecu galben *(f)*, pasre-cu-cioc-încruciat *(f)*
crossbow • *n* arbalet *(f)*
crossroads • *n* rscruce *(f)*, intersecie *(f)*
crow • *n* cioar *(f)*
crowberry • *n* vuietoare *(f)*
crowd • *n* mulime *(f)*, mas de oameni *(f)*, gloat, grmad *(f)*, maldr *(n)*, gloat *(f)*, prostime *(f)*
crowded • *adj* arhiplin *(n)*, înesat *(n)*, ticsit *(n)*, aglomerat *(n)*
crown • *v* încorona, încununa • *n* coroan *(f)*, cunun *(f)*
crucial • *adj* crucial, decisiv, cruciform
crucifix • *n* crucifix
crucify • *v* crucifica
cruel • *adj* crud, crunt, cumplit
cruelty • *n* cruzime *(f)*
cruet • *n* oetar *(n)*
crumb • *n* miez
crumple • *v* cocoloi
crusade • *n* cruciad *(f)*, cruciad
crush • *v* mcina, pulveriza
crushing • *n* strivire *(f)*, turtire *(f)*, zdrobire *(f)* • *adj* copleitor
crustacean • *n* crustaceu
crutch • *n* cârj *(f)*
crux • *n* punct crucial *(n)*, moment decisiv *(n)*
cry • *v* plânge • *n* plânset *(n)*, ipt *(n)*, strigt *(n)*, urlet *(n)*
crystal • *n* cristal, cristal *(m)*
crystallization • *n* cristalizare *(f)*, cristalizaie *(f)*
cub • *n* vulpan *(m)*, pui *(m)*
cube • *n* cub
cubeb • *n* cubeb *(m)*
cubism • *n* cubism *(n)*
cuckold • *n* încornorat *(m)*
cuckoo • *n* cuc
cucumber • *n* castravete *(m)*
cuddle • *n* îmbriare *(f)*
culpable • *adj* culpabil *(m)*
cult • *n* cult *(n)*
cultivation • *n* cultivare *(m)*, cultur agricol *(f)*, cultivaie *(f)*, cultur *(f)*, cultivare *(f)*, instruire *(f)*
cultivator • *n* cultivator *(m)*

cultural • *adj* cultural *(n)*
culture • *v* cultiva • *n* cultur *(f)*
cum • *v* slobozi • *n* sloboz *(m)*
cumin • *n* chimion *(m)*
cumulonimbus • *n* cumulonimbus
cunning • *adj* viclean *(m)*, iret *(m)*, priceput *(m)* • *n* viclenie *(f)*, capacitate *(f)*
cunt • *n* pizd *(f)*
cup • *n* ceac *(f)*, cup *(f)*
cupboard • *n* dulap *(m)*
cupidity • *n* cupiditate *(f)*
curdle • *v* închega
cure • *n* tratament
curettage • *n* chiuretaj *(n)*, chiuretare *(f)*, raclaj *(n)*
curfew • *n* interdicie de ieire din cas *(f)*, or de interdicie *(f)*, semnal de stingere, tocsin, stare de asediu *(f)*, clopot de alarm
curiosity • *n* curiozitate *(f)*
curious • *adj* curios *(n)*, straniu *(m)*, ciudat *(n)*, bizar *(n)*, neobinuit *(n)*
curium • *n* curiu *(n)*
curlew • *n* corl *(f)*, ginu-de-balt *(f)*
curling • *n* curling *(n)*
currency • *n* valut *(f)*
current • *n* curent *(m)*, uvoi *(n)*, flux *(n)*, curs *(n)*, mers *(n)*, manier *(f)*
curry • *n* curry *(m)*
curse • *v* blestema, înjura • *n* blestem *(n)*, maledicie *(f)*
cursive • *adj* cursiv
cursor • *n* cursor *(n)*
curtain • *n* perdea *(f)*, draperie *(f)*, perdele, cortin *(f)*
curvature • *n* curbur *(f)*
curve • *n* curb *(f)*, curbe, linie curb *(f)*, linie curbat *(f)*
curved • *adj* curbat
cushion • *n* pern *(f)*
custom • *n* obicei *(n)*, tradiie *(f)*, obinuin *(f)*, vam *(f)*, acciz *(f)*
customs • *n* vam *(f)*
cut • *v* tia, diminua, reduce • *n* tietur *(f)*, incizie *(f)*, tiere *(f)* • *adj* tiat
cute • *adj* drgu, drgla
cutlet • *n* niel *(n)*
cutoff • *n* scurta *(f)*
cutter • *n* tietor, cuit
cutting • *n* decupare *(f)*
cuttlefish • *n* sepie *(f)*
cyanide • *n* cianura *(f)*
cyborg • *n* cyborg
cyclamen • *n* ciclam *(f)*
cycle • *n* ciclu *(n)*, rotaie *(f)*
cycling • *n* ciclism
cyclist • *n* biciclist *(m)*, ciclist *(m)*
cycloid • *n* cicloid *(f)*
cyclone • *n* ciclon *(n)*
cyclostome • *n* ciclostom *(m)*
cygnet • *n* pui de lebd *(m)*
cylinder • *n* cilindru *(m)*
cylindrical • *adj* cilindric *(m)*, cilindric *(f)*
cynical • *adj* cinic
cynicism • *n* cinism *(n)*
cypress • *n* chiparos *(m)*
cysteine • *n* cistein *(f)*
cytology • *n* citologie *(f)*
cytoplasm • *n* citoplasm *(f)*

D

dacha • *n* dacea *(f)*
dad • *n* tat *(m)*
daddy • *n* ttic
daffodil • *n* narcis *(f)*
dagger • *n* pumnal *(n)*, jungher *(n)*, stilet *(n)*, semn de carte *(n)*
dahlia • *n* dalie *(f)*, gherghin *(f)*
daily • *n* ziar *(n)* • *adj* zilnic, cotidian • *adv* zilnic, cotidian
dairy • *n* untrie *(f)*, lactate
daisy • *n* bnu *(m)*, prlu *(f)*, bnuel *(m)*, margaret *(f)*
dam • *n* baraj *(n)*
damage • *v* defecta, strica, deteriora, avaria • *n* avarie, daun, pagub, avarii, stricciune, pagube, daune
damask • *n* damasc *(n)* • *adj* lie-de-vin
damn • *n* la naiba!
damp • *adj* umed
damsel • *n* fecioar *(f)*, fecior *(m)*
damson • *n* goldan *(m)*, renglot *(m)*, goldan *(f)*, renglot *(f)*
dance • *v* dansa, juca • *n* dans
dancer • *n* dansator *(m)*, dansatoare *(f)*
dandelion • *n* ppdie *(f)*
dandruff • *n* mtrea
danger • *n* pericol, primejdie *(f)*, pericol *(n)*
dangerous • *adj* periculos
dangle • *v* blbni, legna, atârna
daphne • *n* ieder alb *(f)*
dare • *v* îndrzni, încumeta, cuteza
dark • *n* întuneric • *adj* murg, închis, întunecat

darken • *v* întuneca
darkness • *n* întuneric, întunecime *(f)*, întristare *(f)*, tristee *(f)*, negreal *(f)*
darling • *n* drag *(m)*, drag *(f)*, iubit *(m)*, iubit *(f)* • *adj* drag, iubit, scump, încânttor, drgu
darnel • *n* slbie *(f)*
data • *n* date
database • *n* banc de date *(f)*, baz de date *(f)*
date • *n* curmal *(f)*, finic, dat *(f)*, întâlnire • *v* data
daughter • *n* fiic *(f)*
daughter-in-law • *n* nor *(f)*
dauphin • *n* delfin *(m)*
dawn • *n* zori, auror *(f)*, alba *(f)*, rsrit *(n)*
day • *n* zi *(f)*
daybreak • *n* rsrit de soare *(n)*
days • *n* zile *(f)* • *adv* ziua
daytime • *n* zi
daze • *v* ului, stupefia, zpci • *n* uluire *(f)*, stupefacie *(f)*, stupoare *(f)*
deacon • *n* diacon
dead • *adj* mort
deadline • *n* timp limit
deadly • *adj* ucigtor, mortal, letal • *adv* fatalmente, mortal
deaf • *adj* surd
deafen • *v* asurzi
deafening • *adj* asurzitor
dear • *adj* drag, scump *(n)*, stimate, drag
death • *n* moarte *(f)*, moartea *(f)*
deathless • *adj* nemuritor *(n)*
debase • *v* degrada
debate • *n* discuie, dezbatere *(f)*, discuie *(f)*, polemic *(f)*, controvers *(f)*
debauch • *n* destrblare
debt • *n* datorie, datorie *(f)*
decade • *n* deceniu *(n)*, decad *(f)*
decapitate • *v* decapita
decathlon • *n* decatlon *(n)*
deceive • *v* înela, amgi
decency • *n* cuviin, cdere, decen
decibel • *n* decibeli, decibel *(m)*
decide • *v* decide, convinge
decimal • *n* sistem zecimal *(n)*, numr zecimal *(n)*
decision • *n* decizie *(f)*, hotrâre *(f)*, fermitate *(f)*, sentin *(f)*, verdict *(n)*
declaration • *n* declaraie *(f)*, declarare *(f)*
declare • *v* declara
declension • *n* declinare *(f)*, declinaie *(f)*
declivity • *n* înclinaie mare, caracter abrupt *(n)*
decompose • *v* descompune
decomposition • *n* descompunere *(f)*, demontare *(f)*, dezasamblare *(f)*
decorate • *v* decora, orna
decoration • *n* decorare *(f)*, împodobire *(f)*, înfrumuseare *(f)*, decoraie *(f)*, ornament *(n)*, ornamentaie *(f)*
decorator • *n* decorator *(m)*, decoratoare *(f)*
decorous • *adj* cuviincios, decoros
decorum • *n* cuviin, cdere, decen
decrease • *v* descrete, scdea
decree • *n* decret *(n)*
dedication • *n* dedicaie *(f)*
deed • *n* fapt
deep • *n* adâncime *(f)*, adânc *(n)* • *adj* adânc, adânc, adânci, profund • *adv* adânc
deeply • *adv* adânc, profund
deer • *n* cerb *(m)*, ciut *(f)*, cprioar
defame • *v* defima
defeasible • *adj* revocabil *(m)*, anulabil *(m)*, nedefinitiv *(m)*
defeat • *v* învinge, înfrânge, bate
defecate • *v* câca, defeca
defective • *adj* defect *(n)*, defectuos *(n)*, defectiv *(n)*
defend • *v* apra
defender • *n* funda *(m)*, aprtor *(m)*
defense • *n* aprare *(f)*
deference • *n* deferen *(f)*
deferred • *adj* întârziat *(m)*, întârziat *(f)*
deficiency • *n* deficien *(f)*, lips *(f)*, insuficien *(f)*
deficient • *adj* deficient *(n)*
deficit • *n* deficit *(n)*
defile • *v* spurca
defined • *adj* definit *(m)*, definit *(f)*
definition • *n* definire *(f)*, definiie *(f)*, definiie, definire, grad de definire *(n)*, for de definire *(f)*
deflagration • *n* deflagraie *(f)*
deflower • *v* deflora
defraud • *v* frauda, defrauda
defy • *v* sfida
degenerate • *v* degenera, degrada • *adj* degenerat, degradat
degeneration • *n* degenerare *(f)*, degradare *(f)*, degenerri
degradation • *n* degradare *(f)*, retrogradare *(f)*, înjosire *(f)*, deteriorare *(f)*, stricare *(f)*
degree • *n* grad *(n)*, grade, proporie *(f)*, proporii, grad academic *(n)*, diplom academic *(f)*
dehiscence • *n* dehiscen *(f)*
dehiscent • *adj* dehiscent
dehydration • *n* deshidratare
deism • *n* deism
deity • *n* divinitate *(f)*, dumnezeu *(f)*

delay • *v* întârzia, amâna • *n* întârziere *(f)*
deleterious • *adj* deleter, vtmtor, nociv
deliberate • *v* delibera, consftui
deliberation • *n* deliberare *(f)*
delicate • *adj* delicat
delicious • *adj* delicios, gustos
delight • *n* deliciu *(n)*, desftare *(f)*, plcere *(f)*, juisare *(f)*
delightful • *adj* delicios
delirium • *n* delir *(n)*
deliver • *v* livra
delivery • *n* livrare
delphinium • *n* nemior *(m)*
delta • *n* delta *(m)*, delt *(f)*
delude • *v* înela, amgi
delusive • *adj* deluzoriu *(n)*
deluxe • *adj* de lux
demagogue • *n* demagog *(m)*, demagog *(f)*
demagogy • *n* demagogie *(f)*
demand • *v* cere • *n* cerere
demijohn • *n* damigian *(f)*
demimonde • *n* lume interlop *(f)*, prostituie *(f)*
demiurge • *n* demiurg *(m)*
democracy • *n* democraie *(f)*
democratic • *adj* democratic
demolish • *v* drâma
demon • *n* demon *(m)*, drac *(m)*, *(m)*
demonstrable • *adj* demonstrabil
demonstration • *n* demonstraie *(f)*, demonstrare *(f)*
demonstrative • *adj* demonstrativ *(m)*
den • *n* bârlog *(n)*, peter *(f)*
denominator • *n* numitor *(m)*
density • *n* densitate *(f)*
dentist • *n* dentist
deny • *v* nega
deodorant • *n* deodorant *(m)*
deoxyribose • *n* dezoxiriboz
depart • *v* pleca
departure • *n* plecare *(f)*
dependable • *adj* fiabil *(m)*
dependence • *n* dependen *(f)*, subjugare *(f)*, subordonare *(f)*
dependent • *adj* dependent *(n)*
depict • *v* înfia, descrie, picta, ilustra, reprezenta
depiction • *n* reprezentare *(f)*
depleted • *adj* epuizat *(m)*
deplorable • *adj* deplorabil, nenorocit, lamentabil
deplore • *v* plânge
deportation • *n* deportare
depose • *v* depune, detronare *(f)*, mrturisi, a depune mrturie
deposit • *v* a depozita, depune, a lsa în îngrijire • *n* depozit *(n)*, depunere *(f)*, zcmânt *(n)*
depravity • *n* depravare *(f)*, destrblare *(f)*, desfrânare *(f)*, corupie *(f)*, depravaiune *(f)*
depreciation • *n* depreciere
depressed • *adj* deprimat *(m)*, nefericit *(m)*, depresionat *(n)*, deprimat *(n)*
depression • *n* depresiune *(f)*, deprimare *(f)*
depth • *n* adâncime, profunzime
deregulation • *n* dereglare *(f)*
derivation • *n* derivare *(f)*
derivative • *n* derivat *(m)*, derivat *(f)*, derivat *(n)*
derive • *v* deriva
derived • *adj* derivat *(n)*, derivat *(f)*
derogatory • *adj* derogatoriu, defavorabil *(n)*, prejudiciator, duntor, denigrator *(m)*
dervish • *n* dervi *(m)*
descend • *v* coborî, descinde, proveni
descendant • *n* descendent *(m)*, urma *(m)*
describe • *v* descrie
description • *n* descripie, descriere
descriptive • *adj* descriptiv *(n)*
descry • *v* vedea, observa, zri, bga de seam
desecrate • *v* spurca
desert • *n* deert, pustiu
deserted • *adj* abandonat, deert
deserter • *n* dezertor *(m)*
desertion • *n* dezertare *(f)*
deserve • *v* merita
designate • *v* desemna, indica, designa, numi, denumi
desirable • *adj* dorit *(m)*
desire • *v* dori • *n* dorin *(f)*, deziderat *(n)*
desk • *n* birou *(m)*
desolate • *adj* deert, abandonat
despair • *v* despera • *n* desperare *(f)*
desperation • *n* desperare *(f)*
despicable • *adj* dispreuibil *(m)*, abject *(m)*
despoil • *v* despuia
despondency • *n* disperare *(f)*, mâhnire *(f)*, melancolie *(f)*
despotic • *adj* despotic *(n)*
despotism • *n* despotism *(n)*
dessert • *n* desert *(n)*
destiny • *n* soart *(f)*, destin
destitute • *adj* indigent, lipsit, nevoia, srac
destroy • *v* distruge, nimici
destructible • *adj* distructibil *(n)*, nimicibil
destruction • *n* distrugere *(f)*
destructive • *adj* distructiv *(n)*, distrugtor *(n)*

detach • *v* detaa, dezlipi
detachment • *n* separare *(f)*, desprire *(f)*, desprindere *(f)*, detaare *(f)*, indiferen *(f)*, imparialitate *(f)*, obiectivitate *(f)*, detaament *(n)*
detain • *v* a reine
detector • *n* detector *(n)*
detergent • *n* detergent • *adj* detergent
deterioration • *n* deteriorare *(f)*
determination • *n* determinare *(f)*, delimitare *(f)*, fermitate *(f)*
detonate • *v* exploda, detona, a face s explodeze
detonation • *n* detonare *(f)*, explodare *(f)*, explozie *(f)*, detonaie
detonator • *n* detonator
detoxification • *n* dezintoxicare *(f)*
detrimental • *adj* duntor, vtmtor
deuce • *n* doi *(m)*
devastate • *v* devasta
devastation • *n* devastare
develop • *v* dezvolta
developer • *n* creator *(m)*, dezvoltator *(m)*, conceptor, developator *(m)*, lichid developator *(n)*, revelator *(m)*
development • *n* dezvoltare *(f)*
deviate • *v* devia
device • *n* aparat *(n)*, pies *(f)*, dispozitiv *(n)*, element *(n)*, component *(f)*, unitate *(f)*
devil • *n* drac, diavol, satan *(m)*, satan, drac *(m)*
devise • *v* urzi
devoid • *adj* golit, fr de coninut
devotion • *n* devotament *(n)*, devotare *(f)*, devoiune *(f)*, dedicare *(f)*
devour • *v* devora
dew • *n* rou *(f)*
dexterity • *n* dexteritate *(f)*, îndemânare *(f)*, iscusin *(f)*, dibcie *(f)*, abilitate *(f)*
dexterous • *adj* descurcre
diabetes • *n* diabet
diabetic • *adj* diabetic
diagnostic • *adj* de diagnoz, de diagnostic
diagonal • *n* diagonal *(f)*
diagram • *n* diagram *(f)*
dialect • *n* dialect
dialectal • *adj* dialectal
dialogue • *n* dialog, conversaie *(f)*
diameter • *n* diametru
diametral • *adj* diametral, diametric
diametric • *adj* diametral
diamond • *n* diamant *(n)*
diaper • *n* scutec *(n)*
diaphragm • *n* diafragm *(f)*, membran *(f)*
diarrhea • *n* diaree, urdinare *(f)*
diary • *n* jurnal intim
diastole • *n* diastol *(f)*
diatribe • *n* diatriba
dick • *n* pul *(f)*, miel *(m)*
dicotyledonous • *adj* dicotiledonat *(f)*
dictator • *n* dictator *(m)*, dictatori
dictatorship • *n* dictatur *(f)*, guvernare dictatorial *(f)*
dictionary • *n* dicionar *(n)*
die • *v* muri • *n* zar *(m)*
diesel • *n* motorin *(f)*
difference • *n* diferen *(f)*
different • *adj* diferit, deosebit
differentiation • *n* difereniere
difficult • *adj* greu, difícil, anevoios, complicat
difficulty • *n* dificultate, piedic, obstacol *(n)*
diffusion • *n* difuzie *(f)*
dig • *v* spa, escava
digest • *v* digera, mistui
digestible • *adj* digerabil *(n)*, digestibil
digestion • *n* digestie
digit • *n* deget *(n)*, cifr *(f)*
digital • *adj* digital *(m)*, digital *(f)*, numeric *(m)*
digitigrade • *n* digitigrad *(n)* • *adj* digitigrad
dignity • *n* demnitate *(f)*
digress • *v* devia, ofensa
digression • *n* digresiune *(f)*
dike • *n* dig *(n)*
dildo • *n* dildo *(n)*
dilemma • *n* dilem *(f)*
dilettante • *n* diletant *(m)*, amator *(m)*
diligence • *n* sârguin *(f)*, diligen *(f)*, potalion *(n)*, hrnicie *(f)*
diligent • *adj* harnic *(m)*
dill • *n* mrar *(m)*
diluted • *adj* diluat *(m)*
dim • *adj* tern *(n)*, vag *(n)*
dimension • *v* dimensiona • *n* dimensiune *(f)*, dimensiuni
dimensional • *adj* dimensional *(n)*
diminution • *n* diminuare *(f)*, micorare *(f)*, scdere *(f)*
diminutive • *n* diminutiv *(n)*, diminutive • *adj* diminutiv *(n)*, diminutiv *(f)*
dimple • *v* cresta • *n* adâncitur *(f)*, cufundtur *(f)*, scobitur *(f)*, scufundtur *(f)*, gropi *(f)*
dine • *v* cina
dingo • *n* dingo *(m)*
dinner • *n* cin, mas de sear *(f)*, nutre *(n)*, prânz *(n)*, banchet *(n)*, dineu *(n)*
dinnertime • *n* cin
dinosaur • *n* dinozaur *(m)*
diocese • *n* diocez *(f)*

diorama • *n* dioram *(f)*
diphthong • *n* diftong *(m)*
diplomacy • *n* diplomaie *(f)*
direct • *adj* direct
direction • *n* direcie *(f)*
director • *n* director *(m)*, directori, regizor *(m)*, regizori
dirt • *n* pmânt *(n)*, mizerie *(f)*, murdrie *(n)*
dirty • *v* spurca, murdri • *adj* murdar
disabled • *adj* dezactivat *(m)*
disadvantage • *n* dezavantaj
disadvantageous • *adj* dezavantajos *(m)*
disagreeable • *adj* dezagreabil *(n)*, neagreabil *(m)*
disagreement • *n* ceart *(f)*, discuie *(f)*, dezacord *(n)*
disappear • *v* disprea
disappearance • *n* dispariie
disappointed • *adj* dezamgit
disappointment • *n* dezamgire *(f)*, decepie *(f)*
disapprobation • *n* dezaprobare *(f)*
disapproval • *n* dezaprobare *(f)*
disarm • *v* a dezarma
disarray • *v* dezorganiza, zpci, dezbrca • *n* dezordine *(f)*
disaster • *n* nenorocire, dezastru *(n)*, catastrof *(f)*
disbelief • *n* necredin *(f)*, neîncredere *(f)*, uimire *(f)*, surprindere *(f)*
discern • *v* discerne, percepe
discernment • *n* discernere *(f)*, discernmânt *(n)*
discharge • *v* descrca
discipline • *n* disciplin *(f)*
discomfiture • *n* jen *(f)*, stinghereal *(f)*, stânjeneal *(f)*
discomfort • *n* disconfort *(n)*
discontented • *adj* nemulumit *(n)*, nesatisfcut *(n)*
discord • *n* discordie *(f)*
discount • *n* rabat *(n)*, reducere de pre *(f)*
discourage • *v* descuraja
discourse • *n* discurs *(n)*, conversaie *(f)*
discover • *v* descoperi
discredit • *v* discredita
discreet • *adj* discret
discretion • *n* discreie *(f)*, rezerv *(f)*, maturitate *(f)*, libertate de decizie *(f)*
discrimination • *n* discriminare *(f)*, difereniere
discussion • *n* discuie *(f)*, discutare *(f)*, dezbatere *(f)*
disdain • *n* desconsiderare *(f)*, dispre *(n)*
disease • *n* boal *(f)*, maladie *(f)*
disembark • *v* descrca
disequilibrium • *n* dezechilibru *(n)*, instabilitate *(f)*, dezechilibrare *(f)*
disgrace • *v* dizgraia • *n* dizgraie *(f)*, ruine *(f)*, ocar *(f)*
disguise • *v* deghiza, masca • *n* deghizare, mascare
disgust • *v* dezgusta, îngreoa, scârbi • *n* dezgust
disgusting • *adj* dezgusttor, respingtor, scârbos
dishonest • *adj* necinstit
dishwasher • *n* main de splat vase
disingenuous • *adj* necinstit
disintegrate • *v* dezintegra, dezagrega
disintegration • *n* dezintegrare *(f)*
disinterest • *n* dezinteres *(n)*
disk • *n* disc *(n)*, plac de gramofon *(f)*
dislike • *v* displcea, nu-i plcea • *n* aversiune *(f)*, antipatie *(f)*
dislocate • *v* disloca
dismal • *adj* dezamagitor de inadecvat, deprimant
dismay • *n* desperare *(f)*, spaim *(f)*
dismiss • *v* a destitui, a concedia, a revoca (din funcie), a demite, alunga
disobedient • *adj* neasculttor, neobedient, dezobedient, nesupus
disorganization • *n* dezorganizare *(f)*
disorganized • *adj* dezorganizat *(n)*, neorganizat *(n)*
dispel • *v* spulbera
dispersion • *n* dispersare
displacement • *n* deplasament, dezlocuire, dislocare
displeasure • *n* nemulumire *(f)*, indispoziie *(f)*, jen, stinghereal *(f)*, dezaprobare *(f)*, nemulumire
disposition • *n* înclinaie *(f)*, dispoziie *(f)*, dispozitiv *(n)*
dispute • *n* disput *(f)*, disput
disquietude • *n* frmântare *(f)*
disregard • *v* desconsidera, ignora • *n* desconsiderare *(f)*, dispre *(n)*, discreditare *(f)*, nepsare *(f)*, indiferen *(f)*
disrespect • *v* dispreui • *n* lips de respect
disrobe • *v* dezbrca
dissatisfaction • *n* insatisfacie *(f)*, nemulumire *(f)*, neplcere *(f)*
dissatisfied • *adj* nesatisfcut *(n)*, nemulumit *(n)*
dissect • *v* diseca
dissension • *n* disensiune *(f)*
dissipation • *n* disipare *(f)*, dispersie *(f)*, disipaie *(f)*, dezm *(n)*, desfrâu *(n)*
dissociation • *n* disociere *(f)*, disocieri, disociere
dissolution • *n* dizolvare *(f)*
distance • *v* distana • *n* distan *(f)*

distant • *adj* departe
distasteful • *adj* dezgusttor, neplcut *(m)*, dezagreabil, neplcut, ofensator
distillation • *n* distilare *(f)*
distillery • *n* distilerie *(f)*
distinct • *adj* distinct
distinction • *n* distincie *(f)*, deosebire *(f)*, diferen *(f)*, distingere *(f)*, distingibilitate *(f)*
distinctive • *adj* distinctiv
distinguish • *v* distinge, recunoate
distinguishable • *adj* distingibil
distinguished • *adj* distinct *(m)*
distraint • *n* sechestru *(n)*
distress • *v* deranja • *n* suferin *(f)*, primejdie *(f)*, pericol *(n)*
distribute • *v* distribui, împri, repartiza, livra, clasifica
distribution • *n* distribuire, parte distribuit *(f)*, distribuie *(f)*, împrire, aranjament *(n)*, distribuie
distributive • *adj* distributiv
district • *n* district, raion, jude *(n)*, regiune *(f)*, district *(n)*
distrust • *v* suspecta, mefia • *n* neîncredere *(f)*, difiden *(f)*
disturb • *v* deranja
disturbance • *n* deranjare *(f)*, tulburare *(f)*, deranj *(n)*, încomodare *(f)*, perturbare *(f)*, perturbaie *(f)*, deranjament *(n)*
ditch • *n* an *(m)*
dive • *v* sri • *n* plonjare, scufundare, alunecare
diver • *n* scufundtor *(m)*, scafandru *(m)*, scafandrier *(m)*, cufundar *(m)*, bodârlu *(m)*, corcodel *(m)*
divergence • *n* divergen *(f)*
divide • *v* despri, divide, diviza, împri, se diviza
divisible • *adj* divizibil *(m)*
division • *n* divizare *(f)*, diviziune *(f)*, parte *(f)*, împrire *(f)*, impartire *(f)*, divizie *(f)*
divisor • *n* divizor *(m)*
divorce • *v* divora, despri • *n* divor *(n)*, desprire *(f)*
divulge • *v* divulga, denuna
do • *v* face
dobra • *n* dobra
docile • *adj* docil
docility • *n* docilitate
doctor • *n* medic *(m)*, doctor *(m)*, doctori *(f)*, doctor *(f)*
doctrinal • *adj* doctrinal
doctrine • *n* doctrin
document • *v* documenta • *n* document *(n)*
documentary • *n* documentar *(n)* • *adj* documentar *(m)*
documentation • *n* documentaie
dodecagon • *n* dodecagon *(n)*
dodo • *n* pasrea dodo *(f)*, dront *(m)*
doe • *n* ciut *(f)*, cprioar
dog • *n* câine, cîine, câini, câine *(m)*
doge • *n* doge *(m)*
dogma • *n* dogm *(f)*, doctrin *(f)*
dogmatic • *adj* dogmatic *(n)*
dogwood • *n* sânger *(m)*, corn *(m)*
doll • *n* ppu *(f)*
dollar • *n* dolar *(m)*
dolphin • *n* delfin *(m)*
domain • *n* domeniu
domesticate • *v* domestici
domestication • *n* domesticire *(f)*
domicile • *n* domiciliu *(n)*
dominance • *n* dominan *(f)*, domnie *(f)*
dominant • *adj* dominant *(n)*, dominant *(f)*, predominant, preponderent
dominate • *v* domina
domineering • *adj* dominant, dominator *(m)*
dominion • *n* dominaie *(f)*
donation • *n* donaie *(f)*, donaii
donkey • *n* mgar *(m)*, asin *(m)*
donor • *n* donator *(m)*
door • *n* u *(f)*, ui
doorbell • *n* sonerie *(f)*
doorkeeper • *n* portar *(m)*
dormant • *adj* inactiv, suspendat
dormouse • *n* oarece de pdure
dotterel • *n* prundra-de-munte *(m)*, ploier-de-munte *(m)*
double • *v* dubla, îndoi • *adj* dublu *(n)*, dublat *(n)*
doubt • *n* dubiu, îndoial
dough • *n* aluat, mlai *(m)*
doughnut • *n* gogoa *(f)*
douse • *v* muia
dove • *n* porumbel *(m)*
dovecote • *n* porumbar *(m)*, porumbrie *(f)*
down • *adj* czut, deprimat • *adv* jos, în jos, spre-n jos, la sud
downstream • *adv* în aval, la vale, în josul apei
downtown • *n* centru *(n)*
downward • *adj* coborâtor *(m)*, coborâtoare *(f)*, descendent *(m)* • *adv* în jos, în coborâre
dowry • *n* zestre
doze • *v* dormita, aipi, a moi
dozen • *n* duzin *(f)*
drab • *adj* splcit
draft • *n* ciorna *(f)*, schi *(f)*, concept *(n)*,

plan *(n)*, pescaj *(n)*, suflare, tiraj *(f)*, curent de aer *(m)*, cec, recrutare, înrolare *(f)*
dragon • *n* balaur *(m)*, dragon, zmeu
dragonfly • *n* libelul *(f)*
dragoon • *n* dragon
drain • *v* goli, scurge, asana • *n* conduct *(f)*, canal de scurgere *(n)*
drake • *n* roi *(m)*
drama • *n* dram *(f)*
dramaturgic • *adj* dramaturgic *(m)*
draught • *n* tras *(n)*, tragere *(f)*, înghiitur *(f)*, gur *(f)*
draughts • *n* dame, table
draw • *v* desena • *n* egalitate *(f)*, tragere *(f)*
drawer • *n* sertar *(n)*
drawing • *n* desen *(n)*, tragere *(f)*
drawl • *v* trgna
dread • *v* teme • *n* fric *(f)*, team *(f)*, temere *(f)*, sperietoare *(f)*
dream • *v* visa, imagina • *n* vis *(n)*
dreamer • *n* vistor *(m)*, vistoare *(f)*
dreamy • *adj* de vis
dress • *v* îmbrca • *n* rochie *(f)*, rochii, hain
dressing • *n* imbracat
dressmaker • *n* croitor *(m)*, croitoreas *(f)*
drill • *v* gauri • *n* burghiu, sfredel
drink • *v* bea • *n* butur *(f)*
drinkable • *adj* potabil
drinker • *n* butor *(m)*, butoare *(f)*
drip • *v* pica
drive • *v* mâna, conduce, ghida
driver • *n* conductor, ofer *(m)*, conductor auto *(m)*
drizzle • *v* bura, ârâi • *n* burni *(f)*
dromedary • *n* dromader
drone • *n* trântor *(m)*
drop • *v* scpa • *n* pictur *(f)*, cdere *(f)*, prbuire *(f)*, drajeu *(n)*, bomboan *(f)*
drought • *n* secet
drown • *v* îneca
drum • *n* tob *(f)*
drunk • *n* alcoolic *(m)*, beiv *(m)*, beiv *(f)*, beivan *(m)*, beivan *(f)* • *adj* beat, but, îmbtat
drunkard • *n* beiv *(m)*, beiv *(f)*, beivan *(m)*, beivan *(f)*
drunken • *adj* beat, but, îmbtat
drunkenness • *n* beie *(f)*
dry • *adj* uscat, sec, uscat *(n)*, deshidratat *(n)*, arid *(n)*
dubious • *adj* dubios
duchy • *n* ducat *(m)*
duck • *v* ghemui • *n* ra *(f)*, roi *(m)*
duckling • *n* ruc *(f)*, rioar *(f)*, ruc *(f)*, boboc *(m)*
duckweed • *n* linti *(f)*
dude • *n* tip *(m)*
dugong • *n* dugong *(m)*
duke • *n* duce *(m)*
dulcimer • *n* ambal *(m)*
dull • *adj* banal
dullness • *n* obtuzitate *(f)*, plictiseal *(f)*
duma • *n* duma *(f)*
dumping • *n* dumping, vânzare sub valoarea mrfii *(f)*
dune • *n* dun *(f)*
dung • *n* gunoi *(m)*, baleg *(f)*
duplicate • *v* duplica, dubla • *n* duplicat, copie, dublare *(f)*
duplicator • *n* copiator *(m)*, main de copiat *(f)*, duplicator *(m)*
durable • *adj* trainic *(n)*, durabil *(n)*
duration • *n* durat *(f)*
durative • *adj* durativ
duress • *n* obligare prin for *(f)*, constrângere *(f)*
dusk • *v* însera, amurgi • *n* crepuscul, apus, amurg *(n)*
dust • *v* scutura • *n* praf *(n)*, pulbere *(f)*, colb *(n)*
dustpan • *n* fra
duty • *n* datorie *(f)*, sarcin, tax *(f)*, impozit *(n)*
duty-free • *adj* scutit de vam *(m)*, fr vam, scutit de taxe *(m)*
dwarf • *v* minimiza • *n* pitic *(m)*, prichindel *(m)* • *adj* minuscul
dwell • *v* tri
dying • *adj* muribund, pe moarte, de moarte
dynamite • *n* dinamit
dynasty • *n* dinastie *(f)*
dysphoria • *n* disforie *(f)*
dysprosium • *n* disprosiu *(n)*

E

eager • *adj* doritor, amator, avid, dornic, nerbdtor
eagle • *n* acvil *(f)*, acer, vultur, pajur
eaglet • *n* vulturel *(m)*, vultura *(m)*
ear • *n* ureche *(f)*, informator *(m)*, ciripitor *(m)*, spic • *v* ara
earache • *n* durere de ureche *(f)*
earl • *n* conte *(m)*

early • *adj* devreme, timpuriu • *adv* devreme
earn • *v* câtiga
earring • *n* cercel *(m)*
earth • *n* pmânt *(n)*, sol *(n)*, pmânt
earthquake • *n* cutremur *(n)*
earthworm • *n* râm *(f)*
earwig • *n* urechelni *(f)*
ease • *v* alina, uura, liniti, micora, potoli, reduce • *n* confort *(n)*, linite *(f)*, pace *(f)*, uurina *(f)*, uurare *(f)*, dexteritate *(f)*, facilitate *(f)*, repaus *(n)*
easel • *n* evalet *(n)*
east • *n* est
eastern • *adj* estic *(n)*, oriental *(n)*, de est
easy • *adj* uor
eat • *v* mânca, îngrijora, roade
eater • *n* mânctor
ebb • *n* reflux *(n)*
ebony • *n* abanos *(m)*, negru-abanos, negru de abanos • *adj* negru-abanos
eccentricity • *n* excentricitate *(f)*
echidna • *n* echidn *(f)*, echidneu
echo • *v* rsuna • *n* ecou *(n)*
echolocation • *n* ecolocaie *(f)*
eclipse • *v* eclipsa • *n* eclips *(f)*
ecological • *adj* ecologic *(n)*
ecology • *n* ecologie *(f)*
econometric • *adj* econometric *(n)*
econometrician • *n* econometrist *(m)*, econometrician *(m)*
econometrics • *n* econometrie *(f)*
economics • *n* economie
economy • *n* economie *(f)*
ecosystem • *n* ecosistem *(n)*
ecstasy • *n* extaz *(n)*, ecstasy *(n)*
edacious • *adj* lacom
eddy • *n* contracurent *(m)*, bulboan, volbur *(f)*, vârtej *(n)*
edelweiss • *n* floare-de-col *(f)*, edelvais *(m)*, albumeal *(f)*
edentate • *n* edentate
edge • *n* margine, ti, ascui
edible • *adj* comestibil *(n)*, comestibil *(f)*, mâncabil *(n)*
edification • *n* edificare *(f)*
edifice • *n* edificiu *(n)*
edit • *v* edita, modifica, schimba • *n* modificare *(f)*, corectare *(f)*, redactare *(f)*
edition • *n* ediie
editor • *n* editor *(m)*, monteuz *(f)*, editor de text *(m)*
educate • *v* educa, instrui
education • *n* educaie *(f)*, educare *(f)*, învmânt *(n)*
eel • *n* anghil *(f)*, ipar *(m)*
eerie • *adj* straniu, superstiios
efface • *v* a terge
effect • *n* efect, efect sonor
effective • *adj* efectiv *(m)*, eficient *(m)*, efectent *(m)*, eficace *(f)*, plin de efect
effectiveness • *n* eficacitate *(f)*, eficien *(f)*
effeminate • *adj* afemeiat
effete • *adj* slbit
efficacy • *n* eficacitate *(f)*
efflorescence • *n* eflorescen *(f)*
effort • *n* efort *(n)*, solicitare *(f)*
effrontery • *n* sfruntare *(f)*, neruinare *(f)*, insolen *(f)*
effusive • *adj* efuziv *(n)*, efuziv *(f)*
egg • *n* ou, ovul *(n)*
eggplant • *n* vânt *(f)*
eggshell • *n* coaj de ou *(f)*
egret • *n* egret *(f)*, stârc alb *(m)*
eider • *n* eider *(m)*
eighth • *n* cel al optulea *(m)*, cea a opta *(f)*
einsteinium • *n* einsteiniu *(n)*
either • *adv* nici
ejaculate • *n* ejaculaie *(f)*
ejaculation • *n* ejaculare *(f)*, ejaculaie *(f)*
ejaculatory • *adj* ejaculator
elastic • *adj* elastic
elasticity • *n* elasticitate *(f)*
elbow • *n* cot *(n)*
elder • *n* soc *(m)*
elderberry • *n* soc *(m)*
elderly • *adj* vârsta a treia, btrân *(n)*, btrân *(f)*, btrâni, vârstnici
elecampane • *n* iarb-mare *(f)*
elect • *v* alege, hotrî
election • *n* alegere *(f)*, selecie *(f)*, desemnare *(f)*
electorate • *n* electorat *(n)*, alegtori
electric • *adj* electric, electric *(m)*, electronic *(m)*
electrical • *adj* electric
electricity • *n* electricitate
electrobiology • *n* electrobiologie
electrocardiogram • *n* electrocardiogram *(f)*
electrocution • *n* electrocutare *(f)*
electrodynamometer • *n* electrodinamometru *(n)*
electrolysis • *n* electroliz
electromagnetic • *adj* electromagnetic
electromagnetism • *n* electromagnetism *(n)*
electromechanical • *adj* electromecanic
electron • *n* electron *(m)*
electronic • *adj* electronic, de Internet, electronic *(m)*
electronics • *n* electronic *(f)*, electronic
electrostatic • *adj* electrostatic *(n)*
elegance • *n* elegan *(f)*, graie *(f)*, finee *(f)*

element • *n* element *(n)*, elemente, particul *(n)*, prticic *(f)*, pies *(f)*
elementary • *adj* elementar *(n)*, fundamental *(n)*, elementar *(f)*
elephant • *n* elefant *(m)*
elephantine • *adj* elefantin *(n)*, elefantin *(f)*, elefantini
eleventh • *n* cel al unsprezecelea *(m)*, cea a unsprezecea *(f)*
eligibility • *n* eligibilitate *(f)*
eligible • *adj* eligibil *(n)*
elimination • *n* eliminare *(f)*
elite • *n* elit *(f)*
ellipse • *n* elips *(f)*
ellipsoid • *n* elipsoid
elm • *n* ulm *(m)*
elongate • *v* alungi, lungi, prelungi
elsewhere • *adv* aiurea
elude • *v* eluda
elusive • *adj* evaziv
emaciated • *adj* epuizat *(n)*, istovit *(n)*, vlguit *(n)*, sectuit *(n)*
emancipate • *v* emancipa, dezrobi, elibera
emancipation • *n* emancipare
embark • *v* a se îmbarca
embarrassment • *n* jen *(f)*
embassy • *n* ambasad *(f)*
embattled • *adj* înarmai
ember • *n* tciune *(f)*
embers • *n* tciune
embrace • *v* îmbria • *n* îmbriare *(f)*
embryo • *n* embrion *(m)*
emerald • *n* smarald *(n)*, smarand *(n)*, smaragd *(n)*, smaraldiu *(m)* • *adj* smaraldiu
emigrant • *n* emigrant *(m)*, emigrant *(f)*
emigration • *n* emigrare *(f)*, emigraie, emigrare
emission • *n* emisiune *(f)*, emisie *(f)*
emit • *v* emite
emotion • *n* emoie
emotional • *adj* emoional, emoionabil
emotionless • *adj* fr emoii
empathy • *n* empatie *(n)*, empatie *(f)*
emperor • *n* împrat *(m)*
empire • *n* imperiu, împrie
empirical • *adj* empiric
empiricism • *n* empirism
empiricist • *n* empirist
employ • *v* angaja
employee • *n* angajat *(m)*, angajat *(f)*
employer • *n* angajator *(m)*
empress • *n* împrteas *(f)*
empty • *v* goli, descrca, deerta, liber *(n)* • *adj* vid, gol, deert, golit *(n)*
emu • *n* emu *(m)*
emulsifier • *n* emulgator *(m)*, emulsificator *(m)*
emulsion • *n* emulsie *(f)*
enamored • *adj* amorezat, înamorat, îndrgostit
enchanting • *adj* încânttor *(m)*, încânttoare *(f)*, încântant
enchantment • *n* încântare *(f)*, delectare *(f)*, desftare *(f)*, farmec *(n)*, magie *(f)*, vraj *(f)*
encounter • *v* întâlni
encourage • *v* încuraja, îmbrbta, însuflei
encouragement • *n* încurajare *(f)*, încurajare, stimulare *(f)*
encumber • *v* încurca
encyclopedia • *n* enciclopedie *(f)*
end • *v* sfâri, termina • *n* sfârit, terminaie, capt
endanger • *v* compromite, periclita, risca, primejdui
endearment • *n* afeciune *(f)*, dezmierdare *(f)*, îndrgire *(f)*
endeavor • *n* tentativ *(f)*
endemic • *adj* endemic
ending • *n* sfârit *(n)*, încheiere *(f)*, final *(n)*, sfârit
endive • *n* andiv *(f)*
endless • *adj* fr sfîrit, nesfîrit. *(m)*, interminabil *(m)*
endoderm • *n* endoderm
endogenous • *adj* endogen
endosperm • *n* endosperm *(n)*
endure • *v* îndura, rbda, trainic *(n)*, trainic *(f)*, trainici
enemy • *n* duman *(m)*, inamic *(m)*, vrjma *(m)*
energetic • *adj* energetic *(m)*
energy • *n* energie *(f)*
enforce • *v* întri, obliga
engagement • *n* angajament *(n)*, logodire *(f)*, logodn *(f)*
engine • *n* motor *(n)*, locomotiv *(f)*
engineer • *n* inginer *(m)*, inginer *(f)*, ingenios *(m)*, mecanic *(f)*
engineering • *n* inginerie *(f)*
english • *n* english
enigmatic • *adj* enigmatic
enjoy • *v* savura, a se bucura de, a se distra
enlighten • *v* lmuri
enliven • *v* înviora
enmity • *n* dumnie *(f)*, inimiciie *(f)*
enormity • *n* enormitate *(f)*, imensitate *(f)*
enormous • *adj* enorm, uria, gigant *(n)*
enough • *adv* destul, suficient, de ajuns • *interj* ajunge
enrage • *v* înfuria

enslave • *v* robi, înrobi
ensnare • *v* ademeni, a prinde în capcan
ensure • *v* asigura
entangle • *v* zpci, încurca, a vârî în bucluc
entanglement • *n* încurctur, complicaie (*f*), situaie complicat (*f*)
enter • *v* intra, introduce
enteric • *adj* enteric (*m*), intestinal (*m*)
enteritis • *n* enterit (*f*)
entertainment • *n* divertisment (*n*), distracie (*f*), petrecere (*f*), spectacol (*n*)
enthusiasm • *n* entuziasm (*n*)
enthusiast • *n* entuziast (*m*)
enticing • *adj* seductor, tentant, încânttor, atrgtor
entire • *adj* întreg
entomology • *n* entomologie
entrails • *n* mae
entrance • *n* intrare
entrepreneur • *n* antreprenor (*m*), întreprinztor (*m*)
entropy • *n* entropie (*f*)
envelope • *n* plic (*n*), învelitur (*f*), înveli (*n*), sac (*m*), pung (*f*), anvelop (*f*), înfurtoare (*f*)
envious • *adj* invidios, pizma
environment • *n* mediu (*n*), ambient (*n*), ecosistem (*n*), mediu ambiant (*n*), ambient, climat (*n*), ambian (*f*), sistem de operare (*n*)
envy • *v* invidia • *n* invidie (*f*)
epicycloid • *n* epicicloid (*f*)
epidemic • *n* epidemie (*f*), epidemii • *adj* epidemic (*m*)
epidemiologist • *n* epidemiolog (*m*)
epidemiology • *n* epidemiologie (*f*)
epidermis • *n* epiderm (*f*)
epigraph • *n* epigraf
epiphany • *n* epifanie (*n*)
epistle • *n* epistol (*f*), epistole
epithelium • *n* esut epitelial (*n*)
epoch • *n* epoc (*f*), er (*f*), eveniment (*n*)
epochal • *adj* epocal (*m*)
epopee • *n* epopee
equal • *adj* egal
equality • *n* egalitate
equally • *adv* egal, în mod egal
equanimity • *n* linite (*f*)
equation • *n* ecuaie (*f*)
equator • *n* ecuator (*n*)
equilibrium • *n* echilibru (*n*), stabilitate (*f*), echilibru mintal (*n*), ponderaie (*f*)
equinox • *n* echinox (*n*), echinociu (*n*)
equipment • *n* echipare (*f*), echipament (*n*)
equitable • *adj* echitabil, echitabil (*n*)
equity • *n* imparialitate (*f*), echitate, neprtinire (*f*)
equivalent • *adj* echivalent (*m*), echivalent (*f*)
equivocal • *adj* echivoc, ambiguu, echivoc (*n*)
era • *n* er (*f*), epoc (*f*), perioad (*f*)
eradicate • *v* dezrdcina, eradica, elimina, stârpi, extirpa
eraser • *n* radier (*f*), gum de ters (*f*), burete (*m*)
erbium • *n* erbiu (*n*)
erection • *n* erecie (*f*)
ergonomic • *adj* ergonomic (*m*), ergonomic (*f*)
ermine • *n* hermelin (*f*), hermin (*f*), herminat (*n*)
erogenous • *adj* erogen
erosion • *n* eroziune, eroziune (*f*)
erotic • *adj* erotic
err • *v* grei, se înela
erudition • *n* erudiie (*f*)
eruption • *n* erupere (*f*), erupie (*f*)
escalade • *v* escalada
escape • *v* scpa, eluda • *n* scpare, fug, esc
eschew • *v* evita, ocoli
esoteric • *adj* ezoteric
especially • *adv* mai ales
esprit • *n* spirit (*n*)
essayist • *n* eseist (*m*)
essential • *adj* necesar (*n*), esenial (*n*), important (*n*), important (*f*), esenial (*f*), de baz, fundamental
essentiality • *n* esenialitate (*f*)
essentially • *adv* esenial, în esen
establish • *v* stabili
establishment • *n* stabilire (*f*), aezare (*f*), instalare (*f*), instituire (*f*), stabiliment (*n*), întreprindere (*f*), aezmânt (*n*), instituie (*f*), colonie (*f*)
esteem • *v* stima, aprecia • *n* stim (*f*)
estimation • *n* estimare
eternity • *n* eternitate (*f*), venicie (*f*)
ethane • *n* etan
ethereal • *adj* eteric
ethical • *adj* etic
ethnography • *n* etnografie (*f*)
ethos • *n* etos (*n*)
etymological • *adj* etimologic
etymology • *n* etimologie (*f*)
eucalyptus • *n* eucalipt (*m*)
eulogy • *n* elogiu (*n*)
euphemism • *n* eufemism (*n*)
euphoria • *n* euforie (*f*)
eureka • *interj* évrica
europium • *n* europiu (*n*)
euthanasia • *n* eutanasie (*f*)

evaporate • *v* evapora
eve • *n* ajun *(n)*, preziu *(f)*
even • *adj* plat, egal, par *(m)*, par *(f)* • *adv* chiar, exact, i
evening • *n* sear
event • *n* eveniment *(n)*
eventful • *adj* plin de evenimente *(m)*, memorabil *(m)*
eventuality • *n* eventualitate *(f)*
eventually • *adv* în fine, la urma urmei
everlasting • *adv* etern, nemuritor, interminabil, perpetuu, continuu
everybody • *pron* fiecine, toat lumea, oricine, toi oamenii *(m)*
everyday • *adj* de fiecare zi, cotidian *(m)*
everyone • *pron* oricine, toi, fiecare
everything • *pron* tot
evict • *v* evinge, expulza
evident • *adj* evident
evil • *n* ru, rutate *(f)* • *adj* ru, rutcios, hain, câinos, depravat, deczut, desfrânat
evolution • *n* evoluie *(f)*
evolutionary • *adj* evoluional *(n)*, evoluial *(n)*, evoluionar *(n)*
evolve • *v* evolua
ewe • *n* oaie *(f)*, oi *(f)*
ex • *n* fostul *(m)*
exaggerate • *v* exagera
exaggerated • *adj* exagerat *(n)*
exaggeration • *n* exagerare
examination • *n* examinare *(f)*, examen *(n)*, examen medical *(n)*, consult medical *(n)*
example • *n* exemplu
exasperated • *adj* exasperat *(m)*
exasperation • *n* exasperare *(f)*
exceed • *v* depi
exceedingly • *adv* extrem *(n)*
excellent • *adj* excelent *(m)*, excelent *(f)*
excess • *n* exces *(n)*, exagerare *(f)*, abuz *(n)*, prisos *(n)*
excessive • *adj* excesiv, excesiv *(f)*
exchange • *n* schimb *(n)*, troc • *v* schimba
excitation • *n* excitare *(f)*
excited • *adj* entuziasmat *(n)*, înflcrat *(n)*, emoionat *(n)*, exaltat *(n)*, excitat *(n)*
excitement • *n* excitare *(f)*, excitaie *(f)*
exclamation • *n* exclamare *(f)*, exclamaie *(f)*
exclusion • *n* excludere *(f)*, eliminare *(f)*
excrement • *n* excrement, materii fecale, fecale
excrete • *v* a excreta, a elimina
excuse • *v* scuza
execrable • *adj* execrabil
execute • *v* executa
execution • *n* execuie *(f)*, execuie
executioner • *n* clu *(m)*
executor • *n* executor
exempt • *v* scuti, dispensa • *n* scutire *(f)*, dispensare *(f)* • *adj* scutit *(m)*, dispensat *(m)*
exercise • *n* exerciiu
exert • *v* fora, exercita
exhausted • *adj* epuizat *(n)*, vlguit *(n)*, sectuit *(n)*, obosit *(n)*, istovit *(n)*
exhaustion • *n* epuizare *(f)*, extenuare *(f)*
exhibit • *v* expoza, arta
exhibition • *n* expoziie *(f)*
exhibitionist • *n* exhibiionist
exile • *v* exila • *n* exil *(n)*, exilare *(f)*, exilat *(m)*
exist • *v* exista
exit • *v* iei • *n* ieire
exodus • *n* exod *(n)*
exogamy • *n* exogamie *(f)*
exophthalmos • *n* exoftalmie
expand • *v* mri, expanda, crete, factoriza
expectancy • *n* anticipare *(f)*, ateptare *(f)*
expectation • *n* ateptare *(f)*, anticipare *(f)*, expectativ *(f)*, anticipaie *(f)*, ateptat *(n)*
expedient • *adj* expeditiv *(n)*, expeditiv *(f)*, expeditivi, expeditive
expensive • *adj* scump, costisitor
experience • *v* pi • *n* experienta, experien *(f)*
experienced • *adj* experimentat *(n)*, încercat *(n)*
experimental • *adj* experimental
expert • *n* expert *(m)* • *adj* expert, de expert
explain • *v* explica
explanation • *n* explicare *(f)*, explicaie *(f)*
explicable • *adj* explicabil, explicabil *(f)*, explicabile, explicabili
explication • *n* explicare *(f)*
explicit • *adj* explicit, vulgar
exploit • *v* exploata, a abuza (de) • *n* fapt de vitejie *(f)*, fapt eroic *(f)*
explosion • *n* explozie *(f)*, detuntur
exponentiation • *n* exponeniere *(f)*
export • *n* export, marf exportat *(f)*, bun exportat, exportare *(f)*
exporter • *n* exportator *(n)*
expose • *v* expune
exposition • *n* expoziie *(f)*, expunere *(f)*
exposure • *n* expunere, prezentare, poziie, înfiare, dezgolire
express • *n* expres *(n)*, exprese, tren expres *(n)*
expressible • *adj* exprimabil
expression • *n* expresie, expresie *(f)*
expressionism • *n* expresionism *(n)*
expressive • *adj* expresiv *(n)*, plin de ex-

presie *(n)*
expropriation • *n* expropriere *(f)*
expurgate • *v* expurga
extant • *adj* existent *(m)*
extendible • *adj* extensibil *(n)*
extension • *n* extindere *(f)*, întindere *(f)*, extensie *(f)*, prefix telefonic *(n)*, extensie de fiier *(f)*
extent • *n* mrime, întindere, volum
exterminate • *v* exterminare *(f)*
external • *adj* extern
externalization • *n* externizare *(f)*
extinguish • *v* stinge
extirpate • *v* dezrdcina
extract • *n* extract *(n)*, extras
extragalactic • *adj* extragalactic *(n)*
extraordinary • *adj* extraordinar, ieit din comun *(n)*, neobinuit *(n)*
extrapolation • *n* extrapolare *(f)*
extraterrestrial • *n* extraterestru *(m)* • *adj* extraterestru
extravagance • *n* extravagan, risip *(f)*
extremely • *adv* în mod extrem
extremism • *n* extremism *(n)*
extremity • *n* capt, extremitate
eye • *n* ochi *(m)*
eyebrow • *n* sprâncean *(f)*, arcad *(f)*
eyelash • *n* gean *(f)*
eyelid • *n* pleoap *(f)*
eyesight • *n* vedere *(f)*, vz *(n)*
eyesore • *n* oroare vizual *(f)*, dezgust vizual *(n)*

F

fable • *n* poveste
fabled • *adj* legendar, faimos
fabric • *n* structur *(f)*, estur *(f)*, material esut *(n)*, textile
fabrication • *n* fabricare *(f)*
fabulous • *adj* mitic, legendar, incredibil, fabulos, extraordinar, foarte bun, extrem de bun
face • *v* înfrunta, confrunta • *n* fa, fa *(f)*
facilitate • *v* facilita, uura
facilitation • *n* uurare *(f)*, facilitare *(f)*, promovare *(f)*, încurajare *(f)*
facility • *n* facilitate
facing • *n* vipuc *(f)*, tres *(f)*, galon *(n)*
fact • *n* fapt, fapt *(n)*, fapt *(f)*
faction • *n* faciune, fraciune *(f)*, dezbinare *(f)*, rivalitate *(f)*, vrajb *(f)*
factory • *n* fabric *(f)*, uzin *(f)*
factual • *adj* efectiv, faptic
faculty • *n* facultate *(f)*, putin *(f)*, abilitate *(f)*, capacitate *(f)*
fade • *v* apune
fag • *n* poponar *(m)*, bulangiu *(m)*
faience • *n* faian *(f)*
fail • *v* a rata, a se strica, a strica
failing • *n* defect
failure • *n* eec *(n)*
fairy • *n* zân *(f)*
faith • *n* credin *(f)*
falcon • *n* oim *(m)*
fall • *v* cdea • *n* cdere *(f)*
false • *adj* fals, neadevr, artificial, contrafcut, fals *(n)*
falsehood • *n* falsitate *(f)*
falsify • *v* denatura, falsifica
falsity • *n* falsitate *(f)*, neadevr *(n)*, necinste *(f)*
fame • *n* faim
familiarity • *n* familiaritate *(f)*, intimitate *(f)*, impertinen *(f)*
family • *n* familie, familie *(f)*, familiar
famine • *n* foamete *(n)*, foamete *(f)*
famished • *adj* înfometat *(n)*, înfometat *(f)*, înfometai, înfometate, hmesit *(m)*
famous • *adj* celebru, faimos
fan • *v* vântura • *n* ventilator *(n)*
fantastic • *adj* fantastic
far • *adj* departe, îndeprtat, extrem • *adv* departe
far-flung • *adj* distant *(n)*
fare • *n* tarif *(n)*, bilet *(n)* • *v* cltori
farewell • *interj* la revedere
farm • *n* ferm
farmer • *n* ran *(m)*, fermier *(m)*
farrow • *v* fta
farsighted • *adj* hipermetrop
fart • *v* bi, pârâi • *n* vânt *(n)*, flatulen *(f)*, bin *(f)*, pâr *(n)*
fascism • *n* fascism *(m)*
fast • *adj* rapid, iute, grbit, repede • *adv* repede • *v* ajuna, posti
fasten • *v* fixa, ataa
fastidious • *adj* minuios, cusurgiu *(m)*, mofturos *(m)*
fat • *n* grsime • *adj* gras, gros
fatalism • *n* fatalism *(n)*
fate • *n* soart, destin
father • *v* procrea, procreare • *n* tat *(m)*
father-in-law • *n* socru *(m)*
fatherland • *n* patrie

fathom • *v* îmbria, apuca, msura, sonda, ptrunde, înelege • *n* bra *(n)*, fathom *(m)*
fatigue • *v* extenua • *n* extenuare *(f)*, oboseal *(f)*, corvad *(f)*
fatigued • *adj* obosit *(n)*, extenuat *(n)*
fatten • *v* îngra
fault • *n* hib *(f)*, vin *(f)*, greeal *(f)*, culp *(f)*
fauna • *n* faun *(f)*, regnul animal *(n)*
favor • *n* favoare *(f)*
favorite • *adj* favorit *(m)*, favorit *(f)*
fawn • *n* ied *(m)*, cafeniu • *adj* cafeniu • *v* alinta, rsfa, lingui, flata, mguli, gudura
fax • *n* fax
fear • *n* fric *(f)*, team *(f)*, fobie, spaim *(f)*
fearful • *adj* groaznic *(m)*
fearlessness • *n* curaj *(n)*, temeritate *(f)*, cutezan *(f)*, neînfricare *(f)*
feasibility • *n* fezabilitate *(f)*, posibilitate de realizare *(f)*, facibilitate *(f)*
feasible • *adj* fezabil, facibil *(n)*
feast • *n* banchet *(n)*, festin *(n)*, osp *(n)*
feather • *n* fulg *(n)*, pan *(f)*
feature • *n* caracteristic, particularitate, proprietate, foileton, reportaj, trstur
federal • *adj* federal
federalism • *n* federalism *(n)*
federalization • *n* federalizare *(f)*
federation • *n* federaie *(f)*
feeble • *adj* plpând, lânced, slab, debil
feed • *v* hrni • *n* strânsur, nutre
feedback • *n* reacie *(f)*, efect retroactiv *(n)*, conexiune invers *(f)*
feel • *v* simi
feeling • *n* sentiment *(n)*, sentimente • *adj* sentimental *(m)*
feisty • *adj* tenace
felicity • *n* fericire *(f)*
feline • *adj* felin *(m)*, felin *(f)*
fellatio • *n* felaie *(f)*
feminine • *adj* feminin, femeiesc
femininity • *n* feminitate *(f)*
fence • *v* scrima • *n* gard
fencing • *n* scrim
fennel • *n* fenicul
fenugreek • *n* fenugrec *(m)*, fân grecesc *(n)*, schinduf *(m)*
ferment • *v* fermenta, dospi • *n* ferment *(m)*, enzim *(f)*
fermentation • *n* fermentare *(f)*, fermentaie *(f)*
fermium • *n* fermiu *(n)*
fern • *n* ferig *(f)*
ferocity • *n* ferocitate *(f)*
ferret • *n* nevstuic *(f)*
ferry • *n* bac *(m)*
fertilization • *n* fertilizare, fecundare *(f)*
fertilize • *v* fertiliza, însmâna
fertilizer • *n* îngrmânt *(n)*, fertilizant *(m)*, fertilizator *(n)*
fervor • *n* fervoare *(f)*, ardoare *(f)*
fester • *v* supura, puroia
festive • *adj* festiv
fetid • *adj* fetid
fetishism • *n* fetiism
fetus • *n* ft *(m)*
feud • *n* feud
feudalism • *n* feudalism *(n)*
fever • *n* temperatur *(f)*, febr *(f)*
fictitious • *adj* fictiv, nscocit
fidelity • *n* fidelitate *(f)*
fief • *n* fief *(n)*
field • *n* câmp *(n)*, câmp, câmp de btaie *(n)*, domeniu *(n)*, teren, sfer, teren *(n)*, câmp de joc *(n)*, depozit de minerale, câmp mineral, zon de memorie *(f)*
fiendish • *adj* sinistru, ru, demonic
fierce • *adj* feroce, fioros
fiery • *adj* de foc, arzând *(n)*, ardent, ardent *(f)*, incandescent, incandescent *(f)*, aprins *(n)*, aprins *(f)*, focos
fifth • *n* cel al cincilea *(m)*, cea a cincea *(f)* • *adj* cincilea *(m)*, cincea *(f)*
fig • *n* smochin *(m)*, smochin *(f)*
fight • *v* lupta, se bate, combate, a • *n* lupt *(f)*, btaie
fighter • *n* combatant *(m)*, lupttor *(m)*, combatant *(f)*, persoan combativ *(f)*, persoan btioas *(f)*, lupttoare *(f)*
figurative • *adj* figurativ *(n)*
figuratively • *adv* (în mod) figurat
figure • *n* figur
figurine • *n* statuet *(f)*, figurin *(f)*
figwort • *n* iarb-neagr *(f)*, buberic *(m)*, scrofulare *(f)*
filamentous • *adj* filamentos *(n)*
filch • *v* terpeli, fura, ciordi
file • *n* fiier *(n)*, pil *(f)*
filigree • *n* filigran *(n)*
fill • *v* umple, împlini, plomba
fillet • *n* file *(n)*
filling • *n* plomb *(f)*
fillip • *n* bobârnac *(n)*
filly • *n* mânz *(f)*
filter • *v* filtra, strecura
filth • *n* murdrie *(f)*
financial • *adj* financiar
finch • *n* cintez *(f)*, fringilid *(f)*, fringilid *(n)*
find • *v* gsi • *n* descoperire *(f)*
finger • *n* deget *(n)*
fingernail • *n* unghie *(f)*
finish • *v* termina • *n* sfârit, final *(n)*, lac *(n)*
finite • *adj* finit, limitat, care are limit

finiteness • *n* finitate *(f)*
fir • *n* brad *(m)*
fire • *n* foc *(n)*, incendiu *(n)*, sob *(f)*
firearm • *n* arm de foc *(f)*
fireball • *n* minge de foc *(f)*
firecracker • *n* petard *(f)*, pocnitoare *(f)*
firefly • *n* licurici
fireplace • *n* cmin *(n)*, emineu, vatr *(f)*, focar *(n)*
fireproof • *adj* rezistent la daune de la foc, ignifug
firework • *n* artificiu *(n)*, foc de artificiu *(n)*
first • *n* primul *(m)* • *adj* prim *(m)*, prim *(f)*, primul *(m)*, prima *(f)*
fish • *n* pete *(m)*, pescuit *(n)*, pescuire *(f)* • *v* pescui
fisher • *n* pescar *(m)*, pescari, jder-pescresc *(m)*
fisherman • *n* pescar *(m)*
fishing • *n* pescuire
fishmonger • *n* negustor de pete *(m)*, pescar *(m)*, pete *(m)*
fishy • *n* petior *(m)*
fission • *n* fisiune
fissionable • *adj* fisionabil
fissure • *n* fisur *(f)*
fist • *n* pumn
fit • *v* încpea
fitting • *n* a proba
five • *n* cinci, bancnot de cinci
fjord • *n* fiord *(n)*
flag • *v* semnaliza, marca, semnala, debilita, slbi, pava • *n* drapel *(n)*, steag *(n)*, stindard *(n)*, flamur *(f)*, flag *(n)*, iris *(m)*, dal *(f)*, lespede *(f)*
flamboyant • *adj* flamboiant
flame • *v* înflcra • *n* flacr *(f)*, par *(f)*, vpaie *(f)*, iubit *(m)*, iubit *(f)*
flamethrower • *n* arunctor de flcri *(m)*
flank • *n* flanc *(n)*, latur *(f)*
flashlight • *n* lantern
flat • *adj* plan, es, neted, plat, monoton *(n)*, monoton *(f)*
flatten • *v* nivela, netezi, aplatiza
flaunt • *v* parada
flautist • *n* flautist *(m)*, flautist *(f)*
flax • *n* in *(m)*, in *(n)*
flay • *v* beli
flea • *n* purice *(m)*
fledgling • *n* psrea *(f)*, psric *(f)*, novice *(f)*, ageamiu *(m)*
flee • *v* scpa, evada, fugi, a se evapora, disprea
fleece • *v* stoarce • *n* lân
fleeting • *adj* fugaci, fugitiv
flesh • *n* carne *(f)*
fleshy • *adj* crnos
flex • *v* a contracta
flexibility • *n* flexibilitate *(f)*
flexible • *adj* flexibil *(n)*
flicker • *v* licri, pâlpâi • *n* licr *(n)*, scânteiere *(f)*, licrire *(f)*, sclipire *(f)*, clip *(f)*
flight • *n* zbor *(n)*, zburare *(f)*
fling • *v* arunca
flint • *n* silex, cremene *(n)*
flip • *v* întoarce, rsturna
flip-flop • *n* bistabil *(n)*, lap
float • *v* pluti • *n* plut *(f)*, plutitor *(n)*
floating • *adj* plutitor *(n)*, flotant *(n)*
flock • *n* stol *(n)*, turm *(f)*, scam, floc
flood • *v* revrsa, inunda • *n* inundaie *(f)*
floor • *n* podea *(f)*, planeu *(n)*
flora • *n* flor *(f)*, flor microbial *(f)*, flor bacterial, flor intestinal *(f)*
florist • *n* florar *(m)*
floss • *n* a dentar *(f)*
flour • *n* fin *(f)*
floury • *adj* finos
flow • *v* curge • *n* curgere *(f)*, flux *(n)*
flower • *v* înflori • *n* floare *(f)*
flu • *n* grip
fluency • *n* fluiditate *(f)*, fluen *(f)*
fluff • *n* scam
fluid • *n* fluid *(n)* • *adj* fluid
fluorine • *n* fluor *(n)*
fluorite • *n* fluorit *(m)*
flurry • *n* freamt
flute • *n* flaut *(n)*
fluvial • *adj* fluvial
fly • *n* musc *(f)*, momeal *(f)*, fermoar *(n)*
flyer • *n* foaie volant *(f)*
foal • *v* fta • *n* mânz *(m)*, mânz *(f)*
foam • *v* spumega, spuma • *n* spum *(f)*
fodder • *n* furaj, nutre, strânsur
fog • *v* înnegura, înceoat, înceoa • *n* cea *(f)*, negur *(f)*, abureal *(f)*
foggy • *adj* înceat *(m)*
fold • *v* îndoi, plia
folder • *n* dosar *(n)*, folder *(n)*, director *(n)*
follow • *v* urma, urmri
fondle • *v* dezmierda, mângâia
font • *n* font *(n)*
food • *n* aliment *(n)*, mâncare *(f)*, hran *(f)*, alimentare *(f)*, nutriie *(f)*
fool • *v* pcli, prosti • *n* prost *(m)*, bufon *(m)*
foot • *n* picior *(n)*
football • *n* fotbal *(n)*
footbridge • *n* punte
footpath • *n* crare *(f)*, potec *(f)*
footwear • *n* înclminte *(f)*
for • *conj* pentru c, cci • *prep* pentru

forbid • *v* interzice
forbidden • *adj* interzis
force • *v* fora, supune, violenta • *n* for *(f)*
ford • *n* vad *(n)*
forearm • *n* antebra
foreboding • *n* presimire rea *(f)*, presentiment ru *(n)*, piaz *(f)*
forefinger • *n* deget arttor *(n)*, arttor *(n)*
forehead • *n* frunte *(f)*
foreign • *adj* strin
foreigner • *n* strin *(m)*
foremast • *n* trinchet *(m)*, arbore mic *(m)*
foreplay • *n* preludiu *(n)*
forest • *v* împduri • *n* pdure *(f)*, codru *(m)*, silv *(f)*, mulime *(f)*
forge • *n* forj *(f)* • *v* forja, furi
forget • *v* uita
forget-me-not • *n* nu-m-uita, miozotis *(m)*
forgetful • *adj* uituc *(m)*
forgive • *v* ierta
forgiveness • *n* iertare *(f)*, scuz *(f)*, pardon *(n)*
forint • *n* forint *(m)*
fork • *n* furc *(f)*, furculi *(f)*, bifurcaie
form • *v* forma • *n* form, formular *(n)*
formal • *adj* formal *(n)*, oficial *(n)*
formalism • *n* formalism *(n)*
formalist • *adj* formalist *(m)*
format • *n* format *(n)*
formidable • *adj* formidabil, groaznic
formula • *n* formul, formul chimic
formulation • *n* formulare
forsake • *v* abandona, renuna, lepda, prsi, lsa
forsythia • *n* forsiia *(f)*
fortieth • *adj* patruzecilea
fortification • *n* fortificare *(f)*, fortificaie *(f)*, fortrea *(f)*
fortnight • *adv* dou sptmâni
fortress • *n* cetate *(f)*, fortrea *(f)*
fortuitous • *adj* fortuit, accidental, întâmpltor
fortune • *n* soart *(n)*, ans *(m)*, noroc *(m)*, avere *(f)*
forward • *adj* înainte
fossil • *n* fosil *(f)*
fossilization • *n* fosilizare *(f)*, fosilizaie *(f)*
foundation • *n* fondare *(f)*, întemeiere *(f)*, înfiinare *(f)*, fundamentare *(f)*, fundaie *(f)*, temelie *(f)*, fundament *(n)*, temei *(n)*, baz *(f)*, fond *(n)*, fond de ten *(n)*
founder • *n* fondator *(m)*, întemeietor *(m)*
fountain • *n* fântân *(f)*
four-dimensional • *adj* cvadridimensional *(n)*
fourth • *n* cel al patrulea *(m)*, cea a patra *(f)* • *adj* patrulea *(m)*, patra *(f)*
fox • *n* vulpe *(f)*
foxglove • *n* degetar *(n)*, degetari *(f)*, degeel *(n)*
foxtail • *n* coada-vulpii *(f)*
fraction • *n* fracie, fracie *(f)*, fraciune *(f)*
fractional • *adj* fracionar *(m)*, fracional *(m)*
fracture • *v* fractura • *n* fractur *(f)*, fracturare *(f)*, rupere *(f)*
fractured • *adj* frânt
fragment • *v* fragmenta • *n* bucat, fragment
frame • *v* încadra, înrma • *n* cadru *(n)*, ram *(f)*, structur *(f)*, schelet *(n)*, osatur *(f)*
framework • *n* ram *(f)*, structur *(m)*, schelet *(n)*
franc • *n* franc *(m)*
francium • *n* franciu *(n)*
frankincense • *n* tmâie
fraternal • *adj* de frate, fratern, fresc
fraternity • *n* fraternitate *(f)*, frie *(f)*
fraternize • *v* fraterniza, înfri
fraudulent • *adj* fraudulos, fals
freckle • *n* pistrui *(n)*
free • *v* elibera • *adj* liber, slobod, neîmpiedicat, nelegat, neocupat, liber *(m)*, gratuit
freedom • *n* libertate *(f)*, slobod *(f)*
freesia • *n* frezie *(f)*
freeze • *v* înghea, congela
frenzy • *n* frenezie
frequency • *n* frecven *(f)*, desime *(f)*
frequent • *adj* frecvent
frequently • *adv* în mod frecvent, frecvent, deseori
fresco • *n* fresc *(f)*
fresh • *adj* proaspt
freshen • *v* împrospta
freshwater • *adj* de ap dulce
friction • *n* frecare *(m)*, friciune *(f)*, dezacord *(n)*, neînelegere *(f)*, divergen *(f)*, frecare *(f)*
friend • *n* amic *(m)*, amic *(f)*, prieten *(m)*, prieten *(f)*, prieten, iubit, amic, *(m)*
friendliness • *n* amabilitate *(f)*, prietenie *(f)*, atitudine prietenoas *(f)*
friendly • *adj* prietenos, amical *(m)* • *adv* prietenete, (în mod) prietenos
friendship • *n* prietenie *(f)*, amiciie *(f)*
fright • *n* spaim
frighten • *v* speria, înspimânta
frightened • *adj* temtor *(m)*, speriat *(m)*
fringe • *n* breton *(n)*
fritillary • *n* bibilic *(f)*
frog • *n* broasc *(f)*, brotac *(m)*
from • *prep* de, din, de la

frontispiece • *n* frontispiciu
frost • *v* bruma • *n* brum *(f)*, ger *(n)*
frown • *v* încrunta • *n* încruntare *(f)*
frozen • *adj* îngheat
fructose • *n* fructoz *(f)*
frugality • *n* cumptare, frugalitate *(f)*
fruit • *n* fruct *(n)*, poam *(f)*, rod *(n)*, fruct
fruitful • *adj* roditor, rodnic, fertil, fructuos *(m)*
fruitfulness • *n* rodnicie, fertilitate, fecunditate
fruitless • *adj* neproductiv, nefructuos
frump • *n* cineva care este ru îmbrcat()
frustration • *n* frustrare *(f)*, frustraie *(f)*
fry • *v* frige, prji • *n* cartofi prjii, cartofi pai, petior *(m)*, caracud *(f)*
fuchsia • *n* cercelu *(m)*, fucsie *(f)*
fuck • *v* fute, bga, strica • *n* futai, futere
fucking • *n* futere *(f)* • *adv* pula
fuel • *n* combustibil *(m)*, carburant *(m)*
fugacious • *adj* trector *(m)*, efemer *(m)*, care zboar
fugitive • *n* fugar, evadat, trector *(m)* • *adj* fugitiv, fugar, trector
fulfill • *v* împlini, satisface
fulfillment • *n* îndeplinire *(f)*, satisfacere *(f)*, satisfacie *(f)*
full • *adj* plin, complet, terminat, întreg, total, sturat, stul • *v* umple
fume • *v* fumega
fumitory • *n* fumri *(f)*, fumric *(f)*, safterea *(f)*
fun • *n* distracie *(f)*, amuzament *(n)*, divertisment *(n)*, plcere *(f)* • *adj* distractiv, vesel *(n)*, plcut *(n)*
function • *v* funciona • *n* funcie *(f)*, funcie
fundamental • *adj* fundamental *(n)*, de baz
fundamentalism • *n* fundamentalism
funeral • *n* înmormântare *(f)*, îngropare *(f)*, înhumare *(f)*, mormântare *(f)* • *adj* funerar, sepulcral, mormântal
funerary • *adj* funerar
fungible • *adj* fungibil *(n)*
fungus • *n* ciuperc *(f)*
funicular • *n* funicular *(n)*
funnel • *n* pâlnie *(f)*
funny • *adj* caraghios, amuzant *(m)*
fur • *n* blan *(f)*
furious • *adj* furios
furnish • *v* a mobila
furniture • *n* mobil *(f)*
furrow • *v* brzda • *n* brazd *(f)*, rid *(n)*
fury • *n* furie, mânie
fuss • *n* freamt *(n)*, agitaie *(f)*, frmântare *(f)*, indispoziie *(f)*, zgomot *(n)*, glgie *(f)*, entuziasm *(n)*
fusty • *adj* muced
future • *n* viitor • *adj* viitor
futurism • *n* futurism *(n)*

G

gadolinium • *n* gadoliniu *(n)*
gaffe • *n* gaf *(f)*
gaillardia • *n* fluturei
gain • *v* primi, câtiga
gait • *n* pas
galaxy • *n* galaxie *(f)*, galaxii
gall • *v* deranja, incomoda, enerva, tracasa, molesta, sâcâi, zgâria, roade, exaspera • *n* mizerie *(f)*, exasperare *(f)*, tupeu *(n)*, impertinen *(f)*, rostur *(f)*, gal *(f)*, cecidie *(f)*
gallant • *adj* galant
gallantry • *n* curaj *(n)*, bravur *(f)*, cutezan *(f)*, galanterie *(f)*, curtoazie *(f)*
galleon • *n* galion
gallium • *n* galiu *(n)*
gallop • *v* galopa • *n* galop *(n)*
gallows • *n* spânzurtoare *(f)*
galvanometer • *n* galvanometru *(n)*
game • *n* joc *(n)*
gamey • *adj* ca de vânat, ca vânatul
gamut • *n* gam *(f)*, palet *(f)*
gander • *n* gâscan *(m)*, gânsac *(m)*, ochead *(f)*, privire *(f)*, ochire *(f)*
gang • *n* band *(f)*
ganglion • *n* ganglion *(m)*
gangrene • *n* cangren *(f)*
garage • *n* garaj *(n)*, autoservice *(n)*
garbage • *n* gunoi *(n)*
garden • *v* face grdinrie, grdinri • *n* grdin *(f)*, parc *(n)*, grdina public *(f)*, curte *(f)*, iarb *(f)*
gardener • *n* grdinar *(m)*, grdinar *(f)*, grdinreas *(f)*
gardenia • *n* gardenie *(f)*
gardening • *n* grdinrit
garganey • *n* sarsel de var *(f)*
gargoyle • *n* gargui *(n)*
garish • *adj* bttor la ochi, iptor, strident
garlic • *n* usturoi *(m)*, ai
garment • *n* rufe, hain, vemânt, articol de îmbrcminte *(n)*

garnet • *n* granat *(n)*
garrison • *n* garnizoan
garrulous • *adj* limbut, guraliv, gure, flecar
gas • *n* gaz *(n)*, gaze, benzin
gaseous • *adj* gazos *(n)*
gasify • *v* gazifica
gasoline • *n* benzin *(f)*
gasometer • *n* gazometru *(n)*
gastric • *adj* gastric *(n)*
gastrointestinal • *adj* gastrointestinal *(n)*
gastronomy • *n* gastronomie *(f)*
gastrulation • *n* gastrulaie *(f)*
gasworks • *n* fabric de gaze i cocs *(f)*
gate • *n* poart *(f)*, poart
gather • *v* aduna, culege, colecta, conchide
gatherer • *n* aduntor *(m)*
gaur • *n* gaur *(m)*
gauze • *n* voal, tifon *(n)*
gay • *n* homosexual *(m)*, homo *(m)*, poponar *(m)*
gazelle • *n* gazel *(f)*
gear • *n* roat dinat *(f)*, cutie de viteze *(f)*, schimbtor de vitez *(n)*
gearbox • *n* cutie de viteze *(f)*
gem • *n* nestemat *(f)*, piatr preioas *(f)*, gem *(f)*, giuvaier
gendarme • *n* jandarm *(m)*, jandarmi
gender • *n* gen *(n)*, gen, sex
genealogy • *n* genealogie *(f)*
general • *n* general *(m)* • *adj* general *(m)*, comun *(m)*
generate • *v* genera, procrea, zmisli, reproduce, da natere, produce, crea
generation • *n* generare *(f)*, generaie *(f)*
generator • *n* generator *(m)*
generosity • *n* generozitate *(f)*, buntate, abunden *(f)*, noblee *(f)*
generous • *adj* generos, darnic, mrinimos
genet • *n* genet *(f)*, ginet *(f)*
genetic • *adj* genetic
geneticist • *n* genetician *(m)*
genetics • *n* genetic
genitive • *n* cazul genitiv *(m)*, genitiv *(n)*
genius • *n* geniu *(n)*, genialitate *(f)*
genocide • *n* genocid *(n)*
genome • *n* genom *(n)*
genotype • *n* genotip *(n)*
gentian • *n* genian *(f)*
gentile • *adj* pgân
gentleman • *n* domn *(m)*, gentlemen *(m)*, domnilor!, domnii mei!, brbai, domni
gentleness • *n* blândee, gentilee *(f)*
genuflection • *n* genuflexiune *(f)*, genuflexare
geocentric • *adj* geocentric *(m)*
geochemistry • *n* geochimie *(f)*
geographic • *adj* geografic *(n)*
geography • *n* geografie *(f)*
geologist • *n* geolog *(m)*
geometry • *n* geometrie *(f)*
geophysics • *n* geofizic *(f)*
geranium • *n* geraniu *(m)*, mucat *(f)*, pelargonie *(f)*
gerbil • *n* gerbil *(m)*
germanium • *n* germaniu *(n)*
germinate • *v* germina, încoli
gesticulation • *n* gesticulaie *(f)*
gesture • *n* gest *(n)*
get • *v* primi
geyser • *n* gheizer *(n)*
ghastly • *adj* oribil, groaznic, lamentabil
gherkin • *n* cornion *(m)*
ghetto • *n* ghetou *(n)*
giant • *n* uria, gigant • *adj* uria
giantess • *n* uria *(f)*, gigant *(f)*, zmeoaic *(f)*, zmeoaie *(f)*
gibbon • *n* gibon *(m)*
gift • *v* drui • *n* cadou *(n)*, dar *(n)*
gigantic • *adj* uria, gigantic
gigantism • *n* gigantism
gigolo • *n* gigolo *(m)*
gild • *v* auri
gilded • *adj* auriu
gill • *n* branhie
ginger • *n* ghimber *(m)*
gingerbread • *n* turt dulce *(f)*
gingerly • *adv* cu precauie, cu bgare de seam
gingivitis • *n* gingivit *(f)*
ginkgo • *n* ginkgo *(m)*
ginseng • *n* ginseng *(m)*
giraffe • *n* giraf *(f)*
girder • *n* grind *(f)*, bârn *(f)*
girl • *n* fat *(f)*, copil *(f)*
girlfriend • *n* prieten *(f)*, amic *(f)*
give • *v* da
giver • *n* dttor
gizzard • *n* pipota *(f)*
glacier • *n* ghear *(m)*
glad • *adj* bucuros, vesel
glade • *n* poian *(f)*
gladiolus • *n* gladiol *(f)*
gland • *n* gland *(f)*
glass • *n* sticl *(f)*, pahar *(n)*
glaucoma • *n* glaucom
glaucous • *adj* glauc
glaze • *n* emailat *(n)*, glazurat *(n)*
gleam • *n* urm *(f)*, strlucire *(f)*
glider • *n* planor *(n)*
glimmer • *v* scânteia
glint • *n* scânteie
gloat • *v* jubila

globe • *n* Pmânt, glob
globeflower • *n* bulbuc *(m)*
glockenspiel • *n* glockenspiel *(n)*
glorify • *v* glorifica
glorious • *adj* glorios
glory • *n* glorie *(f)*, slav *(f)*
glove • *n* mnu *(f)*
glow • *v* iradia
glowworm • *n* licurici
glucose • *n* glucoz *(f)*
glucoside • *n* glucozid *(f)*
glue • *n* clei *(n)*, lipici *(n)*
gluey • *adj* lipicios
glume • *n* glum *(f)*
glutamine • *n* glutamin *(f)*
gluttony • *n* voracitate *(f)*, lcomie *(f)*
glycine • *n* glicin *(f)*
gnaw • *v* roade
gnu • *n* gnu *(m)*
go • *v* merge, duce, disprea, distruge • *n* tentativ *(f)*
goad • *v* îndemna • *n* strmurare
goal • *n* scop, obiectiv, poart *(f)*, gol
goalkeeper • *n* portar *(m)*, portri *(f)*
goat • *n* capr *(f)*, ap *(m)*
goblet • *n* cup *(f)*
goblin • *n* iazm *(f)*
god • *n* zeu *(m)*, dumnezeu *(m)*, idol *(m)*
goddaughter • *n* fin *(f)*
goddess • *n* zei *(f)*
godfather • *n* na *(m)*, nun *(m)*
godlike • *adj* dumnezeiesc, divin
godmother • *n* na *(f)*, nun *(f)*
godson • *n* fin *(m)*
goggle • *v* holba
gold • *n* aur *(n)*, auriu, medalie de aur *(f)* • *adj* de aur, auriu
goldcrest • *n* auel *(m)*
golden • *adj* de aur, din aur, aurit, auriu, prosper, favorabil, norocos
goldeneye • *n* ra suntoare *(f)*
goldenrod • *n* splinu *(f)*, splin *(f)*, varg-de-aur *(f)*
goldfinch • *n* sticlete *(m)*
goldfish • *n* petior auriu
goldsmith • *n* aurar
gondola • *n* gondol
gondolier • *n* gondolier *(m)*
goniometer • *n* goniometru *(n)*, radio-goniometru *(n)*, goniometru
good • *adj* bun *(m)*, bun *(f)*, bun • *n* bine, bun *(n)*
goodbye • *interj* la revedere, pa
goodness • *n* buntate
goods • *n* marf *(f)*
goodwill • *n* bunvoin *(f)*
goon • *n* papagal *(m)*
goose • *n* gâsc *(f)*, gânsac *(m)*
gooseberry • *n* agri *(f)*
goosefoot • *n* frag-ttreasc *(f)*
goral • *n* goral *(m)*
gorge • *v* înfuleca
gorgeous • *adj* magnific *(n)*, splendid *(n)*, superb *(m)*
gorilla • *n* goril *(f)*
goshawk • *n* uliu *(m)*
gosling • *n* boboc *(m)*
gospel • *n* evanghelie *(f)*
gossamer • *n* funigel
gout • *n* gut *(f)*, podagr *(f)*
govern • *v* guverna, regla, reglementa, regulariza, conduce, dirija, cârmui
government • *n* guvern *(m)*
governmental • *adj* guvernamental *(m)*
governor • *n* regulator *(m)*
grab • *v* apuca
grace • *v* onora, împodobi • *n* graie *(f)*, elegan *(f)*, har, rugciune de mulumire *(f)*, termen de graie *(n)*
gracious • *adj* indulgent, îngduitor
gradually • *adv* treptat, în mod gradat, progresiv, în mod treptat
graft • *v* altoi • *n* altoi, grefon
grain • *n* grunte, bob
gram • *n* gram *(n)*
grammar • *n* gramatic *(f)*
grammatical • *adj* gramatical
gramophone • *n* gramofon *(n)*
granary • *n* grânar
granddaughter • *n* nepoat
grandfather • *n* bunic *(m)*, tataie *(m)*, tata mare *(m)*, strbunic *(m)*, strmo *(m)*, strmoi, strbun *(m)*
grandmother • *n* bunic *(f)*, mamaie *(f)*, mama mare *(f)*
grandson • *n* nepot
granny • *n* bab *(f)*
grape • *n* strugure *(m)*, vi de vie
grapevine • *n* vi de vie
graph • *n* grafic *(m)*
graphic • *n* grafic *(f)*
graphite • *n* grafit *(n)*
grass • *n* iarb *(f)*
grasshopper • *n* lcust *(f)*
grassy • *adj* ierbos
grateful • *adj* recunosctor *(m)*
gratefulness • *n* gratitudine *(f)*, recunotin *(f)*
gratis • *adv* gratis
gratitude • *n* gratitudine *(f)*
grave • *n* mormânt
gravedigger • *n* groparul
gravitation • *n* gravitaie *(f)*
gravitational • *adj* gravitaional

gravure • *n* gravur *(f)*
gravy • *n* zeam *(f)*
gray • *n* gri • *adj* brumriu, cenuiu, sur
graze • *v* pate, pstori
grease • *v* unge • *n* grsime *(f)*
great • *adj* mare, superb *(n)*, minunat *(n)*, foarte bun *(n)*
greatness • *n* mreie *(f)*, grandoare *(f)*, mrire *(f)*, mrime *(f)*, mândrie *(f)*, trufie *(f)*
grebe • *n* cufundar *(m)*, corcodel *(m)*
greed • *n* aviditate *(f)*, lcomie *(f)*, avariie *(f)*
green • *n* verde • *adj* verde
greenhorn • *n* mucos *(m)*
greenhouse • *n* ser *(f)*
greenish • *adj* verzui, verziu, verzuriu
greet • *v* saluta, întâmpina
gregarious • *adj* sociabil, gregar
grenade • *n* grenad *(n)*
grief • *n* tristee *(f)*, întristare *(f)*, mâhnire *(f)*
griffin • *n* grifon *(m)*
grill • *v* frige
grimace • *n* grimas *(f)*
grind • *v* mcina, pisa
gristle • *n* zgârci
grit • *v* scrâni
groan • *v* geme
grocer • *n* negustor *(m)*, negustoreas *(f)*, bcan *(m)*, bcneas *(f)*
grope • *v* mînui, bîjbîi, mîngîia
gross • *adj* scârbos, dezgusttor, brut
grotesque • *adj* grotesc *(n)*
ground • *n* sol *(n)*, pmânt, pmânt *(n)*, potenial zero *(n)*
group • *v* grupa • *n* grup *(n)*, grup
grouse • *n* coco-de-munte *(m)*, coco-slbatic *(m)*
grove • *n* pdurice *(f)*, crâng *(n)*, arboret *(n)*, tufi *(n)*, dumbrav *(f)*
grow • *v* crete
grudge • *n* pic *(f)*, pizm *(f)*, ranchiun *(f)*
guaiacum • *n* guaiac *(m)*
guanaco • *n* guanaco *(m)*
guar • *n* fasolea de guar *(f)*
guarantee • *v* garanta • *n* garanie *(f)*, garant *(m)*, cheza *(m)*
guarantor • *n* garant *(m)*
guard • *v* feri, proteja, pzi • *n* gard, paznic *(m)*, gardian *(m)*, pzitor *(m)*, gard *(f)*, paz *(f)*, aprare *(f)*, protecie *(f)*, apratoare *(f)*
guerrilla • *n* gheril *(f)*
guess • *v* bnui, presupune
guest • *n* oaspete *(m)*, musafir *(m)*
guidance • *n* direcionare *(f)*, ghidare *(f)*
guide • *n* ghid *(m)*, ghid *(n)*
guillotine • *v* ghilotina • *n* ghilotin *(f)*
guilt • *n* pcat, vin *(f)*
guitar • *n* ghitar *(f)*, chitar *(f)*
gules • *n* rou • *adj* rou
gulf • *n* golf *(n)*
gull • *n* pescru • *v* pcli, înela
gum • *n* gingie *(f)*
gun • *n* pistol *(n)*, revolver *(n)*, puc *(f)*, tun *(n)*
gunpowder • *n* praf de puc *(n)*
gurnard • *n* rândunic-de-mare *(f)*
guts • *n* mae, mruntaie, inim *(f)*, suflet *(n)*
gutter • *n* jgheab
guy • *n* tip *(m)*
gymnasium • *n* sal de gimnastic *(f)*, hal de gimnastic *(f)*, gimnaziu *(n)*
gymnast • *n* gimnast *(m)*, gimnast *(f)*
gymnastic • *adj* de gimnastic, gimnastic *(n)*
gymnastics • *n* gimnastic *(f)*
gynecological • *adj* ginecologic *(m)*
gypsy • *n* igan *(m)*, iganc *(f)*
gyrfalcon • *n* oim islandez *(m)*

H

habit • *n* obicei *(m)*, habitudine *(f)*
habitable • *adj* locuibil
habitat • *n* habitat
habitual • *adj* de obicei
habitually • *adv* uzual, regulat
hackberry • *n* sâmbovin *(f)*
hacksaw • *n* bomfaier
haddock • *n* eglefin *(m)*
hafnium • *n* hafniu *(n)*
hag • *n* vrjitoare *(f)*, bab *(f)*, cotoroan *(f)*, baborni
haggard • *adj* epuizat *(n)*, istovit *(n)*, sec-tuit, obosit *(n)*, slbatic *(n)*, nedomesticit *(n)*, neîmblânzit *(n)*
haggle • *v* negua, igni
hail • *v* grindina, saluta • *n* grindin
hair • *n* pr *(m)*, blan *(f)*, fir de pr *(n)*
haircut • *n* frizur *(f)*, frez *(f)*, coafur *(f)*, tunsoare
hairdresser • *n* frizer *(m)*, coafor *(m)*
hairy • *adj* pros
half • *n* jumtate *(f)* • *adj* semi-, emi-

half-moon • *n* semilun *(f)*
hallelujah • *interj* aleluia
hallucinogenic • *adj* halucinogen
halo • *n* nimb *(n)*, aureol *(f)*
halogen • *n* halogen *(m)*
halter • *n* cpstru
ham • *n* unc *(f)*
hammer • *n* ciocan *(n)*
hammock • *n* hamac *(n)*
hamster • *n* hamster, hârciog
hand • *n* mân *(f)*, ac indicator, limb, parte, latur, îndemânare, abilitate, dibcie
handball • *n* handbal *(n)*, hen *(n)*
handcuff • *v* înctua, fereca • *n* ctu *(f)*
handcuffs • *n* ctue
handful • *n* mnunchi
handicraft • *n* meserie
handkerchief • *n* batist *(f)*, nfram *(f)*
handlebar • *n* ghidon *(n)*, mâner *(n)*
handshake • *n* strângere de mân *(f)*
handsome • *adj* abil, frumos, artos, chipe
handwriting • *n* scriere de mân, scris de mân
handy • *adj* îndemânatic, la îndemân
hang • *v* atârna, aga, spânzura
hangar • *n* hangar *(n)*
hanger • *n* cuier *(f)*
hanging • *adj* atârnat
hangman • *n* clu *(m)*, gâde *(m)*, gealat *(m)*, spânzurtoarea *(f)*
hangover • *n* mahmureal *(f)*
happen • *v* întâmpla, petrece
happiness • *n* bucurie *(f)*, fericire *(f)*
happy • *adj* fericit, bucuros, norocos, priceput, mulumit, satisfcut
harassment • *n* distrugere *(f)*, pustiire, deranj *(n)*, imoportunare *(f)*
hard • *adj* tare, dur, greu, vârtos, sever *(m)*, dur *(n)*, dur *(f)*
hardhearted • *adj* insensibil, nemilos, aspru
hardly • *adv* abia
hardship • *n* greutate *(f)*, dificultate *(f)*, adversitate *(f)*
hardware • *n* echipament *(n)*, dotare tehnic *(f)*, hardware *(n)*, aparatur *(f)*, aparataj *(n)*
hardworking • *adj* harnic, sârguincios, muncitor, laborios, diligent
hare • *n* iepure-de-câmp *(m)*
harm • *v* vtma, strica, duna
harmonious • *adj* armonic *(m)*, armonios *(m)*
harmony • *n* armonie *(f)*
harness • *n* ham *(n)*, harnaament *(n)*
harp • *n* harf *(f)*, harp *(f)*
harpist • *n* harpist *(m)*
harpoon • *n* harpon *(n)*
harpsichord • *n* clavecin
harpy • *n* harpie
harrier • *n* erete *(m)*
harrow • *n* grap *(f)*
harsh • *adj* aspru, sever
harvest • *v* recolta, secera, strânge, culege • *n* recolt *(f)*, cules, rod, strânsur *(f)*, seceri
hashish • *n* hai *(n)*
hastily • *adv* prompt
hat • *n* plrie *(f)*
hatch • *v* cloci, urzi
hatchet • *n* bard, toporic
hate • *v* urî
hatred • *n* ur *(f)*
haughty • *adj* mândru
have • *v* avea
hawfinch • *n* botgros *(m)*, cirear *(m)*
hawk • *n* mala *(f)* • *v* vinde
hawthorn • *n* pducel *(m)*, albaspin *(f)*
hay • *v* a întoarce fînul, a cosi fînul • *n* fân *(n)*
hayfield • *n* fânea
hazard • *n* hazard *(n)*, întâmplare *(f)*
hazel • *n* alun *(m)* • *adj* cprui, castaniu, cpriu, aluniu
hazelnut • *n* alun *(f)*
he • *pron* dumnealui, el
head • *n* cap *(n)*, ef *(m)*, cap *(m)*, lider *(m)*, cpetenie *(f)*
headache • *n* durere de cap
headlight • *n* far *(n)*
headline • *n* titlu *(n)*
headmaster • *n* director *(m)*
headquarters • *n* cartier general *(n)*, sediu *(n)*, central *(f)*
headstone • *n* piatr de mormânt
heal • *v* vindeca
health • *n* sntate *(f)*, sntate
healthy • *adj* sntos, zdravn
hear • *v* auzi
hearing • *n* auz *(n)*, auzit *(n)*
heart • *n* inim *(f)*, cord *(n)*, inim, suflet, cup *(f)*, centru *(n)*, mijloc *(n)*
hearts • *n* cup *(f)*
heat • *n* cldur *(f)*, rut *(n)*
heathen • *n* pgân • *adj* pgân
heaven • *n* cer, rai
heavy • *adj* greu *(m)*, grea *(f)*
hectare • *n* hectar *(n)*
hedgehog • *n* arici
hedonism • *n* hedonism *(n)*
heedless • *adj* nepstor
heel • *n* clcâi
heft • *v* ridica
heifer • *n* junc, viea, juninc
height • *n* înlime *(f)*, culme

helicopter • *n* elicopter
heliocentric • *adj* heliocentric *(n)*
heliometer • *n* heliometru *(n)*
heliotrope • *n* heliotrop *(m)*, heliotrop *(n)*
helium • *n* heliu *(n)*
hellebore • *n* elebor *(m)*, spânz *(m)*, cucurig *(m)*
hello • *interj* salut, bun, noroc, bun ziua, servus, alo, haló, aloo, ia uite
helm • *n* cârm *(f)*, timon *(f)*
helmet • *n* casc *(f)*, coif *(m)*
help • *n* ajutor *(n)*, asisten *(f)*, ajutor *(m)*, ajutoare *(f)* • *v* ajuta, asista
helpful • *adj* util, ajuttor *(m)*
helpless • *adj* neajutorat *(m)*
hemisphere • *n* emisfer *(f)*
hemlock • *n* cucut
hemorrhoid • *n* hemoroid *(m)*
hemp • *n* cânep *(f)*
hen • *n* gin
henbane • *n* mselari *(f)*
hence • *adv* de aici, aadar
henna • *n* henna *(f)*, cana *(f)*
hepatic • *adj* hepatic
hepatica • *n* crucea-voinicului *(f)*, trei-ri
hepatitis • *n* hepatit *(f)*
heptagon • *n* heptagon *(n)*
herald • *v* anuna • *n* mesager *(m)*, herald *(m)*, vestitor *(m)*
heraldry • *n* heraldic *(f)*
herbaceous • *adj* erbaceu *(m)*, erbacee *(f)*, ierbos *(m)*
herbivore • *n* erbivor *(n)*
herbivorous • *adj* erbivor
herd • *n* turm, cârd
here • *adv* aici, aci, încoace
hereafter • *adv* în viitor, de acum încolo, mai târziu
hereby • *adv* prin aceasta
hereditary • *adj* ereditar *(n)*, ereditar
heredity • *n* ereditate *(f)*
heritage • *n* tradiie *(f)*
hermaphrodite • *n* hermafrodit • *adj* hermafrodit *(n)*
hermeneutics • *n* hermeneutic *(f)*
hero • *n* erou *(m)*, eroin *(f)*
heroic • *adj* eroic
heroine • *n* eroin *(f)*
heron • *n* stârc *(m)*, bâtlan *(m)*
herring • *n* hering *(m)*
herself • *pron* se, ea însi
hesitate • *v* ezita, ovi, pregeta, codi
heterogeneous • *adj* eterogen *(n)*, eterogen *(f)*, neuniform *(n)*, eterogen
heterosexual • *n* heterosexual *(m)*, heterosexual *(f)* • *adj* heterosexual
heterosexuality • *n* heterosexualitate *(f)*
hetman • *n* hatman *(m)*
heuristic • *adj* euristic
hew • *v* ciopli, sculpta
hexadecimal • *n* sistem hexazecimal *(n)*
hey • *interj* hei, hop
hi • *interj* bun, salut
hibiscus • *n* hibiscus *(m)*
hiccup • *v* sughia • *n* sughi
hick • *n* rnoi *(m)*, ran *(m)*
hickory • *n* hicori *(m)*
hide • *v* ascunde • *n* blan *(f)*
hideout • *n* ascunztoare
hierarchical • *adj* ierarhic *(n)*
hierarchy • *n* ierarhie *(f)*
high • *adj* înalt *(m)*, înlat *(n)*, ridicat *(n)*, înalt, drogat, mare, înalt *(f)*, mare *(f)*
highfalutin • *adj* pompos
highway • *n* autostrad *(f)*, osea
highwayman • *n* tâlhar de drum mare *(m)*, bandit *(m)*, ho *(m)*
hilarious • *adj* ilar *(n)*, ilariant *(n)*
hilarity • *n* râsete, ilaritate *(f)*
hill • *n* deal *(f)*, colin *(f)*
hilum • *n* hil *(n)*
himself • *pron* se, el însui *(m)*
hinder • *v* împiedica, reine, stânjeni
hindrance • *n* piedic, impediment *(n)*, obstacol *(n)*
hinge • *n* balama *(f)*, arnier *(f)*, tâân *(f)*
hinny • *n* bardou *(m)*
hip • *n* old
hippopotamus • *n* hipopotam *(m)*
hire • *v* angaja
hiss • *v* uiera • *n* sâsâit
histidine • *n* histidin *(f)*
historic • *adj* istoric
historical • *adj* istoric *(n)*, istoric *(f)*, istorici
historically • *adv* istoricete
history • *n* istorie, istorie *(f)*, povestire *(f)*
hit • *v* lovi, bate • *n* lovitur *(f)*, lagr *(n)*
hitchhiker • *n* autostopist *(m)*, autostopist *(f)*
hither • *adv* încoace, aici
hitherto • *adv* pân acum, pân în acest moment
hoarse • *adj* rguit *(n)*
hoarseness • *n* rgueal *(f)*
hoax • *n* cioara vopsita
hockey • *n* hochei
hoe • *v* pri, spa • *n* sap
hold • *v* ine, conine • *n* cal *(f)*, hambar *(n)*
hole • *n* gaur
holiday • *n* srbtoare *(f)*
holly • *n* ilice *(f)*, laur *(m)*
hollyhock • *n* nalb, nalb-de-grdin *(f)*
holmium • *n* holmiu *(n)*

holocaust • *n* holocaust *(n)*, genocid *(n)*, exterminare, în, mas *(f)*
holography • *n* holografie *(f)*
holy • *adj* sfânt *(n)*, sfânt *(f)*
homage • *n* omagiu *(n)*, omagiu *(f)*
home • *n* cas *(f)* • *adv* acas
homeless • *adj* fr cas, fr adpost, vagabond
homeopathic • *adj* homeopatic
homeopathy • *n* homeopatie
homework • *n* tem *(f)*
hominid • *n* hominid *(m)*
homogeneous • *adj* omogen *(m)*, omogen *(f)*
homologous • *adj* omolog *(m)*
homology • *n* omologie *(f)*, omologie
homonym • *n* omonim *(m)*
homophobia • *n* homofobie *(f)*
homosexual • *n* homosexual *(m)* • *adj* homosexual *(m)*
homosexuality • *n* homosexualitate *(f)*
honest • *adj* cinstit, onest
honesty • *n* onestitate, pana-zburtorului *(f)*
honey • *n* miere *(f)*, iubit *(m)*, iubit *(f)*, drag *(m)*, drag *(f)*, mieriu • *adj* mieriu
honeycomb • *n* fagure
honeysuckle • *n* caprifoi *(m)*
honor • *v* onora, cinsti • *n* respect *(n)*, onoare *(f)*, demnitate *(f)*, onoare, cinste, privilegiu *(n)*
honorable • *adj* onorabil
hoof • *n* copit
hook • *v* aga • *n* cârlig *(n)*
hookah • *n* narghilea
hooker • *n* taloner
hooligan • *n* huligan *(m)*
hoop • *v* fereca • *n* cerc *(n)*, co *(n)*
hoopoe • *n* pupz
hop • *n* salt *(n)*, hamei
hope • *n* speran *(f)*, ndejde *(f)* • *v* spera, ndjdui
hopelessness • *n* desperare *(f)*, desperaie *(f)*
hora • *n* hor
horehound • *n* ungura *(m)*, voronic *(m)*
horizon • *n* orizont *(n)*, orizonturi
horizontal • *n* orizontal *(f)* • *adj* orizontal *(n)*
horizontally • *adv* orizontal
horn • *n* corn *(m)*, corn *(n)*, coarne, corn, cornuri, claxon
hornbeam • *n* carpen
hornbill • *n* calao *(m)*
horned • *adj* cornut
hornet • *n* grgun *(m)*
horny • *adj* excitat
horrible • *n* înfiorare *(f)*, înfricoare *(f)*, groaz *(f)* • *adj* oribil, groaznic, îngrozitor
horrify • *v* înfiora, îngrozi, oripila
horse • *n* cal, cabalin, cavaler, capr, cal *(m)*, cal alb *(m)*, clu *(m)*
horsefly • *n* tun *(m)*
horseman • *n* clre *(m)*, cavaler *(m)*
horsepower • *n* cal-putere *(m)*
horseradish • *n* hrean *(m)*, hrean
horseshoe • *n* potcoav *(f)*
horsetail • *n* coada-calului *(f)*, barba-ursului *(f)*
horticultural • *adj* horticol, de horticultur
horticulture • *n* horticultur *(f)*
horticulturist • *n* horticultor *(m)*, horticultoare *(f)*, grdinar *(m)*
hospital • *n* spital *(n)*
host • *n* gazd *(f)*, amfitrion *(m)*, moderator *(m)*, moderatoare *(f)*, prezentator *(m)*
hostage • *n* ostatic *(m)*, ostatic *(f)*
hostile • *adj* ostil *(n)*
hostility • *n* ostilitate *(f)*, dumnie *(f)*
hot • *adj* cald, fierbinte, febril, iute, picant, bun
hotel • *n* hotel *(m)*
hour • *n* or *(f)*, ceas *(n)*
hourglass • *n* ceas cu nisip *(n)*, clepsidr *(f)*
house • *n* cas *(f)*, camer, dinastie, familie dinastic
housewife • *n* gospodin *(f)*, casnic *(f)*
hovel • *n* cocioab *(f)*
hover • *v* pluti, oscila, plasa cursorul peste link
how • *adv* cât, cum, ce
however • *adv* totui, oricum, oricât de
howl • *v* urla, rage
hubris • *n* hybris *(n)*
hug • *v* îmbria • *n* îmbriare *(f)*
huge • *adj* uria, enorm, imens, gigantic
huh • *interj* a
hull • *n* coc *(f)*, caren *(f)*
hum • *v* fredona
human • *n* om *(m)* • *adj* om *(m)*, uman, omenesc, omenete
humaneness • *n* omenie *(f)*, umanitate *(f)*
humanism • *n* umanism *(n)*, umanism
humanity • *n* umanitate *(f)*, omenire, buntate *(f)*, benevolen *(f)*
humanly • *adv* omenete
humble • *adj* umil
humid • *adj* umed *(m)*, umed *(f)*
humidity • *n* umezeal *(f)*, umidiitate *(f)*
humiliate • *v* jigni, umili
humiliation • *n* umilire *(f)*, înjosire *(f)*, ruine *(f)*
humility • *n* umilin *(f)*, umilitate *(f)*
hummingbird • *n* colibri

hump • *n* cocoa *(f)*
humus • *n* humus *(n)*
hundred • *n* bancnot de o sut *(f)*
hundredth • *n* sutlea, sutime *(f)* • *adj* sutlea *(m)*, suta *(f)*
hung • *adj* pulos
hunger • *n* foame *(f)*
hungry • *adj* flmând
hunk • *n* armsar *(m)*
hunt • *v* vâna • *n* vântoare
hunter • *n* vântor
hurdle • *n* obstacol *(n)*
hurricane • *n* uragan *(n)*
hurt • *v* durea, rni, vtma
husband • *v* pstra, conserva • *n* so *(m)*
hustler • *n* excroc *(m)*
hut • *n* caban *(f)*, barac *(f)*, colib *(f)*, cocioab
hyacinth • *n* zambil *(f)*, iacint *(m)*
hydra • *n* hidr *(f)*
hydrangea • *n* hortensie *(f)*
hydrargyrum • *n* hidrargir
hydrate • *n* hidrat *(m)*
hydrocarbon • *n* hidrocarbur *(f)*, hidrocarburi
hydrogen • *n* hidrogen *(n)*
hydroxide • *n* hidroxid *(m)*
hyena • *n* hien *(f)*, hiene
hygiene • *n* igien *(f)*
hygienic • *adj* igienic
hygrometer • *n* higrometru
hygroscopic • *adj* higroscopic *(n)*
hymn • *n* imn *(n)*
hyperglycemia • *n* hiperglicemia
hypersomnia • *n* hipersomnie *(f)*
hypertrophy • *v* hipertrofia • *n* hipertrofie
hyphen • *n* liniu *(f)*
hypocrisy • *n* ipocrizie *(f)*
hypocrite • *n* ipocrit *(m)*, ipocrit *(f)*
hypocritical • *adj* ipocrit
hyponym • *n* hiponim *(n)*
hypostasis • *n* hipostaz *(f)*, esen *(f)*
hypotenuse • *n* ipotenuz *(f)*
hypothesis • *n* ipotez *(f)*, prezumie *(f)*
hypothetical • *adj* ipotetic *(n)*
hyrax • *n* daman *(m)*
hyssop • *n* isop *(m)*
hysteria • *n* isterie *(f)*

I

i • *n* i
ibex • *n* capra de stânc, ibex
ibis • *n* ibis *(m)*
ibuprofen • *n* ibuprofen
ice • *v* rci, înghea, congela, glasa • *n* ghea, ghea carbonic *(f)*, îngheat *(f)*
iceberg • *n* aisberg *(n)*
ichneumon • *n* ihneumon *(m)*
ichthyosaur • *n* ihtiozaur *(m)*
icicle • *n* urur *(m)*
icing • *n* glazur *(f)*, acoperire cu ghea *(f)*
icon • *n* icoan *(f)*, iconi *(f)*
idea • *n* idee *(f)*, prere *(f)*, bnuial *(f)*
idealism • *n* idealism *(n)*
idealization • *n* idealizare *(f)*
idealize • *v* idealiza
ideally • *adv* ideal, în mod ideal
identifiable • *adj* identificabil
identity • *n* identitate *(f)*
ideogram • *n* ideogram *(f)*
ideological • *adj* ideologic, ideologic *(m)*
ideologist • *n* ideologist *(n)*, ideologiste, ideolog *(m)*, ideologi
ideology • *n* ideologie *(f)*, ideologii
idiolect • *n* idiolect *(n)*
idiom • *n* idiom
idiomatic • *adj* idiomatic
idiosyncrasy • *n* particularitate *(f)*, idiosincrazie, trstur *(f)*, idiosincrasie *(f)*, caracteristic *(f)*
idiosyncratic • *adj* idiosincratic, idiosincrazic
idiot • *n* idiot *(m)*, idioat *(f)*, idioi, idioate
idol • *n* idol *(m)*
if • *conj* dac
ignominy • *n* ignominie *(f)*
ignorance • *n* ignoran *(f)*
ignorant • *adj* ignorant *(n)*, ignorant *(f)*
ill • *adj* bolnav, abtut
illegal • *adj* ilegal, nelegal *(n)*
illegally • *adv* ilegal *(m)*, nelegal *(m)*
illegitimate • *adj* ilegitim *(m)*, nelegal *(m)*
illiterate • *adj* analfabet *(m)*, anaflabet *(f)*
illness • *n* boal *(f)*
illogical • *adj* ilogic *(n)*, nelogic *(n)*
illuminate • *v* ilumina, lumina
illumination • *n* iluminaie *(f)*
illusion • *n* iluzie *(f)*
illusory • *adj* iluzoriu
illustrate • *v* ilustra
image • *n* imagine *(f)*, poz *(f)*
imagination • *n* imaginaie *(f)*, fantezie *(f)*, for de imaginare *(f)*, închipuire *(f)*, imaginare *(f)*, iluzionare *(f)*, imagine *(f)*

imagine • *v* imagina, închipui
imam • *n* imam *(m)*
imbalance • *n* dezechilibru
imbecile • *n* imbecil
imbibe • *v* bea, îmbiba
imbue • *v* a îmbiba, a impregna
imitation • *n* imitare *(f)*, imitaie *(f)*
immaculate • *adj* imaculat *(m)*, imaculat *(f)*
immaturity • *n* imaturitate *(f)*
immeasurable • *adj* nemsurabil *(n)*, de nemsurat
immediate • *adj* imediat
immediately • *adv* imediat, fr întârziere, numaidecât, de îndat
immense • *adj* imens, uria
immerse • *v* scufunda
immigrant • *n* imigrant *(m)*
immigration • *n* imigraie *(f)*, imigrare
imminent • *adj* iminent *(m)*
immiscible • *adj* neamestecabil
immoral • *adj* imoral *(n)*
immorality • *n* imoralitate *(f)*
immortal • *adj* nemuritor, imortal
immovable • *n* bunuri imobiliare, imobil *(n)* • *adj* imobil, nemicabil *(m)*, nemicat *(m)*, ferm, fix, neclintit, impasiv, netulburat
immunology • *n* imunologie *(f)*
immutable • *adj* imuabil
impaired • *adj* înrautit *(n)*, slbit *(n)*, diminuat *(n)*
impala • *n* impala *(f)*
impart • *v* împri
impartial • *adj* imparial, neprtinitor *(m)*
impartiality • *n* imparialitate, neprtinitate *(f)*, obiectivitate *(f)*
impatience • *n* nerbdare *(f)*, impacien *(f)*
impediment • *n* impediment, piedic, obstacol
impenetrable • *adj* impenetrabil, de neptruns, de nestrpuns
imperfect • *adj* imperfect *(n)*
imperfection • *n* imperfeciune *(f)*
imperial • *adj* imperial *(m)*
imperialism • *n* imperialism
imperiousness • *n* imperiozitate *(f)*
impertinence • *n* irelevan *(f)*, impertinen *(f)*
imperturbability • *n* imperturbabilitate
impervious • *adj* indiferent *(m)*, insensibil *(m)*, impenetrabil *(m)*, impermeabil *(m)*, impermeabil *(f)*
implacable • *adj* implacabil, imobil, nemicabil, nemicat, ferm, de neclintit
implant • *v* implanta • *n* implantat *(n)*, implant *(n)*, implanturi
implantation • *n* implantare *(f)*, implantaie *(f)*, implantri, implantare embrional *(f)*, implantare de embrion *(f)*, inserie ionic
implicit • *adj* implicit, inerent, absolut
impoliteness • *n* impolitee *(f)*
importance • *n* importan *(f)*, însemntate *(f)*
important • *adj* important
impose • *v* impune, dicta
imposing • *adj* impozant, mre, impuntor, falnic
impossibility • *n* imposibil *(n)*, imposibilitate *(f)*
impossible • *adj* imposibil
impost • *n* impozit
imposture • *n* impostur
impotence • *n* impoten, lips de putere
impoverish • *v* srci, pauperiza
impracticability • *n* impractibilitate
impracticable • *adj* impracticabil, nepracticabil
impregnable • *adj* inexpugnabil, impenetrabil
impression • *n* imprimare *(f)*, impresie, aparen
impressionism • *n* impresionism
impressive • *adj* impresionant, mictor, atrgtor
impressiveness • *n* caracter impresionant, caracter mictor
imprison • *v* întemnia, încarcera
imprisonment • *n* întemniare, încarcerare
improbable • *adj* improbabil *(n)*
improper • *adj* impropriu
improve • *v* îmbunti, a se îmbunti
improved • *adj* îmbuntit
improvement • *n* îmbuntire *(f)*
improvisation • *n* improvizare *(f)*
impudence • *n* obrznicie *(f)*, impudoare *(f)*, impuden *(f)*
impulse • *n* impuls *(n)*
impurity • *n* impuritate, necurenie
impute • *v* imputa
in • *prep* în
inability • *n* incapacitate *(f)*, incapabilitate *(f)*, neputin *(f)*
inaccessible • *adj* inaccesibil *(n)*, neaccesibil *(n)*, inaccesibil, de neatins, neatingibil
inadequate • *adj* inadecvat *(n)*, neadecvat *(n)*, inadecvat *(f)*, neadecvat *(f)*, nepotrivit *(n)*
inadmissible • *adj* inadmisibil *(n)*, inadmisibil *(f)*, neadmisibil *(m)*
inanition • *n* goliciune *(f)*, inanitie *(f)*
inappropriate • *adj* inadecvat, necore-

spunztor, impropriu *(n)*, inoportun *(n)*, nepotrivit *(n)*
inaudible • *adj* neauzibil, inauzibil
incantation • *n* descântare *(f)*, incantaie *(f)*, descântec *(n)*
incapable • *adj* incapabil
incense • *n* tmâie *(f)*
incest • *n* incest
inch • *n* ol *(m)*
incident • *n* incident *(n)*, caz *(n)*, episod *(n)*, mic incident, minor incident *(n)*, deranjament *(n)* • *adj* incidental, incident
incidentally • *adv* apropo
incision • *n* incizie *(f)*
incisor • *n* incisiv *(m)*
incite • *v* îndemna, atâa
inclination • *n* înclinaie, înclinaie *(f)*, pant *(f)*, povârni *(n)*, înclinare *(f)*, tendin *(f)*
incline • *v* apleca
incomparable • *adj* incomparabil, necomparabil
incompatibility • *n* incompatibilitate
incomplete • *adj* incomplet
inconceivable • *adj* de neconceput, de neînteles, de nepriceput, neconceptibil *(m)*, neverosimil *(m)*
inconsistency • *n* inconsisten
inconsistent • *adj* neconsistent, inconsistent
inconvenience • *v* deranja, incomoda, importuna • *n* deranj *(n)*, incomodare *(f)*, neplcere *(f)*, inconvenien *(f)*
incorrect • *adj* incorect
incorrectly • *adv* incorect, în mod incorect
increase • *v* crete, mri, spori, urca • *n* cretere *(f)*, sporire *(f)*, mrire *(f)*
incredible • *adj* incredibil
incredulity • *n* incredulitate *(f)*, scepticism *(n)*, necredin *(f)*
incubation • *n* incubaie *(f)*
incubator • *n* incubator *(n)*, incubatoare
incubus • *n* incub *(m)*
inculcate • *v* inculca, înrdcina
incumbent • *adj* obligatoriu *(m)*, impus *(m)*, titular *(m)*, beneficiar *(m)*
incus • *n* nicoval *(f)*
indebted • *adj* dator, îndatorat
indecent • *adj* indecent, indecent *(f)*
indeed • *adv* într-adevr
indefensible • *adj* neaprabil *(m)*, de neaprat, imposibil de aprat, nefundamentat *(m)*, nejustificabil, de neiertat
independence • *n* independen *(f)*
independent • *adj* independent, liber
indescribable • *adj* indescriptibil, inexprimabil
indestructible • *adj* indestructibil *(n)*
index • *n* a cresta *(f)*, index
indicator • *n* indicator *(m)*, semnalizator *(n)*
indifference • *n* indiferen *(f)*
indifferent • *adj* indiferent *(n)*, apatic *(n)*
indigenous • *adj* indigen *(n)*, autohton *(n)*
indigenousness • *n* indigenitate *(f)*
indigestion • *n* indigestie *(f)*
indignation • *n* indignare *(f)*
indigo • *adj* indigo
indiscretion • *n* indiscreie *(f)*
indisputable • *adj* indisputabil
indistinguishable • *adj* indistingibil *(m)*, nedistingibil *(m)*
indium • *n* indiu *(n)*
individual • *n* individ • *adj* individual *(n)*, individual *(f)*, individuali, individual
individualism • *n* individualism *(n)*
indoctrinate • *v* îndoctrina
indoctrination • *n* îndoctrinare
inductance • *n* inductan *(f)*
indulgence • *n* îngduire *(f)*, tolerare *(f)*, indulgen *(f)*
indulgent • *adj* indulgent *(n)*, indulgent *(f)*
industrial • *adj* industrial, de industrie, industrial *(m)*, industrializat *(m)*
industrious • *adj* industrios, harnic, laborios
industry • *n* industrie, bran industrial
inedible • *adj* incomestibil, necomestibil
ineffable • *adj* inefabil
inelastic • *adj* neelastic *(n)*
inequality • *n* inegalitate, inecuaie *(f)*
inessential • *adj* neesenial *(n)*, neimportant *(n)*
inevitability • *n* inevitabilitate, inevitabilitate *(f)*
inevitable • *adj* inevitabil *(n)*, neocolibil *(n)*
inevitably • *adv* inevitabil, în mod inevitabil
inexplicable • *adj* inexplicabil *(n)*, inexplicabil *(f)*, neexplicabil *(n)*
inexpressible • *adj* inexprimabil, neexprimabil
infamous • *adj* infam, neruinat
infant • *n* bebelu *(m)*
infantry • *n* infanterie *(f)*, regiment de infanterie *(n)*
infantryman • *n* infanterist *(m)*
infect • *v* infecta, contamina
infection • *n* infectare, infecie
infectious • *adj* infecios *(n)*, infecios
infer • *v* motiva, deduce, infera, conchide, concluziona

inferior • *adj* inferior
infertile • *adj* infertil
infestation • *n* infestaie *(f)*
infidel • *n* necredincios *(m)*
infidelity • *n* infidelitate *(f)*
infinite • *adj* infinit *(m)*, fr limit, infinit, nelimitat, nesfârit
infinitive • *n* infinitiv *(n)*
infinity • *n* infinitate *(f)*, infinit *(n)*, nesfârit *(n)*, infinit
infirm • *adj* infirm *(m)*, infirm *(f)*, instabil
infirmity • *n* infirmitate *(f)*, debilitate *(f)*
inflammable • *adj* inflamabil
inflammation • *n* aprindere, inflamare *(f)*
inflatable • *n* barc pneumatic *(f)* • *adj* inflaionabil *(n)*, umflabil *(n)*
inflate • *v* umfla
inflated • *adj* umflat *(n)*
inflation • *n* inflaie *(f)*
inflexible • *adj* neflexibil *(n)*, inflexibil *(n)*, rigid *(n)*
inflorescence • *n* inflorescen *(f)*
influence • *v* influena, înrâuri • *n* influen *(f)*, influenare *(f)*, influentor *(n)*, inducie *(f)*, influen
influenza • *n* grip *(f)*
influx • *n* afluen *(f)*, aflux *(n)*
information • *n* informaie *(f)*
infrared • *adj* infrarou *(n)*, infraroie *(f)*, infraroii
infrasonic • *adj* infrasonic *(m)*
infrastructure • *n* infrastructur *(f)*, infrastructur
infrequently • *adv* rar
infringe • *v* înclca
infringement • *n* violare *(f)*, infraciune *(f)*, înclcare *(f)*
infusion • *n* infuzie *(f)*, infuzare *(f)*
ingenious • *adj* cu iscusin, iscusit, ingenios, genial
ingot • *n* lingou *(n)*
ingredient • *n* ingredient
inhabitant • *n* locuitor *(m)*, locuitoare *(f)*
inhalation • *n* inhalare *(f)*
inhale • *v* inspira, aspira, inhala
inherently • *adv* inerent, inalienabil
inherit • *v* moteni
inheritance • *n* motenire *(f)*
inhibit • *v* inhiba
inhibition • *n* inhibare, inhibiie
inhibitor • *n* inhibitor
inhumanity • *n* neomenie *(f)*, neumanitate *(f)*
initiative • *n* iniiativ *(f)*
injectable • *n* injectabil *(m)*
injurious • *adj* pgubitor *(m)*, prejudicios, duntor
injury • *n* ran *(f)*
ink • *n* cerneal *(f)*
inn • *n* han
innocent • *adj* inocent *(m)*, nevinovat *(m)*
inopportune • *adj* inoportun *(n)*, neoportun *(n)*
inorganic • *adj* anorganic
insane • *adj* nebun *(m)*, nebun *(f)*, alienat mintal *(m)*, dezechilibrat psihic *(m)*, demenial *(n)*, înnebunitor *(n)*, himeric *(n)*, nebunesc *(n)*, delirant *(n)*
insanity • *n* demen *(f)*, alienaie mintal *(f)*, nebunie *(f)*
inscrutable • *adj* inscrutabil, neexaminabil, necercetabil, neanchetabil, de necercetat
insect • *n* insect *(f)*, nimeni, zero
insecticide • *n* insecticid *(n)*
insectivorous • *adj* insectivor *(m)*
insemination • *n* însmânare
insert • *v* a bga
inside • *adv* înuntru
insidious • *adj* insidios
insignificance • *n* nesemnifican *(f)*, neimportan *(f)*
insignificant • *adj* nesemnificant *(n)*, nesemnificativ *(n)*, neimportant *(n)*, nesemnificant *(f)*
insincere • *adj* nesincer
insincerity • *n* nesinceritate
insipid • *adj* fr gust, insipid, fad, searbd, fr caracter, anost, fr spirit, nesensibil, nesimitor, nespiritual
insolence • *n* insolen, obrznicie
insomnia • *n* insomnie *(f)*
insouciance • *n* impasibilitate *(f)*, nepsare *(f)*, indiferen *(f)*, nonalan *(f)*, degajare *(f)*, dezinvoltur *(f)*
inspection • *n* inspecionare *(f)*, controlare *(f)*, inspectare *(f)*
inspiration • *n* inspiraie
inspire • *v* inspira
installation • *n* instalare *(f)*, instalaie *(f)*
instance • *n* caz *(n)*, exemplu *(n)*, întâmplare *(f)*, circumstan *(f)*, incident *(n)*, ocazie *(f)*, instan *(f)*
instant • *n* instant
instantaneous • *adj* instantaneu *(m)*, momentan *(m)*
instead • *adv* în loc de
institute • *n* institut *(n)*
institution • *n* instituie *(f)*
instruction • *n* instruire *(f)*, învare, învmânt *(n)*, instruciune *(f)*, indicaie, învtur *(f)*, îndrumare *(f)*
instructor • *n* instructor *(m)*
instrument • *n* instrument *(n)*, aparat *(n)*

instrumental • *adj* instrumental
insubstantial • *adj* nesubstanial *(m)*
insufferable • *adj* insuportabil, nesuportabil, nerbdabil, nesuferibil
insufficient • *adj* insuficient *(n)*, neîndestultor *(n)*, nesuficient *(n)*
insulation • *n* izolare *(f)*, separare *(f)*, izolaie *(f)*
insulator • *n* izolator *(n)*, material de izolare *(n)*
insulin • *n* insulin
insult • *v* jigni, insulta • *n* insult, jignire, injurie
insulting • *adj* insulttor, ofensator
insurance • *n* asigurare *(f)*, asigurare
insurmountable • *adj* insurmontabil *(m)*
intangible • *adj* intangibil *(m)*, de neatins, nepalpabil *(m)*
integer • *n* întreg *(m)*, numr întreg *(n)*
integral • *n* integral *(f)* • *adj* integral
integrate • *v* integra
integrated • *adj* integrat *(n)*
integration • *n* integrare *(f)*
integrity • *n* integritate *(f)*
integument • *n* tegument *(n)*, înveli *(n)*
intellect • *n* intelect *(m)*, intelectual *(m)*, intelectual *(f)*
intellectual • *n* intelectual *(m)*, intelectual *(f)* • *adj* intelectual *(n)*
intelligence • *n* inteligen, judecat
intelligent • *adj* inteligent *(n)*, detept
intelligible • *adj* inteligibil *(m)*
intense • *adj* intens
intensity • *n* intensitate *(f)*
intention • *n* intenie *(f)*
intentionally • *adv* intenionat, premeditat *(m)*
interaction • *n* interaciune *(f)*, interacionare *(f)*
intercalation • *n* intercalare *(f)*
interconnection • *n* interconectare, interconexiune
interdisciplinary • *adj* interdisciplinar
interest • *v* interesa • *n* dobând *(f)*, interes *(n)*, interes material *(n)*, preocupare *(f)*
interested • *adj* interesat *(m)*
interesting • *adj* interesant
intergalactic • *adj* intergalactic *(n)*, intergalactic *(f)*
interior • *adj* intern, interior
interlineation • *n* adugire la un act *(f)*
intermediary • *n* intermediar *(m)*
interment • *n* înhumare *(f)*, înmormântare *(f)*
interminable • *adj* interminabil
intermolecular • *adj* intermolecular *(n)*
international • *adj* internaional
interplanetary • *adj* interplanetar
interpretation • *n* interpretare *(f)*
interpreter • *n* interpret, interpret *(f)*, translator *(m)*, translatoare *(f)*, traductor *(m)*, interpretor *(n)*
interrupt • *v* întrerupe
interruption • *n* întrerupere *(f)*
intersection • *n* intersecie *(f)*, intersectare *(f)*
interstellar • *adj* interstelar *(n)*, interastral *(n)*
interval • *n* interval *(n)*, distan *(f)*
intervertebral • *adj* intervertebral *(n)*
interview • *v* intervieva *(f)* • *n* interviu *(n)*, interviuri, interviu de prezentare *(n)*
intestine • *n* intestin, ma, intestine
intimacy • *n* intimitate *(f)*
intimate • *adj* intim
intolerance • *n* intoleran *(f)*
intoxicate • *v* intoxica
intoxicated • *adj* beat, ameit *(n)*, alcoolizat *(n)*, îmbtat, but, intoxicat *(n)*, otrvit *(n)*
intoxication • *n* intoxicaie *(f)*
intracranial • *adj* intracranial
intransitive • *adj* intransitiv
introduction • *n* introducere *(f)*, prezentare *(f)*
inundation • *n* inundare *(f)*, inundaie *(f)*
invader • *n* invadator
invariable • *adj* invariabil *(n)*, invariabil *(f)*, nevariabil *(n)*, neschimbabil *(n)*
invariant • *n* invariant *(n)* • *adj* constant, invariabil
invent • *v* scorni, nscoci, inventa
invention • *n* invenie *(f)*, invenii
inventive • *adj* de invenie, invenial, inventiv
inventiveness • *n* inventivitate *(f)*
invertebrate • *n* nevertebrat *(f)*, nevertebrat *(m)* • *adj* nevertebrat *(n)*
inverter • *n* invertor *(n)*
investigator • *n* investigator *(m)*
invisibility • *n* invizibilitate *(f)*
invisible • *adj* invizibil *(m)*, ascuns *(m)*
invite • *v* invita
invoice • *n* factur *(f)*, facturi
involucre • *n* involucru *(n)*
iodine • *n* iod *(n)*
ionization • *n* ionizare *(f)*, ionizaie *(f)*
ionosphere • *n* ionosfer *(f)*
iota • *n* iota
irascible • *adj* irascibil
ire • *v* înfuria, mânia • *n* mânie *(f)*, furie *(f)*
iridium • *n* iridiu *(n)*
iris • *n* iris *(m)*, stânjen *(m)*, stânjenel *(m)*,

iris *(n)*
irksome • *adj* enervant, suprtor, plictisitor, fastidios
iron • *v* clca • *n* fier *(n)*, fier de clcat *(m)* • *adj* fier, de fier
ironic • *adj* ironic
irony • *n* ironie *(f)* • *adj* feros *(n)*
irrational • *adj* iraional *(n)*, neraional *(n)*
irredeemable • *adj* iremediabil *(m)*, nerestaurabil *(m)*
irredentist • *n* iredentist *(m)*, iredentist *(f)* • *adj* iredentist, iredent
irregular • *adj* iregular *(n)*, nereglementar *(n)*, neregulat *(n)*
irregularity • *n* iregularitate *(f)*, neregularitate *(f)*, violare de regulament
irrelevance • *n* irelevan *(f)*
irrelevant • *adj* nerelevant *(m)*, irelevant *(m)*
irreproachable • *adj* ireproabil *(n)*
irresistible • *adj* irezistibil *(n)*
irresolute • *adj* nehotrât *(n)*, indecis *(n)*, indecis *(f)*, ovitor *(n)*
irritable • *adj* iritabil *(n)*
irritate • *v* irita, enerva, agasa, sâcâi
irritation • *n* iritare *(f)*, iritaie *(f)*
is • *v* este, e
island • *n* insul *(f)*
isolate • *v* izola
isolated • *adj* izolat *(n)*
isoleucine • *n* izoleucin *(f)*
isotope • *n* izotop *(m)*
issue • *n* emisiune *(f)*, problem *(f)*
isthmus • *n* istm *(n)*
itch • *n* mâncrime *(f)*, dorin *(f)*
item • *n* articol *(n)*, exemplar *(n)*, bucat *(f)*, punct de agend *(n)*
itemize • *v* specifica, detalia
ivory • *n* filde *(n)*, ivoriu *(n)*, alb-ivoriu • *adj* de filde, din filde, alb-ivoriu
ivy • *n* ieder *(f)*

J

jack • *n* conector-fi *(m)*, tecr *(n)*, conector-pin *(m)*
jackal • *n* acal *(m)*
jackdaw • *n* stncu *(f)*
jade • *n* jad *(n)*, verde ca jadul • *v* epuiza, extenua, obosi
jaded • *adj* epuizat
jaguar • *n* jaguar *(m)*
jam • *v* bruia • *n* gem *(n)*, marmelad *(f)*
janissary • *n* ienicer *(m)*
jar • *n* vas *(n)*, castron *(n)*, blid *(n)*
jargon • *n* jargon
jasmine • *n* jasmin *(m)*, iasomie *(f)*
jasper • *n* jasp
jaundice • *n* glbinare, glbenare, icter
javelin • *n* suli *(f)*
jaw • *n* mandibul *(f)*, mandibule, falc, maxilar
jay • *n* gai *(f)*
jealous • *adj* gelos
jealousy • *n* gelozie *(f)*
jelly • *n* jeleu *(n)*, marmelad *(f)*
jellyfish • *n* meduz *(f)*
jerboa • *n* jerboa *(m)*
jet • *n* jet *(n)*, duz *(f)*, motor cu reacie *(n)*, jiclor *(n)*, jais *(n)*, gagat *(n)* • *adj* cu reacie
jewel • *n* nestemat *(f)*, nestemate, pietre scumpe, bijuterie *(f)*, bijuterii, giuvaeruri
jeweler • *n* bijutier *(m)*, bijutieri, giuvaergiu *(m)*
jihad • *n* jihad *(n)*
jockey • *n* jocheu *(m)*
jocose • *adj* glume
join • *v* altura, împreuna, uni
jointly • *adv* împreun
joke • *n* banc *(n)*, glum
joule • *n* joule
journal • *n* ziar
journalism • *n* jurnalism
journalist • *n* ziarist *(m)*, gazetar *(m)*
journey • *v* cltori • *n* voiaj *(n)*, cltorie *(f)*
joy • *n* fericire *(f)*, bucurie *(f)*, jovialitate *(f)*, veselie *(f)*, voioie
judge • *v* judeca • *n* judector
judgment • *n* judecare *(f)*, judecat *(f)*
judo • *n* judo
jug • *n* urcior *(n)*, bidon *(n)*
juice • *n* suc *(n)*
jump • *v* sri, slta, tresri
junction • *n* jonciune
jungle • *n* jungl *(f)*
juniper • *n* ienupr *(m)*, jneapn
juridical • *adj* juridic *(n)*
jurisdiction • *n* jurisdicie *(f)*
jury • *n* juriu *(n)*
just • *adv* doar, numai, tocmai, întocmai
justice • *n* justiie, dreptate *(f)*, justee *(f)*, justiie *(f)*, judector *(m)*
justification • *n* justificare *(f)*, justificaie *(f)*
jute • *n* iut *(f)*

K

kale • *n* varz verde *(f)*
kangaroo • *n* cangur *(m)*, cangur *(f)*
kaput • *adj* stricat, distrus
karate • *n* carate
kava • *n* kava *(f)*
keep • *v* pstra, ine
kelp • *n* laminaria *(f)*, varec *(n)*
kelvin • *n* kelvin *(m)*
kerosene • *n* petrol lampant *(n)*
kestrel • *n* vindereu *(m)*, vânturel *(m)*
key • *n* cheie *(f)*, legend, tast *(f)*, clap *(f)*, manipulator *(n)*, cheie
keyboard • *n* tastatur *(f)*, claviatur *(f)*
khaki • *n* kaki • *adj* kaki
khan • *n* han *(m)*
kick • *v* lovi
kid • *n* ied *(m)*
kidney • *n* rinichi
kike • *n* jidan *(m)*, jidov *(m)*, târtan *(m)*
killer • *n* uciga, uciga *(f)*, asasin *(m)*, uciga *(m)*
kilobyte • *n* kilobyte *(m)*, kilooctet *(m)*
kilogram • *n* kilogram *(n)*
kilogram-meter • *n* kilogram-metru *(m)*
kind • *n* fel, gen • *adj* bun, amabil
kindergarten • *n* grdini *(f)*
kindle • *v* a aâa
kindness • *n* buntate, amabilitate *(f)*, bunvoin *(f)*
kinematics • *n* cinematic *(f)*
kinetic • *adj* cinetic *(n)*
king • *n* rege, pop
kingdom • *n* regat *(n)*, regn *(n)*
kingfisher • *n* pescru albastru *(m)*
kinkajou • *n* kinkaju *(m)*
kinship • *n* înrudire *(f)*, rudenie *(f)*
kiosk • *n* chioc *(n)*
kiss • *v* sruta, pupa, se sruta • *n* srut *(n)*, pupic *(n)*
kitchen • *n* buctrie *(f)*
kite • *n* milan *(m)*, erete *(m)*, gaie *(f)*, zmeu *(n)*
kitten • *n* pisoi, pisicu
kiwi • *n* kiwi *(m)*
kleptomania • *n* cleptomanie *(f)*
knead • *v* frmânta
knee • *n* genunchi
kneel • *v* îngenunchea
knife • *v* a da o lovitur de cuit • *n* cuit *(n)*
knight • *n* cavaler *(m)*, cal *(m)*
knock • *v* ciocni
knot • *v* înnoda • *n* nod
knotgrass • *n* troscot *(m)*
knotty • *adj* nodos
know • *v* ti, cunoate
knowledge • *n* cunoatere *(f)*, tire *(f)*, cunoatere, cunotine, tiin *(f)*
koala • *n* koala *(f)*
kob • *n* kob *(m)*
kohlrabi • *n* gulie *(f)*
kolkhoz • *n* colhoz *(n)*
kopek • *n* copeic *(f)*
kosher • *adj* cuer
krypton • *n* kripton *(n)*
kudu • *n* kudu *(m)*
kumquat • *n* kumquat *(n)*
kvass • *n* cvas

L

label • *v* eticheta, categorisi
labium • *n* labie *(f)*
laboratory • *n* laborator *(m)*
labyrinth • *n* labirint
lace • *n* dantel *(f)*, iret *(m)*
lachrymose • *adj* lcrimos
lack • *n* lips *(f)*
laconic • *adj* laconic
lacquer • *n* lac *(n)*
lad • *n* biat *(m)*
ladder • *n* scar
ladle • *n* polonic *(n)*
lady • *n* doamn *(f)*, doamn, lady *(f)*, dame, femei
ladyfinger • *n* picot *(n)*
lair • *n* vizuin *(f)*
lake • *n* lac *(n)*
lama • *n* lama *(m)*
lamb • *n* miel *(m)*, mioar *(f)*, mia *(f)*, mieluel *(m)*
lame • *adj* chiop *(m)*, olog *(m)*, handicapat *(m)*, schiopatand, jalnic *(m)*, slab *(m)*, lipsit de gust *(m)*, anost *(m)*, plictisitor *(m)*, sters *(m)*
lament • *v* lamenta, boci
lamentation • *n* lamentare *(f)*, lamentaie *(f)*, doliu *(n)*
lamina • *n* lamin *(f)*
lamp • *n* lamp *(f)*, lamp electric *(f)*, lmpi
lamprey • *n* chicar *(m)*

lampshade • *n* abajur *(n)*
lance • *n* lance, suli, fute, lncier *(m)*
land • *v* a ateriza • *n* uscat *(n)*, pmânt *(n)*, teren *(n)*, ar *(f)*
landing • *n* aterizare
landlocked • *adj* continental *(n)*, închis (terestru) *(n)*
landlord • *n* gazd *(f)*
landmark • *n* punct de reper *(n)*, punct de orientare *(n)*
landscape • *n* peisaj *(n)*
landslide • *n* alunecare de teren *(f)*
lane • *n* uli *(f)*
language • *n* limb *(f)*, vorbire *(f)*, limbaj *(n)*, jargon *(n)*
languid • *adj* lânced
languor • *n* langoare *(f)*, moleeal *(f)*
lantern • *n* lantern *(f)*, felinar *(n)*
lanthanum • *n* lantan *(n)*
lap • *v* îmbuca
laptop • *n* computer portabil *(n)*, laptop *(n)*, notebook *(n)*, calculator portabil *(n)*
lapwing • *n* nagâ *(m)*
larboard • *n* babord *(n)*
larceny • *n* furt
larch • *n* zad *(f)*, larice *(f)*
lard • *n* untur
large • *adj* mare
lark • *n* ciocârlie *(f)*, persoan matinal *(f)*
larkspur • *n* nemior *(m)*
larva • *n* larv *(f)*
larynx • *n* laringe *(n)*
lascivious • *adj* lasciv
laser • *n* laser *(n)*
last • *adj* ultim • *v* dura
latch • *n* zvor *(n)*, zvoare
late • *adj* târziu • *adv* târziu
latency • *n* laten
lateness • *n* întârziere *(f)*, zbav *(f)*
latest • *adj* ultim, cel mai din urm
latex • *n* latex *(n)*, latex *(m)*
lathe • *n* strung *(n)*
latitude • *n* latitudine *(f)*
latrine • *n* latrin *(f)*, privat *(f)*
lattice • *n* reea, latice
laud • *v* luda
laugh • *v* râde • *n* râs, râset
laughter • *n* râs *(n)*, râset
laundry • *n* splare *(f)*, splat *(n)*, spltorie *(f)*, camer de splat *(f)*, rufe, lucruri de splat
laurel • *n* laur *(m)*, dafin *(m)*, coroan de lauri
lava • *n* lav
lavatory • *n* camer de baie *(f)*, WC *(n)*, closet *(n)*
lavender • *n* levnic *(f)*, lavand *(f)* • *adj* liliachiu, violaceu
law • *n* lege *(f)*, drept, drept comun *(n)*
lawful • *adj* legal *(m)*
lawn • *n* peluz *(f)*
lawrencium • *n* lawrenciu *(n)*
lawsuit • *n* caz judiciar *(n)*, proces, cauz *(f)*
lawyer • *n* avocat, advocat
lay • *v* culca, oua
layer • *n* strat
layout • *n* plan *(n)*
lazy • *adj* lene, puturos, indolent
lea • *n* pune *(f)*, pajite *(f)*
lead • *n* plumb *(n)* • *v* duce, conduce
leader • *n* conductor, lider *(m)*
leaf • *n* frunz *(f)*, folie *(f)*, foaie *(f)*
leafy • *adj* frunzos
league • *v* a se alia, a se coaliza • *n* alian *(f)*, coaliie *(f)*, lig, lig *(f)*, leghe
leakage • *n* pierdere *(f)*, scurgere de curent *(f)*
lean • *v* inclina, rezema, ine • *adj* subire, slab
lean-to • *n* opron *(n)*
leap • *v* sri, slta • *n* sltare *(f)*, salt *(n)*
leapfrog • *n* capr *(f)*
learn • *v* înva, studiu, afla
learned • *adj* învat *(n)*, erudit *(m)*
learner • *n* învcel *(m)*
learning • *n* instruire *(f)*, învare *(f)*, învtur *(f)*
leather • *n* piele *(f)*, piele de animal *(f)*
leatherette • *n* scai *(n)*
lechery • *n* desfrâu
ledger • *n* registrul mare *(n)*, registrul mare , registru principal *(n)*
leech • *n* lipitoare *(f)*
leek • *n* praz *(m)*
left • *n* stâng *(f)* • *adj* stâng • *adv* la stânga • *v* rmas
left-handed • *n* stângaci
leg • *n* picior *(n)*, gamb
legacy • *n* motenire *(f)*
legal • *adj* legal, juridic
legality • *n* legalitate *(f)*
legally • *adv* legal *(m)*
legend • *n* legend, mit
legendary • *adj* legendar *(m)*, legendar *(f)*, mitic *(n)*
legible • *adj* lizibil, cite, deluit, descifrabil
legion • *n* legiune
legislative • *adj* legislativ *(m)*
legislator • *n* legiuitor *(m)*, legislator *(m)*
legislature • *n* corp legislativ *(n)*
legitimacy • *n* legitimitate *(f)*
legume • *n* leguminoas *(f)*
leguminous • *adj* leguminoas *(f)*
leisure • *n* rgaz *(n)*, timp liber

lemming • *n* leming *(m)*
lemon • *n* lmâie *(f)*, lmâi *(m)* • *adj* galben-verziu
lemur • *n* lemur *(m)*
lend • *v* împrumuta
length • *n* lungime
lengthen • *v* lungi
leniency • *n* blândee *(f)*, toleran *(f)*, indulgen *(f)*, îngduin *(f)*
lenient • *adj* tolerant *(n)*, tolerant *(f)*, indulgent *(n)*, blând *(n)*, îngduitor *(n)*
lens • *v* filma • *n* lentil *(f)*, linte *(f)*, cristalin *(n)*
lentil • *n* linte, linte *(f)*
leopard • *n* leopard *(m)*
lesbian • *n* lesbian *(f)*, lesbi *(f)*
lesion • *n* leziune *(f)*
less • *adj* mai puin
lesson • *n* lecie *(f)*, lecie
lest • *conj* în caz c, care
let • *v* lsa
lethargy • *n* letargie *(f)*
letter • *n* liter *(f)*, caracter *(n)*, scrisoare *(f)*
lettuce • *n* lptuc *(f)*, salat
leu • *n* leu
leucine • *n* leucin *(f)*
leukemia • *n* leucemie *(f)*
level • *n* nivel *(n)*, nivele, grad *(n)*, grade, etaj *(n)*, etaje, nivel, cat *(n)* • *adj* plan, plat, es, nivelat
leveret • *n* iepura
levy • *v* impozita, taxa, recruta • *n* impozitare *(f)*, taxare *(m)*
lewd • *adj* lasciv *(m)*, indecent *(m)*
lexeme • *n* lexem *(n)*
lexicon • *n* lexicon *(n)*
liability • *n* responsabilitate
liable • *adj* rspunztor, responsabil, pasibil
liana • *n* lian *(f)*
liar • *n* mincinos *(m)*, mincinoas *(f)*
libel • *v* defima
liberal • *adj* liberal *(f)*
liberty • *n* libertate *(f)*
libidinous • *adj* libidinos
library • *n* bibliotec *(f)*
lichen • *n* lichen *(m)*
lick • *v* linge
lid • *n* capac *(f)*
lie • *v* sta culcat, zcea, a sta întins, a sta orizontal, a fi situat, a se gsi, mini • *n* minciun *(f)*
liege • *n* vasal *(m)*
life • *n* via *(f)*, durat *(f)*
lifetime • *n* durat de via, eternitate
lift • *v* ridica • *n* lift *(n)*, ascensor *(n)*
ligature • *n* legare *(f)*, legtur *(f)*, frânghie *(f)*, nur *(n)*, sfoar *(f)*, funie *(f)*, ligatur *(f)*
light • *n* lumin *(f)*, corp de iluminat *(n)*, far *(n)* • *v* aprinde, lumina, ilumina • *adj* uor
lighten • *v* uura
lighter • *n* brichet *(f)*
lighthouse • *n* far *(n)*
lightning • *n* fulger *(n)*
lightweight • *adj* uor
like • *v* plcea • *n* preferin *(f)*
likelihood • *n* probabilitate, verosimilitate
lilac • *n* liliac *(m)* • *adj* liliachiu, lila, violet
lily • *n* crin *(m)*, lilie *(f)*
limb • *n* mdular, ciolan, membru
lime • *v* vrui • *n* oxid de calciu *(m)*, var *(n)*, limet *(f)*, lmâie verde *(f)*
limestone • *n* calcar
limit • *n* limit *(f)*, limit, valoare extrem *(f)*, grani *(f)*, margine *(f)*, valoare limit *(f)* • *v* limita, restrânge
limited • *adj* limitat *(n)*, mrginit *(n)*
limousine • *n* limuzin
limp • *v* chiopta
limpid • *adj* limpede
linden • *n* tei
line • *n* funie *(f)*, frânghie *(f)*, sfoar *(f)*, nur *(n)*, a *(f)*, dreapt *(f)*, linie deapt *(f)*, segment (de dreapt) *(n)*, muchie *(f)*, cant *(n)*, latitudine *(f)*, longitudine *(f)*, ecuator *(n)*, linie (de portativ) *(f)*, metru (de msur) *(m)*, direcie *(f)*, linie directoare *(f)*, linie, coad
linen • *n* in *(n)*, lenjerie *(f)*
linger • *v* sta, rmâne, lenevi
lingonberry • *n* merior *(m)*, merior *(n)*
linguistic • *adj* lingvistic, de lingvistic, computero-lingvistic
linguistics • *n* lingvistic *(f)*
lining • *n* acoperire
link • *n* legtur *(f)*, verig *(f)*, za *(f)*, hyperlink *(n)*
lint • *n* scam *(f)*
lion • *n* leu *(m)*
lioness • *n* leoaic *(f)*
lip • *n* buz *(f)*, buze
lips • *n* buze
lipstick • *n* ruj *(n)*, rou de buze *(m)*
liquid • *n* lichid *(m)* • *adj* lichid *(m)*, lichid *(f)*
liquidity • *n* lichiditate *(f)*
liquor • *n* lichior *(n)*, lichioruri
list • *n* list *(f)*
listen • *v* asculta
listener • *n* asculttor, auditor
listless • *adj* apatic, atonic
literacy • *n* alfabetizare *(f)*, alfabetism *(n)*, instruire *(f)*, colire *(f)*
literal • *adj* literally *(n)*, literal *(f)*

literally • *adv* literalmente
literary • *adj* literar *(n)*, literar *(f)*, literari
literature • *n* literatur *(f)*
lithium • *n* litiu *(n)*
litter • *v* fta • *n* lectic, litier, pui *(m)*
little • *adj* mic, mic *(f)* • *adv* puin
liturgy • *n* liturghie *(f)*
live • *v* tri, locui, a avea locuin, supravieui • *adj* viu, în direct • *adv* în direct
liveliness • *n* vitalitate *(f)*, vioiciune *(f)*, însufleire *(f)*, vivacitate *(f)*
liver • *n* ficat *(n)*, mai
liverwort • *n* crucea-voinicului
livery • *n* livrea *(f)*
lizard • *n* opârl *(f)*
llama • *n* lam *(f)*
load • *v* încrca • *n* sarcin *(f)*
loaded • *adj* încrcat *(n)*
loaf • *n* pâine *(f)* • *v* trândvi
loan • *v* împrumuta • *n* împrumut *(n)*
loanword • *n* cuvânt împrumutat *(n)*, împrumut *(n)*
loathsome • *adj* detestabil, odios, dezgusttor
lob • *v* loba
lobe • *n* lob
lobelia • *n* lobelie *(f)*
lobster • *n* homar *(m)*
local • *adj* local, local *(n)*, local *(f)*
localization • *n* localizare
lock • *v* încuia • *n* încuietoare *(f)*, lact, broasc *(f)*, zvor, clan, stvilar, bucl *(f)*
locus • *n* localitate *(f)*, loc *(n)*, locuri
locust • *n* lcust *(f)*
lodge • *n* caban *(f)*, cabin *(f)*, gheret *(f)*, loj *(f)*, barac *(f)*, adpost *(n)*, colib *(f)*
lodging • *n* gzduire *(f)*, camere de închiriat
log • *n* butean *(m)*, trunchi *(n)*
logarithm • *n* logaritm *(m)*, logaritmi
logbook • *n* jurnal de bord *(n)*, registru de bord *(n)*, jurnal de cltorie *(n)*
logging • *n* tiere forestier *(f)*, înregistrare
logic • *n* logic *(f)*
logical • *adj* logic *(m)*, logic *(f)*, rezonabil *(n)*, logic *(n)*, rezonabili, logic
logistics • *n* logistica
logogram • *n* logogram *(f)*
logogriph • *n* logogrif *(m)*
logwood • *n* bcan *(n)*
long • *adj* lung • *v* dori
longing • *n* dor *(n)*
longitude • *n* longitudine *(f)*
look • *v* privi, uita, prea • *n* aspect *(n)*
loom • *n* rzboi de esut *(n)*
loose • *v* dezlega
loosen • *v* desface
loot • *v* prda • *n* prad
lopsided • *adj* strâmb *(m)*, oblic *(m)*
loquacious • *adj* vorbre, limbut, flecar, gure, guraliv
lose • *v* pierde
lost • *adj* pierdut
lotion • *n* loiune *(f)*
lottery • *n* loterie *(f)*
lotus • *n* lotus *(m)*
loud • *adj* tare, glgios
loudspeaker • *n* difuzor *(n)*
louse • *n* pduche *(m)*
lousy • *adj* pduchios, plin *(n)*
lovage • *n* leutean *(m)*
love • *n* iubire, dragoste, amor, iubit, iubit
love-in-a-mist • *n* chica-voinicului *(f)*, nigelu *(f)*
love-lies-bleeding • *n* trompa elefantului *(f)*, amarant *(m)*
lovebird • *n* papagal amorez *(m)*
loved • *adj* iubit, drag, scump
lover • *n* iubit *(m)*, iubit *(f)*
low • *adj* jos
lowland • *n* es
loyalty • *n* loialitate *(f)*
lubricant • *n* lubrifiant *(m)*
lubricate • *v* lubrifia
lucidity • *n* luciditate *(f)*
luck • *n* noroc *(n)*, ans *(f)*, soart
lucky • *adj* norocos *(m)*
lucrative • *adj* lucrativ
ludicrous • *adj* absurd, ridicol
luggage • *n* bagaj *(n)*
lugubrious • *adj* lugubru
lullaby • *n* cântec de leagn *(n)*
luminescence • *n* luminiscen *(f)*
luminosity • *n* luminozitate
luminous • *adj* luminos
lunar • *adj* lunar *(m)*, lunar *(f)*
lunch • *v* prânzi • *n* prânz *(n)*
lung • *n* plmân *(m)*, pulmon, plmâni
lupine • *adj* lupesc
lupus • *n* lupus *(n)*
lush • *adj* luxuriant, delicios, savuros, atrgtor, sexy, extraordinar, minunat, grozav, mito • *n* beiv *(m)*, alcoolic *(m)*
lust • *n* luxur *(f)*, desfrânare *(f)*, concupiscen *(f)*
luster • *n* lustru
lute • *n* lut *(f)*
lutetium • *n* luteiu *(n)*
luxurious • *adj* luxurios *(m)*
lye • *n* leie
lymphocyte • *n* limfocit, limfocit *(f)*
lynx • *n* linx *(m)*, râs *(m)*
lysine • *n* lizin *(f)*

M

macaque • *n* macac *(m)*
macaw • *n* ara *(m)*
mace • *n* buzdugan *(n)*
machine • *n* main *(f)*, main electric *(f)*, main mecanic *(f)*, automobil
machinist • *n* mainist
mackerel • *n* macrou
macrocosm • *n* macrocosm *(n)*, macrocosmos *(n)*
macromolecular • *adj* macromolecular
macromolecule • *n* macromolecul
macroscopic • *adj* macroscopic *(n)*
madder • *adj* roz pal
magazine • *n* revist *(f)*
maggot • *n* larv, vierme
magic • *n* magie, magie *(f)* • *adj* magic, minunat, fermector
magical • *adj* magic, fermector, încânttor
magician • *n* vrjitor *(m)*, magician *(m)*
magnesium • *n* magneziu *(n)*
magnet • *n* magnet *(m)*
magnetic • *adj* magnetic, atractiv
magnetism • *n* magnetism *(n)*
magnetization • *n* magnetizare *(f)*, magnetizaie *(f)*
magnify • *v* mri
magnitude • *n* mrime *(f)*, cantitate *(f)*, mrime stelar *(f)*, magnitudine *(f)*
magnolia • *n* magnolie *(f)*
magpie • *n* coofan *(f)*
mahogany • *n* mahon *(m)*, acaju *(m)*
maiden • *adj* inaugural *(m)*
mailbox • *n* cutie postal *(f)*
mailman • *n* pota *(m)*
maim • *v* mutila
mainland • *n* continent
mainly • *adv* îndeosebi, mai ales, mai cu seam
majesty • *n* mreie, maiestate
major • *n* maior *(m)*, maiori
majority • *n* majoritate *(f)*, majorat *(n)*
make • *v* face
maker • *n* fctor *(m)*, fabricant *(m)*
makeup • *n* machiaj *(n)*
malachite • *n* malahit *(n)*
malaise • *n* indispoziie
male • *n* brbat *(m)*, mascul *(m)*, brbtu *(m)* • *adj* mascul, masculin
malefactor • *n* rufctor *(m)*
malevolence • *n* reavoin *(f)*, ostilitate *(f)*, pizm *(f)*
malice • *n* maliie *(f)*, maliiozitate *(f)*
malicious • *adj* malitios *(m)*
mallard • *n* ra slbatic *(f)*, ra mare *(f)*
malleability • *n* maleabilitate *(f)*
malleable • *adj* maleabil
mallet • *n* mai *(n)*
malleus • *n* ciocan *(n)*
mallow • *n* nalb
mammal • *n* mamifer *(n)*
mammalogy • *n* mamalogie *(f)*
mammoth • *n* mamut *(m)*
man • *n* om *(m)*, brbat *(m)*
manacle • *v* înctua • *n* ctue
manageable • *adj* maniabil, mânuibil
manager • *n* director, ef, impresar *(m)*
manatee • *n* lamantin *(m)*
mandarin • *n* mandarin *(m)*
mandola • *n* mandol *(f)*
mandolin • *n* mandolin *(f)*
mandrake • *n* mandragor *(f)*
mandrill • *n* mandril *(m)*
mane • *n* coam *(f)*
maneuver • *v* manevra
maneuverable • *adj* manevrabil *(m)*
manganese • *n* mangan *(n)*
mange • *n* jigodie, râie, scabie
mangle • *v* mutila, desfigura, sfârtica, manglui • *n* mangl *(n)*
mango • *n* mango *(n)*
mangosteen • *n* mangustan *(m)*
mania • *n* mânie
manifestation • *n* manifestare *(f)*, manifestaie *(f)*
manipulate • *v* manipula
manipulative • *adj* manipulator *(n)*
mankind • *n* omenire *(f)*
manliness • *n* virilitate *(f)*
manly • *adj* masculin, brbtesc, viril
manna • *n* man *(f)*
mannequin • *n* manechin *(n)*
manner • *n* stil *(n)*, fel *(n)*, manier *(f)*, mod, purtare *(f)*, comportament *(n)*, conduit *(f)*
mansion • *n* palat *(n)*, conac *(n)*, curte *(f)*
mantis • *n* clugri *(f)*
mantle • *n* manta *(f)*, mantie *(f)*
manual • *n* manual *(n)*, cutie de viteze *(f)* • *adj* manual *(n)*
manufacture • *v* fabrica, produce • *n* fabricare *(f)*
manufacturer • *n* fabricant, productor
manure • *n* balig *(f)*
manuscript • *n* manuscris
many • *pron* mulime *(f)*
map • *n* hart *(f)*, harta oraului *(f)*
maple • *n* paltin *(m)*, arar *(m)*
mar • *v* strica
marabou • *n* marabu *(m)*

marathon • *n* maraton
marathoner • *n* maratonist
marble • *n* marmur *(f)*
march • *v* mrlui, mrui
mare • *n* iap *(f)*
margarine • *n* margarin *(f)*
marigold • *n* filimic *(f)*, glbenele, cri *(f)*, vâzdoag *(f)*
marijuana • *n* marijuana *(f)*
marimba • *n* marimba *(f)*
marine • *adj* marin, maritim
marionette • *n* marionet *(f)*
mark • *n* marc *(f)*, semn *(n)*, born *(f)*, not *(f)*, scor *(n)*, urm *(f)*, pat *(f)*
market • *n* târg *(n)*, pia *(f)*
marketable • *adj* comerciabil *(m)*, vandabil
marmalade • *n* marmelad *(f)*
marmot • *n* marmot *(f)*
maroon • *n* naufragiat *(m)*, maro • *adj* maro
marriage • *n* cstorie *(f)*, csnicie *(f)*, cstorie, cununie *(f)*, nunt *(f)*
marrow • *n* mduv, dovlecel *(m)*
marry • *v* cstori, însura, cununa, mrita
marshmallow • *n* nalb, bezea *(f)*
marsupial • *n* marsupial • *adj* marsupial
marten • *n* jder
martin • *n* rândunic de cas *(f)*, lstun *(m)*
martyr • *v* martiriza • *n* mucenic, martir
marzipan • *n* maripan *(m)*
mascara • *n* mascara *(f)*
masculine • *adj* masculin *(m)*, masculin, brbtesc, viril
masculinity • *n* masculinitate *(f)*
masculinization • *n* masculinizare *(f)*
mask • *v* masca, deghiza, ascunde, se masca • *n* masc *(f)*
mason • *v* zidi • *n* zidar *(m)*
mass • *n* mas *(f)*
massage • *v* masa, a face masaj, manipula • *n* masaj *(n)*, masare *(f)*
masseur • *n* maseur *(m)*, maseuz *(f)*
mast • *n* catarg, arbore
master • *v* stpâni, conduce, controla, excela • *n* stpân *(m)*, proprietar *(m)*, patron *(m)*, maestru *(m)*, jupân *(m)*, original *(n)*
masterpiece • *n* capodoper *(f)*
mastodon • *n* mastodont *(m)*
masturbation • *n* masturbaie *(f)*, masturbare *(f)*
masturbator • *n* masturbator *(m)*, onanist *(m)*, malahian *(m)*, malahist
mat • *n* rogojin *(f)*
match • *n* meci *(n)*, partid *(f)*, întâlnire *(f)*, joc *(n)*, egal *(m)*, egal *(f)*, chibrit
material • *n* material *(n)*, materie *(f)*, stof *(f)*, material textil *(n)*, pânz *(f)* • *adj* material *(n)*, material *(f)*
materialism • *n* materialism *(n)*
materialist • *n* materialist *(m)*, materialist *(f)*
materialistic • *adj* materialist *(m)*, materialist
maternal • *adj* matern
mathematical • *adj* matematic *(n)*, matematic *(f)*
mathematically • *adv* în mod matematic
mathematics • *n* matematic *(f)*
matricide • *n* matricid *(n)*
matriculation • *n* înmatriculare
matrix • *n* matrice *(f)*
matter • *n* materie *(f)*, problem *(f)*, chestiune *(f)*, subiect *(n)*, fond *(n)*, material *(n)*, cauz, substan *(f)*
mattress • *n* saltea
mature • *adj* matur
maturity • *n* maturitate *(f)*
matutinal • *adj* matinal
mausoleum • *n* mausoleu *(n)*
mauve • *adj* mov, liliachiu
maverick • *adj* individualist
maxim • *n* maxim *(f)*, maxime
maximal • *adj* maximal
maximum • *n* maximum
may • *v* putea, se poate, s • *n* pducel *(m)*, gherghin *(m)*
maybe • *adv* poate
mayonnaise • *n* maionez
mayor • *n* primar *(m)*
mayoress • *n* primri *(f)*
me • *pron* mine, m, imi
mead • *n* hidromel *(m)*, mied
meadow • *n* livad
meal • *n* mas *(f)*, fin *(f)*
mealy • *adj* finos
mean • *v* vrea, avea intenia, gândi, a semnifica, indica, însemna, a vrea s spun, am convingerea • *n* mijloc, mediu, medie • *adj* mediu
measles • *n* rujeol *(f)*
measurable • *adj* msurabil *(n)*
measure • *v* msura • *n* msur, msur *(f)*, distan *(f)*, msurare *(f)*, tact *(n)*, rigl *(f)*, linie *(f)*
measurement • *n* msurare *(f)*, msurtoare, msur *(f)*, mrime *(f)*
meat • *n* carne *(f)*
meatball • *n* chiftea *(f)*
mechanic • *n* mecanic *(f)*
mechanical • *adj* mecanic
mechanism • *n* mecanism *(n)*
medal • *n* medalie *(f)*
medallion • *n* medalion
mediate • *v* media

mediation • *n* mediere *(f)*
mediator • *n* mediator *(m)*
medication • *n* medicaie
medicinal • *adj* medicinal, vindector
medicine • *n* medicament *(n)*, terapie *(f)*, tratament *(n)*, medicin
mediocre • *adj* mediocru *(m)*, mediocr *(f)*
medium • *n* mediu *(n)*, medium *(m)* • *adj* mediu
medley • *n* amestec *(n)*, amestectur *(f)*, potpuriu *(n)*
meerschaum • *n* spum-de-mare, piatr ponce, pipã din spum-de-mare
meet • *v* întâlni, atinge
meeting • *n* edin
megabyte • *n* megabyte *(m)*, megaoctet *(m)*
megalomania • *n* megalomanie *(f)*, grandomanie *(f)*
megalomaniacal • *adj* megaloman
megaspore • *n* megaspor *(m)*, macrospor *(m)*
melancholy • *n* melancolie *(f)*, tristee *(f)* • *adj* melancolic
melange • *n* melanj *(n)*
melodic • *adj* melodic, melodios
melodious • *adj* melodios
melodrama • *n* melodram *(f)*
melodramatic • *adj* melodramatic
melody • *n* melodie *(f)*
melon • *n* pepene, pepene galben
melt • *v* topi
member • *n* membru *(m)*, membru, mdular
membrane • *n* membran *(f)*, membrane
meme • *n* mem *(f)*
memorable • *adj* memorabil
memorize • *v* memoriza
memory • *n* memorie *(f)*, amintire *(f)*
menacing • *v* amenintor
menacingly • *adv* amenintor *(m)*
menagerie • *n* menajerie *(f)*
mend • *v* repara, drege
mendacious • *adj* mincinos
mendacity • *n* falsitate
mendelevium • *n* mendeleviu *(n)*
menhir • *n* menhir
mental • *adj* mintal, mental *(n)*
mentally • *adv* mintal
menu • *n* meniu, meniu *(n)*
meow • *v* mieuna, miorli • *interj* miau
merchandise • *n* marf *(f)*
merchant • *n* negustor, comerciant
mercilessness • *n* cruzime *(f)*, ferocitate *(f)*
mercury • *n* mercur *(n)*, hidrargir *(n)*, argint viu
mercy • *n* mizericordie *(f)*, îndurare *(f)*, comptimire *(f)*, compasiune *(f)*, iertare *(f)*, mil *(f)*, indulgen *(f)*, binecuvântare *(f)*
merely • *adv* doar, abia
meridian • *n* meridian *(n)*, meridian
meridional • *adj* de meridian, meridional
mermaid • *n* siren *(f)*
mesophyte • *n* mezofit *(f)*
metabolism • *n* metabolism *(n)*
metal • *n* metal *(n)*
metalloid • *n* metaloid *(m)*
metamorphosis • *n* metamorfoz *(f)*
metaphor • *n* metafor *(f)*
meteor • *n* meteor
meteoric • *adj* meteoric
meter • *n* metru *(m)*, contor *(n)*, ritm *(n)*
methamphetamine • *n* metanfetamin *(f)*
methane • *n* metan *(n)*
methanol • *n* metanol *(m)*
methionine • *n* metionin *(f)*
method • *n* metod *(f)*
methodical • *adj* metodic *(n)*
methodological • *adj* metodologic *(n)*
methodology • *n* metodologie *(f)*
methyl • *n* metil *(m)*
meticulous • *adj* meticulos *(n)*
meticulousness • *n* meticulozitate *(f)*
metis • *n* metis
metonymy • *n* metonimia *(f)*
metric • *adj* metric
metro • *n* metrou *(m)*, metropolitan *(m)*
metropolis • *n* metropol *(f)*
metropolitan • *n* mitropolit *(m)*
mezereon • *n* tulichin *(f)*
microbe • *n* microb *(m)*
microcosm • *n* microcosm *(n)*, microcosmos *(n)*
micrometer • *n* micrometru
microorganism • *n* microorganism *(n)*
microphone • *n* microfon
microprocessor • *n* microprocesor *(n)*
microscope • *n* microscop *(n)*
microscopic • *adj* microscopic *(n)*
microwave • *n* microunde *(f)*
middle • *n* mijloc, miez • *adj* mediu
midnight • *n* miezul nopii, miez de noapte, mijloc de noapte *(n)*,
midwife • *n* moa
mignonette • *n* rezed *(f)*, rozet *(f)*
migration • *n* migrare, migraie
mildew • *n* mucegai
mile • *n* mil *(f)*
milieu • *n* mijloc *(n)*
military • *adj* militar, militar *(n)*
militia • *n* miliia *(f)*
milkman • *n* lptar *(m)*
milkwort • *n* amreal *(f)*, poligal *(f)*

milky • *adj* lptos
mill • *n* moar • *v* mcina
millennium • *n* mileniu *(n)*
miller • *n* morar *(m)*
millet • *n* mei *(m)*
milligram • *n* miligram *(n)*
millipede • *n* miriapod
millisecond • *n* milisecund *(f)*
millstone • *n* piatr de moar *(f)*
mimosa • *n* mimoz *(f)*
mince • *v* toca • *n* carne tocat *(f)*
mind • *v* fi atent, psa • *n* minte *(f)*, atenie *(f)*, memorie, concentrare, nebun, judecat
mine • *pron* al meu *(m)*, a mea *(f)* • *v* mina • *n* min
miner • *n* miner *(m)*
mineral • *n* mineral *(n)*, minerale, ap mineral *(f)*
mineralogist • *n* mineralog *(m)*
mineralogy • *n* mineralogie *(f)*
minimal • *adj* minimal
minimum • *n* minimum
minion • *n* rsfat
minister • *n* ministru *(m)*, ministr *(f)*
ministry • *n* minister *(m)*
mink • *n* nurc *(f)*
minority • *n* minoritate
minstrel • *n* menestrel *(m)*
mint • *v* bate moned, emite • *n* monetria *(f)*, ment *(f)*
minuet • *n* menuet *(n)*
minute • *n* minut *(n)* • *adj* minuscul, mrunt, minuios, amnunit
miracle • *n* miracol *(n)*, minune *(f)*, minunie *(f)*
miraculous • *adj* miraculos
mirage • *n* miraj *(n)*
mirror • *n* oglind *(f)*
misanthropy • *n* mizantropie *(f)*
miscellaneous • *adj* amestecat *(n)*, divers *(n)*
mischievous • *adj* ru, rutcios, ruvoitor, obraznic
miser • *n* zgârcit
miserable • *adj* nenorocit
miserly • *adj* ciufut
misery • *n* mizerie *(f)*
misfortune • *n* ghinion *(n)*, neans *(f)*, peal *(f)*, panie *(f)*
misogyny • *n* misoginie *(f)*
missile • *n* proiectil *(n)*, proiectile, rachet *(f)*
mission • *n* misiune, însrcinare *(f)*, misiuni, misiune *(f)*
missionary • *n* misionar *(m)*
mist • *n* cea *(f)*, negur *(f)*
mistake • *v* confunda, grei • *n* greeal *(f)*, eroare *(f)*
mister • *n* domn *(m)*
mistletoe • *n* vâsc
mistrust • *n* neîncredere *(f)*, difiden *(f)*
mite • *n* acarian *(m)*
mix • *v* amesteca, mesteca • *n* amestec *(n)*, mixtur *(f)*, amestectur *(f)*
mixed • *adj* amestecat *(n)*, mixt *(n)*, impur *(n)*
mixture • *n* amestecare, amestec, mixtur, amestectur *(f)*, compus *(m)*, compoziie *(f)*
moan • *v* geme • *n* geamt
moat • *n* an *(f)*
mobile • *adj* mobil
mobilization • *n* mobilizare *(f)*
mocha • *n* moca *(f)*, moca
modality • *n* modalitate *(f)*
modem • *n* modem *(n)*
moderate • *v* modera • *n* centrist *(m)*, centrist • *adj* moderat *(n)*, moderat *(f)*, mediocru *(n)*, mediocr *(f)*, mijlociu *(n)*, mijlocie *(f)*, mediu *(n)*, centrist *(n)*
moderation • *n* moderaie, cumptare, moderare *(f)*, prezidare *(f)*, regulare *(f)*
modest • *adj* modest
modesty • *n* modestie *(f)*, rezerv *(f)*, castitate *(f)*, puritate *(f)*
modification • *n* modificare *(f)*, modificare
modified • *adj* modificat *(n)*
modify • *v* modifica
modulation • *n* modulaie *(f)*
moist • *adj* umed *(m)*, umed *(f)*
moisten • *v* uda, umezi
moisture • *n* umezeal *(f)*
molarity • *n* molaritate *(f)*
mold • *n* mucegai
mole • *n* aluni *(f)*, cârti *(f)*, sobol *(m)*
molecular • *adj* molecular
molecule • *n* molecul *(f)*
molest • *v* molesta, necji
molten • *adj* topit
molybdenum • *n* molibden *(n)*
moment • *n* clip *(n)*, moment
monarch • *n* monarh *(m)*
monarchist • *n* monarhist *(n)*
monarchy • *n* monarhie *(f)*
monastery • *n* mânstire *(f)*, mnstire *(f)*
monetarism • *n* monetarism *(n)*
monetary • *adj* monetar *(n)*
money • *n* ban *(m)*
mongoose • *n* mangust *(f)*
mongrel • *n* corcitur
monism • *n* monism
monitor • *n* monitor *(n)*
monk • *n* clugr *(m)*, monah *(m)*
monkey • *n* maimu *(f)*, simie *(f)*

monochrome • *adj* monocrom
monocle • *n* monoclu *(n)*
monogamy • *n* monogamie *(f)*
monograph • *n* monografie *(f)*
monolith • *n* monolit *(n)*
monomer • *n* monomer *(m)*
monopoly • *n* monopol *(n)*
monotheism • *n* monoteism
monotone • *adj* monoton
monotony • *n* monotonie
monotreme • *n* monotrem *(n)*, monotrem *(f)*
monoxide • *n* monoxid
monster • *n* monstru
monstera • *n* filodendron *(m)*
monstrosity • *n* monstruozitate *(f)*
monstrous • *adj* monstruos, hidos, oribil, enorm, colosal, cumplit, atroce, groaznic
month • *n* lun *(f)*
monthly • *adv* lunar, mensual
monument • *n* monument
moo • *v* mugi • *n* muget *(n)* • *interj* mu
moon • *n* lun *(f)*
moonlight • *n* lumin de lun *(f)*
moonwort • *n* limba-cucului *(f)*
moorhen • *n* ginu *(f)*, ginu-de-balt *(f)*
moose • *n* elan *(m)*
moped • *n* moped
moraine • *n* moren *(f)*
morality • *n* moralitate, moralitate *(f)*
morass • *n* mlatin
morel • *n* zbârciog *(m)*
morgue • *n* morg *(f)*, camer mortuar *(f)*
morning • *n* diminea *(f)*
morose • *adj* morocnos, moros, ursuz
morpheme • *n* morfem *(n)*
morphology • *n* morfologie *(f)*
mortal • *adj* muritor, mortal, pieritor
mortar • *n* mortar *(n)*, mortier *(n)*, piuli *(f)*, piu *(f)*, mojar *(n)*
mortgage • *n* ipotec *(f)*
mosaic • *n* mozaic *(n)*
mosque • *n* moschee *(f)*
mosquito • *n* ânar *(m)*
moss • *n* muchi *(n)*
moth • *n* molie *(f)*
mother • *n* mam *(f)*, maic *(f)*
mother-in-law • *n* soacr *(f)*
motherwort • *n* talpa-gâtei *(f)*
motion • *n* micare
motivation • *n* motivaie *(f)*, motivare *(f)*
motive • *n* motiv, raiune, motiv *(n)*
motor • *n* motor *(n)*
motorcycle • *n* motociclet *(f)*
motto • *n* deviz *(f)*
mouflon • *n* muflon *(m)*
mound • *n* movil *(f)*
mount • *n* munte • *v* încleca, monta
mountain • *n* munte *(m)*, grmad *(f)*, munte *(f)*, noian *(n)*
mouse • *n* oarece *(m)*, maus *(n)*, oricel *(m)*
mousetrap • *n* curs de oareci
moussaka • *n* musaca
moustache • *n* musta *(f)*
mouth • *n* gur *(f)*, *(f)*, orificiu *(n)*, deschiztur *(f)*
mouthful • *n* gur *(f)*
movable • *adj* mobil, micabil
move • *v* mica, muta, actiona, emoiona, însuflei, propune, recomanda • *n* micare *(f)*, mutare *(f)*
movement • *n* micare *(f)*, micare
movie • *n* film *(n)*
moving • *adj* mictor *(n)*, emoionant *(n)*, emoionant *(f)*
mow • *v* tunde
much • *adv* mult
mucous • *adj* mucos
mucus • *n* muci, mucus
mud • *v* noroi, înnmoli • *n* noroi *(n)*
muddle • *v* încurca, încâlci, a face confuz
muffin • *n* brio *(f)*
mug • *n* can *(f)*
mulberry • *n* dud *(m)*, dud *(f)*
mule • *n* catâr *(m)*, mul *(m)*
mullein • *n* lumânric *(f)*, coada-mielului *(f)*
multicultural • *adj* multicultural
multidimensional • *adj* multidimensional *(m)*
multimedia • *n* multimedia *(f)* • *adj* multimedia *(f)*
multiple • *n* multiplu *(m)*
multiplexer • *n* multiplexor *(n)*
multiplicand • *n* înmulit *(m)*, multiplicat *(m)*
multiplication • *n* multiplicare *(f)*, înmulire, înmulire *(f)*
multiplier • *n* multiplicator *(m)*, înmulit *(m)*
multiply • *v* multiplica, înmuli
mum • *n* mmic *(f)*, micu *(f)*
mummy • *n* mumie *(f)*, mmic *(f)*, micu *(f)*, mam *(f)*
municipality • *n* municipalitate *(f)*
murder • *n* crim *(f)*, asasinat *(n)*
murderer • *n* criminal *(m)*
murky • *adj* tulbure
murmur • *n* freamt
muscle • *n* muchi, muchi *(m)*
muscular • *adj* muscular, muchiular, muchiulos, musculos
museum • *n* muzeu *(n)*
mushroom • *n* ciuperc *(f)*

music • *n* muzic *(f)*, melodie *(f)*, partitur *(f)*
musician • *n* muzician *(m)*, muzician *(f)*
musk • *n* mosc *(n)*
musket • *n* muschet *(f)*, muschet *(n)*
muskrat • *n* bizam *(m)*
must • *v* trebui • *n* must
mustard • *n* mutar *(m)*, mutar *(n)*
musty • *adj* muced
mutable • *adj* muabil
mutant • *n* mutantului
mute • *adj* mut
muteness • *n* muenie *(f)*
mutilate • *v* mutila, schilodi, devasta
mutton • *n* oaie *(f)*
mutual • *adj* mutual *(n)*, reciproc *(n)*
mutually • *adv* (în mod) mutual
mycelium • *n* miceliu *(n)*
myocardium • *n* miocard *(n)*, muchi al inimii *(m)*
myopia • *n* miopie *(f)*
myrtle • *n* mirt *(m)*
myself • *n* eu însumi *(m)*, eu însmi *(f)*
mysterious • *adj* misterios
mystery • *n* mister *(n)*
myth • *n* mit *(n)*, legend *(f)*
mythological • *adj* mitologic *(n)*, mitologic *(f)*, mitic *(n)*, legendar *(n)*, legendar *(f)*, mitic *(m)*, fabulos *(n)*, fabuloas *(f)*
mythologist • *n* mitolog *(m)*, mitolog *(f)*, mitologist *(m)*
mythology • *n* mitologie *(f)*, colecie mitologic *(f)*

N

nag • *v* cicli
nail • *n* unghie *(f)*, cui *(n)*
naked • *adj* dezbrcat, gol
name • *n* nume *(n)*, reputaie *(f)*, renume *(n)*, faim
namely • *adv* adic
namesake • *n* tiz *(m)*
nap • *v* dormita • *n* pui de somn *(m)*, somnior *(n)*, somnule *(n)*
nape • *n* ceaf *(f)*, grumaz *(f)*, cerbice
napkin • *n* erveel *(n)*
narcissus • *n* narcis *(f)*
narcolepsy • *n* narcolepsie
narcotic • *n* narcotic *(f)* • *adj* narcotic
nark • *v* a turna
narrow • *v* îngusta • *adj* strâmt, îngust
narwhal • *n* narval *(m)*
nasturtium • *n* cluna *(m)*
natal • *adj* natal, de natere
nation • *n* naiune, stat *(n)*
national • *adj* naional
nationalism • *n* naionalism *(m)*
nationality • *n* naionalitate *(f)*
native • *n* indigen, autohton • *adj* nativ, de la natere, matern, originar *(n)*, originar *(f)*, localnic *(n)*, localnic *(f)*, autohton
nativity • *n* natere *(f)*, natalitate *(f)*
natural • *adj* natural *(m)*, natural *(f)*, natural *(n)*
naturalism • *n* naturalism *(n)*
naturalize • *v* naturaliza
naturally • *adv* natural, firete, desigur, bineîneles
naturalness • *n* naturalitate *(f)*, naturalee *(f)*
nature • *n* natur *(f)*
nausea • *n* grea *(f)*, nausea *(f)*
nave • *n* naos *(n)*, nav *(f)*
navel • *n* buric *(n)*
navigation • *n* navigaie, navigaie *(f)*
navy • *n* marin *(f)*, flot *(f)*, for naval *(f)*, marin militar *(f)*, bleumarin *(n)* • *adj* bleumarin, marin, maritim
near • *adj* aproape
nebula • *n* nebuloas *(f)*
nebulosity • *n* nebulozitate *(f)*
necessary • *adj* necesar
necessity • *n* necesitate
neck • *v* strangula, sugruma • *n* gât *(n)*, guler *(n)*
necklace • *n* colan, colier, salb
necktie • *n* cravat *(f)*
necromancy • *n* necromania *(f)*
necropolis • *n* necropol *(f)*
necrosis • *n* necroz *(f)*
necrotic • *adj* necrotic *(m)*
nectarine • *n* nectarin *(f)*
need • *n* necesitate *(f)*, cerin *(f)*, nevoie • *v* trebui
needle • *n* ac, ac *(n)*
negation • *n* negare *(f)*, negaie *(f)*
neglect • *v* neglija, a nu ine cont de
negligence • *n* neglijen, delsare
neigh • *v* râncheza • *n* nechezat *(n)*
neighborhood • *n* vecintate
neither • *adv* nici
neoclassicism • *n* neoclasicism *(n)*
neocolonialism • *n* neocolonialism *(n)*
neodymium • *n* neodim *(n)*
neologism • *n* neologism *(n)*

neon • *n* neon *(n)*
neonatal • *adj* de noi nscui, neonatal
nephew • *n* nepot *(m)*
nepotism • *n* nepotism *(n)*
neptunium • *n* neptuniu *(n)*
nerve • *n* nerv *(m)*, nervur *(f)*, curaj *(n)*, rbdare *(f)*, putere *(f)*, rezisten *(f)*, tupeu *(n)*, insolen *(f)*, neruinare *(f)*, nervi
nervous • *adj* nervos, emoionat, nerbdtor
nervousness • *n* nervozitate *(f)*
nest • *n* cuib
net • *n* reea, plas, net *(m)*, net *(f)* • *v* câtiga, lucra
nether • *adj* sub, subteran
nettle • *n* urzic *(f)*
network • *n* reea *(f)*, reele, reea computeric *(f)*, reea de computere *(f)*, reea de calculatoare
neurological • *adj* neurologic *(m)*, neurologic *(f)*
neurologist • *n* neurolog *(m)*
neurology • *n* neurologie *(f)*
neurosarcoma • *n* neurosarcom *(n)*
neuroscience • *n* neurotiin *(f)*
neutral • *n* stat neutru, stat nealiniat, persoan neutr, conductor neutru, born neutr • *adj* neutru, imparial, ters, cenuiu, neutru *(n)*
neutrino • *n* neutrino *(m)*
neutron • *n* neutron *(m)*
never • *adv* niciodat, nicicând
nevertheless • *adv* totui, cu toate acestea
new • *adj* nou, nou *(n)*
newborn • *n* nou-nscut *(m)*, nou-nscut *(f)* • *adj* nou-nscut *(m)*, nou-nscut *(f)*
newness • *n* noutate
news • *n* tire, noutate
newspaper • *n* ziar, ziare
newsstand • *n* chioc de ziare *(n)*
newt • *n* triton *(m)*
newton • *n* newton *(m)*
next • *adj* urmtor
niche • *n* ni *(f)*
nickel • *v* nichela • *n* nichel *(n)*
nickname • *v* porecli • *n* porecl *(f)*
nicotine • *n* nicotin *(f)*
niece • *n* nepoat *(f)*
nigella • *n* chica-voinicului *(f)*, negruc *(f)*, negrilic *(f)*
nigger • *n* cioar *(f)*
night • *n* noapte *(f)*, noapte, înserare *(f)*, întuneric
nightfall • *n* cderea serii *(f)*, înserare *(f)*, amurg *(n)*, venirea nopii *(f)*, cderea nopii *(f)*, înnoptare *(f)*
nightingale • *n* privighetoare
nightmare • *n* comar *(n)*
nihilism • *n* nihilism
nimble • *adj* ager
nineteenth • *n* nousprezecelea *(m)*
ninetieth • *adj* nouzecilea
ninth • *n* cel al noulea *(m)*, cea a noua *(f)*
niobium • *n* niobiu *(n)*
nipple • *n* sfârc *(n)*, biberon *(n)*, tetin *(f)*
nit • *n* lindin *(f)*
nitrogen • *n* azot *(n)*
no • *n* nu
nobelium • *n* nobeliu *(n)*
nobility • *n* nobilime, noblee *(f)*
noble • *n* nobil, aristocrat
nobody • *n* nimeni
nod • *v* a da din cap, dormita
node • *n* nod *(n)*, punct de jonciune *(n)*, punct nodal *(n)*
nodule • *n* nodul *(n)*
noise • *n* glgie *(f)*, larm *(f)*, vacarm *(n)*, zgomot *(n)*, sunet *(n)*, perturbaie *(f)*, rsunet *(n)*, zgomot de semnal *(n)*
noiseless • *adj* silenios *(n)*, nezgomotos *(n)*
noisome • *adj* nuizibil, vtmtor, duntor, insalubru, nesntos, dezgusttor, respingtor, scârbos
nomenclature • *n* nomenclatur *(f)*
nominal • *adj* nominal
nominative • *adj* nominativ
nonchalance • *n* nonalan *(f)*
nonconformist • *n* nonconformist *(m)*, nonconformist *(f)*
none • *pron* nimeni, nici unul *(m)*, nici una *(f)*
nonexistent • *adj* neexistent, nonexistent, inexistent
nonlinear • *adj* neliniar *(n)*, neliniar *(f)*
nonmagnetic • *adj* nemagnetic *(m)*
nonsense • *n* nonsens *(n)*, absurditate *(f)*, nonsens, nerozie *(f)*, nerozii, prostie *(f)*
nonstructural • *adj* nestructural *(n)*
noodle • *n* tiei
nook • *n* col *(n)*
noon • *n* amiaz *(f)*, miezul zilei *(n)*, mijloc de zi *(n)*
noose • *n* la, treang *(n)*
nor • *conj* nici
norm • *n* norm *(f)*, regul *(f)*
normal • *adj* normal, obinuit, uzual
normality • *n* normalitate *(f)*
normally • *adv* de obicei
normative • *adj* normativ *(n)*
north • *n* nord *(n)*
northeast • *adj* nordestic, de nord-est, nord-vestic *(m)*
northern • *adj* nordic *(n)*
northwest • *n* nord-vest *(n)* • *adj* de nord-

vest, nordvestic
nose • *v* a-i bga nasul, mirosi • *n* nas, bot *(n)*, vârf *(n)*, cioc *(n)*, lungime de nas *(f)*, arom *(f)*, buchet *(n)*, nas *(n)*
nostril • *n* nar
not • *adv* nu
notary • *n* notar public
note • *v* nota, adnota, însemna pe margine • *n* not *(f)*, semn *(n)*, marcaj *(n)*, comentariu *(n)*, adnotare *(f)*, noti *(f)*, not de informare *(f)*, not informaional *(f)*
nothing • *pron* nimic, nimic *(n)*, fleac *(n)*, bagatel *(f)*
notice • *n* observare *(f)*, percepere *(f)*, întiinare *(f)*, aviz *(n)*, notificare *(f)*, avertisment *(n)*
notification • *n* notificare *(f)*
notion • *n* noiune *(f)*, opinie *(f)*, înclinaie *(f)*
notwithstanding • *prep* in ciuda faptului ca
noun • *v* substantiviza • *n* substantiv *(n)*, nume *(n)*
nourish • *v* nutri
nova • *n* nov *(f)*
novel • *adj* nou *(m)*, original *(m)*, original • *n* roman *(n)*
novelty • *n* noutate
novice • *n* începtor, debutant
now • *adv* acum
nowhere • *adv* nicieri, niciunde
noxious • *adj* nociv *(n)*, vtmtor *(n)*, nesntos *(n)*
nuance • *n* nuan *(f)*, nuane
nucellus • *n* nucel *(f)*
nuclear • *adj* nuclear *(n)*, atomic *(n)*
nucleon • *n* nucleon *(m)*
nucleotide • *n* nucleotide
nucleus • *n* nucleu *(n)*, miez *(n)*
nude • *adj* nud, nud *(f)*, gol *(n)*
nudism • *n* nudism *(n)*
nudist • *adj* nudist
nudity • *n* nuditate *(f)*
nullify • *v* anula
numb • *v* amori • *adj* amorit *(n)*
number • *v* numra, numerota • *n* numr *(n)*, numr întreg *(n)*, cantitate *(f)*
numerator • *n* numrtor
numeric • *adj* numeric *(m)*, numeric *(f)*
numerous • *adj* numeros *(n)*
nun • *n* clugri *(f)*
nuptial • *adj* de nunt, nupial, nupial *(f)*
nurse • *n* infirmier *(f)*
nursery • *n* cre *(f)*
nurture • *n* educare *(f)*, cretere *(f)*, cultivare
nut • *n* nuc *(f)*, alun, piuli *(f)*, nebun *(m)*, icnit *(m)*, cap *(m)*, coi *(n)*
nutcracker • *n* sprgtor de nuci *(m)*, alunar *(m)*
nuthatch • *n* scorar *(m)*, iclete *(m)*
nutmeg • *n* nucor *(m)*, nucoar *(f)*
nutrition • *n* nutrire, nutriie *(f)*
nymph • *n* nimf *(f)*

O

oak • *n* stejar *(m)*
oar • *n* ram *(f)*, vâsl *(f)*
oasis • *n* oaz *(f)*
oat • *n* ovz
oath • *n* jurmânt, legmânt
oatmeal • *n* fin de ovz *(f)*
oats • *n* ovz *(n)*
obedience • *n* ascultare
obedient • *adj* asculttor, obedient, docil, supus
obese • *adj* obez
obesity • *n* obezitate
obfuscate • *v* întuneca, umbri, confunda, încurca, zpci
obituary • *n* necrolog *(n)*
object • *v* obiecta, opune • *n* obiect *(n)*, lucru *(n)*
objection • *n* obiectare *(f)*, obiecie *(f)*, protest, protest *(n)*
objective • *n* obiectiv *(m)*, obiectiv *(n)* • *adj* obiectiv, obiectiv *(f)*
objectivity • *n* obiectivitate
obligation • *n* obligare *(f)*, obligaie, obligaie *(f)*
obliged • *adj* obligat, îndatorat
obligee • *n* creditor obligatar *(m)*
obligor • *n* debitor obligatar
oblong • *adj* prelung
obnoxious • *adj* respingtor, insuportabil, greos, neplcut, dezagreabil, nesuferit *(m)*
oboe • *n* oboi *(m)*
obscene • *adj* obscen *(n)*, obscen *(m)*, imoral *(m)*
obscurantism • *n* obscurantism *(n)*
obscure • *v* obscura, întuneca, ascunde, oculta • *adj* obscur, întunecos, retras, ascuns
obscurity • *n* obscuritate *(f)*

obsequious • *adj* obsecvios, servil
observant • *adj* observator *(n)*
observation • *n* observare *(f)*, observaie *(f)*
observatory • *n* observator *(n)*
observe • *v* observa
obsession • *n* idee fix *(f)*, obsesie *(f)*
obsidian • *n* obsidian *(n)*
obstacle • *n* obstacol, piedic
obstetric • *adj* obstetric
obstetrics • *n* obstetric *(f)*
obstinacy • *n* încpânare *(f)*, obstinaie *(f)*
obstinate • *adj* obstinat, încpânat, persistent
obstruct • *v* înfunda, obtura, astupa, bloca, împiedica, întârzia
obstruction • *n* împiedicare, obstrucionare
obtain • *v* obine, avea, reui, avea succes, a se stabili
obvious • *adj* evident, clar, limpede, vdit
occasion • *n* întâmplare *(f)*, hazard *(n)*, ocazie *(f)*, situaie, favorabil *(f)*
occasional • *adj* ocazional *(n)*
occasionally • *adv* ocazional, câteodat, uneori
occur • *v* trece
occurrence • *n* caz *(n)*, eveniment *(n)*, întâmplare *(f)*
ocean • *n* ocean *(n)*
oceanography • *n* oceanografie *(f)*, oceanologie *(f)*
ocelot • *n* ocelot *(m)*
octopus • *n* caracati *(f)*
ocular • *adj* ocular *(m)*
odd • *adj* impar
oddity • *n* raritate
ode • *n* od
of • *prep* de
offense • *n* act sancionabil *(n)*, ofens *(f)*, ofensiv *(f)*, atacant
offensive • *n* ofensiv *(f)*, atac *(n)* • *adj* ofensant *(n)*, ofensant *(f)*
offer • *v* oferi
office • *n* birou *(n)*, minister *(n)*, departament *(n)*, oficiu *(n)*, funcie *(f)*
officer • *n* ofier *(m)*, funcionar *(m)*
official • *n* funcionar oficial *(m)*, funcionar oficial *(f)* • *adj* oficial *(n)*
offshoot • *n* ramur *(f)*
often • *adv* des
ogle • *v* holba
ogre • *n* cpcun *(m)*
oil • *n* ulei, petrol, pcur, benzin, iei *(n)*
okapi • *n* okapi *(f)*
okra • *n* bam *(f)*
old • *adj* vechi, btrân, antic, fost
old-fashioned • *adj* demodat *(n)*, demodat *(f)*, vechi-modic *(n)*, învechit *(n)*
old-timer • *n* veteran *(m)*, vechi locuitor btina *(m)*
oleander • *n* leandru *(m)*, oleandru *(m)*
oligosaccharide • *n* oligozaharid *(f)*
olive • *n* mslin *(f)*, oliv *(f)*
omega • *n* omega *(m)*
ominous • *adj* sinistru, prevestitor, fatidic, de ru augur
omit • *v* omite, a lsa la o parte, neglija
omnibus • *n* autobuz *(n)*
omnipotent • *adj* omnipotent, atotputernic
omnipresence • *n* omniprezen *(f)*
omnipresent • *adj* omniprezent
omniscient • *adj* omniscient, atottiutor
on • *prep* deasupra, pe
once • *adv* odat
one • *n* unu *(m)*
one-eyed • *adj* cu un singur ochi, chior *(m)*
one-sided • *adj* partinic *(m)*, unilateral *(m)*, unilateral
oneness • *n* unitate *(f)*
ongoing • *adj* neîntrerupt, continuu, necontenit
onion • *n* ceap *(f)*
only • *adj* singur, unic • *adv* numai
onomatopoeia • *n* onomatopee *(f)*
onomatopoeic • *adj* onomatopeic
ontological • *adj* ontologic
ontology • *n* ontologie, ontologie *(f)*
onyx • *n* onix *(m)*
opaque • *adj* netransparent, opac
opera • *n* oper *(f)*
operable • *adj* operabil
operand • *n* operand
operation • *n* operaie *(f)*, operaiune *(f)*, operare *(f)*
operational • *adj* operaional *(n)*
operator • *n* operator, operatoare *(f)*, telefonist *(f)*
ophthalmologist • *n* oftalmolog *(m)*, oftalmolog *(f)*
opinion • *n* prere *(f)*, opinie *(f)*
opium • *n* opiu *(n)*
opossum • *n* oposum *(m)*, sarig *(f)*
opponent • *n* adversar *(m)*, oponent *(m)*
opportune • *adj* oportun *(n)*, potrivit *(n)*, adecvat *(n)*
opportunity • *n* oportunitate *(f)*
oppose • *v* opune, contrazice
opposed • *adj* opozant *(n)*, contrar *(n)*
opposite • *adj* opus, opus *(n)*, opus *(f)*
opposition • *n* opoziie *(f)*, împotrivire *(f)*, opunere *(f)*, oponent *(n)*

opt • *v* opta
optic • *n* ochi *(m)* • *adj* optic *(m)*
optionally • *adv* opional, facultativ
opulence • *n* opulen *(f)*
opuntia • *n* opunia *(f)*
or • *conj* ori, sau • *n* aur • *adj* auriu
orange • *n* portocal *(m)*, portocal *(f)*, portocaliu *(n)*, oranj *(n)* • *adj* portocaliu, oranj
orangutan • *n* urangutan *(m)*
orator • *n* orator *(m)*, oratoare *(f)*
orbit • *n* orbit *(f)*
orbital • *adj* orbital *(n)*, orbital *(f)*
orc • *n* orc *(m)*
orchard • *n* pomet *(n)*, livad *(f)*
orchestral • *adj* orchestral, de orchestr
orchid • *n* orhidee *(f)*
ordeal • *n* calvar *(n)*, chin *(n)*, ordalie *(f)*
order • *v* comanda, ordona, porunci • *n* ordine *(f)*, rânduial *(f)*, ordin *(n)*, comand *(f)*, porunc *(f)*
ordinance • *n* ordonan *(f)*
ordinary • *adj* normal *(m)*, uzual *(m)*, ordinar *(m)*
ore • *n* minereu *(n)*
oregano • *n* oregano *(m)*, sovârf *(m)*
organ • *n* organ *(n)*, org *(f)*
organism • *n* organism *(n)*
organization • *n* organizaie *(f)*, organizare *(f)*
organize • *v* organiza
orgasm • *n* orgasm *(n)*
orgy • *n* orgie *(f)*
orientalist • *n* orientalist *(m)*
origin • *n* origine *(f)*, origin *(f)*
originality • *n* originalitate *(f)*
originator • *n* promotor *(m)*, iniiator *(m)*
ornament • *v* ornamenta, înfrumusea, aduga • *n* ornament *(n)*, ornament muzical *(n)*
ornamental • *adj* ornamental *(n)*
ornamentation • *n* ornamentare *(f)*, ornamentaie *(f)*
ornithine • *n* ornitin *(f)*
orphan • *n* orfan *(m)*, orfan *(f)*
orthoclase • *n* ortoz *(f)*
orthoepy • *n* ortoepie *(f)*
orthogonality • *n* ortogonalitate *(f)*
orthographic • *adj* ortografic *(m)*
orthography • *n* ortografie *(f)*
ortolan • *n* ortolan *(m)*
oryx • *n* oryx *(m)*
oscillate • *v* oscila
oscillation • *n* oscilare *(f)*
oscillator • *n* oscilator *(n)*
osmium • *n* osmiu *(n)*
osprey • *n* vultur-pescar *(m)*
osseous • *adj* osos
ossified • *adj* neadaptabil *(m)*, anchilozat *(n)*, învechit *(n)*
ossify • *v* osifica
ossuary • *n* osuar *(n)*
ostentation • *n* ostentaie *(f)*
ostentatious • *adj* ostentativ *(n)*, provocator *(n)*, ostentaios *(n)*, împopoonat, iptor
ostracism • *n* ostracism
ostrich • *n* stru
other • *adj* alt
others • *n* alii, altele
otter • *n* lutr *(f)*, vidr *(f)*
ouch • *interj* ai, au, ah, vai, aoleu
ours • *pron* al nostru *(m)*, a noastr *(f)*, ai notri, ale noastre
outfit • *n* costum *(n)*
outlaw • *n* fugar *(m)*, persoan fr de lege *(f)*
outlook • *n* vedere *(f)*, punct de vedere *(n)*, perspectiv *(f)*
outpost • *n* avanpost *(n)*, avanposturi
output • *v* produce, crea, trimite la ieire (date) *(f)* • *n* producie *(f)*
outrage • *v* ultragia • *n* atrocitate *(f)*, ultraj *(n)*, furie *(f)*, mânie *(f)*
outright • *adv* complet, desvârit *(m)*, deschis, sincer
outside • *n* exterior *(n)* • *adj* afar • *adv* afar
outstanding • *adj* extraordinare
outward • *adj* în afara
outweigh • *v* a cântri mai greu decât, a excede în valoare
oval • *n* oval *(n)*
ovary • *n* ovar, ovar *(n)*
oven • *n* cuptor
over • *prep* deasupra, peste
over-the-counter • *adj* fr reet, cu vânzare liber, extrabursier *(m)*
overabundant • *adj* supraabundent
overcoat • *n* pardesiu
overflow • *n* revrsare *(f)*
overload • *v* supraîncrca, supraînsrcina • *n* sarcin excesiv *(f)*
overtake • *v* întrece, depi
overtime • *n* ore suplimentare, prelungire *(f)*, ore suplimentare pltite
overvalue • *v* supraevalua
overwhelming • *adj* copleitor, covâritor
ovum • *n* ovul
owl • *n* bufni
own • *v* deine
ownership • *n* proprietate *(f)*, posesiune *(f)*, proprieti
ox • *n* bou *(m)*
oxide • *n* oxid *(m)*
oxlip • *n* ciuboica-cucului *(f)*

oxygen • *n* oxigen *(n)*
oxymoron • *n* oximoron *(n)*
oystercatcher • *n* scoicar *(m)*, ostrigar *(m)*
ozone • *n* ozon *(m)*

P

pace • *v* umbla • *n* pas, ritm *(n)*, pas *(m)*, tempo *(n)*
pack • *n* sarcin *(f)*, hait *(f)*
package • *n* pachet *(n)*
packet • *n* pachet *(n)*, pachete, pachet de date *(n)*
padlock • *n* lact *(n)*
pagan • *n* pgân *(m)* • *adj* pgân
paganism • *n* pgânism, pgântate
page • *n* pagin *(f)*, *(f)*
pagoda • *n* pagod *(f)*
pain • *v* durea, îndurera • *n* durere *(f)*, chin *(f)*, suferin *(f)*, chin *(n)*, pislog *(m)*, om plictisitor *(m)*, persoan enervant *(f)*, necaz *(n)*, suprare *(f)*
painless • *adj* nedureros, fr durere
paint • *v* picta, vopsi • *n* culoare *(f)*, vopsea *(f)*
paintbrush • *n* pensul *(f)*
painter • *n* pictor *(m)*, pictori *(f)*
painting • *n* pictur *(f)*, pictare *(f)*
pair • *n* pereche
pajamas • *n* pijama *(f)*
palace • *n* palat *(n)*
palanquin • *n* palanchin *(n)*
palate • *n* palat *(n)*
pale • *adj* pal
paleness • *n* paliditate *(f)*, glbinare *(f)*
paleontological • *adj* paleontologic *(n)*
paleontologist • *n* paleontolog *(m)*
paleontology • *n* paleontologie *(f)*
palimpsest • *n* palimpsest *(n)*
palladium • *n* paladiu *(n)*
pallor • *n* paliditate *(f)*, glbinare *(f)*
palm • *n* palm *(f)*
pamper • *v* rsfa, alinta
pancake • *n* cltit *(f)*
pancreas • *n* pancreas
pandemonium • *n* pandemoniu *(n)*, haos *(n)*
panel • *n* panou *(n)*, tblie *(f)*
panic • *v* a se panica
panicky • *adj* panicat
pannier • *n* crinolin
pansy • *n* pansea *(f)*, panselu *(f)*
pantheon • *n* panteon *(n)*
panther • *n* panter neagr, panter *(f)*
pantry • *n* cmar
pants • *n* pantalon
papaya • *n* papaia *(f)*
paper • *n* hârtie *(f)*, document *(n)* • *adj* hârtie
pappus • *n* papus *(n)*
paprika • *n* papric *(f)*, boia *(f)*
parachute • *n* paraut *(f)*
parade • *n* parad *(f)*
paradise • *n* rai *(n)*, paradis
paradox • *n* paradox *(n)*
paraffin • *v* parafina
paragon • *n* pild *(f)*, luceafr *(m)*, model de perfeciune *(n)*
paragraph • *n* paragraf *(n)*
parakeet • *n* peru *(m)*
parallax • *n* paralax
parallel • *adj* paralel
parallelism • *n* paralelism *(n)*, paralelitate *(f)*
paralysis • *n* paralizie *(f)*
paralytic • *n* paralitic *(m)*, paralitic *(f)* • *adj* paralitic
parameter • *n* parametru
parametric • *adj* parametric
paramilitary • *n* paramilitar *(m)*, paramilitar • *adj* paramilitar *(m)*
paramount • *adj* suprem
paramour • *n* amant *(m)*, amanta *(f)*
paraphrase • *v* parafraza, perifraza
paraplegic • *adj* paraplegic *(m)*
parasite • *n* parazit *(m)*, parazit *(f)*
parasitic • *adj* parazitar *(n)*, parazitar *(f)*
parcel • *n* pachet *(n)*, colet *(n)*, parcel *(f)*, lot *(n)*
parchment • *n* pergament *(m)*
pardon • *interj* poftim *(n)*, pardon
parenchyma • *n* parenchim *(n)*
parent • *n* printe
parentage • *n* prini, descenden *(f)*
parish • *n* parohie *(f)*, enorie *(f)*, comun *(f)*
park • *v* parca • *n* parc *(n)*
parliament • *n* parlament *(n)*
parliamentarian • *n* parlamentar *(m)*
parliamentary • *adj* parlamentar *(n)*
parmesan • *n* parmezan *(n)*
parochial • *adj* parohial
parquet • *v* parcheta • *n* parchet *(n)*
parrot • *v* papagaliza • *n* papagal *(m)*
parsimony • *n* cumptare, parcimonie *(f)*

parsley • *n* ptrunjel *(m)*
parsnip • *n* pstârnac *(m)*
part • *n* parte *(f)*
partake • *v* participa
partial • *adj* parial *(n)*, prtinitor *(n)*, neobiectiv *(n)*
participate • *v* participa
particle • *n* particul *(f)*
particular • *adj* particular *(n)*, specific *(n)*, caracteristic *(n)*, special *(n)*
particularity • *n* particularitate *(f)*
parting • *n* crare
partner • *n* partener *(m)*, partener *(f)*
partridge • *n* potârniche *(f)*
party • *v* petrece • *n* parte *(f)*, participant *(m)*, participant *(f)*, partid *(n)*, petrecere *(f)*
pass • *v* trece
passenger • *n* cltor, pasager
passion • *n* pasiune *(f)*, patimi
passionate • *adj* înflcrat *(m)*
passive • *adj* pasiv *(n)*
passport • *n* paaport *(n)*, document de identitate
password • *n* parol *(f)*
past • *n* trecut *(n)* • *adj* trecut *(n)*, trecut *(f)*, trecut
pasta • *n* paste finoase
paste • *v* lipi
pasteurize • *v* pasteuriza
pastiche • *n* pasti *(f)*
pastrami • *n* pastram *(f)*
pasture • *v* pstori, puna, pate • *n* pune
paternal • *adj* patern
path • *n* crare, potec, drum *(n)*, mers *(n)*, curs *(n)*
pathetic • *adj* patetic, emoionant, disperat
pathogen • *n* agent patogen
pathological • *adj* patologic *(n)*
pathologically • *adv* în mod patologic
pathology • *n* patologie *(f)*
patience • *n* rbdare *(f)*
patina • *n* patin *(f)*
patriot • *n* patriot *(m)*
patriotism • *n* patriotism *(n)*
patrol • *n* patrulare
pattern • *n* model *(n)*, ablon *(n)*
pause • *n* pauz
pavement • *n* caldarâm *(n)*
paw • *n* lab *(f)*
pawn • *n* pion *(m)* • *v* amaneta
pawnshop • *n* amanet *(n)*
pay • *v* plti, merita, a fi profitabil
payment • *n* plat *(f)*, pltire
payslip • *n* flutura *(m)*
pea • *n* mazre *(f)*, mazre
peace • *n* pace, pace *(f)*, linite *(f)*, armonie *(f)*
peaceful • *adj* panic
peach • *n* piersic *(m)*, piersic, piersiciu
peacock • *n* pun *(m)*
peafowl • *n* pun *(m)*
peak • *n* vârf, culme
peanut • *n* arahid, alun de pmânt *(f)*, alun american *(f)*
pear • *n* par *(f)*, pr *(m)*
pearl • *n* perl *(f)*, mrgritar *(n)*
peasant • *n* ran *(m)*
pebble • *n* pietri *(m)*, prundí *(m)*
peccary • *n* pecari *(m)*
pectin • *n* pectin *(f)*
pectoral • *adj* pectoral
pecuniary • *adj* monetar *(n)*
pedagogue • *n* pedagog *(m)*, pedagog *(f)*, învtor *(m)*, pedant *(m)*, dogmatic *(m)*
pedantic • *adj* meticulos, pedant
pederast • *n* pederast *(m)*
pederastic • *adj* pederastic
pederasty • *n* pederastie *(f)*
pedestal • *n* piedestal *(n)*
pedestrian • *n* pedestru • *adj* pedestru, pentru pietoni, prozaic *(n)*, comun *(n)*, neinspirat *(n)*
pee • *v* pia, face pipi, urina • *n* pipi *(n)*
pelargonium • *n* pelargonie *(f)*, mucat *(f)*
pelican • *n* pelican *(m)*
pen • *n* stilou *(n)*
penalty • *n* penalizare *(f)*, pedeaps *(f)*
penance • *n* pocin
pencil • *n* creion *(n)*
pendant • *n* pandantiv *(n)*
pendulum • *n* pendul *(n)*
penetrable • *adj* penetrabil *(m)*
penetrate • *v* penetra, ptrunde
penguin • *n* pinguin *(m)*
penicillin • *n* penicilin *(f)*
peninsula • *n* peninsul *(f)*
penis • *n* penis *(m)*, pul
pennant • *n* fanion *(n)*
penultimate • *adj* penultim
peony • *n* bujor *(m)*
people • *n* oameni, lume *(f)*, popor *(n)*, neam *(n)*, naiune *(f)*, popor
pepper • *v* pipera • *n* piper *(m)*, ardei *(m)*
peptide • *n* peptid *(f)*
perceive • *v* realiza, pricepe, înelege
perception • *n* percepie, percepere, discernere, discernmânt, sesizare
perceptive • *adj* perspicace, perceptiv
perch • *n* biban *(m)*
perfect • *adj* perfect, perfect *(n)*, perfectul simplu • *v* perfecta
perfectibility • *n* perfectibilitate *(f)*
perfection • *n* perfeciune *(f)*
performance • *n* performan *(f)*, randa-

ment *(n)*, îndeplinire *(f)*, desvârire *(f)*, realizare *(f)*, realizri, prestaie *(f)*
perhaps • *adv* poate
pericarditis • *n* pericardit *(f)*
pericardium • *n* pericard *(n)*
pericarp • *n* pericarp *(n)*
peridot • *n* olivin
perigee • *n* perigeu *(n)*
perineal • *adj* perineal
perineum • *n* perineu *(n)*
periodical • *n* periodic *(n)*, publicaie periodic *(f)*
peripheral • *adj* periferic *(n)*, secundar *(n)*, neimportant *(n)*, auxiliar *(n)*
periphery • *n* periferie *(f)*
perish • *v* pieri
peristalsis • *n* peristaltic *(f)*, peristaltism *(n)*
peristaltic • *adj* peristaltic
periwinkle • *n* saschiu *(m)*, pervinc *(f)*, litorin *(f)*
permanganate • *n* permanganat
permeability • *n* permeabilitate
permit • *n* permis *(n)*
pernicious • *adj* pernicios, vtmtor, duntor
perpetrate • *v* comite
perpetrator • *n* fpta *(m)*, fptuitor *(m)*
perplexity • *n* perplexitate *(f)*
persecution • *n* persecutare *(f)*
perseverance • *n* perseveren *(f)*
persevere • *v* persevera
persistence • *n* persisten *(f)*
person • *n* persoan *(f)*
personality • *n* personalitate *(f)*
personnel • *n* personal
perspicacious • *adj* perspicace
perspicacity • *n* perspicacitate *(f)*
persuade • *v* convinge
pervade • *v* ptrunde
perverse • *adj* pervers
perversity • *n* perversitate *(f)*
pestiferous • *adj* pestifer, pestilenial, plictisitor, sâcâitor, pislog
pestilence • *n* cium
pestle • *n* pistil *(n)*
pet • *v* mângâia
petal • *n* petal *(f)*
petition • *n* petiie
petrify • *v* petrifica, împietri
petrochemical • *adj* petrochimic *(m)*, petrochimic *(f)*
petty • *adj* mrunt
petunia • *n* petunie *(f)*
pewter • *n* aliaj alb *(n)*
phalarope • *n* notti *(f)*
phallic • *adj* falic
phallus • *n* falus *(n)*
phantom • *n* fantom *(f)*
pharaoh • *n* faraon *(m)*
pharmacist • *n* farmacist *(m)*
pharmacologist • *n* farmacolog *(m)*
pharmacology • *n* farmacologie *(f)*
pharmacy • *n* farmacie *(f)*
phase • *n* faz *(f)*, faze
pheasant • *n* fazan *(m)*
phenomenon • *n* fenomen *(n)*
phenotype • *n* fenotip *(n)*
phenylalanine • *n* fenilalanin *(f)*
phi • *n* fi
philanthropic • *adj* filantropic *(n)*
philanthropy • *n* filantropie *(f)*
philology • *n* filologie *(f)*
philosopher • *n* filozof *(m)*
philosophical • *adj* filozofic
philosophically • *adv* în mod filozofic
philosophy • *n* filozofie *(f)*
phlegmatic • *adj* apos *(n)*, apoasa *(f)*, aposi, apoase
phlox • *n* flox *(m)*
phobia • *n* fobie
phoenix • *n* fenix *(m)*
phone • *n* telefon *(n)*
phoneme • *n* fonem *(n)*
phonetic • *adj* fonetic
phosphate • *v* fosfata • *n* fosfat *(m)*
phosphorus • *n* fosfor *(n)*
photo • *n* fotografie *(f)*, poz *(f)*, foto *(n)*
photograph • *v* fotografia • *n* fotografie *(f)*, poz *(f)*
photography • *n* fotografie *(f)*, fotografia *(f)*
photomontage • *n* fotomontaj
photon • *n* foton *(m)*
photovoltaic • *adj* fotovoltaic
phrase • *n* expresie *(f)*, fraz *(f)*, sintagm *(f)*
phylloxera • *n* filoxer *(f)*
phylum • *n* încrengtur *(f)*
physical • *adj* corporal *(n)*, fizic *(n)*, fiziologic *(n)*, fiziologic *(f)*, fizic *(f)*, material *(n)*, fizic *(m)*
physicist • *n* fizician *(m)*
physiognomy • *n* fiziognomonie *(f)*
physiological • *adj* fiziologic
physiologist • *n* fiziolog
physiology • *n* fiziologie *(f)*
pi • *n* pi *(m)*
pianist • *n* pianist *(m)*, pianist *(f)*
piano • *n* pian *(n)*
picket • *n* pichet *(n)*
pickle • *v* mura
pickpocket • *n* ho de buzunare *(m)*
picture • *n* imagine, fotografie
picturesque • *adj* pitoresc
pie • *n* plcint *(f)*

piece • *n* bucat
pierce • *v* strpunge
pietist • *n* pietist *(m)*
piety • *n* evlavie, pietate
pig • *n* porc *(m)*
pigeon • *n* porumbel *(m)*, porumb *(f)*
piglet • *n* purcel
pigmentation • *n* pigmentare *(f)*
pigsty • *n* cocin *(f)*
pike • *n* tiuc *(f)*
pilaf • *n* pilaf *(n)*
pilgrim • *n* pelerin *(m)*
pillage • *v* prda
pillar • *n* stâlp *(f)*
pillow • *n* pern *(f)*, perin
pilot • *n* pilot
pimp • *n* proxenet *(m)*, pete *(m)*
pimple • *n* co
pin • *n* bold *(n)*, pin *(m)*, contact-pin *(m)*
pincers • *n* clete *(m)*
pinch • *v* pica, ciupi
pine • *n* pin *(m)*, dor *(n)* • *v* dori
pineapple • *n* ananas *(m)*
pink • *n* garoaf, roz • *adj* roz *(f)*, trandafiriu
pioneer • *n* pionier *(m)*
piper • *n* fluierar *(m)*
pipit • *n* fâs *(f)*
piquant • *adj* picant *(m)*
pique • *v* supra, ofensa • *n* pic *(f)*
piranha • *n* pirania *(f)*
pirate • *n* pirat *(m)*
piss • *v* pia
pistol • *n* pistol *(n)*
piston • *n* piston *(n)*
pit • *n* groap *(f)*, sâmbure *(f)*
pitch • *n* rin *(f)*, smoal *(f)*, aruncare, teren, prezentare, pas, inclinare, ton, înlime *(f)*
pitcher • *n* brdac *(n)*
pitchfork • *n* furc *(f)*
pity • *n* compasiune *(f)*, mil *(f)*, comptimire *(f)*, pcat *(n)*
pivot • *n* pivot, pivotare *(f)*, pivotri
pizza • *n* pizza *(f)*
place • *v* pune • *n* loc *(n)*, ptrat *(n)*, pia *(f)*
placenta • *n* placent *(f)*
placental • *n* placentar *(n)* • *adj* placentar
plagiarize • *v* plagia
plague • *n* cium, pest, cium *(f)*, pest *(f)*
plain • *n* es, câmpie
plait • *v* împleti
planar • *adj* planar *(m)*
plane • *v* rabota • *n* rindea *(f)*, platan *(m)*
planet • *n* planet *(f)*
planetarium • *n* planetariu *(n)*
planetary • *adj* planetar
planetoid • *n* planetoid *(m)*
plank • *n* scândur *(f)*
plant • *v* planta • *n* plant *(f)*
plantain • *n* ptlagin *(f)*
plasma • *n* plasm *(f)*
plate • *n* farfurie *(f)*, platou *(n)*, plac *(f)*, plcu de înmatriculare *(f)*, anod *(m)*
plateau • *n* platou *(n)*, podi *(n)*
platform • *n* podium *(n)*, scen *(f)*, estrad *(f)*, peron *(n)*, chei *(n)*
platinum • *n* platin *(f)*
platypus • *n* ornitorinc *(m)*
plausibility • *n* plauzibilitate, plauzibilitate *(f)*
plausible • *adj* plauzibil *(n)*
play • *v* juca, cânta • *n* joc *(f)*
player • *n* juctor *(m)*, juctori, juctoare *(f)*, actor *(m)*, actri *(f)*, interpret *(m)*, solist instrumentist *(m)*, muzician *(m)*, lene *(m)*
playground • *n* teren de joc *(n)*, loc de joac *(n)*
playwright • *n* dramaturg
plaza • *n* pia *(f)*
plead • *v* pleda, implora
pleasant • *adj* plcut *(m)*, plcut *(f)*, savurabil *(n)*, agreabil *(n)*
pleasantness • *n* agreabilitate *(f)*, caracter plcut *(n)*, savurabilitate *(f)*
please • *v* a mulumi, a satisface, a incânta, plcea • *adv* v rog, te rog
pleasure • *n* plcere *(f)*
pleat • *v* plisa
plebeian • *n* plebe
pledge • *v* promite, garanta • *n* legmânt, promisiune
plenary • *adj* plenar
plenipotentiary • *n* plenipoteniar
plenty • *n* belug *(n)*
plethoric • *adj* pletoric
pliability • *n* pliabilitate *(f)*
pliable • *adj* pliabil *(m)*, pliant *(m)*
pliers • *n* clete *(m)*
plosive • *n* oclusiv *(f)*
plot • *v* urzi • *n* subiect *(n)*, complot *(n)*
plough • *v* ara • *n* plug *(f)*
plover • *n* ploier *(m)*, fluierar *(m)*
plowshare • *n* brzdar *(n)*
pluck • *v* trage, scoate, ciupi, smulge, jumuli, peni, scrmna, jefui, prda, jecmni • *n* smulgere *(f)*, jumulire *(f)*, mruntaie *(f)*, perseveren *(f)*
plug • *v* astupa, închide • *n* fi *(f)*, tecr *(n)*, pin *(m)*
plum • *n* prun *(f)*, prun *(m)*, ou • *adj* prun *(f)*
plumbing • *n* evrie
plume • *n* fulg *(m)*, pan *(f)*, mnunchi de pene *(n)*, pmtuf (de pene) *(n)*

plunder • *v* prda, despuia • *n* prad
plural • *n* plural *(n)* • *adj* plural *(f)*
pluralism • *n* pluralism *(n)*
pluralist • *n* pluralist *(m)*
plurality • *n* pluralitate *(f)*
plutocratic • *adj* plutocratic
plutonium • *n* plutoniu *(n)*
pocket • *n* buzunar *(n)*
pocketknife • *n* briceag *(n)*
pococurante • *adj* nepstor, indiferent, insensibil, impasibil
pod • *v* capsul • *n* pstaie *(f)*
poem • *n* poem
poet • *n* poet *(m)*, poet *(f)*
poetess • *n* poet *(f)*
poetic • *adj* poetic
poetry • *n* poezie
pogrom • *n* pogrom *(n)*
poinsettia • *n* steaua Crciunului *(f)*
point • *n* punct *(n)*, punct
poison • *v* otrvi, învenina, intoxica • *n* otrav *(f)*, venin *(n)*
poisonous • *adj* otrvitor, veninos
poker • *n* vtrai *(n)*, poker *(n)*
pole • *n* pol *(m)*
polecat • *n* dihor
police • *n* poliie *(f)*
policeman • *n* poliist *(m)*
politburo • *n* Birou Politic *(n)*
polite • *adj* politico
politeness • *n* politee *(f)*, amabilitate *(f)*, civilitate *(f)*
political • *adj* politic *(n)*, politic *(f)*
politician • *n* politician
politics • *n* politic *(f)*
polka • *n* polc *(f)*
pollen • *n* polen *(n)*
pollination • *n* polenizare *(f)*, polenizaie *(f)*
polonium • *n* poloniu *(n)*
polychromatic • *adj* policromatic
polychrome • *adj* policrom
polyethylene • *n* polietilen *(f)*
polygamy • *n* poligamie
polygon • *n* poligon
polyhedron • *n* poliedru *(n)*, poliedre
polymer • *n* polimer *(m)*
polymerization • *n* polimerizare *(f)*
polynomial • *n* polinom *(n)* • *adj* polinomial *(m)*, polinomic *(m)*
polyphosphate • *n* polifosfat *(m)*
polytheism • *n* politeism *(n)*
pomegranate • *n* rodiu *(m)*, rodier *(m)*, rodie *(f)*
pomelo • *n* pomelo
pomp • *n* pomp *(f)*
pompous • *adj* pompos
pond • *n* balt *(f)*
pontiff • *n* pontif
pontoon • *n* ponton *(n)*, ponton
pony • *n* ponei *(m)*
ponytail • *n* coad
poodle • *n* pudel
poor • *n* sraci, nevoiai • *adj* srac, srman, pauper, mizer, nevoia, amrât *(m)*, biet *(m)*, prost *(m)*, slab *(m)*
popcorn • *n* floricelele de porumb, cocoei, pop-corn
pope • *n* pap *(m)*
poplar • *n* plop *(m)*
poppy • *n* mac *(m)*
popular • *adj* popular *(n)*, agreat *(n)*, popular *(f)*
popularity • *n* popularitate *(f)*
population • *n* populaie *(f)*
porcelain • *n* porelan *(n)*
porcupine • *n* porc spinos, porc-ghimpos *(m)*
pork • *n* carne de porc
pornographer • *n* pornograf *(m)*
pornographic • *adj* pornografic
pornography • *n* pornografie *(f)*
porpoise • *n* marsuin *(m)*
porridge • *n* psat *(n)*, terci *(n)*
port • *n* port *(n)*
portability • *n* portabilitate *(f)*
portion • *n* poriune *(f)*, bucat *(f)*, porie *(f)*, fragment *(n)*, cot-parte *(f)*
portrait • *n* portret *(n)*
position • *v* poziiona • *n* poziie, funcie *(f)*, poziie *(f)*
positional • *adj* poziional
positive • *n* pozitiv grad *(n)*, pozitiv film *(n)* • *adj* pozitiv *(m)*, HIV pozitiv
positivism • *n* pozitivism *(n)*
positron • *n* pozitron *(m)*
possess • *v* avea, deine, poseda
possession • *n* posesie *(f)*, proprietate *(f)*, posesiune *(f)*, proprietate, stpânire *(f)*, drept de proprietate *(n)*, demonism *(n)*, demonie *(f)*
possibility • *n* posibil *(n)*, posibilitate *(f)*
possible • *adj* posibil
post • *n* stâlp *(m)*
postcard • *n* carte potal *(f)*
poster • *n* afi *(n)*, poster *(n)*
posterity • *n* posteritate *(f)*
postmodernism • *n* postmodernism *(m)*
postpone • *v* amâna
postponement • *n* amânare *(f)*
postscript • *n* postscriptum *(n)*
posture • *n* postur *(f)*, inut *(f)*
pot • *n* oal *(f)*
potable • *adj* potabil

potassium • *n* potasiu *(n)*, kaliu *(n)*
potato • *n* cartof *(m)*, barabul *(f)*
potency • *n* poten *(f)*, putere *(f)*
potential • *n* potenial *(n)*
potion • *n* poiune *(f)*
potter • *n* olar *(m)*
pottery • *n* olrie *(f)*, olrit
pound • *n* livr *(f)*, pfund *(m)*, lir *(f)* • *v* pisa, bate
pour • *v* turna
poverty • *n* srcie *(f)*, mizerie *(f)*, paupertate *(f)*
powder • *n* pudr *(f)*, pulbere *(f)*
power • *n* putere *(f)*, for *(f)*, trie *(f)*, electricitate *(f)*, randament *(n)*, poten *(f)*, mrire *(f)*
practicability • *n* practicabilitate
practicable • *adj* practicabil, funcional, folosibil *(n)*, funcionabil *(n)*
practical • *adj* practic
practice • *n* practic *(f)*, aplicare *(f)*, antrenament *(n)*
pragmatic • *adj* pragmatic *(n)*, pragmatic *(f)*
pragmatism • *n* pragmatism *(n)*
praise • *v* luda • *n* laud *(f)*, elogiu *(n)*, glorificare *(f)*, devoiune *(f)*, adorare *(f)*, venerare *(f)*, divinizare *(f)*
praline • *n* pralin *(f)*
praseodymium • *n* praseodim *(n)*
prawn • *n* crevet *(f)*
pray • *v* ruga, închina
prayer • *n* rugciune
preacher • *n* predicator
precede • *v* preceda
precedence • *n* preceden
precedent • *n* precedent
precinct • *n* incint
precious • *adj* preios
precipice • *n* prpstie *(f)*, genune, râp *(f)*
precipitate • *v* accelera, precipita, grbi, condensa, a se depune
precipitation • *n* precipitaie *(f)*
precision • *n* precizie *(f)*, exactitate *(f)*
predicate • *n* predicat *(n)* • *v* (a) predica
predict • *v* prezice
predictability • *n* previzibilitate *(f)*, anticipabilitate *(f)*
predictable • *adj* predictibil *(n)*, anticipabil *(n)*, previzibil *(n)*
prediction • *n* predicie *(f)*, previziune *(f)*, prevestire *(f)*
predilection • *n* predilecie *(f)*
predisposition • *n* predispoziie *(f)*
prefecture • *n* prefectur
prefer • *v* prefera
preferably • *adv* (în mod) preferabil, (în manier) preferabil
preference • *n* preferin *(f)*, preferin, 'preferat *(m)*, preferat *(f)*
prefix • *n* prefix *(n)*
pregnancy • *n* graviditate
pregnant • *adj* gravid *(f)*, însrcinat *(f)*, boroas *(f)*, pregnant *(m)*
prehistoric • *adj* preistoric
prejudice • *v* prejudicia, duna • *n* prejudecat *(f)*, prejudiciu *(n)*, daun *(f)*
prejudiced • *adj* prejudiciat *(n)*, dunat *(n)*
preliminary • *adj* introductiv *(n)*, preliminar *(n)*, pregtitor *(n)*
prematurely • *adv* prea devreme, în mod prematur, înainte de vreme
premeditated • *adj* premeditat *(m)*, deliberat *(m)*
premise • *n* premis *(f)*
prenatal • *adj* prenatal, de pân la natere
prenuptial • *adj* prenupial *(m)*, înainte de nunt
preparation • *n* preparare *(f)*, pregtire *(f)*, preparat *(n)*
preparatory • *adj* pregtitor *(m)*, preliminar *(m)*, preparator *(m)*
prepare • *v* prepara, pregti
preponderance • *n* preponderen *(f)*
preposition • *n* prepoziie *(f)*
prepuce • *n* prepu *(n)*
preschool • *adj* precolar *(n)*, precolar *(f)*
prescribe • *v* prescrie
prescription • *n* prescripie *(f)*, recomandare *(f)*, reet *(f)*
prescriptive • *adj* prescriptiv *(n)*
presence • *n* prezen *(f)*
present • *adj* prezent *(n)*
presentation • *n* prezentare *(f)*
preservative • *n* conservant *(m)*
preserve • *v* proteja, întreine
preside • *v* prezida
president • *n* preedinte *(f)*, preedinte *(m)*
pressure • *n* presiune *(f)*
presume • *v* presupune
presumption • *n* presupunere *(f)*, prezumie *(f)*
pretend • *v* preface, pretinde
pretension • *n* pretenie, preteniozitate *(f)*
pretentious • *adj* pretenios
pretty • *adj* drgu *(m)*, drgu *(f)* • *adv* cam
pretzel • *v* covrigel *(m)*, covrig *(m)*
prevalent • *adj* prevalent, preponderent
prevention • *n* prevenire, anticipare, preîntâmpinare
prey • *n* prad
price • *n* pre *(n)*
prick • *n* pula
prickle • *n* spin *(m)*
prickly • *adj* iritabil

pride • *n* îngâmfare *(f)*, mândrie *(f)*, trufie, orgoliu *(n)*
priest • *n* preot
primarily • *adv* în primul rând, înainte de toate, în principal
primitive • *adj* primitiv
primitivism • *n* primitivism *(n)*, primitivitate *(f)*
primrose • *n* primul *(f)*, ciuboica-cucului *(f)*
prince • *n* prin
princess • *n* prines *(f)*
principal • *n* director *(m)* • *adj* principal
principality • *n* principat *(n)*
print • *v* Imprima
printer • *n* imprimator *(m)*, tipograf *(m)*, imprimant *(f)*
printing • *n* tipar, tipografiere, imprimerie, tipritur
priority • *n* prioritate
priory • *n* priorat *(n)*
prism • *n* prism *(f)*, prisme
prismatoid • *n* prismatoid
prison • *n* închisoare, pucrie, temni
prisoner • *n* pucria *(m)*
pristine • *adj* virgin
privet • *n* lemn-câinesc *(n)*
privilege • *n* privilegiu *(n)*, drept *(n)*
prize • *n* premiu *(n)*
probability • *n* probabilitate *(f)*
probable • *adj* probabil *(n)*
probably • *adv* probabil
problem • *n* problem *(f)*
procedure • *n* procedur *(f)*, procedeu *(n)*, funciune *(f)*, funcie *(f)*, subrutin *(f)*
proceed • *v* proceda
process • *n* proces *(n)*, procese
processing • *n* prelucrare *(f)*, procesare *(f)*
processor • *n* procesor
procrastinate • *v* amâna, trgna, procrastina
procrastination • *n* amânare *(f)*
procreate • *v* procrea
prodigious • *adj* enorm *(n)*, gigantic, prodigios, vast, neobinuit *(n)*
produce • *v* produce, face
product • *n* produs *(n)*, producie *(f)*
production • *n* producere, producie, reprezentare, înscenare
productive • *adj* productiv, fertil, rodnic
profanity • *n* înjurtur *(f)*
profession • *n* profesiune *(f)*, jurmânt *(n)*, legmânt *(n)*, profesie, meserie
professional • *n* profesional *(m)* • *adj* profesional *(n)*, profesionist *(n)*
professionalism • *n* profesionalism *(n)*
professionally • *adv* profesional, în mod profesional
professor • *n* profesor *(m)*, profesoar *(f)*
professorial • *adj* de profesor, profesoral
profit • *v* profit *(n)*, profituri, profita, beneficia • *n* câtig *(n)*, profit *(f)*
profound • *adj* profund, care e în adânc, adânc
profusion • *n* profuziune *(f)*, abunden *(f)*, extravagan *(f)*
progenitor • *n* strmo *(m)*, strbun *(m)*, predecesor *(n)*, precursor *(n)*
prognathous • *adj* proeminent
program • *n* program
programmer • *n* programator, programatoare *(f)*
programming • *n* programare
progress • *v* progresa
progressive • *adj* progresist, progresist *(f)*, avansat *(n)*, înaintat *(n)*, progresiv *(n)*, de progres, progresiv
prohibit • *v* interzice
project • *n* proiect *(n)*
projectile • *n* proiectil *(n)*
projection • *n* proiectare *(f)*, proiecie
proline • *n* prolin *(f)*
prolong • *v* prelungi, lungi, alungi, amâna
prolonged • *adj* prelung, îndelungat
promethium • *n* promeiu *(n)*
prominence • *n* proeminen *(f)*
prominent • *adj* proeminent
promise • *v* promite • *n* promisiune *(f)*, legmânt
promoter • *n* promotor
prompt • *adj* rapid, prompt, punctual
promulgate • *v* promulga
promulgation • *n* promulgare *(f)*
pronghorn • *n* antilocapr *(f)*
pronoun • *n* pronume *(n)*
pronounce • *v* pronuna
pronunciation • *n* pronunie *(f)*, pronunare *(f)*, pronunie
proof • *n* prob, dovad
propeller • *n* elice *(f)*
proper • *adj* propriu
property • *n* proprietate *(f)*, posesie *(f)*, drept de proprietate *(n)*, posesiune *(f)*, însuire *(f)*, atribut *(n)*, caracter *(n)*
prophesy • *v* profetiza, profei, prezice
prophet • *n* proroc *(m)*
proportional • *adj* proporional *(n)*, proporional *(f)*
proposal • *n* propunere *(f)*
propose • *v* propune, sugestiona, pei, a cere în cstorie
proposition • *n* afirmaie *(f)*, declaraie, propunere *(f)*, sugestie *(f)*

proprietary • *adj* proprietar, de proprietate
proprietor • *n* proprietar *(m)*
propriety • *n* decen *(f)*, cuviin, corectitudine *(f)*
propulsion • *n* propulsare *(f)*, propulsie *(f)*
proscribe • *v* interzice
prosody • *n* prosodie *(f)*, metric *(f)*
prosperity • *n* prosperitate *(f)*
prostate • *n* prostat *(f)*
prosthesis • *n* protez *(f)*, proteze
prostitute • *v* prostitua • *n* prostituat *(f)*, curv *(f)*, târf *(f)*
protactinium • *n* protactiniu *(n)*
protect • *v* ocroti
protected • *adj* protejat
protection • *n* protejare *(f)*, ocrotire *(f)*, protecie *(f)*
protective • *n* protector *(m)*
protector • *n* protector *(n)*, protectoare *(f)*
protein • *n* protein *(f)*
protest • *v* protesta
protocol • *n* protocol *(n)*
proton • *n* proton *(m)*
prototype • *n* prototip *(n)*, prim-model *(n)*
prove • *v* proba, dovedi, stabili, arta
proverb • *n* proverb *(n)*, proverbe
province • *n* provincie
provision • *n* provizie *(f)*
prow • *n* pror *(f)*, prov *(f)*
proximity • *n* proximitate *(f)*, vecintate *(f)*
prude • *n* pudic *(m)*
prudence • *n* pruden *(f)*
prune • *n* prun uscat *(f)* • *v* cur, emonda
prurience • *n* lascivitate *(f)*
prurient • *adj* lasciv, libidinos
psalm • *n* psalm *(m)*
psychedelic • *adj* psihedelic
psychiatrist • *n* psihiatru *(m)*, medic psihiatru *(m)*
psychiatry • *n* psihiatrie *(f)*
psychoanalysis • *n* psihoanaliz *(f)*
psychological • *adj* psihologic *(n)*
psychology • *n* psihologie *(f)*
psychometry • *n* psihometrie
psychosis • *n* psihoz *(f)*
ptarmigan • *n* coco polar *(m)*, ptarmigan *(m)*, potârniche alb *(f)*
ptomaine • *n* ptomain *(f)*
pub • *n* cârcium *(f)*
publication • *n* publicare *(f)*, publicaie *(f)*, revist *(f)*
puddle • *n* balt *(f)*
puffin • *n* furtunar *(m)*
puku • *n* puku *(m)*
pull • *v* trage
pullet • *n* puic *(f)*
pulley • *n* scripete *(m)*
pulp • *n* pulp, pulp *(f)*
pulpit • *n* amvon *(m)*
pulsar • *n* pulsar *(m)*
pulsate • *v* pulsa
puma • *n* pum *(f)*
pumice • *n* piatr ponce
pump • *v* pompa • *n* pomp, pompare, pomp *(f)*, pantof cu toc
pumpkin • *n* bostan *(m)*, dovleac *(m)*, dovleac
pun • *n* calambur, joc de cuvinte
punctuality • *n* punctualitate *(f)*
punctuation • *n* punctuaie *(f)*
punish • *v* pedepsi
punishable • *adj* penalizabil *(n)*, pedepsibil *(n)*, penalizabil *(f)*
punishment • *n* pedepsire *(f)*, pedeaps *(f)*, penalizare, pedeaps punitiv *(f)*
punitive • *adj* punitiv *(m)*
pup • *n* cel *(m)*, celu *(m)*, novice *(f)*
pupa • *n* pup *(f)*
pupil • *n* elev *(m)*, eleva *(f)*, pupil *(f)*
puppet • *n* ppu *(f)*, marionet *(f)*
puppy • *n* cel *(m)*, celu *(m)*, raton *(m)*
purchase • *v* cumpra
pure • *adj* pur, curat *(n)*, cast
purgatory • *n* purgatoriu *(n)*
purification • *n* purificare *(f)*, curire *(f)*
purity • *n* puritate *(f)*
purpose • *n* scop *(n)*, rost, el *(n)*, int *(f)*, obiectiv *(n)*, determinare *(f)*, subiect *(n)*, tem *(f)*, cauz, motiv *(n)*, rost *(n)*
purpure • *adj* purpuriu
purr • *v* toarce • *n* tors *(n)*
purslane • *n* agurijoar *(f)*, iarb-gras *(f)*, portulac *(f)*
pursue • *v* urmri
pursuit • *n* vântoare
pus • *n* puroi *(n)*
push • *v* împinge, apsa
pussy • *adj* purulent, supurant • *n* pisic *(f)*, pizd *(f)*, psric *(f)*
pustule • *n* pustul *(f)*
put • *v* pune
putrid • *adj* putred
pygmy • *n* pigmeu *(m)*, pitic *(m)*
pyramid • *n* piramid *(f)*
pyre • *n* rug *(n)*
pyrite • *n* pirit *(f)*
python • *n* piton *(m)*, arpe piton *(m)*

Q

quack • *v* mci • *n* mac, mac-mac, mcit *(n)*, mcnit *(n)*, mcitur *(f)*
quadrature • *n* cvadratur *(f)*
quadrilateral • *n* patrulater, cadrilater • *adj* cvadrilateral *(m)*
quadriplegia • *n* tetraplegie *(f)*, cvadriplegie *(f)*
quadriplegic • *n* tetraplegic *(m)*, cvadriplegic *(m)*
quadruple • *adj* cvadruplu
quail • *n* prepelia
qualification • *n* calificare *(f)*
qualified • *adj* calificat, competent
qualitative • *adj* calitativ *(n)*
quality • *n* calitate *(f)*
qualm • *n* grea *(f)*, scrupul *(n)*, compunciune *(f)*
quantify • *v* cuantifica
quantity • *n* cantitate *(f)*, mulime *(f)*, mare cantitate *(f)*
quarrel • *v* certa • *n* ceart *(f)*
quarry • *n* carier *(f)*, vânat *(n)*
quarter • *n* sfert, ptrime *(f)*, ptrar *(n)*, trimestru *(n)*
quartet • *n* cvartet
quartz • *n* cuar *(n)*
quaver • *n* tremur, tremolo
quay • *n* chei
queen • *n* regin *(f)*, dam *(f)*
question • *v* întreba • *n* întrebare *(f)*
queue • *n* coad *(f)*
quick • *adj* repede, rapid, iute, vioi, vioaie, sprinten, ager, energic, violent, aprig, înfocat, învpiat
quickly • *adv* rapid, repede
quicksilver • *n* mercur *(n)*, argint viu *(n)*, hidrargir
quiet • *adj* încet, tcut
quince • *n* gutuie *(f)*, gutui *(m)*
quinsy • *n* anghin *(f)*, amigdalit, gâlci
quintet • *n* cvintet *(n)*, cvintet
quirk • *n* particularitate *(f)*
quiver • *n* tolb *(f)*
quorum • *n* cvorum *(m)*
quotation • *n* citat *(n)*
quotidian • *n* cotidian *(n)* • *adj* cotidian *(m)*, de fiece zi, cotidian *(n)*, obinuit *(n)*, banal *(m)*

R

rabbi • *n* rabin *(m)*
rabbit • *n* iepure, iepure de vizuin
rabid • *adj* turbat
rabies • *n* turbare *(f)*, rabie *(f)*
raccoon • *n* raton *(m)*, ursule spltor *(m)*
race • *n* curs *(f)*, curent de ap *(m)*, ambalare *(f)*, supraturare *(f)*, ras *(f)*, neam *(n)*
racehorse • *n* cal de curse *(m)*, cai de curse
raceme • *n* racem *(n)*
rachis • *n* rahis *(n)*
racing • *n* curs
racism • *n* rasism *(n)*
racist • *n* rasist *(n)*, rasist *(f)*
racket • *n* rachet *(f)*
radar • *n* radar *(n)*
radial • *adj* radial *(m)*
radiance • *n* strlucire *(f)*, lucire *(f)*, iradiere *(f)*, radian *(f)*, emitan *(f)*
radiate • *v* iradia, ilumina
radiation • *n* radiaie *(f)*
radiator • *n* radiator, calorifer *(n)*
radical • *adj* de rdcin, rdcinal
radicchio • *n* radicchio *(m)*
radio • *n* radio, radio *(n)*, radioreceptor *(n)*, aparat de radio *(n)*
radioactive • *adj* radioactiv *(m)*, radioactiv *(f)*
radioactivity • *n* radioactivitate
radish • *n* ridiche, ridiche *(f)*
radium • *n* radiu *(n)*
radon • *n* radon *(n)*
raft • *n* plut *(f)*
rafter • *n* cprior *(m)*
raftsman • *n* pluta *(m)*
rag • *n* cârp *(f)*, zdrean *(f)*, cârpitur *(f)*, vechitur *(f)*
rage • *v* turba • *n* mânie, furie
rail • *n* in *(f)*
railing • *n* balustrada, mana curenta
railway • *n* cale ferat *(f)*, reea feroviar *(f)*, ci ferate
rain • *v* ploua • *n* ploaie *(f)*
rainbow • *n* curcubeu *(m)*, spectru *(n)*, varietate *(f)*, multitudine *(f)* • *adj* multicolor, policrom
raincoat • *n* hain de ploaie *(f)*, impermeabil *(n)*, mant de ploaie *(f)*, trenci *(n)*
raindrop • *n* pictur de ploaie

rainy • *adj* ploios
raisin • *n* stafid *(f)*
rake • *n* grebl *(f)*
ram • *n* berbec *(m)*, arete *(m)*
ramie • *n* ramie *(f)*, ramia *(f)*
rancid • *adj* rânced
rancor • *n* ranchiun *(f)*, pic *(f)*, rancoare *(f)*
rank • *adj* rânced
ransack • *v* prda
rapacity • *n* rapacitate *(f)*
rape • *v* rpi, viola • *n* rpire *(f)*, viol *(n)*
rapid • *adj* repede, rapid
rapt • *adj* fascinat
rapture • *n* rpirea
rare • *adj* rar, rarefiat
rarely • *adv* rar, rareori
rareness • *n* raritate
rarity • *n* raritate *(f)*, rariti
rascal • *n* miel, ticlos
raspberry • *n* zmeur *(m)*, zmeur *(f)*, zmeuriu • *adj* zmeuriu
rational • *adj* raional *(n)*
rationalism • *n* raionalism
rattlesnake • *n* arpe cu clopoei
ravage • *v* prda • *n* ravagiu *(n)*, devastare *(f)*
raven • *n* corb, rapacitate *(f)*, prad *(f)* • *adj* corbiu
ravine • *n* raven *(f)*, râp *(f)*
raw • *adj* crud
ray • *n* raz *(f)*
razor • *n* brici *(n)*
razorbill • *n* alc *(f)*, pinguin nordic *(m)*
reach • *v* extinde, alungi, prelungi, întinde, lungi, aterne, atinge, ajunge, nimeri
reactance • *n* reactan
reactant • *n* reactiv *(m)*, reactant, reactani
reaction • *n* reacia *(f)*, reacie *(m)*
read • *v* citi, lectura, a putea citi, a lectura, a fi citit, a fi lecturat • *n* citire *(f)*, lecturare, intonare *(f)*
real • *adj* real, adevrat, actual *(n)*, real *(n)*, adevrat *(n)*, prea, super
realism • *n* realism
realistic • *adj* realist
reality • *n* realitate *(f)*
realize • *v* realiza
really • *adv* pe bune
reap • *v* secera
rearrangement • *n* rearanjare *(f)*
reason • *n* raiune
reasonableness • *n* raiune
rebuke • *v* mustra, certa
recall • *v* aminti
recapitulate • *v* recapitula
recede • *v* retrage
receivable • *adj* recepionabil *(m)*
receive • *v* primi, recepiona
recent • *adj* recent
recently • *adv* recent, de curând, în ultimul timp
receptive • *adj* receptiv *(n)*, primitor *(n)*
recess • *n* vacan *(f)*, pauz
recession • *n* retragere *(f)*, recesiune, recesie *(f)*, îndeprtare, recesiune *(f)*
recipe • *n* reet *(f)*
reciprocal • *adj* reciproc, reciproc *(f)*, invers *(m)*
reciprocally • *adv* (în mod) reciproc, (în manier) reciproc
reciprocity • *n* reciprocitate *(f)*
recklessness • *n* neglijen *(f)*
recognition • *n* recunoatere *(f)*, recunotin *(f)*, apreciere *(f)*
recognize • *v* recunoate
recognized • *adj* conoscut
recollection • *n* reamintire *(f)*, amintire
reconcile • *v* reconcilia, împca
reconciliation • *n* reconciliere *(f)*, împcare *(f)*
reconnaissance • *n* recunoatere *(f)*, cercetare *(f)*
reconstruct • *v* reconstrui, restaura
reconstructed • *adj* reconstruit, recldit
reconstruction • *n* reconstrucie *(f)*, reconstruire, restaurare *(f)*, restauraie, reconstituire *(f)*
record • *n* disc *(n)*, discuri, disc-audio *(n)*, disc de gramofon *(n)*, disc-video *(n)*, record *(n)*, recorduri
recover • *v* recupera
recovery • *n* recuperare *(f)*
recreate • *v* recrea
rectangle • *n* dreptunghi
rectifier • *n* redresor *(n)*
rectify • *v* rectifica, corecta
rectitude • *n* rectitudine *(f)*, echitate *(f)*, rigoare *(f)*
rector • *n* paroh *(m)*, rector *(m)*
recurrence • *n* repetare *(f)*, reîncepere *(f)*, reîntoarcere *(f)*
recurrent • *adj* recurent *(m)*, reînceput *(m)*, repetat *(m)*
recycling • *n* reciclare *(f)*
red • *n* rou • *adj* rou
reddish • *adj* rocat
redeemable • *adj* rambursabil *(m)*, restituibil *(n)*, reformabil *(n)*, reformabili
redoubt • *n* redut
redpoll • *n* inri *(f)*, intar *(m)*
redress • *v* redresa
redshank • *n* fluierar-cu-picioare-roii *(m)*
reduce • *v* reduce, diminua, micora

reduced • *adj* redus *(n)*, micorat *(n)*
reducible • *adj* reductibil, micorabil, diminuabil
redwing • *n* mierl *(f)*
reed • *n* stuf
reef • *n* recif *(n)*
reference • *n* referin *(f)*, surs de referin *(f)*
refinement • *n* rafinare *(f)*, rafinaj *(n)*, rafinament *(n)*, finee *(f)*, delicatee *(f)*
reflecting • *n* reflectare *(f)*, chibzuire *(f)*
reflection • *n* reflectare *(f)*, reflecie *(f)*, reflexie *(f)*
reflective • *adj* reflectiv
reflector • *n* reflector *(n)*
reflexive • *adj* reflexiv, reflexiv *(n)*
reform • *n* reform
refraction • *n* refracie *(f)*
refractometer • *n* refractometru *(n)*
refresh • *v* împrospta
refrigerate • *v* refrigera
refrigerator • *n* frigider
refund • *n* rambursare
refute • *v* refuta
regal • *adj* regal *(n)*, regal *(f)*
regale • *v* ospta
regent • *n* regent *(m)*
regicide • *n* regicid *(n)*
regiment • *n* regiment *(n)*
region • *n* regiune
register • *v* înregistra • *n* registru *(n)*, registru, înregistrare *(f)*
registered • *adj* înregistrat *(m)*
regress • *v* regresa
regret • *n* regret *(n)*
regulation • *n* reglare *(f)*, regul *(f)*, reglementare *(f)*, regulament *(n)*, regulament
reign • *v* domni
reimburse • *v* rambursa
reimbursement • *n* rambursare
reindeer • *n* ren *(m)*
reinstall • *v* reinstala
reinvigorate • *v* revigora
reject • *v* respinge, refuza
rejoice • *v* bucura
relapse • *v* recidiva
related • *adj* relaionat *(n)*
relation • *n* relaie, legtur *(f)*, relatare *(f)*, povestire *(f)*, narare *(f)*
relationship • *n* relaie *(f)*, legtur *(f)*, raport *(n)*, asociere, rudenie *(f)*, înrudire *(f)*, relaie *(n)*
relative • *adj* relativ
relatively • *adv* în mod relativ
relativism • *n* relativism
relativity • *n* relativitate *(f)*
relax • *v* relaxa, destinde, desface
relaxation • *n* relaxare *(f)*, repaus *(n)*
relaxed • *adj* relaxat *(m)*
relay • *n* releu *(n)*, tafet *(f)*
relent • *v* a se înmuia
relentless • *adj* sever
relevance • *n* relevan *(f)*, pertinen *(f)*
relevant • *adj* relevant *(m)*, pertinent *(m)*
reliability • *n* fiabilitate *(f)*
reliable • *adj* fiabil *(m)*, sigur *(m)*
relic • *n* relicv *(f)*, moate
relief • *n* uurare *(f)*, alinare *(f)*, asisten umanitar *(f)*, ajutor umanitar *(n)*, relief *(n)*, basorelief *(n)*, altorelief *(n)*
religion • *n* religie *(f)*
reliquary • *n* relicvariu *(n)*
reluctance • *n* repulsie *(f)*, ezitare *(f)*, codire *(f)*, reluctan *(f)*
reluctant • *adj* prevztor
remain • *v* rmâne
remand • *n* arest preventiv *(m)*
remark • *n* remarc *(f)*, observaie *(f)*
remarkable • *adj* remarcabil *(m)*, notabil *(m)*
remember • *v* aminti
remembrance • *n* reamintire *(f)*, memorie *(f)*, amintire *(f)*
reminiscence • *n* reamintire *(f)*, reminiscen *(f)*, amintire *(f)*
remodel • *v* remodela
remorse • *n* remucare *(f)*, regret *(n)*
remove • *v* scoate, îndeprta
remuneration • *n* remuneraie *(f)*, rambursare *(f)*, salariu *(n)*, retribuie *(f)*, plat *(f)*, compensaie *(f)*, despgubire *(f)*
renew • *v* înnoi, reînnoi, renova
rennet • *n* cheag
renounce • *v* lepda, renuna, abandona
renown • *n* renume, faim *(f)*
renowned • *adj* renumit, faimos
rent • *v* închiria, arenda • *n* chirie *(f)*, locaiune *(f)*, rent *(f)*
repair • *v* repara
reparation • *n* reparare, reparaie
repatriation • *n* repatriere
repellent • *adj* respingtor *(m)*, repulsiv *(m)*, antipatic *(m)*, antipatic *(f)*
repetition • *n* repetare *(f)*, repetiie *(f)*, repetare
replace • *v* înlocui, substitui
replica • *n* copie *(f)*, copii, replic *(f)*, reproducere *(f)*
replication • *n* copiere *(f)*, copieri, duplicare *(f)*, reproducere *(f)*, replicare *(f)*
reply • *v* rspunde
report • *v* reporta
repose • *n* repaus
represent • *v* reprezenta
representable • *adj* reprezentabil *(m)*

representation • *n* reprezentare *(f)*, înfiare *(f)*, închipuire *(f)*
representative • *adj* reprezentativ *(n)*
reprimand • *v* mustra
reproach • *v* reproa, imputa • *n* repro
reprobate • *v* reproba
reproduce • *v* reproduce
reproduction • *n* reproducere *(f)*, reproducie *(f)*, duplicat *(n)*, duplicare
reproductive • *adj* reproductiv *(m)*, reproductor *(m)*
reprove • *v* mustra, certa
reptile • *n* reptil
republic • *n* republic *(f)*
republican • *adj* republican *(m)*, republican *(f)*
republicanism • *n* republicanism *(n)*
repugnant • *adj* repugnant
repulsion • *n* repulsie *(f)*, dezgust *(n)*, respingere *(f)*, recul *(n)*
reputable • *adj* reputabil *(m)*
reputation • *n* faim
request • *v* cere, ruga • *n* cerere *(f)*
requirement • *n* condiie *(f)*, cerin *(f)*
rerun • *v* relua
research • *n* cercetare *(f)*
resemble • *v* semna
resentment • *n* resentiment *(n)*
residence • *n* reedin *(f)*, reziden *(f)*
resident • *n* rezident *(m)*
resin • *n* rin *(f)*
resinous • *adj* rinos
resist • *v* rezista
resistance • *n* rezistare *(f)*, opunere *(f)*, rezisten
resistant • *adj* rezistent *(n)*, rezistent *(f)*
resistible • *adj* rezistibil
resoluteness • *n* hotrâre *(f)*, fermitate *(f)*, neovin *(f)*, decizie *(f)*
resolve • *v* rezolva, conchide, hotrî
resonance • *n* rezonan *(f)*
resonate • *v* rsuna
resorb • *v* resorbi
resound • *v* rsuna
resource • *n* resurs *(f)*, resurse
respect • *v* respecta • *n* respect
respectability • *n* respectabilitate *(f)*
respectable • *adj* respectabil *(m)*
respectful • *adj* respectos *(m)*
respond • *v* rspunde
responsibility • *n* responsabilitate *(f)*
responsible • *adj* responsabil *(m)*
responsive • *adj* sensibil *(n)*, simitor *(n)*, rspundent *(n)*
rest • *n* odihn, repaus, pace *(f)*, odihn *(f)*, semn de pauz *(n)*, rest *(n)* • *v* odihni, repauza
restaurant • *n* restaurant *(n)*
restless • *adj* nelinitit *(n)*, agitat *(n)*, agitat *(f)*
restlessness • *n* neastâmpr *(n)*, nerbdare *(f)*, înfrigurare *(f)*, nelinite *(f)*, agitaie *(f)*
restrain • *v* reine, înfrâna, a ine închis, , a deine, restrânge, opri, împiedica, îngrdi
restricted • *adj* restricionat *(n)*
restriction • *n* restricie *(f)*
restrictive • *adj* restrictiv
result • *n* rezultat *(n)*
resultant • *adj* rezultant
resurrection • *n* reînviere *(f)*, înviere *(f)*
resuscitate • *v* reanima, reînvia, resuscita, renate
resuscitation • *n* reanimare *(f)*, resuscitare, reînviere
retail • *n* vânzare cu amnuntul *(f)*, vânzare cu bucata
retailer • *n* vânztor cu amnuntul *(m)*, vânztor cu bucata *(m)*, vînztor detaliist *(m)*
retain • *v* reine
retention • *n* reinere *(f)*, retenie *(f)*, memorare *(f)*, memorie *(f)*, amintire *(f)*
retina • *n* retin *(f)*
retort • *n* retort
retract • *v* retrage, retracta, dezice
retribution • *n* rzbunare
retrospective • *adj* retrospectiv
return • *v* întoarce, restitui, înapoia, returna • *n* reîntoarcere *(f)*, înapoiere *(f)*, revenire *(f)*
revelation • *n* revelaie *(f)*, revelare *(f)*
revenge • *v* rzbuna • *n* rzbunare *(f)*
reverse • *v* inversa, rsturna, bascula, întoarce, revoca, abroga, anula • *n* spate, revers *(n)*, dos *(n)*, verso *(n)*, contrariu *(n)* • *adj* invers *(n)*, rsturnat *(n)*, invers *(f)*
reviewer • *n* recenzent *(m)*
revocation • *n* revocare
revolt • *v* revolta • *n* revolt
revolution • *n* revoluie *(f)*
revolutionary • *n* revoluionar • *adj* revoluionar
revolver • *n* revolverul
rhea • *n* nandu *(m)*
rhenium • *n* reniu *(n)*
rheum • *n* urdoare
rhinitis • *n* rinit *(f)*
rhinoceros • *n* rinocer *(m)*
rhodium • *n* rodiu *(n)*
rhododendron • *n* rododendron *(m)*
rhombus • *n* romb
rhubarb • *n* rubarb *(f)*, revent *(m)*
rhyme • *v* rima • *n* vers *(n)*, rim *(f)*
rhythm • *n* ritm

rib • *n* coast
ribbon • *n* fund *(f)*
rice • *n* orez, orez *(n)*
rich • *adj* bogat *(m)*, bogat *(f)*, avut *(m)*, avut *(f)*
rickets • *n* rahitism *(n)*
rictus • *n* rictus
rider • *n* clre
ridge • *n* creast *(f)*
ridicule • *v* a batjocori, a ridiculiza
ridiculous • *adj* ridicol *(m)*
ridiculously • *adv* în mod ridicol
rifle • *n* flint *(f)*, puc *(f)*, ghintuit *(f)*
rigging • *n* tachelaj *(n)*
right • *n* drept, dreapta *(f)* • *adj* drept, corectitudine *(f)*, sntos *(m)*, dreapta • *adv* la dreapta, pe dreapta • *interj* e drept, aa-i, nimic de zis, sigur, aa-i, nu-i aa?, i atunci?
right-handed • *n* dreptaci *(m)*
rigid • *adj* rigid, bos, eapn
rime • *n* brum
ring • *n* inel *(n)*, inel *(f)* • *v* suna, bate
ripe • *adj* copt, matur
ripen • *v* coace
rise • *v* rsri
risk • *v* risca • *n* risc *(n)*
risotto • *n* rizoto *(n)*
rite • *n* ritual *(n)*, rit *(n)*
rival • *n* rival
river • *n* râu *(n)*, fluviu *(n)*
riverbed • *n* albie
road • *n* drum *(n)*, cale *(f)*
roadrunner • *n* cucul alergtor *(m)*
roadstead • *n* rad *(f)*
roam • *v* hoinri
roar • *v* urla, rage, mugi, zbiera
roast • *v* frige • *n* friptur *(f)*
rob • *v* fura
robin • *n* gu-roie *(f)*, mcleandru *(m)*
robotics • *n* robotica
robust • *adj* robust *(n)*, puternic *(n)*, vânjos *(n)*, robust *(f)*
robustness • *n* robustee *(f)*, soliditate, vânjoie *(f)*
rock • *n* stânc, roc, stan *(f)* • *v* legna
rocket • *n* rachet *(f)*, rucol *(f)*, aragul *(f)*, ruchet *(f)*
rod • *n* varg, nuia, vergea, b, undi *(f)*
rodent • *n* roztor *(n)*
roe • *n* icre
roebuck • *n* cprior *(m)*
roil • *v* enerva, irita, supra
roll • *n* ruliu *(n)*
romanticism • *n* romantism
roof • *n* acoperi *(n)*, acopermânt *(n)*
roofer • *n* acoperitor *(m)*
rook • *n* cioar de semntur *(f)*, turn *(n)*
room • *n* spaiu, loc *(n)*, camer *(f)*, odaie *(f)*, încpere *(f)*
rooster • *n* coco *(m)*
root • *n* rdcin *(f)*, rdcin de dinte *(f)*, rdcin dentar (dental) *(f)*, rdcin de pr *(f)*
rootstock • *n* portaltoi
rope • *n* frânghie *(f)*, coard, funie
rosary • *n* mtnii
rose • *n* trandafir *(m)*, roz *(f)*, rozacee *(f)* • *adj* roz
roselle • *n* trandafirul de Abisinia *(m)*
rosemary • *n* rozmarin *(m)*
rot • *v* putrezi, descompune
rotate • *v* roti
rotor • *n* rotor *(n)*
rotten • *adj* putred
rouge • *v* farda
rough • *adj* dur, aspru
roughness • *n* asprime *(f)*, asperitate
round • *adj* rotund
routine • *n* rutin *(f)*
row • *n* rând *(n)*, linie *(f)* • *v* vâsli, certa
rowan • *n* scoru-de-munte *(m)*, scoru-psresc *(m)*
rowdiness • *n* debandad
royal • *adj* regal *(m)*, regal *(f)*
royalty • *n* regalitate *(f)*, monarhie *(f)*
rub • *v* freca
rubber • *n* cauciuc *(n)*, cauciucuri
rubidium • *n* rubidiu *(n)*
ruble • *n* rubl *(f)*, *(f)*
ruby • *n* rubin • *adj* rubiniu
rudder • *n* cârm *(f)*
ruddy • *adj* rocat
rue • *n* regret *(n)*, compasiune *(f)*, virnan *(m)*, rut *(f)*
rufous • *adj* armiu
ruin • *v* strica • *n* ruin *(f)*
rule • *v* domni • *n* regul
ruler • *n* rigl *(f)*, linie *(f)*
ruling • *n* conducere
rum • *n* rom *(m)*
ruminant • *n* rumegtoare *(f)*
ruminate • *v* rumega
rumination • *n* rumega
rumor • *n* zvon *(n)*, zvonuri
run • *v* alerga, fugi, conduce, concura • *n* fug, rut, flux, golf, tiraj, pas, trap, arc, cârm
rung • *n* treapt
runner • *n* alergtor *(m)*
rupture • *n* ruptur
rural • *adj* rural, rnesc, câmpenesc
rush • *n* papur *(f)*, pipirig *(m)*
rust • *v* rugini, oxida • *n* rugin *(f)*, ruginiu
rustle • *n* freamt
rusty • *adj* ruginit, rocat

rutabaga • *n* nap suedez *(m)*
ruthenium • *n* ruteniu *(n)*
rutherfordium • *n* rutherfordiu *(n)*
rye • *n* secar *(f)*

S

sable • *n* zibelin *(f)*, samur *(m)*, neagr • *adj* negru
sabotage • *n* sabotaj *(n)*, sabotare *(f)*, subminare *(f)*
sack • *v* prda • *n* sac
sacred • *adj* sacru
sacrifice • *v* sacrifica, jertfi • *n* sacrificiu *(n)*, jertf *(f)*
sacrosanct • *adj* sacrosanct
sad • *adj* trist, trist *(f)*, abtut *(n)*, abtut *(f)*
sadden • *v* întrista, mâhni
saddle • *n* a *(f)*
sadism • *n* sadism *(n)*
sadistic • *adj* sadic *(n)*
sadness • *n* tristee *(f)*
safeguard • *v* salvgarda
safety • *n* siguran *(f)*, securitate *(f)*
safflower • *n* ofrna *(m)*, ofrnel *(m)*
saffron • *n* ofran *(m)* • *adj* ofrniu
saga • *n* legend nordic
sage • *adj* înelept • *n* salvie *(f)*, jale *(f)*
saiga • *n* saiga *(f)*
sail • *n* vel *(f)*, pânz *(f)* • *v* naviga
sailor • *n* marinar, matelot, matroz *(m)*
sainfoin • *n* sparcet *(f)*
saint • *n* sfânt *(m)*, sfânt *(f)*, sânt *(m)*, sânt *(f)*, sânt
sainthood • *n* sfinenie *(f)*, caracter sfânt *(n)*
salad • *n* salat
salamander • *n* salamandr
salami • *n* salam *(n)*
salary • *n* salariu *(n)*
sale • *n* vânzare *(f)*, vindere *(f)*
salesman • *n* vânztor *(m)*
salient • *adj* proeminent
saliva • *n* saliv *(f)*
salmon • *n* somon *(m)*
salt • *v* sra • *n* sare *(f)*
salutation • *n* salut *(n)*
salute • *n* salut *(n)*, salutare *(f)*
salvation • *n* salvare *(f)*
salvo • *n* salv *(f)*
samarium • *n* samariu *(n)*
same • *adj* acelai, la fel
sameness • *n* asemnare perfect *(f)*, identitate, monotonie *(f)*, uniformitate *(f)*
samovar • *n* samovar *(n)*
sample • *n* mostr *(f)*
samurai • *n* samurai *(m)*
sanctuary • *n* sanctuar *(n)*, refugiu *(n)*, adpost *(n)*, rezervaie *(f)*, azil *(n)*
sand • *v* sabla, acoperi cu nisip, nisipi • *n* nisip *(f)*, arin *(f)*, plaj *(f)*, curaj *(n)* • *adj* nisipiu
sandalwood • *n* santal *(m)*
sandblast • *v* sabla
sandbox • *n* groap cu nisip *(f)*, cutie cu nisip
sandpiper • *n* fugaci *(m)*
sandstone • *n* gresie
sandwich • *n* sandvi *(n)*
sandy • *adj* nisipos, arinos, nisipiu
sane • *adj* sntos *(m)*
sanguinary • *adj* sângeros, sanguinar, sangvin
sanicle • *n* snioar *(f)*
sapphire • *n* safir *(n)*
sapwood • *n* alburn *(n)*
sarcasm • *n* sarcasm
sarcophagus • *n* sarcofag
sardine • *n* sardin *(f)*
sartorial • *adj* vestimentar
satanic • *adj* satanic, diavolesc, diabolic, drcesc
satchel • *n* ghiozdan *(n)*
sate • *v* stura
satellite • *n* satelit
satiate • *v* stura
satiety • *n* saietate *(f)*
satire • *n* satir *(f)*
satirical • *adj* satiric
satisfaction • *n* satisfacie *(f)*, satisfacere
satisfactory • *adj* satisfctor
satisfied • *adj* satisfcut *(n)*, mulumit *(n)*
saturate • *v* satura
saturated • *adj* plin, saturat *(n)*
sauce • *n* sos *(n)*
saucepan • *n* crati *(f)*, oal *(f)*
sauerkraut • *n* varz acr *(f)*
sauna • *n* saun *(f)*, baie de abur *(f)*
sausage • *n* cârnat *(m)*
save • *v* ajuta, salva, aproviziona
saving • *n* economie *(f)*, sum economisit, economisire *(f)*
savor • *v* da gust
savory • *n* cimbru *(m)*
saw • *n* ferstru *(n)*

sawdust • *n* rumegu *(n)*
sawhorse • *n* capr *(f)*
saxifrage • *n* saxifrag *(f)*
saxophonist • *n* saxofonist *(m)*
say • *v* zice, spune
saying • *n* zical *(f)*, proverb
scabbard • *n* teac *(f)*
scabies • *n* scabie, râie
scaffold • *n* eafod *(n)*
scaffolding • *n* eafodaj *(n)*
scalar • *adj* scalar
scale • *n* solz, cântar *(n)*
scalp • *v* scalpa
scammony • *n* scamonee *(f)*
scan • *v* a baleia imaginea, explora, scana, sonda, numeriza, scaneriza, scruta, cerceta • *n* scanare, scanerizare, numerizare, scanat *(n)*
scandium • *n* scandiu *(n)*
scanner • *n* scaner *(n)*, numerizor, scaner, aparat scaner, scanerizor
scanty • *adj* redus
scape • *n* scap *(m)*
scar • *n* cicatrice *(f)*
scarab • *n* scarabeu *(m)*
scare • *v* speria
scarecrow • *n* sperietoare *(f)*, momâie *(f)*
scaremonger • *n* alarmist *(m)*
scarf • *n* earf *(f)*, al *(n)*
scarlet • *adj* stacojiu, desfrânat, stricat, dezmat
scenery • *n* decor, peisaj, culise
scherzo • *n* scherzo *(n)*
schizophrenia • *n* schizofrenie *(f)*
school • *v* înva, educa, instrui, colariza, antrena • *n* coal *(f)*, coal medie *(f)*, gimnaziu, coal superiar *(f)*, universitate *(f)*, facultate *(f)*, colegiu *(n)*
schoolboy • *n* elev *(m)*
schooling • *n* instruire *(f)*, colarizare, învtur, educaie
schooner • *n* goelet *(f)*
science • *n* tiin *(f)*, materie *(f)*
scientific • *adj* tiinific
scientist • *n* om de tiin *(m)*, savant *(m)*
scion • *n* motenitor *(m)*
scissors • *n* foarfece, foarfec
scold • *v* certa
scoop • *n* msur *(f)*, cup *(f)*
scooter • *n* scuter *(n)*
score • *n* scor *(m)*
scorn • *v* dispreui, urî, respinge, refuza • *n* dispre *(n)*
scorpion • *n* scorpion *(m)*
scoundrel • *n* miel
scourge • *n* flagel
scowl • *v* încrunta
scramble • *v* amesteca
scrape • *v* zgâria
scraper • *n* rachet *(f)*, rzuitoare *(f)*
scratch • *v* scrpina, zgâria
scream • *v* ipa, striga, urla
screen • *n* ecran *(n)*
screw • *v* înuruba, pcli • *n* urub *(n)*, elice *(f)*, înurubare *(f)*
screwdriver • *n* urubelni *(f)*
scribe • *n* scrib *(m)*, copist *(m)*
scroll • *v* derula
scrotal • *adj* scrotal
scrotum • *n* scrot *(n)*
scrum • *n* meleu *(n)*
scrupulously • *adv* scrupulos, cu scrupulozitate
scuff • *v* lufta
sculptor • *n* sculptor *(m)*, sculptori *(f)*
sculpture • *v* sculpta • *n* sculptur *(f)*
scythe • *n* coas *(f)*
sea • *n* mare *(f)*
seal • *n* foc *(f)*
seaman • *n* marinar *(m)*
search • *v* cuta
seashell • *n* scoic *(f)*
season • *v* condimenta • *n* sezon *(n)*, anotimp *(n)*
seat • *n* scaun
secant • *n* secant *(f)*
second • *adj* secund *(m)*, al doilea *(m)* • *n* secund • *v* susine, secunda
secondary • *adj* secundar
secrecy • *n* secretism *(n)*, secretee *(f)*
secret • *n* secret *(n)*, tain *(f)* • *adj* secret *(m)*, secret *(f)*, tainic *(m)*, tainic *(f)*
secretary • *n* secretar *(m)*, secretar *(f)*, pasre secretar *(f)*
secretion • *n* secreie *(f)*, secretare *(f)*, secreionare, secreiere *(f)*
secretive • *adj* secretos
section • *n* secionare *(f)*, tiere *(f)*, seciune *(f)*, tietur *(f)*, parte, secie *(f)*, sector *(n)*, subdiviziune *(f)*, despritur *(f)*, segment *(n)*, departament *(n)*, incizie *(f)*, secionare
sector • *n* sector *(n)*
secure • *adj* sigur *(m)*, protejat, asigurat *(m)*, stabil *(m)*
security • *n* securitate *(f)*, siguran, securitate
sedentary • *adj* sedentar
sedge • *n* rogoz *(n)*
seduce • *v* seduce
sedulous • *adj* asiduu, struitor, perseverent
see • *v* vedea
seed • *n* smân *(f)*
seedling • *n* rsad *(n)*

seek • *v* cuta
seem • *v* prea
segment • *v* segmenta • *n* segment *(n)*
seizure • *n* confiscare *(f)*
seldom • *adv* rar, rareori
selection • *n* selectare *(f)*, selecie *(f)*, selecie, culegere, alegere
selective • *adj* selectiv, de selecie
selenium • *n* seleniu *(n)*
self-control • *n* autocontrol *(n)*, stpânire de sine *(f)*
self-educated • *adj* autodidact *(m)*
self-love • *n* amor propriu *(n)*
self-pollination • *n* autopolenizare *(f)*
selfish • *adj* egoist
sell • *v* vinde
seller • *n* vânztor *(m)*, vânztoare *(f)*
semen • *n* sperm *(f)*
semester • *n* semestru *(n)*
semicircle • *n* semicerc *(n)*, semicercuri
semicircular • *adj* semicircular *(m)*
semicolon • *n* punct i virgul
semiconductor • *n* semiconductor *(n)*
semivowel • *n* semivocal
semolina • *n* gri *(m)*
send • *v* trimite, expedia
sender • *n* expeditor *(m)*, expeditoare *(f)*, expeditori, emitor *(m)*
senility • *n* senilitate *(f)*
sense • *v* simi • *n* sim *(n)*, sens *(n)*
sensible • *adj* perceptibil *(n)*, observabil *(n)*, sesizabil *(n)*, considerabil, apreciabil, mare, simitor, sensibil, raional *(n)*, contient *(n)*, inteligent *(n)*, rezonabil *(n)*, practic *(n)*, logic *(n)*, chibzuit *(n)*
sensitive • *adj* sensibil *(n)*, susceptibil *(n)*, impresionabil *(n)*, receptiv *(n)*, simitor *(n)*, sensibil, de precizie
sensitivity • *n* sensibilitate *(f)*
sensitization • *n* sensibilizare *(f)*
sensuality • *n* senzualitate *(f)*
sent • *v* trimis
sentence • *n* sentin *(f)*, opinie *(f)*, verdict *(n)*, propoziie *(f)*
sentiment • *n* sentiment *(n)*
sentimental • *adj* sentimental, romantic
sentimentality • *n* sentimentalitate
separate • *v* despri, separa • *adj* separat *(n)*, separat *(f)*
separation • *n* separare *(f)*, izolare *(f)*, divorare *(f)*, divor *(n)*
sepia • *n* sepie *(f)*, sepia *(f)* • *adj* sepia
sequence • *n* secven *(f)*
sequester • *v* sechestra, pune sub sechestru
sequoia • *n* sequoia *(m)*
sere • *adj* veted
serenade • *n* serenad *(f)*
serendipity • *n* serendipitate *(f)*
serene • *adj* senin
serenity • *n* senintate
serf • *n* iobag *(m)*, erb *(m)*
sergeant • *n* sergent *(m)*
serial • *adj* serial *(n)*
series • *n* serie *(f)*
serin • *n* scatiu *(m)*
serine • *n* serin *(f)*
serious • *adj* serios
seriousness • *n* seriozitate
sermon • *n* predic *(f)*, propovedanie *(f)*, cazanie *(f)*
serotonin • *n* serotonin *(f)*
serpent • *n* arpe *(m)*
servant • *n* servitor *(m)*, slug *(f)*, slujitor *(m)*
serve • *v* servi
service • *n* serviciu *(n)*
servile • *adj* servil *(n)*
servility • *n* servilism *(n)*, servilitate *(f)*
sesame • *n* susan *(m)*, sesam *(m)*
set • *v* aeza, pune, fixa, stabili, regla, bate, introduce, descrie, pregti, potrivi, pasa, trimite, întri, solidifica, apune, asfini, scpta • *n* aparat *(n)*, receptor *(n)*, set *(n)*, colecie *(f)*, ansamblu *(n)*, trus *(f)*, mulime *(f)*, grup *(n)*, platou *(n)*, platou de filmare *(n)* • *adj* pregtit, gata, hotrât, stabilit, fixat, aezat
seta • *n* set *(f)*
seven • *n* apte
seventh • *n* cel al aptelea *(m)*, cea a aptea *(f)*
severity • *n* severitate *(f)*, asprime *(f)*
sew • *v* coase
sex • *n* relaii sexuale, sex *(n)*
sexism • *n* sexism *(n)*
sextant • *n* sextant *(n)*
sextet • *n* sextet *(m)*, sextet
sexton • *n* paracliser *(m)*
sexual • *adj* sexual *(n)*, sexual *(f)*
sexy • *adj* sexy, sexos
shade • *n* umbr *(f)* • *v* adumbri, umbri
shadow • *n* umbr
shady • *adj* umbros
shah • *n* ah *(m)*
shake • *v* agita, scpa, da mâna, dansa • *n* scuturare *(f)*
shallot • *n* ham *(f)*
shallow • *adj* plat, puin adânc
sham • *v* pcli • *adj* pcleal *(f)*
shamanism • *n* amanism *(n)*
shame • *n* ruine *(f)*
shampoo • *n* ampon *(n)*, amponare *(f)*
shamrock • *n* trifoi *(n)*

shape • *v* modela • *n* stare *(f)*, form, form *(f)*
share • *v* partaja, împri, împrti, distribui • *n* parte *(f)*, pri
shared • *adj* distribuit *(n)*, împrit *(n)*
shark • *n* rechin *(m)*
sharp • *adj* ascuit, diez *(m)* • *adv* fix *(m)*
sharpen • *v* ascui
shave • *v* rade, brbieri, a se brbieri
shawl • *n* al *(m)*
she • *pron* dumneaei, ea
sheaf • *n* mnunchi *(n)*, fascicul *(n)*, legtur *(f)*
shear • *v* tunde
shears • *n* foarfece
sheath • *n* teac *(f)*
sheepfold • *n* stân *(f)*, arc *(n)*, oierie *(f)*
sheepish • *adj* bleg
sheer • *adj* sadea
sheet • *n* foaie
sheik • *n* eic
shelduck • *n* clifar *(m)*
shelf • *n* poli *(f)*
shell • *n* scoic, cochilie, carapace
shepherd • *n* cioban *(m)*, dohotar, oier *(m)*, pstor *(m)*, pcurar *(m)*
sheriff • *n* erif *(m)*
shield • *n* scut *(m)*, pavz, protector *(m)*, protectoare *(f)*, scut *(n)*, protectori, indicator *(n)* • *v* a proteja
shilling • *n* iling *(m)*
shine • *v* strluci, luci, lumina, lustrui • *n* strlucire, luciu, lustru
shingle • *v* indrili • *n* indril *(f)*
shining • *adj* strlucitor, reflector *(m)*, strlucitor *(m)*, lucios *(m)*, ilustru *(m)*, reputat *(m)*
shiny • *adj* stralucitor
ship • *n* nav, corabie, vas
shire • *n* judet *(n)*
shirt • *n* cma *(f)*
shirtfront • *n* pieptar *(n)*
shit • *n* excrement *(n)*, ccat *(n)*, rahat *(m)* • *v* cca
shiver • *v* tremura
shocking • *v* ocant *(n)*
shoe • *n* pantof *(m)*, gheat *(f)*, înclminte *(f)*
shoebill • *n* abumarkub *(m)*
shoehorn • *n* încltor de pantofi *(n)*
shoelace • *n* iret *(n)*
shoemaker • *n* pantofar *(m)*
shoot • *v* trage
shop • *v* merge la cumprturi • *n* magazin *(n)*, spaiu comercial, atelier *(n)*
shopping • *n* cumprturi
shore • *n* mal *(f)*, rm *(f)*, coast *(f)*
short • *adj* scurt, scund
shortcut • *n* scurttur *(f)*, scurtare *(f)*, prescurtare *(f)*
shorten • *v* scurta
shorts • *n* pantaloni scuri, ort *(n)*
shoulder • *n* umr *(m)*
shout • *v* striga, urla, ipa
shovel • *n* lopat *(f)*
show • *v* arta, demonstra • *n* spectacol *(n)*, expoziie *(f)*, demonstraie *(f)*, emisiune *(f)*, program *(f)*
showcase • *n* vitrin *(f)*
shower • *v* a face un du • *n* avers *(f)*, ploaie torenial *(f)*, ploaie de var *(f)*, du *(n)*
shrew • *n* chican *(m)*, meger *(f)*, scorpie *(f)*
shriek • *v* ipa, striga, urla • *n* ipt *(n)*, strigt *(n)*, urlet *(n)*
shrimp • *n* crevet *(f)*
shrink • *v* micora
shrub • *n* arbust *(m)*, tuf *(f)*
shudder • *v* tremura • *n* tremur *(n)*, fiori, fior
shun • *v* evita, evada, ascunde, împinge
shyness • *n* timiditate *(f)*
sickle • *v* secera • *n* secer
sickly • *adj* bolnvicios, slab
sickness • *n* maladie *(f)*, boal *(f)*, grea *(f)*
side • *n* fa, latur, fa *(f)*, parte *(f)*
sidewalk • *n* trotuar *(n)*
sienna • *n* pmânt de Siena *(n)* • *adj* siena
sieve • *v* cerne • *n* sit *(f)*
sift • *v* cerne
sigh • *v* suspina • *n* suspin *(n)*, oftat, geamt *(n)*
sight • *n* vedere *(f)*, privelite *(f)*, spectacol *(n)*
sign • *n* semn • *v* semna
signal • *n* semnal, semnal indicator *(n)*, semnalizator *(n)*, semnal *(n)*
signature • *n* semntur
significance • *n* semnifican *(n)*, importan *(f)*, semnificativitate *(f)*
significant • *adj* semnificant *(n)*, important *(n)*, semnificativ *(n)*
significantly • *adv* (în mod) semnificativ, cu îneles, (în mod) considerabil
silence • *n* linite *(f)*, tcere *(f)* • *interj* tcere!, linite!
silhouette • *n* siluet *(f)*
silicle • *n* silicul *(f)*
silicon • *n* siliciu *(n)*
silicone • *n* silicon *(m)*
silique • *n* silicv *(f)*
silk • *n* mtase *(f)*
silkworm • *n* vierme de mtase *(m)*
silo • *n* siloz *(n)*

silver • *n* argint *(n)*, argintrie *(f)*, obiecte argintate *(n)*, argintiu *(n)*, argintie *(f)* • *adj* argintiu
silvery • *adj* argintiu
simian • *n* simian *(m)* • *adj* simian
similar • *adj* similar, asemntor
similarity • *n* similaritate
simony • *n* simonie *(f)*
simple • *adj* simplu *(n)*, necomplicat *(n)*, simplu
simplify • *v* simplifica
simultaneity • *n* simultaneitate *(f)*
simultaneously • *adv* simultan, în mod simultan
sin • *v* pctui • *n* pcat *(n)*
sincere • *adj* sincer
sincerity • *n* sinceritate *(f)*
sine • *n* sinus *(n)*
sinecure • *n* sinecur *(f)*
sing • *v* cânta
singer • *n* cântre *(m)*, cântrea *(f)*
singing • *n* cântare *(f)*
single • *adj* singur, unit, unitar *(n)*, întreg, nedivizat *(n)*, separat *(n)*, individual, singular, celibatar *(m)*, necstorit *(n)*
singlet • *n* maiou *(n)*
singular • *adj* unic *(m)*, singular, singular *(m)*, neobinuit
singularity • *n* singularitate *(f)*, punct de întâlnire *(n)*, punct comun *(n)*
sinister • *adj* sinistru
sink • *v* scufunda, afunda • *n* chiuvet
sinus • *n* sinus *(n)*
sinusitis • *n* sinuzit
sip • *v* sorbi
sir • *n* s trii, domn *(m)*, domnule
sire • *n* domn *(m)*
sister • *n* sor *(f)*, surori, clugri *(f)*
sister-in-law • *n* cumnat *(f)*
sisterly • *adj* ca de sor, de sor • *adv* ca o sor
sit • *v* edea, aeza, se aeza
situation • *n* situare *(f)*, situaie *(f)*, poziie *(f)*, localizare *(f)*, stare *(f)*, situaie, stadiu *(n)*, etap *(f)*, post *(n)*, posturi
six • *n* ase
sixth • *n* cel al aselea *(m)*, cea a asea *(f)*, esime *(f)* • *adj* aselea *(m)*, asea *(f)*
sixtieth • *adj* aizecilea
skeleton • *n* schelet *(n)*
skepticism • *n* scepticism *(n)*
sketch • *n* schi *(f)*
skewer • *n* frigare *(f)*
ski • *v* schia • *n* schi *(n)*
skiing • *n* schi
skill • *n* abilitate *(f)*, pricepere *(f)*, talent *(n)*
skillful • *adj* priceput *(m)*
skim • *v* rsfoi
skin • *v* zgâria • *n* piele *(f)*
skinny • *adj* slab
skirt • *n* fust *(f)*
skull • *n* craniu *(n)*, east
skullcap • *n* gura-lupului *(f)*
sky • *n* cer *(n)*, *(n)*, cer
skylark • *n* ciocârlie *(f)*
skylight • *n* lucarn
skyscraper • *n* zgârie-nori, building *(n)*
slalom • *n* slalom
slander • *v* defima
slang • *n* argou *(n)*, jargon *(n)*, slang *(n)*
slate • *v* programa, planifica, destina • *n* ardezie *(f)*, tbli *(f)*, plac de ardezie *(f)*, not de plat *(f)*, cont *(n)*, list electoral *(f)*
slaughter • *v* mcelri *(m)*, tia, omorî • *n* mcel
slave • *n* sclav, rob, serv
slavery • *n* sclavie *(f)*, robie *(f)*, sclavie
sledge • *n* sanie *(f)*
sleep • *v* dormi • *n* somn *(n)*
sleeper • *n* travers *(f)*
sleepiness • *n* somnolen *(f)*
sleepy • *adj* somnoros, somnolent *(n)*
sleet • *v* lapovia • *n* lapovi *(f)*, flecial *(f)*
sleeve • *n* mânec *(f)*
slender • *adj* subtire *(n)*
slide • *v* aluneca • *n* tobogan *(n)*, alunecare *(f)*, alunecare de teren *(f)*, diapozitiv *(n)*, lam *(f)*
sling • *v* a trage cu pratia • *n* pratie *(f)*
slip • *v* aluneca
slipper • *n* papuc *(m)*
sliver • *n* surcea, achie
slivovitz • *n* libovi, uic, plinc
slobber • *v* saliva
slope • *n* pant *(f)*
sloth • *n* lene *(f)*, lene *(m)*
slow • *adj* încet
slowly • *adv* încet
slowness • *n* lentoare
slug • *n* melc *(m)*, limax *(m)*
sluice • *n* ecluza *(f)*, deschizatura *(f)*
slumber • *v* dormita, somnola
slut • *n* coarda *(f)*, cea *(f)*
small • *adj* mic, tânr, mici
smallness • *n* micime *(f)*
smallpox • *n* variol *(f)*, vrsat *(n)*
smart • *adj* detept, descurcre, iste *(m)*
smear • *v* badijona • *n* frotiu
smell • *v* mirosi • *n* miros *(n)*
smile • *v* zâmbi, surâde • *n* zâmbet *(n)*, surâs
smith • *n* fierar *(m)*, furar *(m)*
smoke • *v* fuma, fumega, afuma • *n* fum

(*n*), fumegar (*f*), igar (*f*), iluzie (*f*), amgire (*f*), himer (*f*), fumuriu • *adj* fumuriu
smoker • *n* fumtor (*m*)
smoking • *n* fumtor (*m*), fumtoare (*f*), fumtori, fumtoare • *adj* fumigen (*m*), fumigen (*f*)
smooth • *adj* neted, lin, lis
smugness • *n* automulumire (*f*), autoîncântare (*f*)
snail • *n* melc (*m*)
snake • *n* arpe (*m*)
snapdragon • *n* gura-leului (*f*)
snare • *n* curs, la
sneeze • *v* strnuta • *n* strnut
snicker • *v* a chicoti
snivel • *n* muci
snob • *n* snob (*m*)
snooker • *n* rsturna
snooze • *v* dormita, aipi
snore • *v* sfori • *n* sforit (*n*), sforial (*f*), sforitur (*f*)
snot • *n* muci
snout • *n* rat (*n*)
snow • *v* ninge • *n* zpad (*f*), nea (*f*), omt (*n*), ninsoare (*f*), cdere de zpad (*f*)
snow-white • *adj* alb ca neaua, alb ca zpada
snowball • *n* bulgre de zpad (*m*)
snowberry • *n* hurmuz (*m*)
snowflake • *n* fulg de nea
snowman • *n* om de zpad (*m*)
snowy • *adj* înzpezit (*m*), alb ca zpada (*m*)
so • *adv* atât, aa • *conj* aadar, deci
soak • *v* muia
soap • *v* spuni • *n* spun (*n*)
soapwort • *n* odagaci (*m*), ciuin (*m*), spunari (*f*)
sob • *n* suspin (*n*)
sobriety • *n* sobrietate, cumptare
soccer • *n* fotbal (*n*)
sociable • *adj* sociabil (*n*)
social • *adj* social (*n*)
socialism • *n* socialism, socialism (*n*)
socialist • *adj* socialist (*m*)
society • *n* societate (*f*), societate, mediu
sociology • *n* sociologie (*f*)
sock • *n* ciorap (*m*)
socket • *n* priz, soclu (*n*), fasung (*n*), dulie (*f*)
soda • *n* buturi rcoritoare, rcoritoare
sodium • *n* sodiu (*n*), natriu (*n*)
sodomy • *n* sodomie (*f*)
sofa • *n* canapea (*f*), canapele
soft • *adj* moale, încet
soften • *v* muia, înmuia
softness • *n* moliciune (*f*)
software • *n* software (*n*), programe de computer (*n*)
soil • *n* sol (*n*), teren (*n*) • *v* spurca
sojourn • *n* sejur (*n*)
sol • *n* sol (*m*), sol (*n*)
solace • *n* consolare (*f*), reconfortare (*f*)
soldier • *n* soldat (*m*), osta (*m*), militar (*m*), gard (*f*), paz (*f*)
sole • *adj* singur • *v* pingeli • *n* talp (*f*), pingea (*f*), sol (*f*), limb-de-mare (*f*)
solemn • *adj* serios, solemn
solemnity • *n* solemnitate
solicitude • *n* solicitudine (*f*)
solid • *adj* solid, masiv, compact, plin, temeinic
solidify • *v* solidifica
solidity • *n* soliditate (*f*)
solitude • *n* singurtate (*f*)
solo • *n* solo • *adj* solo
soloist • *n* solist (*m*), solist (*f*)
solstice • *n* solstiiu (*n*), solstiiul verii (*n*), solstiiul iernii (*n*)
solution • *n* soluie (*f*), rezultat (*n*), soluionare (*f*), rezolvare (*f*)
solvable • *adj* pltibil (*n*), solvabil (*n*), solvabil (*f*), solubil (*n*), dizolvabil (*n*), dizolvabil (*f*)
solve • *v* rezolva, soluiona, lmuri
somebody • *pron* cineva
someday • *adv* într-o zi
somehow • *adv* cumva
somersault • *n* tumb, rostogolire
something • *pron* ceva
sometime • *adj* fost, ex-, anterior • *adv* cândva
sometimes • *adv* uneori, câteodat, ocazional
somewhat • *adv* întrucâtva
somewhere • *adv* undeva
somnambulism • *n* somnambulism (*n*), noctambulism (*n*), selianism (*n*)
somnambulist • *n* somnambul (*m*), somnambulist (*m*)
son • *n* fiu (*m*)
son-in-law • *n* ginere (*m*)
sonata • *n* sonat (*f*)
song • *n* cântec (*n*), cântare (*f*)
sonnet • *n* sonet (*n*)
soon • *adv* curând
soot • *n* funingine
soothe • *v* alina, domoli, liniti, potoli
sophisticated • *adj* sofisticat, complicat (*n*), rafinat, elegant
soprano • *n* sopran (*f*)
sore • *n* plag
sorghum • *n* sorg (*m*)
sororal • *adj* de sor
sorrel • *n* mcri (*m*), acri (*n*) • *adj* roib

sorrow • *n* tristee *(f)*, întristare *(f)*, mâhnire *(f)*, suprare *(f)*, nefericire *(f)*, durere *(f)*
sorry • *interj* îmi pare ru, scuz, scuz-m, scuzai, scuzai-m
sort • *n* fel *(f)*, gen • *v* clasifica, împri, sorta, aranja
soul • *n* suflet *(n)*, spirit *(n)*, muzic soul, unic, singur
sound • *adj* sntos *(n)*, nevtmat *(n)*, teafr *(n)*, zdravn *(n)*, intact *(n)*, complet *(n)*, solid *(n)*, sigur *(n)*, robust *(n)* • *v* suna • *n* sunet
soundness • *n* trinicie *(f)*, soliditate *(f)*, robustee *(f)*
sour • *adj* acru
source • *n* surs *(f)*, izvor *(n)*, fântân *(f)*
south • *n* sud *(n)* • *adj* sudic
south-southwest • *n* sud-sudvest
southeast • *adj* sudestic, de sud-est
southern • *adj* sudic *(n)*, austral *(n)*
southernmost • *adj* cel mai sud
southernwood • *n* lemnul-Domnului *(n)*
southwest • *n* sud-vest *(n)*, sudvest *(n)* • *adj* de sud-vest, sudvestic
sovereign • *n* suveran *(m)* • *adj* suveran, suveran *(m)*
soviet • *n* soviet
sow • *n* scroaf, purcea, poarc • *v* semna
space • *n* spaiu *(n)*
spacecraft • *n* nav cosmic
spaceship • *n* nav cosmic
spacetime • *n* spaiu-timp *(n)*
spade • *n* lopat *(f)*, cazma *(f)*, pic *(f)*, cioroi *(m)*
spadix • *n* spadice *(n)*, spadix *(n)*
spanking • *n* stranic
spark • *n* scânteie
sparkle • *n* scânteie • *v* scânteia
sparrow • *n* vrabie *(f)*
spawn • *n* icre
speak • *v* vorbi, discuta, comunica
speaker • *n* vorbitor *(m)*, vorbitoare *(f)*
spear • *n* lance, suli
species • *n* specie, specie *(f)*
specific • *adj* specific
specificity • *n* specificitate *(f)*
specimen • *n* specimen, exemplar
spectacle • *n* spectacol *(n)*
spectacles • *n* ochelari
spectacular • *adj* spectaculos, spectacular, de spectacol
spectator • *n* spectator *(m)*, privitor *(m)*
spectral • *adj* spectral
spectrum • *n* spectru *(n)*
speech • *n* vorbire *(f)*, discurs *(n)*, cuvântare *(f)*
speed • *n* vitez *(f)*, rapiditate *(f)*, iueal *(f)*, fotosensibilitate
speedometer • *n* vitezometru *(n)*
spell • *n* vraj *(f)*, farmec *(n)*, descântec *(n)*, descânttur *(f)*, interval *(n)* • *v* litera, rosti, se scrie, indica, clarifica, înlocui
spelt • *n* alac *(n)*
spend • *v* cheltui
sperm • *n* spermatozoid *(m)*, sperm *(f)*, smecleu *(n)*, smârcu *(n)*, smahoz *(n)*
spermatozoon • *n* spermatozoid *(m)*
sphere • *n* sfer *(f)*, bil *(f)*, bol *(n)*
spherical • *adj* sferic
spheroid • *n* sferoid
sphinx • *n* sfinx *(m)*
spice • *n* condiment
spicule • *n* spicul *(n)*
spider • *n* pianjen *(m)*
spiderwort • *n* tradescania *(f)*
spike • *n* ru *(m)*, piron *(n)*, spic
spill • *v* vrsa
spin • *v* toarce, învârti
spinach • *n* spanac *(n)*
spindle • *n* fus, salb-moale *(f)*
spinet • *n* spinet *(f)*
spirit • *n* suflet *(n)*, spirit, duh *(n)*, spirit *(n)*, trie *(f)*
spirits • *n* spirt *(n)*, spirturi
spiritual • *adj* sufletesc, spiritual
spiritualism • *n* spiritualism *(n)*, spiritualitate *(f)*
spiritualist • *n* spiritualist *(m)*
spiritually • *adv* sufletete
spit • *n* frigare *(f)*, scuipat • *v* scuipa
spite • *v* urî, maltrata, ofensa, vexa • *n* ciud, rutate, suprare *(f)*, dispre *(n)*, vexaiune *(f)*
spiteful • *adj* malitios *(m)*, ranchiunos *(m)*
spittle • *n* scuipat
spleen • *n* splin *(f)*
splinter • *n* achie, factiune *(f)*, schisma *(f)*
split • *v* despica, diviza, scinda, spinteca, repartiza, separa • *n* spagatul
spoil • *v* strica, ruina, rsfa • *n* prad
spoke • *n* spi *(f)*
sponge • *n* burete *(m)*, spongie *(f)*
sponsor • *v* sponsoriza
spontaneity • *n* spontaneitate *(f)*
spontaneous • *adj* spontan *(m)*
spoon • *n* lingur *(f)*
spore • *n* spor *(m)*, spori
sport • *n* sport *(n)*
spot • *n* pat
sprat • *n* sprot
spread • *v* aterne, întinde
spring • *n* primvar *(f)*, izvor *(n)*, arc *(n)*
springboard • *n* trambulin, trambulin *(f)*

sprint • *v* sprinta • *n* sprint *(n)*
sprinter • *n* sprinter *(m)*, sprinter *(f)*
spruce • *n* molid *(m)*
spur • *v* îndemna
spurge • *n* aior *(m)*, alior
spy • *v* spiona • *n* spion *(m)*, spioan *(f)*
squabble • *v* certa
squalid • *adj* murdar
square • *n* ptrat, cvadrat, echer *(n)*, pia *(f)*, piee, ptrat *(n)* • *adj* ptrat
squared • *adj* ridicat la ptrat
squeeze • *v* strânge, stoarce
squid • *n* calmar *(m)*
squill • *n* viorea *(f)*, scila *(f)*
squint • *v* se chiorî
squire • *n* moier
squirrel • *n* veveri *(f)*
stab • *v* înjunghia, strpunge, a da o lovitur de cuit
stability • *n* stabilitate *(f)*, stabilitate
stable • *n* staul, grajd *(n)*, grajd de cai *(n)*, grajd • *adj* stabil
stack • *v* stivui • *n* cpi *(f)*, stiv *(f)*
stadium • *n* stadion *(n)*
staff • *n* portativ *(n)*, personal *(n)*
stag • *n* cerb *(n)*
stagnation • *n* stagnare *(f)*, nemicare *(f)*
stain • *n* pta
stair • *n* treapt, scar *(f)*
staircase • *n* scar *(f)*
stairs • *n* scar
stake • *n* par *(m)*
stalk • *n* tulpin *(f)*
stall • *n* staul *(m)*
stallion • *n* armsar *(m)*
stamen • *n* stamin *(f)*
stammer • *n* Balbism
stampede • *n* busculad *(f)*, învlmeal *(f)*
stand • *v* sta, sta în picioare, ridica, fi supus • *n* arboret *(n)*
stand-in • *n* dublur
stand-up • *adj* onest, de încredere, vertical *(m)*, drept *(m)*, perpendicular *(m)*
standard • *n* standard *(n)*, standarde, stindard *(n)*
standpoint • *n* punct de vedere *(n)*
standstill • *n* oprit, imobilizat
stanza • *n* strof *(f)*, stan *(f)*
stapes • *n* scri *(f)*
staple • *v* capsa • *n* caps *(f)*
star • *n* stea *(f)*, stelu *(f)*
starboard • *n* tribord *(n)*
starch • *n* amidon
starfish • *n* stea de mare *(f)*, stea-de-mare *(f)*
stark • *adj* dur *(m)*, crud *(m)*, violent, drastic, puternic *(m)*, viguros *(m)*, aspru *(m)*, dezolant *(m)*, rigid *(m)*, total *(m)*, absolut *(m)* • *adv* absolut, in intregime
starling • *n* graur *(m)*
starry • *adj* înstelat
start • *n* început • *v* începe, porni
starter • *n* demaror *(n)*
starvation • *n* foamete
starve • *v* flmânzi, suferi de foame, muri de foame, înfometa
state • *v* declara • *n* stat *(n)*, stare *(f)*, stat
statement • *n* declaraie *(f)*, remarc *(f)*, bilan *(n)*, instruciune *(f)*, instruciuni
static • *adj* static *(n)*
station • *n* staie *(f)*, gar *(f)*
statistical • *adj* statistic *(n)*, de statistic
statistically • *adv* statistic
statistics • *n* statistic
statue • *n* statuie *(f)*
status • *n* statut *(n)*, poziie, stare *(f)*, situaie
stave • *n* doag
stay • *v* sta, rmâne, zbovi, rmâne, dinui, amâna, întârzia
steadfastness • *n* statornicie *(f)*, neclintire *(f)*, fidelitate
steal • *v* fura, însui, eclipsa, strecura, furia • *n* chilipir *(n)*, furt *(n)*, furat *(n)*, furtur *(f)*
stealthily • *adv* pe furi
steam • *n* abur *(m)*
steel • *n* oel *(n)*
steer • *n* bou *(m)*
steerable • *adj* pilotabil *(m)*, dirijabil *(m)*, cârmuibil *(m)*
stele • *n* stel *(n)*, cilindru central *(m)*
stellar • *adj* stelar, strlucitor *(n)*
stem • *n* tulpin *(f)*, trunchi, peduncul, picior, coad
step • *v* pi • *n* pas, treapt, pas *(m)*, pai
stepfather • *n* tat vitreg *(m)*
stepmother • *n* mater *(f)*, mam vitreg *(f)*
stepparent • *n* printe vitreg *(m)*, tat vitreg *(m)*, mam vitreg *(f)*
steppe • *n* step *(f)*
stepson • *n* fiu vitreg *(m)*
sterilization • *n* sterilizare *(f)*, sterilizaie *(f)*
stern • *adj* dur, sever
stethoscope • *n* stetoscop *(n)*
stewardess • *n* stewardes *(f)*, osptar *(f)*
stick • *n* nuia *(f)*, creang *(f)*, b *(m)*, baston *(n)* • *v* lipi, aga, înfige
sticky • *adj* lipicios
stiff • *v* a epui
stiffen • *v* întri
stigmatism • *n* stigmatism *(n)*
still • *adv* înc, i, tot • *v* liniti, calma

stilt • *n* piciorong *(n)*
stimulant • *n* stimulent *(m)*, stimulator *(m)*
stimulate • *v* stimula
stimulus • *n* stimul *(m)*, motiv *(n)*
sting • *v* împunge, înepa, pica
stinginess • *n* avariie *(f)*, zgârcenie *(f)*, parcimonie *(f)*
stingy • *adj* ciufut
stink • *v* pui • *n* putoare *(f)*
stinking • *adj* împuit
stint • *n* fugaci
stirrup • *n* scar *(f)*
stochastic • *adj* stocastic
stockpile • *n* rezerv *(f)*
stocks • *n* butuc *(m)*
stocky • *adj* îndesat, bondoc, scurt i gros, mic i solid
stoicism • *n* stoicism *(n)*
stomach • *n* stomac *(n)*
stone • *n* piatr *(f)*
stonechat • *n* mrcinar *(m)*
stool • *n* taburet *(n)*, scaun *(n)*
stoop • *v* apleca
stop • *v* opri, termina • *n* punct *(n)*, stop *(n)*, minge stopat *(f)*
storage • *n* înmagazinare *(f)*, depozitare *(f)*, acumulare *(f)*, depozit *(n)*, magazie *(f)*, rezervor *(n)*, memorare *(f)*, stocare *(f)*
store • *n* depozit *(n)*, magazie *(f)*, stoc *(n)*
stork • *n* barz *(f)*, barza-alb *(f)*
storm • *n* furtun, vijelie *(f)*, atac *(n)*, asalt *(n)* • *v* ataca, asalta
stormy • *adj* furtunos *(m)*
story • *n* istorie, poveste
stove • *n* sob *(f)*, aragaz *(n)*, reou *(n)*
straight • *adj* drept
straighten • *v* îndrepta
straightforward • *adj* onest, sincer, simplu
strain • *v* strecura
strait • *n* strâmtoare
strand • *n* plaj *(f)*
strange • *adj* ciudat, straniu, neobinuit, nenatural *(n)*
strangely • *adv* ciudat
strategy • *n* strategie *(f)*
straw • *n* pai *(n)*, paie *(f)*
strawberry • *n* cpun *(f)*, cpun *(m)*
stream • *n* pârâu *(f)*, torent *(n)*, uvoi *(n)*, curent *(m)*, iroi *(n)*, flux *(n)*, curs de ap *(n)*, lan *(n)*
street • *n* strad *(f)*
streetlight • *n* felinar *(n)*
stress • *n* tensiune *(f)*, încordare *(f)*, stres *(n)*
stretch • *v* întinde
strew • *v* împrtia, rspândi, aterne
strike • *v* grev • *n* grev *(f)*
string • *n* coard *(f)*, coard, strun, ir, serie, suit
strip • *v* jupui, dezbrca, face, prdui, seca, despuia
stripe • *n* dung
stroke • *v* mângâia
stroll • *v* plimba
strong • *adj* puternic, vârtos
strontium • *n* stroniu *(n)*
structural • *adj* structural *(n)*
structured • *adj* structurat *(n)*
strudel • *n* strudel *(n)*
struggle • *v* lupta, zbate
stubbornness • *n* încpânare *(f)*
stud • *n* armsar *(m)*
student • *n* student *(m)*, student *(f)*
study • *v* studia, înva • *n* studiu *(n)*, studiere *(f)*
stuff • *v* înfunda, înghesui, îndesa, îndopa, îmbuiba
stump • *n* ciot *(n)*
stupa • *n* chedi
stupid • *adj* prost, stupid
stupidity • *n* stupiditate *(f)*
sturgeon • *n* sturion *(m)*
stutter • *v* bâlbâi • *n* bâlbâire
sty • *n* cocin *(f)*
style • *n* stil *(n)*, fel, gen, stil *(m)*
stylus • *n* stil *(n)*
subatomic • *adj* subatomic *(m)*
subconscious • *n* subcontient *(n)*, subcontiin *(f)* • *adj* subcontient
subcontinent • *n* subcontinent
subdivide • *v* subdiviza
subdue • *v* supune, cuceri, subjuga, închina
subfamily • *n* sub-familie *(f)*
subgroup • *n* subgrup *(n)*
subject • *n* subiect *(n)*, tem *(f)*, materie *(f)*, disciplin
subjective • *adj* subiectiv
subjectivity • *n* subiectivitate
subjugate • *v* subjuga
subjugation • *n* subjugare
submarine • *n* submarin *(n)* • *adj* submarin *(n)*
submissive • *adj* supus *(n)*, docil *(n)*, umil *(n)*
submit • *v* închina
subordinate • *adj* subordonat *(m)*, subordonat *(f)*
subscribe • *v* abona, subscrie
subscription • *n* abonament *(n)*
subsistence • *n* subzisten, mijloace de trai

subsonic • *adj* subsonic, subsonic *(f)*
substance • *n* substan *(f)*, drog *(n)*, droguri, narcotic *(n)*
substantial • *adj* substanial *(m)*
substantiality • *n* substanialitate *(f)*
substitute • *v* înlocui, substitui • *n* substitut *(n)*, înlocuitor *(m)*, lociitor *(m)*, substituent *(m)*, substituitor *(m)*
substructure • *n* substructur *(f)*
subtract • *v* scdea, sustrage
subtraction • *n* scdere *(f)*
subtropical • *adj* subtropical *(m)*
suburb • *n* suburbie *(f)*
suburban • *n* suburban *(n)*, suburban *(f)*
subversive • *adj* subversiv
subway • *n* metrou *(n)*
succeed • *v* succeda, succede, reui
success • *n* succes *(n)*, succese
succession • *n* succesiune *(f)*, ir *(n)*
suck • *v* suge
sucker • *n* sugtor *(m)*, fraier *(m)* • *v* fraieri
suckle • *v* alpta, suge
sudden • *adj* subit, brusc, neateptat, neprevzut
suddenly • *adv* subit, brusc, deodat, instantaneu
suffer • *v* suferi
suffering • *n* suferin *(f)*, ps • *adj* suferin *(f)*
sufficiently • *adv* destul, suficient
suffix • *n* sufix *(n)*
sugar • *v* îndulci • *n* zahr *(n)*, zaharuri, glucide
sugary • *adj* mieros
suggest • *v* sugera
suggestible • *adj* sugestionabil *(n)*
suggestion • *n* sugestionare *(f)*, sugestie, propunere, sugestie *(f)*
suicide • *n* sinucidere *(f)*, sinuciga *(m)*, sinuciga *(f)*
suit • *n* costum *(n)*
suitability • *n* potrivire *(f)*, adecvabilitate *(f)*, aptitudine *(f)*
suitable • *adj* adecvat *(n)*, convenabil *(n)*, potrivit *(n)*, nimerit *(n)*
sulfate • *n* sulfat *(m)*
sulfide • *n* sulfur *(f)*
sulfur • *v* sulfurare *(f)* • *n* sulf *(n)*, sulfuri
sulk • *v* îmbufnat
sully • *v* spurca, mânji
sultan • *n* sultan *(m)*
sultanate • *n* sultanat *(n)*
sum • *n* sum *(f)*
summer • *v* vra • *n* var *(f)*, travers *(f)*
summit • *n* culme
sumptuous • *adj* somptuos *(m)*
sun • *v* însori, sori, înclzi • *n* soare *(m)*, rsrit *(n)*, asfinit *(n)*
sunbeam • *n* raza de soare
sundew • *n* roua-cerului *(f)*, roua-soarelui *(f)*
sunflower • *n* floarea soarelui *(f)*
sunglasses • *n* ochelari de soare
sunlight • *n* lumina soarelui *(f)*
sunny • *adj* însorit
sunrise • *n* rsrit de soare *(n)*, crparea zilei *(f)*, realizare *(f)*, trezire *(f)*
sunset • *n* apus *(n)*, asfinire *(f)*, crepuscul *(n)*, declin *(n)*
sunshine • *n* soare *(m)*, lumina soarelui *(f)*
sunspot • *n* pt solar *(f)*
superb • *adj* superb *(n)*, superb *(f)*, excepional *(n)*, excepional *(f)*
superfluity • *n* superfluitate *(f)*
superfluous • *adj* superfluu *(n)*, superflu *(f)*, de prisos
superior • *n* superior *(m)*, superioar *(f)* • *adj* superior *(m)*, mai bun, mai sus
superlative • *adj* suprem, superlativ
supermarket • *n* supermagazin, magazin universal *(n)*
supernatural • *adj* supranatural *(n)*
supersonic • *adj* supersonic
supervise • *v* superviza
supervision • *n* supervizare *(f)*, supraveghere *(f)*
supine • *adj* letargic, pasiv
supper • *v* cina, supa • *n* cin, supeu *(n)*, mas de sear *(f)*, cin *(f)*
supply • *n* aprovizionare, alimentare, provizie, rezerv
support • *v* susine, sprijini, propti • *n* suport *(n)*, suporturi, reazem *(n)*, sprijin *(n)*, sprijinire *(f)*
supporter • *n* suporter *(m)*, partizan
suppose • *v* presupune
supremacy • *n* supremaie *(f)*
supreme • *adj* suprem *(n)*
sure • *adj* sigur, cert • *interj* sigur
surface • *n* suprafa
surface-active • *adj* tensioactiv *(n)*
surgeon • *n* chirurg
surgery • *n* chirurgie *(f)*
surname • *n* nume de familie *(n)*, patronim *(n)*, nume patronimic *(n)*
surpass • *v* depi, întrece
surprise • *v* surprinde • *n* surpriz *(f)*, surprindere *(f)*
surrealism • *n* suprarealism
surround • *v* înconjura
surroundings • *n* jur
survival • *n* supravieuire *(f)*
survive • *v* supravieui

susceptibility • *n* susceptibilitate *(f)*, susceptivitate *(f)*
susceptible • *adj* susceptibil
sushi • *n* sushi
suslik • *n* popându *(m)*
suspend • *v* suspenda, amâna, atârna, aga, întrerupe
suspension • *n* suspendare *(f)*, suspensie *(f)*
suspicious • *adj* suspect, dubios, suspicios
swaddle • *v* înfa
swagger • *n* fanfaronad *(f)*, ludroenie *(f)*, gasconad *(f)*
swallow • *v* înghii • *n* rândunic *(f)*, lstun *(m)*, rândunea *(f)*
swamp • *n* mlatin *(f)*, smârc
swan • *n* lebd *(f)*
sward • *n* gazon *(n)*, iarb, pajite, iarb *(f)*
swarm • *n* roi
swastika • *n* svastic *(f)*
swear • *v* jura, înjura
sweat • *n* sudoare *(f)*, transpiraie *(f)* • *v* transpira, asuda
swede • *n* nap
sweep • *v* mtura
sweet • *n* dulce *(n)*, bomboan *(f)* • *adj* dulce, îndulcit, parfumat, înmiresmat, proaspt, melodios, simpatic, drgu, mito • *adv* dulce
sweetbread • *n* momite
sweeten • *v* îndulci
sweetheart • *n* drag *(m)*, drag *(f)*, iubit *(m)*, iubit *(f)*, drgu *(f)*
sweetish • *adj* dulcior, dulciu, dulceag
sweetness • *n* dulcea
sweets • *n* dulciuri
swell • *v* se umfla • *n* val, valuri • *adj* super, senzaional, minunat
swelling • *n* umfltur *(f)*
swift • *n* drepnea
swim • *v* înota
swimming • *n* înot
swindle • *v* înela
swineherd • *n* porcar
swing • *v* balansa, legna
switch • *v* schimba, comuta • *n* comutator *(n)*, întreruptor *(n)*, punct *(f)*, selector
switchboard • *n* panou cu taste, bord cu taste *(n)*, taste de comutare, taste de apel
sword • *n* sabie *(f)*, spad *(f)*
swordfish • *n* pete spad *(f)*
sycamore • *n* platan *(m)*, sicomor *(m)*
syllable • *n* silab *(f)*
syllogism • *n* silogism *(n)*
symbol • *n* simbol *(m)*
symbolic • *adj* simbolic
symbolically • *adv* simbolic
symbolize • *v* simboliza
symmetrical • *adj* simetric *(n)*
symmetry • *n* simetrie *(f)*
sympathizer • *adj* simpatizant *(n)*, simpatizant *(f)*, simpatizator *(n)*, simpatizani
sympathy • *n* compasiune, comptimire, simpatie, empatie *(f)*
symposium • *n* simpozion *(n)*
symptom • *n* simptom
symptomatic • *adj* simptomatic
synagogue • *n* sinagog *(f)*
synchronization • *n* sincronizare *(f)*
synchronize • *v* sincroniza
synchronous • *adj* sincron *(m)*, în acelai timp
synclinal • *n* sinclinal
synonym • *n* sinonim *(n)*
syntax • *n* sintax *(f)*
synthesis • *n* sintez
synthesizer • *n* sintetizator *(m)*, sintetizator
synthetic • *adj* sintetic *(m)*
syphilis • *n* sifilis *(n)*
syringe • *n* sering *(f)*
syrup • *n* sirop *(n)*
system • *n* sistem *(n)*
systematic • *adj* sistemic *(n)*, sistematic *(n)*
systematization • *n* sistematizare *(f)*
systematize • *v* sistematiza

T

table • *v* a pune (depune) pe mas, a pune masa, amâna • *n* mas *(f)*, tabel *(n)*, tabel *(f)*
tablecloth • *n* fa de mas *(f)*
tacitly • *adv* în mod tacit
tactic • *n* tactic *(f)*
tadpole • *n* mormoloc *(m)*
tag • *n* etichet, leapa
taiga • *n* taiga
tail • *n* coad
tailor • *v* croi • *n* croitor *(m)*, croitoreas *(f)*, lufar
taint • *v* spurca, mânji
take • *v* lua

takeoff • *n* decolare
tale • *n* poveste *(f)*
talisman • *n* talisman, amulet
talk • *v* vorbi
talkative • *adj* vorbre *(m)*, flecar, limbut, guraliv, gure
tall • *adj* înalt
tamandua • *n* tamandua *(m)*
tamarin • *n* tamarin *(m)*
tamarind • *n* tamarin *(m)*
tamarisk • *n* ctin *(f)*, tamarisc *(f)*
tambourine • *n* tamburin *(f)*
tan • *v* bronza, tbci, argsi • *adj* cafeniu, bronzat • *n* bronz *(n)*, bronzare *(f)*
tangent • *n* tangent *(f)*
tangerine • *n* tangerin *(f)* • *adj* portocaliu
tangible • *adj* tangibil *(m)*, palpabil *(m)*
tank • *n* tanc rezervor *(n)*, rezervor *(n)*, recipient, tanc
tanner • *n* tbcar *(m)*, argsitor *(m)*, pielar *(m)*
tansy • *n* vetrice *(f)*
tantalum • *n* tantal *(n)*
tantrum • *n* pandalie *(f)*, toan *(f)*
tapir • *n* tapir *(m)*
tar • *n* gudron *(n)*
target • *v* inti, ochi
tarragon • *n* tarhon *(m)*
tartan • *n* tartan *(n)*
taste • *v* gusta • *n* gust
tasteless • *adj* fr gust
tatter • *n* zdrean *(f)*
tattoo • *v* tatua • *n* tatuaj *(n)*
tautology • *n* tautologie *(f)*, pleonasm *(n)*
tavern • *n* bodeg *(f)*, berrie *(f)*, braserie *(f)*
tax • *n* tax *(f)*, impozit *(n)*, dare
taxi • *n* taximetru
taxonomic • *adj* taxonomic
taxonomy • *n* taxonomie *(f)*, ierarhic clasificare *(f)*
tea • *n* ceai *(m)*
teach • *v* înva, instrui
teacher • *n* profesor *(m)*, profesoar *(f)*, învtor *(m)*
teak • *n* tec *(m)*
teakettle • *n* ceainic, ibric *(n)*
teal • *n* lii *(f)*, sarsel *(f)* • *adj* albastru-verzui
team • *n* echip
teapot • *n* ceainic
tear • *v* rupe, sfâia, scoate, smulge, detaa, demola, drâma, se rupe, alerga, lcrima • *n* rupere *(f)*, ruptur *(f)*, tietur *(f)*, lacrim *(f)*
teardrop • *n* lacrim *(f)*
tearful • *adj* înlcrimat
teaspoon • *n* linguri *(f)*
teat • *n* sfârc, â
technetium • *n* techneiu *(n)*
technical • *adj* tehnic *(n)*, tehnici, tehnic *(f)*
technique • *n* tehnic
technocracy • *n* tehnocraie
technological • *adj* tehnologic *(n)*
technology • *n* tehnologie *(f)*, tehnologie
tedium • *n* plictiseal *(f)*, urât *(n)*, anosteal *(f)*
telecommunication • *n* telecomunicaii
telegraph • *n* telegraf
telemarketing • *n* vânzare prin telefon *(f)*, telemarketing *(n)*
telepathy • *n* telepatie *(f)*
telephone • *n* telefon *(n)*
telescope • *n* telescop *(n)*, lunet *(f)*
telescopic • *adj* telescopic *(n)*
television • *n* televiziune *(f)*, televizor *(n)*
telltale • *n* limbut, denuntor, guraliv
tellurium • *n* telur *(n)*
temerity • *n* temeritate *(f)*
temper • *v* tempera, modera, regula, reveni, cli, amesteca • *n* caracter *(n)*, fire *(f)*, temperament *(n)*, stare *(f)*, dispoziie *(f)*, revenire *(f)*
temperamental • *adj* temperamental *(m)*
temperance • *n* sobrietate *(f)*, cumptare *(f)*
temperature • *n* temperatur *(f)*, febr *(f)*
tempest • *n* furtun *(f)*
template • *n* model *(n)*, format *(n)*, ablon *(n)*
temple • *n* templu *(n)*, tâmpl
temporal • *adj* temporal *(n)*, temporar *(n)*, temporar, trector
tempt • *v* tenta, ispiti
tempting • *adj* tentant
ten • *n* decar *(m)*, zece *(m)*
tenacity • *n* tenacitate *(f)*, adezivitate *(f)*
tend • *v* avea grij
tendency • *n* tendin *(f)*, înclinaie *(f)*
tender • *adj* iubit, gentil, dulce
tenderness • *n* tandree *(f)*, grij *(f)*, pruden *(f)*, sensibilitate *(f)*
tendon • *n* tendon *(n)*, ligament *(n)*, capt de muchi *(n)*
tenebrous • *adj* tenebros, întunecat
tennis • *n* tenis *(n)*
tenrec • *n* tanrec *(m)*
tension • *n* tensiune, încordare
tensional • *adj* tensional, de tensiune
tent • *n* cort *(n)*
tenth • *n* cel al zecelea *(m)*, cea a zecea *(f)*, zecime *(f)* • *adj* al zecelea *(m)*, a zecea *(f)*
tenure • *n* posesie *(f)*, durat de mandat *(f)*, durata posesiei, termen de stpânire *(n)*, ocupare *(f)*, drept de posesie *(n)*

tepid • *adj* dezinteresat
terbium • *n* terbiu *(n)*
term • *n* limit *(f)*, condiie *(f)*, clauz *(f)*, termen, expresie, cuvânt, trimestru
terminable • *adj* terminabil *(n)*
terminal • *n* terminal *(n)*, gar *(f)*, staie *(f)*
termination • *n* terminare *(f)*, sfârire, concediere *(f)*, disponibilizare *(f)*, încheiere *(f)*
terminology • *n* terminologie, terminologie *(f)*
termite • *n* termit *(f)*
tern • *n* rândunic-de-mare *(f)*
terrace • *v* terasa • *n* teras *(f)*
terrain • *n* teren *(n)*
terrestrial • *adj* terestru *(n)*, terestru, neacvatic
terrible • *adj* groaznic, teribil *(m)*, impresionant *(m)*, înspimânttor *(m)*, îngrozitor *(m)*
terrify • *v* înspimânta
territorial • *adj* teritorial *(n)*
territory • *n* teritoriu *(m)*
terror • *n* spaim, teroare *(f)*
terrorism • *n* terorism *(m)*
terrorist • *n* terorist *(m)*, terorist *(f)* • *adj* terorist *(n)*, terorist *(f)*
test • *n* prob, examen, test
testament • *n* testament *(n)*
testicular • *adj* testicular
testify • *v* atesta, declara, adeveri
testimonial • *n* recomandare scris *(f)*, atestat *(n)*, dovad *(f)*, atestat, referin, dovad
testimony • *n* depoziie *(f)*, declaraie *(f)*, depoziie scris *(f)*, mrturie *(f)*
testosterone • *n* testosteron *(m)*
textbook • *n* manual *(n)*
texture • *n* estur *(f)*, textur *(f)*, calitate a esturii *(f)*
thallium • *n* taliu *(n)*
than • *prep* ca, decât
thankful • *adj* recunosctor *(m)*, mulumitor *(m)*
thankfulness • *n* recunotin *(f)*
thanks • *interj* mulumesc, mersi
that • *conj* c • *pron* acel *(m)*, acea *(f)*, la *(m)*, aia *(f)*
thatch • *n* stuf
the • *art* -ul *(n)*, -a *(f)*, -i, -le, cel *(m)*, cea *(f)*, cele
theater • *n* teatru *(m)*
theatrical • *adj* teatral *(n)*
theft • *n* furt *(m)*
theirs • *pron* al lor *(m)*, a lor *(f)*, ai lor, ale lor
theism • *n* teism *(n)*
theme • *n* tem
then • *adv* atunci, apoi
theological • *adj* teologic *(n)*
theology • *n* teologie *(f)*
theory • *n* teorii, teorie *(f)*, teorie
theosophy • *n* teozofie *(f)*
therapeutic • *adj* terapeutic *(n)*
therapist • *n* terapeut
there • *adv* acolo, colo
therefore • *adv* deci, aadar, prin urmare
thermal • *adj* termal, termic
thermistor • *n* termistor
thermometer • *n* termometru *(n)*
thermonuclear • *adj* termonuclear *(n)*
thermosphere • *n* termosfer *(f)*
thesaurus • *n* dicionar de sinonime *(n)*
thesis • *n* tez *(f)*
they • *pron* ei *(m)*, ele *(f)*, dumnealor
thick • *adj* gros, tulbure
thicket • *n* tufi *(n)*, subarboret *(n)*, pdurice *(f)*, crâng *(n)*, arboret *(n)*, desi *(n)*
thief • *n* ho *(m)*, hoa *(f)*
thigh • *n* coaps *(f)*
thimble • *n* degetar *(m)*
thin • *v* subia, slbi • *adj* slab, subire
thine • *pron* al tu, a ta, ai ti, ale tale
thing • *n* lucru *(n)*, chestie *(f)*, obiect *(n)*
think • *v* gândi, cugeta, considera, crede, lua în consideraie, judeca
thinkable • *adj* imaginabil *(m)*, posibil, gândibil
thinker • *n* intelectual
third • *n* cel de al treilea *(n)*, cea de a treia *(f)*, treime *(f)*
thirst • *v* a dori fierbinte • *n* sete *(f)*
thirsty • *adj* setos
thirtieth • *adj* al treizecilea *(m)*, a treizecea *(f)*
this • *pron* acest, sta *(m)*, aceast, asta *(f)*
thistle • *n* scaiete *(m)*, ciulin *(m)*
thither • *adv* încolo
thorium • *n* toriu *(n)*
thorn • *n* spin, ghimpe
thoroughness • *n* meticulozitate
thou • *pron* tu
though • *conj* desi, parca
thought • *n* gând *(n)*, cuget *(n)*, gândire *(f)*, cugetare *(f)*
thoughtful • *adj* cugetat *(m)*
thousandth • *adj* al miilea *(m)*, a mia *(f)*
thread • *n* a *(f)*, tort *(f)*, fir *(f)*
threat • *n* ameninare *(f)*
threaten • *v* amenina
threatened • *adj* ameninat *(n)*
threatening • *adj* amenintor
three • *n* trei *(m)*
three-dimensional • *adj* tridimensional *(n)*, tridimensional *(f)*

thresh • *v* treiera
threshold • *n* prag *(n)*
thrice • *adv* trei oar
thrift • *n* cumptare
thrill • *n* fior
throat • *n* gât *(n)*, gât
throb • *v* pulsa
thrombosis • *n* tromboz *(f)*
thrombus • *n* trombus, cheag de sânge *(n)*
throne • *n* tron *(n)*, scaun *(n)*
through • *prep* prin
throw • *v* arunca, a deplasa
thrush • *n* sturz *(m)*
thrust • *v* împinge, bui, împunge
thulium • *n* tuliu *(n)*
thumb • *n* deget mare *(n)*, policar
thunder • *v* tuna • *n* tunet
thunderbolt • *n* fulger *(n)*
thunderclap • *n* tunet
thunderstorm • *n* furtun *(f)*
thus • *adv* aa, aa cum, în acest fel, astfel, deci, aadar
thyme • *n* lmâioar *(f)*, cimbru *(m)*
tick • *n* cpu *(f)* • *v* tici
ticket • *n* bilet *(n)*, amend *(f)*, amendare contravenional *(f)*, cupon de amend
tickle • *v* gâdila
tide • *n* maree *(f)*
tie • *v* lega
tiger • *n* tigru *(m)*
tighten • *v* strânge
tigress • *n* tigroaic *(f)*
tile • *n* igl *(f)*, olan *(n)*
tillage • *n* artur *(f)*, pmânt arabil *(n)*, pmânt cultivat
time • *n* timp, vreme, timp *(n)*, timpuri, timpi, ceas *(m)*, or *(f)*, ora zilei *(f)*, dat *(f)*, oar *(f)*, er *(f)*, epoc *(f)*
timekeeping • *n* cronometrare *(f)*, cronometraj *(n)*
timer • *n* cronometru *(n)*, cronograf *(n)*, regulator de timp, timpizor *(n)*
timothy • *n* timoftic *(f)*
tin • *n* staniu *(n)*, cositor • *adj* de cositor, din cositor
tinamou • *n* tinamu *(m)*
tincture • *n* tinctur *(f)*
tinder • *n* iasc *(f)*
tiny • *adj* minuscul, micu
tip • *n* baci
tipsy • *adj* beat
tired • *adj* obosit *(m)*, obosit *(f)*
tissue • *n* batist *(f)*, erveel *(n)*, esut *(n)*
tit • *n* mamelon *(n)*, sfârc *(n)*, â *(f)*, sân *(m)*, clu *(m)*, cior *(m)*, feti *(f)*, fetioar *(f)*, fetic *(f)*
titanium • *n* titan *(n)*
tithe • *n* zeciuial
titillate • *v* stimula, excita, gâdila, stârni
title • *n* titlu *(n)*
to • *prep* la, ctre, spre, cu
toad • *n* broasc râioas *(f)*
toadflax • *n* linari *(f)*
tobacco • *n* tutun *(m)*, tutun *(f)*, tabac *(n)*
tocsin • *n* semnal de alarm *(n)*, clopot de alarm
today • *n* astzi, azi • *adv* astzi, azi, ziua de azi, acum
toddler • *n* copil mic *(m)*
toe • *n* deget de la picior *(n)*, deget *(n)*
together • *adv* împreun, laolalt
toilet • *n* toalet *(f)*, closet *(n)*, closet *(f)*, vece *(n)*, privat *(f)*
tolerable • *adj* tolerabil *(n)*
tolerance • *n* rezisten *(f)*, tolerna *(f)*, toleran *(f)*, acceptare *(f)*, conformare
tolerate • *v* tolera, suporta
tom • *n* cotoi *(m)*, motan *(m)*, mascul *(m)*
tomato • *n* tomat *(f)*, roie *(f)*
tomb • *n* mormânt *(m)*
tomfoolery • *n* bufonerie, caraghioslâc *(n)*
tomorrow • *n* mâine *(n)* • *adv* mâine
tongue • *n* limb *(f)*
tonight • *n* ast noapte *(f)* • *adv* disear, desear
tonsil • *n* amigdal *(f)*
tonsillitis • *n* amigdalit *(f)*
too • *adv* i, deasemenea, prea
tool • *n* scul *(f)*, unealt *(f)*, instrument *(n)*, unealt
toolbox • *n* cutie de scule *(f)*, cutie cu instrumente *(f)*, trus de scule *(f)*
tooth • *n* dinte *(m)*
toothache • *n* durere de dini
toothbrush • *n* periu de dini *(f)*
toothless • *adj* edentat
toothpaste • *n* past de dini
toothpick • *n* scobitoare *(f)*
top • *n* culme, vârf
topaz • *n* topaz *(n)*
topgallant • *n* arboret *(m)*
topmast • *n* arboret *(n)*
topology • *n* topologie *(f)*
torch • *n* tor, fclie, fachie, lantern
torment • *v* chinui, tortura • *n* chin *(n)*, turment *(n)*, zbucium *(n)*
tornado • *n* tornad *(f)*
torpedo • *n* torpil *(f)*, torpedo *(n)*
torrent • *n* torent *(n)*, puhoi
tortoise • *n* estoas *(f)*, broasc estoas *(f)*
torture • *v* tortura, chinui • *n* tortur *(f)*, chin *(n)*
totality • *n* totalitate *(f)*

totally • *adv* total *(m)*
totem • *n* totem
totemism • *n* totemism *(n)*
toucan • *n* tucan *(m)*
touch • *v* atinge, emoiona
tourism • *n* turism *(n)*
tourist • *n* turist *(m)*, turiti, turist *(f)*
tout • *v* racola
tow • *n* stup
towel • *n* prosop *(n)*
tower • *n* turn, turl *(f)*, turn *(n)*
town • *n* ora *(n)*, orae
toxic • *adj* toxic
toxicology • *n* toxicologie *(f)*
toy • *n* jucrie *(f)*
trace • *n* urm, cablaj imprimat *(n)*
traceable • *adj* trasabil *(m)*, care poate fi trasat, reperabil *(m)*
track • *n* drum, pist de circulaie, band rutier
tractor • *n* tractor *(n)*
trade • *n* meserie
trademark • *n* marc înregistrat *(f)*, marc *(f)*
tradition • *n* tradiie *(f)*, datin *(f)*
traditional • *adj* tradiional
traffic • *n* trata *(f)*
tragedy • *n* tragedie *(f)*
train • *n* tren *(n)*
training • *n* antrenament *(n)*
traitor • *n* trdtor
trajectory • *n* traiectorie *(f)*
tram • *n* tramvai
trampoline • *n* trambulin *(f)*
transaction • *n* afacere *(f)*, transacie *(f)*, operaie comercial *(f)*
transatlantic • *adj* transatlantic *(n)*, transatlantic *(f)*
transcendental • *adj* transcendental *(n)*
transcribe • *v* transcrie
transducer • *n* transductor *(n)*
transfer • *v* transfera
transform • *v* transforma
transformation • *n* transformare *(f)*, transformri, mutaie *(f)*, mutare *(f)*
transformer • *n* transformator *(n)*
transfusion • *n* transfuzie de sânge *(f)*, transvazare *(f)*
transgress • *v* grei
transgression • *n* infraciune *(f)*, transgresiune *(f)*, înclcare de lege *(f)*
transient • *adj* trector, efemer, tranzient, tranzitoriu
transitional • *adj* tranziional *(n)*
transitive • *adj* tranzitiv
transitivity • *n* tranzitivitate *(f)*
translatable • *adj* traductibil *(m)*
translate • *v* traduce
translation • *n* traducere *(f)*, transmisie *(f)*, translaie *(f)*
translator • *n* traductor *(m)*, interpret *(m)*, translator *(m)*
transliteration • *n* transcripie *(f)*, transliteraie *(f)*
transmission • *n* transmitere *(f)*, transmisie *(f)*, angrenaj *(n)*
transmit • *v* transmite
transmitter • *n* transmiãtor
transmute • *v* a transmuta
transparency • *n* transparen *(f)*
transparent • *adj* transparent *(n)*, clar *(n)*, evident *(n)*, limpede *(n)*, vdit *(n)*
transplant • *n* transplantare *(f)*
transport • *v* transporta, cra • *n* transportare, mijloc de transport
transportation • *n* transportare, transport
transshipment • *n* transbordare *(f)*
transubstantiation • *n* transsubstaniere *(f)*, transsubstaniaie
trash • *n* lucru nevaloros *(n)*, rebut *(n)*, gunoi *(n)*, rmie, reziduu *(n)*, deeu *(n)*, co de hârtii *(n)*
traumatic • *adj* traumatic
travel • *v* cltori • *n* voiaj *(n)*, cltorie *(f)*
traveling • *n* pai
tread • *v* clca
treason • *n* trdare
treasure • *v* preui • *n* comoar *(f)*
treasury • *n* tezaur de stat *(n)*, trezorerie *(f)*, trezorerii, vistierie (de stat) *(f)*, tezaur *(n)*, tezaur literar *(n)*
treat • *v* trata, negocia, implora, conjura, îngriji, ospta • *n* încântare *(f)*, desftare *(f)*, trataie *(f)*, cinste *(f)*, surpriz *(f)*
treatise • *n* tratat *(n)*
treatment • *n* tratament
treaty • *n* tratat *(n)*
tree • *n* arbore *(m)*, copac *(m)*, pom *(m)*
trefoil • *n* trifoi
tremble • *v* tremura
trepidation • *n* trepidaie *(f)*, trepidare *(f)*
trial • *n* proces *(n)*, judecat *(f)*
triangle • *n* triunghi *(n)*
tribal • *adj* tribal *(n)*
tribe • *n* trib *(n)*
tributary • *n* afluent *(m)*, tributar *(m)*
trick • *v* înela, pcli
tricycle • *n* triciclu *(m)*
trifling • *adj* mrunt
trigonometry • *n* trigonometrie *(f)*
trill • *n* consoan vibrant *(f)*
trimester • *n* trimestru *(n)*
trinitarianism • *n* trinitarianism *(m)*
trinity • *n* triad *(f)*

trip • *v* împiedica, cltori • *n* excursie *(f)*, voiaj *(n)*, cltorie *(f)*, împiedicare *(f)*, poticneal *(f)*, piedic *(f)*
triple • *n* triplu *(n)*
triumph • *n* triumf *(n)*, victorie *(f)* • *v* triumfa, învinge
triumphant • *adj* triumftor *(m)*, victorios *(m)*, triumfant *(m)*
troll • *n* trol *(m)*, *(m)*, troll *(m)*
trolley • *n* crucior
trombone • *n* trombon *(n)*
trope • *n* trop *(m)*
trophy • *n* trofeu *(n)*
tropical • *adj* tropical *(n)*, tropical *(f)*
troposphere • *n* troposfer *(f)*
trot • *v* trota
troubadour • *n* trubadur
trouble • *n* necaz *(n)*
trout • *n* pstrv *(m)*
trowel • *n* mistrie *(f)*
truce • *n* armistiiu *(n)*
truck • *n* camion
true • *adj* adevrat, adevrat *(n)*, loial *(n)*, fidel *(n)*, sincer *(n)*
truffle • *n* truf
trump • *n* atu *(n)*
trumpet • *n* trompet *(f)*
trunk • *n* portbagaj *(n)*
trust • *v* încrede • *n* încredere *(f)*, speran *(f)*, sperare *(f)*, credit *(n)*, veridicitate *(f)*, trust *(n)*
trustworthy • *adj* sigur, demn de încredere
truth • *n* adevr *(n)*, corectitudine *(f)*, sinceritate, bun credin *(f)*, veridicitate, adevr, veridicitate *(f)*
truthfulness • *n* veridicitate *(f)*
try • *v* încerca, proba, se fora, strdui, testa, gusta, judeca • *n* încercare *(f)*, tentativ *(f)*, prob *(f)*, probare *(f)*, experimentare *(f)*
tryptophan • *n* triptofan *(m)*
tsar • *n* ar *(m)*
tuberculosis • *n* tuberculoz *(f)*
tuft • *n* smoc *(n)*, floc
tug • *v* trage, smuci
tugboat • *n* remocher
tulip • *n* lalea *(f)*, tulip *(f)*
tumult • *n* freamt, tumult *(n)*, tumulte
tumulus • *n* tumul *(m)*
tuna • *n* ton
tundra • *n* tundr *(f)*
tungsten • *n* tungsten *(n)*, wolfram
tunic • *n* tunic *(f)*
tunnel • *n* tunel *(n)*
turbid • *adj* tulbure *(f)*
turbulence • *n* tulburare *(f)*, turbulen *(f)*
turbulent • *adj* turbulent *(n)*
turkey • *n* curcan *(m)*, curc *(f)*
turn • *v* învârti
turnery • *n* strungrie *(f)*
turnip • *n* navet *(f)*, nap *(m)*
turnstile • *n* turnichet
turpentine • *n* terebentin *(f)*
turquoise • *n* turcoaz *(f)*, peruzea *(f)*, turcoaz • *adj* de turcoaz, de peruzea, turcoaz
turtle • *n* broasc estoas *(f)*
tutor • *n* preceptor *(m)*
twayblade • *n* buhai *(m)*
twenty-eighth • *adj* douzeci i optulea
twenty-fifth • *adj* douzeci i cincilea
twenty-fourth • *adj* douzeci i patrulea
twenty-ninth • *adj* douzeci i noulea
twenty-second • *adj* douzeci i doilea
twenty-seventh • *adj* douzeci i aptelea *(m)*, douzeci i aptea *(f)*
twenty-sixth • *adj* al douzeci i aselea
twenty-third • *adj* douzeci i treilea
twig • *n* rmurea *(f)*, rmuric *(f)*, nuia *(f)*, varg *(f)*, smicea *(f)*
twilight • *n* amurg *(n)*, crepuscul *(n)*
twin • *n* geamn *(m)*
twist • *v* rsuci, învârti, întortochea, stoarce
twit • *v* mustra
two • *n* doi *(m)*
two-dimensional • *adj* bidimensional *(m)*
type • *n* fel, gen
typed • *adj* tiprit
typhoon • *n* taifun *(n)*
typhus • *n* tifos *(n)*
typographical • *adj* tipografic, de tipografie
typography • *n* tipografie, tipar
tyrannical • *adj* tiranic *(n)*, opresiv, tiranic, despotic
tyrannosaur • *n* tiranozaur *(m)*
tyranny • *n* tiranie *(f)*, tiranie
tyre • *n* pneu *(n)*, cauciuc *(n)*
tyrosine • *n* tirozin *(f)*

U

ubiquitous • *adj* ubicuu, omniprezent *(m)*, omniprezent *(f)*
ubiquity • *n* ubicuitate *(f)*
udder • *n* uger
ugh • *interj* câh
ugly • *adj* urât
ulcer • *n* ulcer *(n)*
ultimately • *adv* la urma urmei, în definitiv, recent, nu de mult
ululation • *n* urlet *(n)*
umbel • *n* umbel *(f)*
umbrage • *v* umbri, adumbri • *n* suprare *(f)*, ranchiun *(f)*, umbr *(f)*
umbrella • *n* umbrel *(f)*
unable • *adj* incapabil *(n)*, neputincios *(n)*, incompetent *(n)*
unacceptability • *n* neacceptabilitate *(f)*, inacceptabilitate *(f)*
unacceptable • *adj* neacceptabil *(n)*, inacceptabil, nesatisfctor *(n)*
unacknowledged • *adj* nerecunoscut
unambiguous • *adj* clar *(n)*, neechivoc *(n)*, precis *(n)*, neambiguu *(n)*, univoc
unanticipated • *adj* neanticipat, neateptat, neprevzut
unassured • *adj* nesigur, îndoielnic, neasigurat
unauthorized • *adj* neautorizat, neîmputernicit *(m)*
unavailable • *adj* indisponibil, neutilizabil
unavoidable • *adj* inevitabil, de neocolit
unaware • *adj* netiutor, neprevenit
unbearable • *adj* nesuportabil, insuportabil
unbind • *v* dezlega
unbrushed • *adj* neperiat *(m)*
uncanny • *adj* bizar
uncertain • *adj* nesigur *(n)*, nesiguri, incert *(n)*, nedecis *(n)*, indecis *(n)*, instabil *(n)*, inconstant *(n)*, nestatornic *(n)*, nestabil *(n)*, instabili, neregulat, variabil *(n)*, imprevizibil *(n)*, imprevizibili
uncertainty • *n* incertitudine, nesiguran
unchain • *v* dezlnui
uncle • *n* unchi
unclean • *adj* murdar *(n)*, imoral *(n)*, necurat *(n)*
unclear • *adj* neclar
unclothed • *adj* dezbrcat *(n)*, neîmbrcat *(n)*, gol *(n)*, goal *(f)*
uncommon • *adj* rar, necomun
unconscious • *adj* incontient
unconstructive • *adj* neconstructiv
uncontaminated • *adj* necontaminat, nepoluat
uncontrollable • *adj* incontrolabil, necontrolabil
uncontroversial • *adj* necontroversat
unconventional • *adj* neconvenional *(n)*, atipic
uncritical • *adj* necritic, indulgent
undefined • *adj* nedefinit
under • *prep* sub
undercurrent • *n* curent de adâncime *(m)*, curent submarin *(m)*
underground • *n* micare clandestin, organizaie clandestin
undermine • *v* surpa, submina, spa
underneath • *adv* sub
underpants • *n* chiloi
understand • *v* înelege, pricepe
understatement • *n* declaraie incomplet *(f)*, declaraie atenuant *(f)*
undertake • *v* întreprinde
undertone • *n* ton slab *(n)*, ton reinut *(n)*, semiton *(n)*
underwear • *n* chiloi, lenjerie de corp, izmene, indispensabili
undesirable • *adj* nedorit *(m)*
undo • *v* desface
uneasiness • *n* stinghereal *(f)*, nelinite *(f)*, tulburare *(f)*, anxietate *(f)*
uneasy • *adj* dificil *(n)*, complicat *(n)*
unemployed • *adj* omer
unemployment • *n* omaj *(n)*
unequal • *adj* inegal
unequivocally • *adv* neechivoc *(n)*
uneven • *adj* denivelat
unexceptionable • *adj* incontestabil *(n)*, nereproabil *(n)*, inatacabil *(n)*
unexpected • *adj* neateptat *(n)*, neprevzut *(n)*, neanticipat *(n)*
unfashionable • *adj* demodat
unfavorable • *adj* nefavorabil *(n)*, nefavorabil *(f)*
unfold • *v* desfura
unforgettable • *adj* de neuitat, neuitabil
unfriendly • *adj* neprietenos, ostil
unfruitful • *adj* infructuos, neroditor, nerodnic, sterp, steril
unfruitfulness • *n* nerodnicie, sterilitate
unfurl • *v* desfura
ungrammatical • *adj* negramatical
unhappiness • *n* nefericire *(f)*
unholy • *adj* ru *(n)*, nesfânt *(n)*, afurisit *(n)*, rea *(f)*, afurisit *(f)*
unhygienic • *adj* antiigienic
unicameral • *adj* unicameral
unicorn • *n* unicorn *(m)*
unification • *n* unificare *(f)*
uniform • *n* uniform *(f)*
unilateral • *adj* unilateral *(m)*, unilateral *(f)*

unilaterally • *adv* în mod unilateral
unimaginable • *adj* inimaginabil *(n)*, neimaginabil *(n)*, neînchipuibil
unimpeded • *adj* neîmpiedicat, neobstrucionat *(n)*
unimportant • *adj* neimportant
uninformed • *adj* neinformat *(n)*
unintelligible • *adj* neinteligibil
uninterested • *adj* neinteresat *(n)*, dezinteresat *(n)*, indiferent *(n)*
uninterrupted • *adj* neîntrerupt *(m)*, neîntrerupt *(f)*, fr pauz
union • *n* unire, unitate *(f)*, uniune *(f)*, uniune
unique • *adj* unic *(n)*
unit • *n* unitate *(f)*
unitarianism • *n* unitarianism *(m)*
unite • *v* uni
united • *adj* unit *(n)*, unit *(f)*
unity • *n* unire, unitate *(f)*
universe • *n* univers *(n)*
university • *n* universitate *(f)*
unknown • *adj* necunoscut, netiut, obscur
unleaded • *adj* fara plumb
unlikelihood • *n* improbabilitate, neverosimilitate
unlikely • *adj* improbabil, improbabil *(f)* • *adv* în mod improbabil, puin probabil
unlimited • *adj* nelimitat, nemrginit *(m)*, nelimitat *(f)*
unload • *v* descrca
unlock • *v* descuia, debloca
unlucky • *adj* nenorocos *(m)*
unmarried • *adj* burlac
unnatural • *adj* artificial, nenatural *(n)*
unnecessarily • *adv* în mod nenecesar
unnecessary • *adj* nenecesar *(n)*, inutil *(n)*, netrebuibil *(n)*
unnumbered • *adj* nenumrat *(m)*, nenumrabil
unobvious • *adj* neevident, neclar, nevdit
unofficial • *adj* neoficial *(n)*
unorthodox • *adj* neortodox, neconvenional
unpaid • *adj* nepltit, neachitat, neretribuit, netimbrat, nefrancat
unpleasant • *adj* neplcut *(n)*, nedorit, neagreat
unpleasantness • *n* neagreabilitate *(f)*
unpopular • *adj* nepopular *(n)*
unpopularity • *n* nepopularitate *(f)*
unpredictability • *n* neprevizibilitate *(f)*, neanticipabilitate *(f)*
unpredictable • *adj* neprevizibil *(n)*, neanticipabil *(n)*, neprevizibili, neprevizibil *(f)*
unproductive • *adj* neproductiv, nefructuos
unprotected • *adj* neprotejat
unqualified • *adj* necalificat *(n)*, incompetent *(n)*, necompetent *(n)*, nestudiat *(n)*, necercetat *(n)*
unravel • *v* deira
unreal • *adj* nereal
unrealistic • *adj* nerealist, irealist
unreasonable • *adj* nerezonabil *(m)*
unrequested • *adj* necerut, nesolicitat
unresponsive • *adj* nesensibil *(n)*, nereactiv *(n)*, nereacionant *(n)*, nerspundent *(n)*, apatic *(n)*, indiferent *(n)*
unrestricted • *adj* nerestricionat *(n)*
unrighteous • *adj* injust *(m)*, nedrept *(m)*, necinstit *(m)*
unruly • *adj* nesupus *(m)*, neasculttor *(m)*
unsafe • *adj* nesigur
unskillful • *adj* nepriceput *(m)*
unstable • *adj* instabil, inconstant, variabil
unstoppable • *adj* de neoprit *(m)*, neopribil *(n)*, de nestopat, nestopabil *(n)*
unsuitable • *adj* neadecvat *(n)*, neconvenabil *(n)*, inconvenabil *(n)*, nepotrivit *(n)*, nenimerit *(n)*
unsystematic • *adj* nesistematic *(n)*
unthinkable • *adj* neimaginabil, de neimaginat, incredibil, negândibil *(m)*, imposibil *(m)*, de neconceput, neconcepibil, inimaginabil
untie • *v* desface, dezlega
untraceable • *adj* netrasabil *(m)*, ; nereperabil *(m)*
untranslatable • *adj* netraductibil *(m)*
untrustworthy • *adj* îndoielnic, nesigur
untruthful • *adj* neveridic *(n)*, fals *(n)*, mincinos *(n)*
untruthfulness • *n* neveridicitate *(f)*
unused • *adj* nefolosit *(n)*, neutilizat *(n)*, neîntrebuinat *(n)*
unusual • *adj* ciudat, insolit *(n)*, neobinuit *(n)*, neuzual
unusually • *adv* ciudat
unwanted • *adj* nedorit, nevoit
unwind • *v* deira
up • *adv* sus
upholstery • *n* capitonare *(f)*
uproar • *n* freamt, agitaie *(f)*, tumult *(n)*, larm *(f)*, clamoare *(f)*, glgie *(f)*, zgomot *(n)*
upset • *v* tulbura, supra, necji, deranja, perturba, da peste cap, rsturna • *n* suprare *(f)*, deranjare *(f)*, capotare *(f)*, grea *(f)*, discomfort *(n)* • *adj* suprat, deranjat, greos
upstream • *adv* la deal, în amonte, în susul apei, în contra-curent

upwards • *adv* în sus, la deal
uranium • *n* uraniu *(n)*
urbanity • *n* decen *(f)*, bun-cuviin *(f)*, urbanitate *(f)*, urbanism *(n)*
urbanization • *n* urbanizare *(f)*
urchin • *n* arici *(m)*
us • *pron* ne, nou
use • *n* folosire *(f)*, uz *(f)*, întrebuinare *(f)*, utilitate *(f)*, folosin *(f)*, funcie *(f)* • *v* utiliza, folosi
used • *adj* utilizat *(m)*, folosit *(m)*, întrebuinat *(m)*
useful • *adj* util, folositor, trebuincios *(n)*
useless • *adj* inutil *(n)*, netrebuincios *(n)*, nefolositor *(n)*
user • *n* utilizator *(m)*, consumator *(m)*, narcoman *(m)*, toxicoman *(m)*, utilizatoare *(f)*, exploatator *(m)*
usual • *adj* uzual *(n)*, obinuit *(n)*
usually • *adv* de obicei, în general
usurp • *v* uzurpa, rpi
usurper • *n* uzurpator *(m)*
utility • *n* utilitate, folos
utopia • *n* utopie *(f)*
utterance • *n* vorbi, vorbire
uvula • *n* uvul *(f)*

V

vacant • *adj* gol
vacation • *n* vacan, anulare, golire
vaccine • *n* vaccin
vacuum • *n* vid *(n)*
vagabond • *v* a vagabonda • *n* vagabond *(m)*
vagina • *n* vagin *(n)*
valediction • *n* discurs de adio, discurs de rmas bun, desprire *(f)*, rmas bun, adio, formul de încheiere
valence • *n* valen *(f)*
valerian • *n* valerian *(f)*, odolean *(m)*
valiant • *adj* viteaz, curajos
valid • *adj* valid
validation • *n* validare, confirmare, certificare
validity • *n* validitate *(f)*, valabilitate *(f)*
valine • *n* valin *(f)*
valkyrie • *n* walkirie
valley • *n* vale *(f)*
valuable • *adj* valoros, preios
value • *n* valoare *(f)*
valve • *n* ventil *(n)*, valv *(f)*
vampire • *n* vampir *(m)*, vampir *(f)*, strigoi, vârcolac, vampiri, strigoaie *(f)*
van • *n* furgonet *(f)*
vanadinite • *n* vanadinit *(n)*
vanadium • *n* vanadiu *(n)*
vandalism • *n* vandalism *(n)*
vanguard • *n* avangard *(f)*, antegard *(f)*
vanilla • *n* vanilie *(f)*
vanity • *n* vanitate *(f)*, mândrie, îngâmfare *(f)*
vapor • *n* abur *(m)*
variable • *n* variabil, parametru • *adj* variabil *(n)*, schimbabil *(n)*
variance • *n* variere *(f)*, variaie *(f)*, contradicie *(f)*, diferen *(f)*, discrepan *(f)*
variation • *n* variaie *(f)*, variere *(f)*
variegated • *adj* vrgat, blat
variety • *n* varietate *(f)*, sort *(n)*, fel *(n)*, sortiment *(n)*
vase • *n* vaz *(f)*
veal • *n* carne de viel *(f)*, viel *(m)*
vegetable • *n* vegetal *(f)*, legum, legume, legum *(f)* • *adj* vegetal *(n)*
vegetarian • *n* vegetarian *(f)*, vegetarian *(m)*, ierbivor *(m)* • *adj* vegetarial *(m)*
vegetarianism • *n* vegetarianism *(n)*
vegetation • *n* vegetaie *(f)*
vehemence • *n* vehemen *(f)*
vehicle • *n* vehicul *(n)*, mijloc de transport *(n)*
veil • *n* vl, voal
vein • *n* ven *(f)*, vân
velocipede • *n* velociped *(n)*
velocity • *n* vitez *(f)*
velvet • *n* catifea *(f)*
velvety • *adj* catifelat
vendor • *n* vânztor, vânztoare *(f)*
veneration • *n* venerare *(f)*, veneraie *(f)*
vengeance • *n* rzbunare *(f)*
venom • *n* venin *(n)*, fiere
venomous • *adj* veninos
ventral • *adj* ventral *(n)*
veranda • *n* verand
verb • *n* verb *(n)*
verbal • *adj* verbal *(m)*, oral *(m)*, oral *(n)*
verbena • *n* verbin *(f)*
verdant • *adj* verde, luxuriant, proaspt, ageamiu
verify • *v* verifica
verisimilitude • *n* verosimilitate *(f)*, verosimilitudine *(f)*
vermilion • *n* vermillon *(n)*, cinabru *(n)*, vermillon • *adj* vermeil

versatile • *adj* versatil, multilateral, pivotant, inconstant
verse • *n* vers
verso • *n* verso *(n)*
vert • *n* verde
vertebra • *n* vertebr *(f)*
vertebral • *adj* vertebral
vertebrate • *n* vertebrat *(n)*
vertical • *adj* vertical *(n)*
very • *adj* acelai *(n)* • *adv* foarte
vessel • *n* ambarcaiune *(f)*, recipient, vas *(n)*
vestibule • *n* vestibul *(n)*, antreu *(n)*, hol de intrare *(n)*
vestige • *n* urm *(f)*, indiciu *(n)*, vestigiu *(n)*, rmi *(f)*
vestigial • *adj* vestigial *(m)*
vetch • *n* mzriche *(f)*
veterinarian • *n* doctor veterinar *(m)*
vexation • *n* vexaiune *(f)*, vexare *(f)*
via • *prep* via, prin
vial • *n* fiol *(f)*
vibraphone • *n* vibrafon
vibration • *n* vibrare *(f)*
vice • *n* viciu
vicinity • *n* apropiere *(f)*, vecintate
vicissitude • *n* vicisitudine *(f)*
victim • *n* victim *(f)*, jertf *(f)*
victor • *n* învingtor *(m)*, învingtoare *(f)*, învingtori, învingtoare
victorious • *adj* victorios *(n)*
victory • *n* victorie *(f)*
video • *n* video
videocassette • *n* videocaset *(f)*
vigil • *n* veghe, gard, ateptare, observare
vigilance • *n* vigilen *(f)*
vigilant • *adj* vigilent, precaut, atent
vigorous • *adj* viguros *(n)*, viguroas *(f)*
vileness • *n* infamie *(f)*, ticloie *(f)*, mielie *(f)*, josnicie *(f)*
villa • *n* vil *(f)*
village • *n* sat *(n)*
villain • *n* miel, ticlos, spirit ru *(n)*, viclean *(m)*, rufctor *(m)*, erb *(m)*, iobag *(m)*, vecin *(m)*
vindictive • *adj* vindicativ, rzbuntor, dumnos *(m)*, ranchiunos *(m)*
vine • *n* vi
vinegar • *n* oet *(n)*
vineyard • *n* vie *(f)*
viola • *n* viol *(f)*, alto *(m)*, viorea *(f)*, topora *(m)*
violate • *v* viola, înclca
violence • *n* violen *(f)*
violent • *adj* violent, violent *(m)*
violet • *n* violet *(n)*, violet *(f)*, viorea *(f)* • *adj* violet
violin • *n* vioar *(f)*
violinist • *n* violonist *(m)*
viper • *n* npârc *(f)*, viper
virgin • *n* fecioar *(f)*, virgin *(f)*, virgin *(m)* • *adj* fecioresc, feciorelnic, virgin *(f)*, virgin *(m)*, virgin
virginity • *n* virginitate *(f)*, feciorie *(f)*
virile • *adj* viril
virility • *n* virilitate *(f)*
virology • *n* virusologie
virtually • *adv* în mod virtual
virtue • *n* virtute
virulent • *adj* virulent
virus • *n* virus, virus *(m)*, virus de computer *(m)*, virus computeric *(m)*, virus informatic *(m)*
visa • *n* viz *(f)*
viscometer • *n* viscozimetru *(n)*
viscount • *n* viconte *(m)*
viscountess • *n* vicontes *(f)*
viscous • *adj* vâscos, cleios
visibility • *n* vizibilitate *(f)*
visible • *adj* vizibil *(n)*
vision • *n* vedere *(f)*, viziune *(f)*, obiectiv *(n)*, vedenie *(f)*, apariie *(f)*
visionary • *adj* vizionar
visit • *v* vizita • *n* vizit *(f)*
vista • *n* perspectiv *(f)*, vedere *(f)*
vitamin • *n* vitamin *(f)*
viticulture • *n* viticultur *(f)*
vixen • *n* vulpi *(f)*, vulpoaic *(f)*
vizier • *n* vezír
vocabulary • *n* glosar *(n)*, vocabular *(n)*, lexic *(n)*
vocation • *n* vocaie *(f)*, predispoziie *(f)*, chemare *(f)*, ocupaie *(f)*
vociferation • *n* vociferare *(f)*
vodka • *n* vodc *(f)*
vogue • *n* vog *(f)*
voice • *n* voce, voci, glas *(n)*, glasuri, sonor *(f)*, consoan sonor *(f)*, sunet sonor *(n)*, sunet fonic *(n)*, sunet, ton *(n)*, voce *(f)*, vorbire *(f)*, cuvinte, exprimare *(f)*, expresie *(f)*, vot *(n)*, diatez *(f)*
voiceless • *adj* mut, fr voce
void • *n* vid *(n)* • *adj* nul
voivode • *n* voievod *(m)*
volatile • *adj* volatil *(m)*, efemer *(m)*
volcano • *n* vulcan *(m)*
volcanology • *n* vulcanologie *(f)*
vole • *n* oarece-de-câmp *(m)*
volleyball • *n* volei *(m)*
volt • *n* volt
voltage • *n* tensiune *(f)*, voltaj *(n)*
voltaic • *adj* voltaic
voltmeter • *n* voltmetru *(n)*
volume • *n* volum *(n)*

voluminous • *adj* voluminos *(m)*
volunteer • *n* voluntar *(m)*, voluntar *(f)*
vomit • *v* vomita, borî, vrsa
vortex • *n* vâltoare, vârtej *(n)*, bulboan *(f)*
vote • *v* vota • *n* vot *(n)*
vow • *n* jurmânt
vowel • *n* vocal *(f)*
voyage • *n* cltorie *(f)*
vulgar • *adj* obscen *(n)*, vulgar *(n)*, grosolan *(n)*, comun *(n)*, ordinar *(n)*
vulnerability • *n* vulnerabilitate *(f)*
vulpine • *adj* iret
vulture • *n* vultur *(m)*

W

wage • *n* plat *(f)*, salariu *(n)*, leaf *(f)*
wagon • *n* car *(n)*, cru *(f)*
wagtail • *n* codobatur *(f)*, prunda *(m)*
waist • *n* mijloc, talie
waistcoat • *n* vest *(f)*, jiletc *(f)*
wait • *v* atepta, servi masa • *n* ateptare *(f)*
waiter • *n* chelner *(m)*, osptar *(m)*
waitress • *n* chelneri *(f)*, osptri *(f)*
wake • *v* trezi • *n* priveghi *(n)*, siaj *(n)*
walk • *v* merge, umbla
wall • *n* zid, perete *(m)*
wallet • *n* portofel, portmoneu
wallflower • *n* micsandr-slbatic *(f)*, micsandr-de-munte *(f)*
wallpaper • *n* tapet *(n)*
walnut • *n* nuc *(m)*, nuc *(f)*
walrus • *n* mors *(f)*
wander • *v* umbla, plimba
want • *v* vrea • *n* lips *(f)*
wapiti • *n* wapiti *(m)*
war • *n* rzboi *(n)*, rzbel *(n)*
warbler • *n* silvie *(f)*
warehouse • *v* depozita, înmagazina • *n* magazie *(f)*, antrepozit *(n)*, depozit *(n)*
warm • *adj* cald *(m)*, cald *(f)*, apropiat *(m)*, apropiat *(f)* • *v* înclzi
warmth • *n* cldur *(f)*
warp • *n* urzeal, natr *(f)*
warranted • *adj* garantat *(m)*, în garanie
warranty • *n* garanie *(f)*
warren • *n* vizuin *(f)*
warrior • *n* lupttor *(m)*
warship • *n* nav de rzboi *(f)*, vas de rzboi *(n)*, nav militar *(f)*
wart • *n* neg, gâlm *(f)*
warthog • *n* porc alergtor *(m)*, porc cu negi *(m)*, facocer *(m)*
wash • *v* spla
washbasin • *n* chiuvet
washer • *n* aib *(f)*
wasp • *n* viespe *(f)*
waste • *n* deert *(n)*, pustietate *(f)*, irosire *(f)*, pierdere *(f)*, decdere *(f)*, deeu *(n)*, gunoi *(n)*, rest *(n)*, excrement *(n)* • *adj* deert, pustiu, sterp, prisos, superfluu, inutil • *v* distruge, devasta, decdea, irosi, pierde, risipi, ucide, omorî, emacia, descrna, slbi
watch • *n* ceas *(n)*, straj, gard, tur *(f)*, strjer, gard *(f)* • *v* privi, urmri, veghea, pzi, avea grij
watchful • *adj* vigilent, atent
watchmaker • *n* ceasornicar *(m)*
water • *v* iriga • *n* ap *(f)*, *(f)* *((ap))*
watercress • *n* nsturel *(m)*, creson *(n)*, cardama *(f)*
waterfall • *n* cascad *(f)*
watermelon • *n* pepene verde *(m)*, lubeni *(f)*, pepene *(m)*, pepene verde
watery • *adj* aptos, apos
wavelength • *n* lungime de und *(f)*
wax • *v* cera • *n* cear *(f)* • *adj* cear
way • *n* cale *(f)*, drum *(n)*, fel, mod
we • *pron* noi
weak • *adj* slab, debil, lânced
weaken • *v* slbi
wealth • *n* avere *(f)*, bogie *(f)*
weapon • *n* arm *(f)*
wear • *v* purta • *n* îmbrcminte *(f)*, haine, uzur *(f)*
wearable • *adj* purtabil *(n)*, îmbrcabil *(n)*
weasel • *n* nevstuic *(f)*
weather • *n* vreme, stare atmosferic *(f)*, timp *(n)*, intemperii
weave • *v* ese
wed • *v* cstori, însura, mrita, cununa
wedding • *n* nunt *(f)*
wedge • *n* pan *(f)*, felie *(f)*, cârd *(n)*
weed • *n* buruian, iarb *(f)* • *v* a plivi
week • *n* sptmân *(f)*
weekday • *n* zi a sptmânii *(f)*, zi lucrtoare *(f)*
weekend • *n* sfârit de sptmân *(n)*, weekend *(n)*
weekly • *adj* sptmânal *(n)*
weep • *v* plânge, lcrima
weigh • *v* cântri, evalua, chibzui, cumpni, avea greutate, cântri greu
weight • *v* îngreuna, pondera • *n* greutate *(f)*, halter, haltere, mas *(f)*

weightlifting • *n* solicitare muchiular *(f)*, ridicare de greuti, halterofilie *(f)*
weighty • *adj* greu *(m)*, care atârn greu, serios, important
weird • *adj* straniu, ciudat
welcome • *v* întâmpina • *adj* binevenit *(m)*, binevenit *(f)* • *interj* bine ai venit!, bine ai venit!, bun venit, bine ai venit
well • *adj* bine • *adv* bine, foarte • *n* fântân *(f)*, pu *(n)*
well-behaved • *adj* manierat *(m)*, bine crescut *(m)*
well-being • *n* bunstare *(f)*, prosperitate *(f)*, sntate *(f)*
werewolf • *n* pricolici
west • *n* vest *(n)*
western • *adj* vestic *(n)*, occidental *(n)*, apusean *(n)*
wet • *v* uda, excita • *adj* ud, umed, ploios
wether • *n* batal *(m)*
whale • *n* balen *(f)*
wharf • *n* chei *(n)*
what • *pron* ce, care
wheat • *n* grâu *(m)*, grâne
wheel • *n* roat *(f)*
wheelbarrow • *n* roab *(f)*
whelp • *v* fta • *n* cel *(m)*, lupan *(m)*
when • *n* atunci când • *adv* când • *conj* când • *pron* când
whence • *adv* de unde
where • *adv* unde • *conj* unde, de unde, încotro
whereas • *conj* pe când
whet • *v* ascui, aâa
whether • *conj* dac, în orice caz
whetstone • *n* gresie *(f)*, cute
whey • *n* zer *(f)*
which • *pron* care, ce
while • *n* vreme *(f)* • *conj* în timp ce, dei, cât timp
whim • *n* capriciu *(n)*, toan *(f)*
whip • *n* bici
whippoorwill • *n* caprimulg *(m)*
whirlpool • *n* vâltoare *(f)*, volbur *(f)*
whisker • *n* fir *(n)*, musta *(f)*, vibris *(f)*
whiskey • *n* whisky
whisper • *v* opti, susura • *n* oapt *(f)*
whistle • *v* fluiera, uiera • *n* fluier *(n)*, fluierat *(n)*
whit • *n* iot *(f)*
white • *n* alb • *adj* alb
whiten • *v* albi
whiteness • *n* albiciune *(f)*, albea *(f)*, albitate *(f)*
whither • *adv* încotro
who • *pron* cine, care
whole • *n* tot *(n)*, totalitate *(f)*, întreg *(m)*, total *(n)* • *adj* întreg • *adv* total
wholeness • *n* deplintate, plenitudine *(f)*, caracter complet *(n)*
whoop • *n* urlet *(n)*
whopper • *n* minciun gogonat *(f)*
whore • *n* curv *(f)*, târf *(f)*, prostituat *(f)*
why • *n* pentru ce • *adv* de ce, pentru ce
wick • *n* fitil *(n)*, muc
wicked • *adj* ru *(n)*, rutcios *(n)*, hain *(m)*
wickedness • *n* rutate *(f)*, perversitate *(f)*, ticloie *(f)*
wide • *adj* larg, lat
widen • *v* lrgi
widespread • *adj* rspândit *(m)*, extins *(m)*
widow • *n* vduv *(f)*
widowed • *adj* vduv
widower • *n* vduv
width • *n* lrgime, lime *(f)*, lrgime *(f)*
wife • *n* soie *(f)*, nevast *(f)*, muiere
wig • *n* peruc *(f)*
wild • *adj* slbatic
will • *n* voin *(f)*, testament *(n)*
willow • *n* salcie *(f)*
willowherb • *n* pufuli *(f)*
wimple • *n* vl *(n)*, broboad *(f)*, curbur *(f)*, meandr *(f)*, cotitur *(f)*
win • *n* victorie *(f)*
wince • *n* fior
wind • *n* vânt *(n)*
window • *n* fereastr *(f)*, perioad de timp *(f)*, interval *(n)*
windowpane • *n* geam *(n)*
windpipe • *n* trahee
windshield • *n* parbriz *(n)*, ferastr de fa *(f)*
windy • *adj* vântos
wine • *n* vin *(n)*
wing • *n* arip *(f)*
wink • *v* face cu ochiul • *n* clip *(f)*
winner • *n* câtigtor *(m)*, câtigtoare *(f)*
winter • *v* ierna • *n* iarn *(f)*
wipe • *v* terge
wire • *n* fir *(n)*, sârm *(f)*
wisdom • *n* înelepciune, judecat, sapien
wise • *adj* cu scaun la cap, înelept
wisent • *n* zimbru *(m)*
wish • *v* dori, ura • *n* dorin *(f)*
wisp • *n* uvi *(f)*, uvie
wisteria • *n* glicin *(f)*
wit • *n* schepsis
witch • *n* vrjitoare, vrjitor
with • *prep* cu, alturi
withdraw • *v* preleva, retrage
wither • *v* veteji, ofili
withered • *adj* ofilit, vetejit
without • *prep* fr
witness • *n* martor

wizard • *n* vrjitor *(m)*, mag *(m)*, magician *(m)*
woad • *n* drobuor *(m)*
woe • *n* durere *(f)*, suferin *(f)*, mâhnire *(f)*
wolf • *n* lup *(m)*
wolframite • *n* wolframit *(n)*
wolverine • *n* polifag american *(m)*, gluton *(m)*
woman • *n* femeie *(f)*, muiere *(f)*, doamn
womanizer • *n* afemeiat *(m)*, vântor de fuste *(m)*, crai *(m)*, muieratic *(m)*
womanly • *adj* feminin *(m)*, femeiesc *(m)*
womb • *n* uter *(n)*, matc *(f)*
wombat • *n* wombat *(m)*
wonder • *v* mira • *n* minune, mirare *(f)*, minune *(f)*
wont • *n* obicei *(m)*
woo • *v* curta
woodcock • *n* beca *(f)*, becain *(f)*, sitar *(m)*
wooden • *adj* lemnos, de lemn
woodpecker • *n* ghionoaie *(f)*, ciocnitoare *(f)*
woof • *v* ltra • *n* ham-ham
wool • *n* lân *(f)*
woolly • *adj* lânos
word • *n* cuvânt *(n)*, vorb *(f)*, cuvânt de onoare *(n)*
work • *n* munc *(f)*, serviciu *(n)*, ocupaie *(f)*, îndeletnicire *(f)*, efort *(n)*, lucrare *(f)*, oper *(f)*, creaie *(f)* • *v* face, munci, lucra, opera, aciona, fermenta, folosi, produce, funciona, se manifesta, se comporta, manifesta, simi
workbench • *n* banc
worker • *n* lucrtor *(m)*, lucrtoare *(f)*, muncitor *(m)*, muncitoare *(f)*, albin lucrtoare *(f)*
workhorse • *n* cal de traciune *(m)*
workshop • *n* atelier *(n)*
world • *n* lume, pmânt
worldwide • *adv* în toat lumea, în lumea întreag
worm • *v* a se târî • *n* vierme *(m)*, balaur *(m)*, arpe *(m)*
wormwood • *n* pelin *(m)*
worn • *v* purtat *(n)*
worried • *adj* îngrijorat
worry • *n* grij *(f)*
worship • *v* închina
worsted • *n* lân pieptnat *(f)*, gabardin *(f)*, stof-gabardin *(f)*
worthy • *adj* demn
wound • *v* rni, vtma • *n* ran, plag, leziune *(f)*
wrap • *v* înfura, împacheta • *n* al *(n)*, vemânt *(n)*
wrath • *n* mânie *(f)*, furie *(f)*, urgie *(f)*, rzbunare *(f)*
wreak • *v* a cauza, provoca, varsa nervii
wreath • *n* cunun, coroan
wreck • *v* distruge, avaria, ruina, prgini, drpna • *n* ruin *(f)*, epav *(f)*, drâmtur *(f)*, accident *(n)*, avarie *(f)*, coliziune *(f)*
wren • *n* pitulice *(f)*
wrench • *n* rsucire, cheie fix
wrestler • *n* lupttor
wrestling • *n* lupt
wretch • *n* nenorocit, nefericit
wretched • *adj* nenorocit
wring • *v* stoarce
wrinkle • *v* cuta, rida, încrei, zbârci, plisa
wrist • *n* încheietura mâinii *(n)*
write • *v* scrie, A scrie
writer • *n* scriitor *(m)*, scriitoare *(f)*, autor *(m)*
writing • *n* scriere *(f)*, scris
written • *adj* scris *(n)*, scris *(f)*
wrong • *adj* greit, incorect
wrongly • *adv* în mod imoral, în mod injust
wryneck • *n* capîntortur *(f)*

X

xenon • *n* xenon *(n)*
xenophobia • *n* xenofobie
xylem • *n* xilem *(n)*

Y

yak • *n* iac *(m)*
yam • *n* ignam *(f)*
yard • *n* curte *(f)*, verg *(f)*
yarn • *n* fir *(n)*, basm *(n)*, poveste *(f)*
yarrow • *n* coada oricelui
yawn • *v* csca, deschide, casca
year • *n* an *(m)*
yearly • *adj* anual *(n)*

yearning • *n* dor *(n)*, dorin arztoare *(f)*, nzuin *(f)*
yeast • *n* drojdie *(f)*, levur *(f)*, ferment
yell • *v* urla, ipa, striga
yellow • *v* înglbeni • *n* galben *(m)*, galben *(f)* • *adj* galben, la *(m)*
yesterday • *n* ieri • *adv* ieri
yet • *adv* înc • *conj* totui
yew • *n* tis *(f)*, tis
yield • *v* închina
yogurt • *n* iaurt *(n)*
yoke • *v* înjuga • *n* jug
yokel • *n* ran *(m)*, mojic *(m)*, bdran *(m)*
yolk • *n* glbenu *(n)*
you • *pron* voi, dumneavoastr, tu, dumneata
young • *n* pui • *adj* tânr, june
youth • *n* tineree, junimea, tânr
ytterbium • *n* yterbiu *(n)*
yttrium • *n* ytriu *(n)*
yucca • *n* yucca *(f)*

Z

zeal • *n* zel *(n)*, ardoare *(f)*
zebra • *n* zebr *(f)*
zenith • *n* dric *(m)*
zero • *n* zero *(n)*
zilch • *n* canci, ioc, boac *(f)*
zinc • *n* zinc *(n)*
zircon • *n* zircon
zirconium • *n* zirconiu *(n)*
zither • *n* iter *(f)*
zodiac • *n* zodiac *(n)*
zombie • *n* zombi *(m)*
zoo • *n* zoo *(f)*, parc zoologic *(n)*, grdin zoologic *(f)*, zooparc *(n)*
zoologist • *n* zoolog *(m)*, zoolog *(f)*
zoology • *n* zoologie *(f)*

ROMANIAN-ENGLISH

A

a • *v* fight • *interj* huh
abac • *n* abacus
abac • *n* abacus
abaca • *n* abaca
abajur • *n* lampshade
abandon • *n* abandonment, abortion
abandona • *v* abandon, forsake, renounce
abandonare • *n* abandonment
abandonat • *adj* abandoned, deserted, desolate
abanos • *n* ebony
abaial • *adj* abbatial
abaie • *n* abbey
abatiz • *n* abatis
abator • *n* abattoir
abtut • *adj* ill, sad
abtut • *adj* sad
abces • *n* abscess, boil
abdomen • *n* abdomen, belly
abdominal • *adj* abdominal
abduce • *v* abduct
abductor • *adj* abductive
aberant • *adj* aberrant
aberan • *n* aberrance
aberaie • *n* aberration
abhora • *v* abhor
abhorare • *n* abhorrence
abia • *adv* hardly, merely
abil • *adj* able, handsome
abilitat • *adj* able
abilitate • *n* ability, address, adroitness, dexterity, faculty, hand, skill
abiogenez • *n* abiogenesis
abis • *n* abyss
abisal • *adj* abyssal
abject • *adj* abject, despicable
ablactaie • *n* ablactation
ablaiune • *n* ablation
ablativ • *adj* ablative
ablaut • *n* ablaut
abluiune • *n* ablution
abnegaie • *n* abnegation
abnormalitate • *n* abnormity
aboli • *v* abolish
abolire • *n* abolition
aboliionism • *n* abolitionism
aboliionist • *n* abolitionist
abominabil • *adj* abominable
abominaiune • *n* abomination
abona • *v* subscribe
abonament • *n* subscription
abordabil • *adj* approachable
abortiv • *n* abortive
abraza • *v* abrade
abrevia • *v* abbreviate
abreviat • *adj* abbreviated
abreviaie • *n* abbreviation
abreviere • *n* abbreviation
abroga • *v* abrogate, reverse
abrupt • *adj* abrupt • *adv* abruptly
abscis • *n* abscissa
absciziune • *n* abscission
absent • *adj* absent, away
absen • *n* absence
absent • *adj* absent
absid • *n* apse
absint • *n* absinthe
absolut • *adj* implicit, stark • *adv* stark
absolutism • *n* absolutism
absorbant • *n* absorbent
absorban • *n* absorbency
absorbi • *v* absorb
absorbibil • *adj* absorbable
absorbire • *n* absorption
absorbit • *adj* absorbed
absorbit • *adj* absorbed
absorbie • *n* absorption
abstracie • *n* abstract, abstraction
abstracionism • *n* abstractionism
absurd • *n* absurd, absurdity • *adj* absurd, ludicrous
absurditate • *n* absurdity, nonsense
abine • *v* abstain
abinere • *n* abstention
abumarkub • *n* shoebill
abunda • *v* abound
abundent • *adj* abundant
abunden • *n* abundance, generosity, profusion
abur • *n* steam, vapor
abureal • *n* fog
abuz • *n* abuse, excess
ac • *n* needle
acacia • *n* acacia
academic • *adj* academic
academic • *adj* academic
academie • *n* academy
acaju • *n* cashew, mahogany
acant • *n* acanthus
acarian • *n* mite
acas • *adv* home
accelera • *v* accelerate, precipitate
accelerare • *n* acceleration
acceleraie • *n* acceleration
accelerator • *n* accelerator
accelerometru • *n* accelerometer
accent • *n* accent
accepta • *v* accept

acceptabil • *adj* acceptable
acceptabilitate • *n* acceptability
acceptan • *n* acceptance
acceptare • *n* acceptance, tolerance
acceptat • *adj* acknowledged
accepie • *n* acceptance
acces • *n* access
accesibil • *adj* accessible, approachable
accesoriu • *adj* accessory • *n* accessory
accident • *n* accident, chance, wreck
accidental • *adj* accidental, fortuitous
accidental • *adj* accidental
acciz • *n* custom
acea • *pron* that
aceast • *pron* this
acel • *pron* that
acelai • *adj* same, very
acer • *n* eagle
acerola • *n* acerola
acest • *pron* this
acetabul • *n* acetabulum
acetamid • *n* acetamide
acetilen • *n* acetylene
acetilenic • *adj* acetylenic
aceton • *n* acetone
achen • *n* achene
achilie • *n* achylia
achita • *v* acquit
achiziie • *n* acquisition
achiziionare • *n* acquisition
aci • *adv* here
acid • *n* acid • *adj* acid
acidificare • *n* acidification
acin • *n* acinus
aclamare • *n* acclamation
aclamaie • *n* acclamation
acnee • *n* acne
acolo • *adv* there
acomodare • *n* adjustment
acompania • *v* accompany
acompaniament • *n* accompaniment
aconit • *n* aconite
acopermânt • *n* roof
acoperi • *v* cover
acoperire • *n* lining
acoperi • *n* roof
acoperit • *adj* covered
acoperitor • *n* roofer
acord • *n* accord, chord, concord, concordance
acorda • *v* allow, conform
acordeon • *n* accordion
acrilic • *adj* acrylic
acrimonie • *n* acrimony
acrimonios • *adj* acrimonious
acri • *n* sorrel
acrobat • *n* acrobat
acrobatic • *n* acrobatics
acrobaie • *n* acrobatics
acrocianoz • *n* acrocyanosis
acromion • *n* acromion
acronim • *n* acronym
acropol • *n* acropolis
acrostih • *n* acrostic
acru • *adj* acid, acrid, sour
act • *n* bill
actiniu • *n* actinium
actinometru • *n* actinometer
actinomicoz • *n* actinomycosis
actiona • *v* move
aciona • *v* work
aciune • *n* action
activ • *adj* active
activist • *n* activist
activist • *n* activist
activitate • *n* activity
actor • *n* actor, player
actri • *n* actor, actress, player
actual • *adj* real
actualitate • *n* actuality
acuitate • *n* acuity
acum • *adv* now, today
acumulare • *n* accumulation, storage
acupunctur • *n* acupuncture
acuratee • *n* accuracy
acustic • *n* acoustics
acuzare • *n* charge
acuzativ • *n* accusative • *adj* accusative
acuzator • *adj* accusative
acuzatorie • *adj* accusatory
acuzatorii • *adj* accusatory
acuzatoriu • *adj* accusatory
acvamarin • *n* aquamarine
acvariu • *n* aquarium
acvatic • *adj* aquatic
acvil • *n* eagle
adânc • *n* abyss, deep • *adj* deep, profound • *adv* deep, deeply
adânc • *adj* deep
adânci • *adj* deep
adâncime • *n* abyss, deep, depth
adâncitur • *n* dimple
adaos • *n* addition
adpost • *n* asylum, lodge, sanctuary
adapta • *v* adapt
adaptabil • *adj* adaptable
adaptabil • *adj* adaptable
adaptabilitate • *n* adaptability
adaptare • *n* adaptation
adaptat • *adj* adapt
adaptor • *n* adapter
aduga • *v* add, ornament
adugire • *n* addition
adax • *n* addax

addax • *n* addax
adecvabilitate • *n* suitability
adecvat • *adj* adequate, applicable, opportune, suitable
ademeni • *v* beguile, ensnare
adenin • *n* adenine
adenoid • *n* adenoid
aderent • *n* adherent • *adj* adherent
adevr • *n* truth
adevrat • *adj* authentic, real, true
adeveri • *v* attest, corroborate, testify
adeverire • *n* acknowledgement, attestation
adezivitate • *n* tenacity
adiacent • *adj* adjacent
adic • *adv* namely
adiere • *n* breeze
adio • *interj* adieu • *n* valediction
adipos • *adj* adipose
adiional • *adj* additional
adjectiv • *n* adjective • *adj* adjective
adjectiv • *adj* adjective
adjectival • *adj* adjectival
adjutant • *n* adjutant
administrare • *n* administration
administraie • *n* administration
administrativ • *adj* administrative
administrator • *n* administrator
admirabil • *adj* admirable
admirare • *n* admiration
admiraie • *n* admiration
admisibil • *adj* admissible
admite • *v* allow
admonestare • *v* berate
adnota • *v* note
adnotare • *n* note
adolescent • *n* adolescent • *adj* adolescent
adolescen • *n* adolescence
adolescent • *n* adolescent
adopta • *v* adopt
adoptare • *n* adoption
adopie • *n* adoption
adoptiv • *adj* adoptive
adorabil • *adj* adorable
adorare • *n* adoration, praise
adoraie • *n* adoration
adormit • *adj* asleep
adrenalin • *n* adrenaline
adresa • *v* address
adres • *n* address
adresare • *n* address
aduce • *v* bear, bring
adult • *n* adult • *adj* adult
adult • *n* adult
adumbri • *v* shade, umbrage
aduna • *v* add, gather
adunare • *n* addition
aduntor • *n* gatherer
adverb • *n* adverb
adverbial • *adj* adverbial
advers • *adj* adverse
adversar • *n* adversary, opponent
adversitate • *n* adversity, hardship
advocat • *n* lawyer
aer • *n* air
aera • *v* air
aerare • *n* aeration
aerian • *adj* aerial
aerisi • *v* air
aerisire • *n* airing
aerobic • *adj* aerobic
aerodinamic • *n* aerodynamics
aerodrom • *n* aerodrome
aerometru • *n* aerometer
aeronautic • *n* aeronautics
aeronav • *n* aircraft
aeroplan • *n* airplane
aeroport • *n* airport
aeroscopie • *n* aeroscopy
aerospaial • *adj* aerospace
aerospaiu • *n* aerospace
afabil • *adj* affable, bland
afabilitate • *n* affability, amiability
afacere • *n* affair, bargain, business, transaction
afar • *adj* outside • *adv* outside
afeciune • *n* endearment
afemeiat • *adj* effeminate • *n* womanizer
aferez • *n* apheresis
afid • *n* aphid
afide • *n* aphid
afiliaie • *n* affiliation
afiliere • *n* affiliation
afin • *n* bilberry, blueberry
afin • *n* blueberry
afinitate • *n* affinity
afirmaie • *n* affirmation, proposition
afi • *n* bill, poster
afix • *n* affix
afla • *v* betray, learn
afluent • *n* tributary
afluen • *n* influx
aflux • *n* influx
aforism • *n* aphorism
aforisme • *n* aphorism
afrodisiac • *adj* aphrodisiac
afrodiziac • *n* aphrodisiac
afront • *n* affront
afuma • *v* smoke
afunda • *v* sink
afurisit • *adj* blasted, unholy
afurisit • *adj* unholy
agasa • *v* irritate

aga • *v* clutch, hang, hook, stick, suspend
agav • *n* agave
ageamiu • *n* fledgling • *adj* verdant
agend • *n* calendar
agent • *n* broker
agenie • *n* agency
agentur • *n* agency
ager • *adj* nimble, quick
agita • *v* agitate, shake
agitare • *n* agitation
agitat • *adj* restless
agitat • *adj* restless
agitaie • *n* agitation, bother, fuss, restlessness, uproar
agitator • *n* agitator
aglomerat • *adj* crowded
aglomeraie • *n* agglomeration
aglutinare • *n* agglutination
agnostic • *n* agnostic
agnostic • *n* agnostic
agnosticism • *n* agnosticism
agonie • *n* agony, anguish
agraf • *n* clip
agreabil • *adj* agreeable, pleasant • *adv* agreeably
agreabilitate • *n* pleasantness
agreat • *adj* popular
agresiune • *n* aggression
agresiv • *adj* aggressive
agresivitate • *n* aggressiveness
agricol • *adj* agricultural
agricultur • *n* agriculture
agri • *n* gooseberry
agrobiologic • *adj* agrobiologic
agrobiologie • *n* agrobiology
agrume • *n* citrus
agurijoar • *n* purslane
aguti • *n* agouti
ah • *interj* ouch
ai • *n* aye-aye, garlic • *interj* ouch
aia • *pron* that
aici • *adv* here, hither
aior • *n* spurge
aisberg • *n* iceberg
aiurea • *adv* elsewhere
ajun • *n* eve
ajuna • *v* fast
ajunge • *v* arrive, reach • *interj* enough
ajusta • *v* adjust
ajustabil • *adj* adjustable
ajustare • *n* adjustment
ajuta • *v* aid, assist, help, save
ajuttor • *adj* helpful
ajutoare • *n* help
ajutor • *n* aid, assistance, help
la • *pron* that
alabastru • *n* alabaster
alac • *n* spelt
alam • *n* brass
alambic • *n* alembic
alambicat • *adj* complicated
almuri • *n* brass
alanin • *n* alanine
alpta • *v* suckle
alarmist • *n* scaremonger
altura • *v* join
alturi • *prep* beside, with
alb • *n* white • *adj* white
alb-ivoriu • *n* ivory • *adj* ivory
alba • *n* dawn
albaspin • *n* hawthorn
albstrea • *n* cornflower
albstriu • *adj* bluish
albastru • *n* blue, cerulean • *adj* blue
albastru-verzui • *adj* teal
albstrui • *adj* bluish
albatros • *n* albatross
albea • *n* whiteness
albedo • *n* albedo
albi • *v* whiten
albiciune • *n* whiteness
albie • *n* riverbed
albin • *n* bee
albinar • *n* beekeeper
albinar • *n* beekeeper
albinism • *n* albinism
albitate • *n* whiteness
albumeal • *n* edelweiss
albumin • *n* albumin
alburn • *n* sapwood
albu • *n* albumen
alc • *n* auk, razorbill
alcalin • *adj* alkaline
alcaloid • *n* alkaloid
alctui • *v* compile
alctuire • *n* composition
alctuit • *adj* composite
alcazar • *n* alcazar
alchen • *n* alkene
alchimist • *n* alchemist
alcool • *n* alcohol
alcoolic • *n* alcoholic, drunk, lush • *adj* alcoholic
alcoolic • *n* alcoholic
alcoolism • *n* alcoholism
alcoolizat • *adj* intoxicated
aleatoriu • *adj* aleatory
alee • *n* alley
alegtori • *n* electorate
alege • *v* choose, elect
alegere • *n* election, selection
aleluia • *interj* hallelujah
alen • *n* breath
alerga • *v* run, tear

alergtor • *n* runner
alergie • *n* allergy
alfa • *n* alpha
alfabet • *n* abecedary, alphabet
alfabetic • *adj* alphabetic, alphabetical
alfabetic • *adj* alphabetic
alfabetism • *n* literacy
alfabetizare • *n* literacy
alfanumeric • *adj* alphanumeric
alfanumeric • *adj* alphanumeric
alfanumerici • *adj* alphanumeric
alg • *n* alga
algebr • *n* algebra
algebric • *adj* algebraic
algoritm • *n* algorithm
algoritmi • *n* algorithm
algoritmic • *adj* algorithmic
algoritmic • *adj* algorithmic
aliaj • *n* alloy
alian • *n* alliance, bond, league
aliat • *n* ally
alien • *n* alien
alien • *n* alien
alifatic • *adj* aliphatic
aligator • *n* alligator
alilic • *adj* allylic
aliment • *n* food
alimentare • *n* food, supply
alina • *v* allay, alleviate, assuage, ease, soothe
alinare • *n* relief
alinia • *v* conform
alinta • *v* caress, fawn, pamper
alior • *n* spurge
allegretto • *n* allegretto • *adv* allegretto
alo • *interj* hello
aloca • *v* allot, apportion
aloe • *n* aloe
aloo • *interj* hello
alotropic • *adj* allotropic
alpaca • *n* alpaca
alt • *adj* other
altar • *n* altar
altele • *n* others
alterare • *n* alteration
alteraie • *n* alteration
alternare • *n* alternation
alternator • *n* alternator
alii • *n* others
altitudine • *n* altitude
alto • *n* viola
altoi • *v* graft • *n* graft
altorelief • *n* relief
altruism • *n* altruism
altruist • *adj* altruistic
aluat • *n* dough
alun • *n* hazel
alun • *n* hazelnut, nut
alunar • *n* nutcracker
aluneca • *v* slide, slip
alunecare • *n* avalanche, dive, slide
alunga • *v* banish, dismiss
alungi • *v* elongate, prolong, reach
aluni • *n* birthmark, mole
aluniu • *adj* hazel
aluziv • *adj* allusive
alveolar • *adj* alveolar
alveolar • *n* alveolar
amabil • *adj* kind
amabilitate • *n* amiability, condescension, friendliness, kindness, politeness
amgi • *v* beguile, deceive, delude
amgire • *n* smoke
amâna • *v* adjourn, delay, postpone, procrastinate, prolong, stay, suspend, table
amânare • *n* postponement, procrastination
amanet • *n* pawnshop
amaneta • *v* pawn
amant • *n* paramour
amanta • *n* paramour
amnunit • *adj* minute
amar • *adj* bitter
amrciune • *n* bitterness
amarant • *n* amaranth, love-lies-bleeding
amrât • *adj* poor
amreal • *n* bitterness, milkwort
amarilis • *n* amaryllis
amator • *n* amateur, dilettante • *adj* amateur, eager
amatorism • *n* amateurism
ambalare • *n* race
ambarcaiune • *n* vessel
ambasad • *n* embassy
ambasador • *n* ambassador
ambian • *n* atmosphere, environment
ambidextru • *adj* ambidextrous
ambient • *n* atmosphere, environment
ambiguitate • *n* ambiguity
ambiguu • *adj* ambiguous, equivocal
ambr • *n* amber, ambergris
ambreiaj • *n* clutch
ambulan • *n* ambulance
ameliorare • *n* amelioration
amend • *n* ticket
amenina • *v* threaten
ameninare • *n* threat
ameninat • *adj* threatened
amenintor • *v* menacing • *adv* menacingly • *adj* threatening
ament • *n* catkin
americiu • *n* americium
amestec • *n* composite, medley, mix, mixture

amesteca • *v* mix, scramble, temper
amestecare • *n* mixture
amestecat • *adj* miscellaneous, mixed
amestectur • *n* medley, mix, mixture
ametist • *n* amethyst
ameit • *adj* intoxicated
amfitrion • *n* host
amiaz • *n* noon
amic • *n* friend
amic • *n* friend, girlfriend
amical • *adj* friendly
amiciie • *n* friendship
amid • *n* amide
amidon • *n* starch
amigdal • *n* tonsil
amigdalit • *n* quinsy, tonsillitis
• *n* friend
amin • *adv* amen
amin • *n* amine
aminti • *v* recall, remember
amintire • *n* memory, recollection, remembrance, reminiscence, retention
amiral • *n* admiral
amnezie • *n* amnesia
amoniac • *n* ammonia
amor • *n* love
amorezat • *adj* amorous, enamored
amoros • *adj* amorous
amorsare • *n* bootstrap
amori • *v* numb
amorit • *adj* numb
amper • *n* ampere
amper-or • *n* ampere-hour
amplificare • *n* amplification
amplitudine • *n* amplitude
amplitudini • *n* amplitude
amulet • *n* amulet, charm, talisman
amurg • *n* dusk, nightfall, twilight
amurgi • *v* dusk
amuzament • *n* fun
amuzant • *adj* funny
amvon • *n* pulpit
an • *n* year
anacardier • *n* cashew
anaflabet • *adj* illiterate
anale • *n* annals
analfabet • *adj* illiterate
analgezic • *adj* analgesic
analiza • *v* analyze
analiz • *n* analysis
analizabil • *adj* analyzable
analog • *adj* analog, analogous
analogic • *adj* analog, analogous
analogie • *n* analogy
ananas • *n* pineapple
anarhic • *adj* anarchic
anarhie • *n* anarchy
anarhism • *n* anarchism
anarhisr • *n* anarchist
anarhist • *n* anarchist
anason • *n* anise
anatem • *n* anathema
anatomic • *adj* anatomical
anatomie • *n* anatomy
ancestral • *adj* ancestral
anchilozat • *adj* ossified
ancor • *n* anchor
ancora • *v* anchor
andiv • *n* endive
androgin • *adj* androgynous
anecdotic • *adj* anecdotal
anemie • *n* anemia
anemon • *n* anemone
anevoios • *adj* difficult
anex • *n* appendage, appendix
anexare • *n* annexation
anexat • *v* attach
angaja • *v* employ, hire
angajament • *n* engagement
angajat • *n* employee
angajat • *n* employee
angajator • *n* employer
angelic • *adj* angelic
angelic • *n* angelica
anghil • *n* eel
anghin • *n* quinsy
anghinare • *n* artichoke
angiografie • *n* angiography
angiopatie • *n* angiopathy
angiosperm • *n* angiosperm
angrenaj • *n* transmission
anhidrid • *n* anhydride
anihila • *v* annihilate
anima • *v* animate
animal • *n* animal • *adj* animal
animalic • *adj* animal, bestial
animalic • *adj* bestial
animare • *n* animation
anime • *n* anime
animism • *n* animism
animozitate • *n* animosity
anin • *n* alder
anison • *n* anise
aniversare • *n* anniversary, birthday
anoa • *n* anoa
anod • *n* plate
anomalie • *n* anomaly
anonim • *n* anonymity • *adj* anonymous • *adv* anonymously
anonimitate • *n* anonymity
anorexic • *n* anorexic
anorexica • *n* anorexic
anorganic • *adj* inorganic
anormal • *adj* abnormal

anormalitate • *n* abnormality
anost • *adj* boring, insipid, lame
anosteal • *n* tedium
anotimp • *n* season
ansamblu • *n* set
anoa • *n* anchovy
antafrodisiac • *adj* antaphrodisiac
antagonic • *adj* antagonistic
antagonism • *n* antagonism
antagonist • *n* antagonist • *adj* antagonistic
antebra • *n* forearm
antecedent • *adj* antecedent
antegard • *n* vanguard
anten • *n* aerial, antenna
antepenultim • *adj* antepenultimate
anter • *n* anther
anterior • *adj* anterior, back, sometime
antiafrodisiac • *n* antaphrodisiac
antibacterial • *adj* antibacterial
antic • *adj* old
antichitate • *n* antiquity
anticipa • *v* anticipate
anticipabil • *adj* predictable
anticipabilitate • *n* predictability
anticipare • *n* anticipation, expectancy, expectation, prevention
anticipaie • *n* anticipation, expectation
anticoncepional • *adj* contraceptive
anticorp • *n* antibody
anticorpi • *n* antibody
anticrist • *n* antichrist
antierou • *n* antihero
antigen • *n* antigen
antihrist • *n* antichrist
antiigienic • *adj* unhygienic
antiinflamator • *n* anti-inflammatory
antilocapr • *n* pronghorn
antilop • *n* antelope
antilop-de-pdure • *n* bushbuck
antimoniu • *n* antimony
antiparticul • *n* antiparticle
antipatic • *adj* repellent
antipatic • *adj* repellent
antipatie • *n* antipathy, dislike
antiproton • *n* antiproton
antitetic • *adj* antithetical
antonim • *n* antonym
antrax • *n* anthrax
antrena • *v* school
antrenament • *n* practice, training
antrenor • *n* coach
antrepozit • *n* warehouse
antreprenor • *n* entrepreneur
antreu • *n* vestibule
antropocentrism • *n* anthropocentrism
antropofag • *adj* cannibalistic
antropoid • *adj* anthropoid
antropoid • *n* anthropoid
antropoide • *n* anthropoid
antropologie • *n* anthropology
antropomorf • *adj* anthropoid
antropozofie • *n* anthroposophy
anual • *adj* annual, yearly
anuar • *n* annual
anula • *v* abrogate, annul, cancel, nullify, reverse
anulabil • *adj* defeasible
anulare • *n* annulment, vacation
anulator • *n* annihilator
anume • *adj* certain
anun • *n* advertisement
anuna • *v* announce, bill, herald
anus • *n* anus
anvelop • *n* envelope
anxietate • *n* anxiety, uneasiness
anxios • *adj* anxious
aoleu • *interj* ouch
aorist • *n* aorist
ap • *n* water
apra • *v* defend
aprare • *n* defense, guard
aparat • *n* apparatus, device, instrument, set
aparataj • *n* hardware
apratoare • *n* guard
aprtor • *n* defender
aparatur • *n* apparatus, hardware
aprea • *v* appear
aparen • *n* appearance, impression
apariie • *n* apparition, appearance, vision
apartament • *n* apartment
apsa • *v* push
apatic • *adj* indifferent, listless, unresponsive
apatie • *n* apathy
apatit • *n* apatite
aptos • *adj* aqueous, watery
• *n* water
apeduct • *n* aqueduct
apel • *n* appeal
apela • *v* appeal
apendice • *n* appendix
aperiodic • *adj* aperiodic
apetit • *n* appetite
apicultoare • *n* beekeeper
apicultor • *n* beekeeper
aplatiza • *v* flatten
aplauda • *v* applaud
apleca • *v* bow, incline, stoop
aplicabil • *adj* applicable
aplicabilitate • *n* applicability
aplicare • *n* application, practice
aplicaie • *n* application

apoasa • *adj* phlegmatic
apoase • *adj* phlegmatic
apocaliptic • *adj* apocalyptic
apofonie • *n* ablaut
apogeu • *n* apogee
apoi • *adv* afterwards, then
apos • *adj* phlegmatic, watery
aposi • *adj* phlegmatic
apostazie • *n* apostasy
apostrof • *n* apostrophe
apoziie • *n* apposition
aprecia • *v* esteem
apreciabil • *adj* sensible
apreciere • *n* acknowledgement, adoration, appraisal, appreciation, recognition
aprehensiune • *n* apprehension
aprig • *adj* quick
aprinde • *v* light
aprindere • *n* inflammation
aprins • *adj* fiery
aproape • *adv* almost • *adj* close, near
aprobare • *n* approbation
apropia • *v* approach
apropiat • *adj* warm
apropiat • *adj* warm
apropiere • *n* access, vicinity
apropo • *adv* apropos, incidentally
aproviziona • *v* save
aprovizionare • *n* supply
aproximare • *n* approximation
aproximaie • *n* approximation
aproximativ • *adv* approximately
apt • *adj* apt
aptitudine • *n* suitability
apuca • *v* clasp, clutch, fathom, grab
apune • *v* fade, set
apus • *n* dusk, sunset
apusean • *adj* western
ar • *n* are
ara • *v* ear, plough • *n* macaw
arabil • *adj* arable
aragaz • *n* cooker, stove
aragul • *n* rocket
arahid • *n* peanut
arahnid • *n* arachnid
aram • *n* copper
armar • *n* brazier
armiu • *adj* copper, rufous
aranja • *v* arrange, sort
aranjament • *n* arrangement, distribution
aranjare • *n* arrangement
arta • *v* exhibit, prove, show
arttor • *n* forefinger
artos • *adj* handsome
artur • *n* tillage
arbalet • *n* crossbow
arbitraj • *n* arbitration
arbitrar • *adj* arbitrary
arbitrare • *n* arbitration
arbitri • *n* arbiter
arbitru • *n* arbiter, arbitrator
arbore • *n* mast, tree
arbore-de-cacao • *n* cacao
arbore-de-cafea • *n* coffee
arboret • *n* arboretum, grove, stand, thicket, topgallant, topmast
arbust • *n* bush, shrub
arc • *n* arc, arch, bow, spring
arca • *n* ark
arcad • *n* arcade, cloister, eyebrow
arca • *n* archer
arde • *v* burn
ardei • *n* pepper
ardent • *adj* burning, fiery
ardent • *adj* fiery
arden • *n* ardor
ardere • *n* burning, combustion
arderi • *n* combustion
ardezie • *n* slate
ardoare • *n* appetite, ardor, craving, fervor, zeal
areal • *n* area
aren • *n* arena
arenda • *v* rent
arest • *n* apprehension, arrest
aresta • *v* arrest
arestare • *n* apprehension, arrest
arete • *n* ram
argsi • *v* tan
argsitor • *n* tanner
argil • *n* clay
arginin • *n* arginine
argint • *n* argent, silver
argintrie • *n* silver
argintie • *n* silver
argintiu • *adj* argent, silver, silvery • *n* silver
argon • *n* argon
argou • *n* slang
argument • *n* argument
argumentabil • *adj* arguable
argumentativ • *adj* argumentative
arhaic • *adj* archaic
arhaism • *n* archaism
arhaisme • *n* archaism
arhanghel • *n* archangel
arheolog • *n* archaeologist
arheolog • *n* archaeologist
arheologie • *n* archaeology
arhidiocez • *n* archdiocese
arhiepiscop • *n* archbishop
arhipelag • *n* archipelago
arhiplin • *adj* crowded
arhitect • *n* architect

arhitect • *n* architect
arhitectonic • *adj* architectural
arhitectur • *n* architecture
arhitectural • *adj* architectural
arhiva • *v* archive
arhiv • *n* archive
arici • *n* hedgehog, urchin
arid • *adj* dry
arie • *n* air, area, aria
arii • *n* area
arin • *n* alder
arin • *n* sand
arinos • *adj* sandy
arip • *n* wing
aristocrat • *n* noble
aristocratic • *adj* aristocratic
aristocraie • *n* aristocracy
aritmetic • *adj* arithmetic
aritmetic • *n* arithmetic
arma • *v* arm
arm • *n* arm, weapon
armsar • *n* hunk, stallion, stud
armat • *adj* armed
armat • *n* army
armistiiu • *n* armistice, truce
armonic • *adj* harmonious
armonie • *n* harmony, peace
armonios • *adj* harmonious
armur • *n* armor
arnic • *n* arnica
arogant • *adj* arrogant
arogan • *n* arrogance
arom • *n* bouquet, nose
aromat • *adj* aromatic
aromatic • *adj* aromatic
arsen • *n* arsenic
ari • *n* ardor
arsur • *n* burn
art • *n* art
arar • *n* maple
arter • *n* artery
arterioscleroz • *n* arteriosclerosis
articol • *n* article, item
articula • *v* articulate
articulaie • *n* articulation
artificial • *n* artifice • *adj* artificial, contrived, false, unnatural
artificiu • *n* firework
artilerie • *n* artillery
artiodactil • *n* artiodactyl
artist • *n* artist
artist • *n* artist
artistic • *adj* artistic
artizan • *n* craftsman
artrit • *n* arthritis
artromer • *n* arthromere
artropod • *n* arthropod
artroz • *n* arthritis
arunca • *v* fling, throw
aruncare • *n* pitch
arzând • *adj* fiery
arztor • *adj* burning
as • *n* ace
aa • *adv* so, thus
aa-i • *interj* right
aadar • *adv* hence, therefore, thus • *conj* so
asalt • *n* storm
asalta • *v* storm
asana • *v* drain
asasin • *n* killer
asasina • *v* assassinate
asasinat • *n* murder
asbestoz • *n* asbestosis
asc • *n* ascus
ascenden • *n* ascendancy
ascensor • *n* lift
achie • *n* chip, sliver, splinter
ascomicet • *n* ascomycete
asculta • *v* listen
ascultare • *n* obedience
asculttor • *n* listener • *adj* obedient
ascunde • *v* conceal, hide, mask, obscure, shun
ascuns • *adj* invisible, obscure
ascunztoare • *n* hideout
ascui • *v* sharpen, whet
ascui • *n* edge
ascuit • *adj* acute, sharp
asemntor • *adj* similar
asexual • *adj* asexual
aeza • *v* set, sit
aezmânt • *n* establishment
aezare • *n* establishment
aezat • *adj* set
asfini • *v* set
asfinire • *n* sunset
asfinit • *n* sun
asfodel • *n* asphodel
asiduu • *adj* assiduous, sedulous
asigura • *v* ensure
asigurare • *n* insurance
asigurat • *adj* secure
asimetric • *adj* asymmetrical
asimilare • *n* assimilation
asimilaie • *n* assimilation
asimptot • *n* asymptote
asimptotic • *adj* asymptotic
asin • *n* ass, donkey
asincron • *adj* asynchronous
asista • *v* assist, help
asistent • *n* assistant
asisten • *n* assistance, help
asociat • *n* associate • *adj* associate

asociaial • *adj* associational
asociaie • *n* association
asociaional • *adj* associational
asociere • *n* association, relationship
asparagin • *n* asparagine
aspect • *n* appearance, aspect, look
asperitate • *n* roughness
aspira • *v* inhale
aspirare • *n* aspiration
aspiraie • *n* aspiration
aspirin • *n* aspirin
asprime • *n* roughness, severity
aspru • *adj* coarse, hardhearted, harsh, rough, stark
sta • *pron* this
asta • *pron* this
astâmpra • *v* allay, appease
astatin • *n* astatine
astzi • *n* today • *adv* today
atepta • *v* await, wait
ateptare • *n* expectancy, expectation, vigil, wait
ateptat • *n* expectation
aster • *n* aster
asterisc • *n* asterisk
aterne • *v* reach, spread, strew
asteroid • *n* asteroid
asteroizi • *n* asteroid
astfel • *adv* thus
astigmatism • *n* astigmatism
astm • *n* asthma
astral • *adj* astral
astrofizic • *n* astrophysics
astrologie • *n* astrology
astronaut • *n* astronaut
astronom • *n* astronomer
astronom • *n* astronomer
astronomie • *n* astronomy
astupa • *v* obstruct, plug
asuda • *v* sweat
asurzi • *v* deafen
asurzitor • *adj* deafening
a • *n* line, thread
atac • *n* attack, offensive, storm
ataca • *v* attack, storm
atacant • *n* attacker, offense
atacant • *n* attacker
ataraxie • *n* ataraxia
atârna • *v* dangle, hang, suspend
atârnat • *adj* hanging
ataa • *v* fasten
ataament • *n* attachment
ataare • *n* attachment
atasat • *v* attach
atât • *adv* so
atâa • *v* incite
aâa • *v* whet
atavism • *n* atavism
ateism • *n* atheism
ateist • *n* atheist • *adj* atheistic
ateist • *n* atheist
atelier • *n* shop, workshop
atent • *adj* vigilant, watchful
atenie • *n* attention, attentiveness, mind
atenua • *v* attenuate
atenuare • *n* attenuation
aterizare • *n* landing
atesta • *v* attest, testify
atestare • *n* attestation
atestat • *n* testimonial
ateu • *n* atheist
atinge • *v* meet, reach, touch
atingere • *n* contact, contingence
aipi • *v* doze, snooze
atipic • *adj* atypical, unconventional
atitudine • *n* attitude
atlas • *n* atlas
atlet • *n* athlete
atlet • *n* athlete
atlete • *n* athlete
atlei • *n* athlete
atletic • *adj* athletic
atletism • *n* athletics
atmosfer • *n* air, atmosphere
atmosferic • *adj* atmospheric
atol • *n* atoll
atomic • *adj* nuclear
atonic • *adj* listless
atotputernic • *adj* almighty, omnipotent
atottiutor • *adj* all-knowing, omniscient
atracie • *n* attraction
atractiv • *adj* attractive, magnetic
atrgtor • *adj* enticing, impressive, lush
atrage • *v* appeal, attract
atragere • *n* appeal, attraction
atribui • *v* assign
atribut • *n* property
atributiv • *adj* attributive
atriu • *n* atrium
atrium • *n* atrium
atroce • *adj* atrocious, awful, monstrous
atrocitate • *n* atrocity, outrage
atrofie • *n* atrophy
atrofiere • *n* atrophy
atropin • *n* atropine
atu • *n* trump
atunci • *adv* then
au • *interj* ouch
audio • *adj* audio
audio-vizual • *adj* audiovisual
auditor • *n* listener
augmentativ • *n* augmentative • *adj* augmentative
augmentativ • *adj* augmentative

augur • *n* augury
aur • *n* gold, or
aurar • *n* goldsmith
aureol • *n* aureole, halo
auri • *v* gild
aurit • *adj* golden
auriu • *adj* gilded, gold, golden, or • *n* gold
auror • *n* dawn
auel • *n* goldcrest
auspiciu • *n* augury
auster • *adj* austere
austeritate • *n* austerity
austral • *adj* southern
autentic • *adj* authentic
autentificare • *n* attestation, authentication
autism • *n* autism
autoare • *n* author
autobiografic • *adj* autobiographical
autobiografie • *n* autobiography
autobuz • *n* bus, omnibus
autocontrol • *n* composure, self-control
autodidact • *n* autodidact • *adj* self-educated
autograf • *n* autograph
autohton • *adj* autochthonous, indigenous, native • *n* native
autoîncântare • *n* complacency, smugness
automat • *adj* automatic • *adv* automatically • *n* automaton
automat • *adj* automatic
automatizare • *n* automation
automobil • *n* automobile, car, machine
automulumire • *n* complacency, smugness
autonom • *adj* autonomous
autonom • *adj* autonomous
autopolenizare • *n* self-pollination
autor • *n* author, writer
autoritar • *adj* authoritarian
autoritate • *n* authority, control
autoriti • *n* authority
autorizare • *n* authorization
autorizaie • *n* authorization
autoservice • *n* garage
autostopist • *n* hitchhiker
autostopist • *n* hitchhiker
autostrad • *n* highway
auxiliar • *adj* peripheral
auz • *n* hearing
auzi • *v* hear
auzibil • *adj* audible
auzit • *n* hearing
avalan • *n* avalanche
avangard • *n* avant-garde, vanguard
avanpost • *n* outpost
avanposturi • *n* outpost
avansa • *v* advance
avansat • *adj* progressive
avânt • *n* boom
avantaj • *n* advantage, benefit
avantaja • *v* advantage
avantajos • *adj* advantageous
avar • *adj* avaricious
avaria • *v* damage, wreck
avarie • *n* damage, wreck
avarii • *n* damage
avariie • *n* avarice, greed, stinginess
avea • *v* have, obtain, possess
avenue • *n* avenue
avere • *n* assets, fortune, wealth
avers • *n* shower
aversiune • *n* abhorrence, abomination, aversion, dislike
avertisment • *n* notice
aviaie • *n* aviation
avid • *adj* eager
aviditate • *n* avarice, avidity, greed
avion • *n* airplane
aviz • *n* notice
avocado • *n* avocado
avocat • *n* lawyer
avort • *n* abort, abortion
avut • *adj* rich
avut • *adj* rich
ax • *n* axle
ax • *n* axis
axial • *adj* axial
axial • *adj* axial
axiologic • *adj* axiological
axiologie • *n* axiology
axiomatic • *adj* axiomatic
aye-aye • *n* aye-aye
azalee • *n* azalea
azi • *n* today • *adv* today
azil • *n* asylum, sanctuary
azot • *n* nitrogen
azur • *n* azure
azuriu • *adj* azure, blue

B

bab • *n* crone, granny, hag
babord • *n* larboard
baborni • *n* hag
babuin • *n* baboon
bac • *n* ferry
bac • *n* berry
bacalaureat • *n* baccalaureate
bcan • *n* grocer, logwood
bcneas • *n* grocer
bacil • *n* bacillus
baclava • *n* baklava
bacon • *n* bacon
baci • *n* tip
bacterii • *n* bacteria
bacteriologie • *n* bacteriology
bdran • *n* boor, yokel
badijona • *v* smear
bga • *v* fuck
bagaj • *n* luggage
bagatel • *pron* nothing
bahic • *n* bacchanal
biat • *n* boy, lad
baie • *n* bath, bathroom
baionet • *n* bayonet
blbni • *v* dangle
balad • *n* ballad
balama • *n* hinge
balamuc • *n* bedlam
balans • *n* balance
balansa • *v* swing
balan • *n* balance
balast • *n* ballast
balaur • *n* dragon, worm
bâlbâi • *v* stutter
bâlbâire • *n* stutter
Balbism • *n* stammer
balcon • *n* balcony
baleg • *n* dung
balen • *n* whale
balerin • *n* ballerina
balet • *n* ballet
baletist • *n* ballerina
balig • *n* manure
balistic • *adj* ballistic
balon • *n* balloon, bubble
balsa • *n* balsa
balsam • *n* balsam
balt • *n* pond, puddle
blat • *adj* variegated
balustrad • *n* balustrade
balustrada • *n* railing
balustru • *n* baluster
bam • *n* okra
bambu • *n* bamboo
bambus • *n* bamboo
ban • *n* ban, money
banal • *adj* dull, quotidian
banan • *n* banana
banan • *n* banana
bananier • *n* banana
banc • *n* joke, workbench
banc • *n* bank, bench
bancher • *n* banker
banchet • *n* banquet, dinner, feast
band • *n* gang
bandaj • *n* bandage
bandit • *n* highwayman
bani • *n* cash
banian • *n* banyan
bnui • *v* guess
bnuial • *n* idea
bnu • *n* daisy
bnuel • *n* daisy
baobab • *n* baobab
baptist • *n* baptist
baptist • *n* baptist
bara • *v* bar
barabul • *n* potato
barac • *n* box, hut, lodge
baracud • *n* barracuda
baraj • *n* barrage, dam
barb • *n* beard
barba-ursului • *n* horsetail
barbarism • *n* barbarism
brbat • *n* male, man
brbtesc • *adj* manly, masculine
brbai • *n* gentleman
brbie • *n* bravery
brbtu • *n* cock, male
brbie • *n* chin
brbier • *n* barber
brbieri • *v* shave
brbos • *adj* bearded
barc • *n* boat
bard • *n* hatchet
brdac • *n* pitcher
bardou • *n* hinny
bariu • *n* barium
bârlog • *n* den
bârn • *n* girder
barometru • *n* barometer
barz • *n* stork
barza-alb • *n* stork
baschet • *n* basket, basketball
bascula • *v* reverse
baseball • *n* baseball
bi • *v* fart
bic • *n* bladder, blister, bubble
basidie • *n* basidium
bin • *n* fart
basm • *n* yarn
basorelief • *n* relief
bastard • *n* bastard
bastarde • *n* bastard

bastarzi • *n* bastard
bastion • *n* bastion
baston • *n* bat, cane, stick
b • *n* rod, stick
bât • *n* bat, club
btaie • *n* combat, fight
batal • *n* wether
btlie • *n* battle
batalion • *n* battalion
bttur • *n* callus
bate • *v* bat, beat, defeat, hit, pound, ring, set
baterie • *n* battery
batic • *n* batik
baticul • *n* batik
batist • *n* batiste
batist • *n* handkerchief, tissue
bâtlan-de-stuf • *n* bittern
bos • *adj* rigid
btrân • *adj* elderly, old
btrân • *adj* elderly
btrâni • *adj* elderly
bau • *interj* boo
but • *adj* drunk, drunken, intoxicated
butoare • *n* drinker
butor • *n* drinker
butur • *n* beverage, drink
baz • *n* base, basis, foundation
bazal • *adj* basal
bazalt • *n* basalt
bazilic • *n* basilica
bea • *v* drink, imbibe
beat • *adj* drunk, drunken, intoxicated, tipsy
beatitudine • *n* beatitude, bliss
bebe • *n* baby
bebelu • *n* baby, infant
beca • *n* woodcock
becain • *n* woodcock
beci • *n* cellar
beduin • *n* bedouin
beduini • *n* bedouin
begonie • *n* begonia
behaviorism • *n* behaviorism
bej • *n* beige • *adj* beige
beletristic • *n* belles-lettres
beli • *v* flay
belicos • *adj* belligerent
beligerant • *adj* belligerent
belug • *n* plenty
beluga • *n* beluga
benediciune • *n* blessing
beneficia • *v* profit
beneficiar • *adj* incumbent
beneficii • *n* benefit
beneficiu • *n* benefit
benevolen • *n* humanity
benign • *adj* benign
benzen • *n* benzene
benzin • *n* gas, gasoline, oil
berar • *n* brewer
berrie • *n* tavern
berbec • *n* ram
bere • *n* beer
beret • *n* beret
beril • *n* beryl
beriliu • *n* beryllium
berkeliu • *n* berkelium
bestial • *adj* bestial
bestial • *adj* bestial
bestialitate • *n* bestiality
bestie • *n* beast
beie • *n* drunkenness
beiv • *n* drunk, drunkard, lush
beiv • *n* drunk, drunkard
beivan • *n* drunk, drunkard
beivan • *n* drunk, drunkard
beton • *n* concrete • *adj* concrete
bezea • *n* marshmallow
biban • *n* bass, perch
biber • *n* beaver
biberon • *n* nipple
bibilic • *n* fritillary
Biblie • *n* bible
bibliotec • *n* library
bicameral • *adj* bicameral
biceps • *n* biceps
bici • *n* whip
biciclet • *n* bicycle, bike
biciclist • *n* cyclist
biconvex • *adj* biconvex
biconvex • *adj* biconvex
bidimensional • *adj* two-dimensional
bidon • *n* jug
biet • *adj* poor
bifurca • *v* bifurcate
bifurcare • *n* bifurcation
bifurcaie • *n* fork
big • *n* chariot
bigamie • *n* bigamy
bîjbîi • *v* grope
bijuterie • *n* jewel
bijuterii • *n* jewel
bijutier • *n* jeweler
bijutieri • *n* jeweler
bikini • *n* bikini
bil • *n* ball, bile, sphere
bilan • *n* balance, statement
bilet • *n* fare, ticket
biliard • *n* billiards
bilingv • *adj* bilingual
bilingv • *adj* bilingual
binar • *adj* binary
bine • *n* good • *adj* well • *adv* well

binecuvânta • *v* bless
binecuvântare • *n* blessing, mercy
binecuvântat • *adj* blessed
binecuvântat • *adj* blessed
binefctpr • *adj* altruistic
bineîneles • *adv* certainly, naturally
binevenit • *adj* welcome
binevenit • *adj* welcome
binevoitoare • *adj* benevolent
binevoitor • *adj* benevolent
binoclu • *n* binoculars
binturong • *n* binturong
biochimie • *n* biochemistry
biofizic • *n* biophysics
biograf • *n* biographer
biografie • *n* biography
biologic • *adj* biological
biologie • *n* biology
biomas • *n* biomass
biotit • *n* biotite
birocrat • *n* bureaucrat, clerk
birocratic • *adj* bureaucratic
birocraie • *n* bureaucracy
birou • *n* bureau, desk, office
biscuit • *n* biscuit
biseric • *n* church
biserici • *n* church
bisexualitate • *n* bisexuality
bismut • *n* bismuth
bistabil • *n* flip-flop
bitum • *n* bitumen
bivol • *n* buffalo
bizam • *n* muskrat
bizar • *adj* curious, uncanny
bizon • *n* bison, buffalo
blagoslovi • *v* bless
blagoslovit • *adj* blessed
blama • *v* blame
blan • *n* fur, hair, hide
blând • *adj* benign, bland, lenient
blândee • *n* clemency, gentleness, leniency
bleg • *adj* sheepish
blestem • *n* curse
blestema • *v* blaspheme, curse
blestemat • *adj* blasted
bleumarin • *n* navy • *adj* navy
blid • *n* jar
bloca • *v* obstruct
blond • *n* blond
bluz • *n* blouse
boa • *n* boa
boac • *n* zilch
boal • *n* disease, illness, sickness
boar • *n* cowherd
boare • *n* breeze
boae • *n* balls
bob • *n* bean, grain
bobârnac • *n* fillip
boboc • *n* bud, duckling, gosling
boci • *v* bemoan, bewail, lament
bodârlu • *n* diver
bodeg • *n* tavern
boem • *n* bohemian • *adj* bohemian
bogat • *adj* rich
bogat • *adj* rich
boia • *n* paprika
boier • *n* boyar
bol • *n* sphere
bold • *n* pin
bolnav • *adj* ill
bolnvicios • *adj* sickly
bolovan • *n* boulder
bol • *n* bolt
bomb • *n* bomb
bombardament • *n* bombardment
bombardare • *n* bombardment
bombardier • *n* bomber
bomboan • *n* chocolate, drop, sweet
bomfaier • *n* hacksaw
bompres • *n* bowsprit
bondar • *n* bumblebee
bondoc • *adj* stocky
bonit • *n* bonito
bonomie • *n* bonhomie
bootstrap • *n* bootstrap
bor • *n* boron
bordel • *n* brothel
bordo • *adj* burgundy
bordur • *n* border
boreal • *adj* boreal
borî • *v* vomit
bormain • *n* borer
born • *n* mark
bor • *n* borscht
boroas • *adj* pregnant
bostan • *n* pumpkin
bot • *n* bot, nose
botanic • *adj* botanical
botanic • *n* botany
botanist • *n* botanist
botaniza • *v* botanize
botez • *n* baptism
boteza • *v* baptize
botgros • *n* hawfinch
botro • *n* bullfinch
botulism • *n* botulism
bou • *n* ox, steer
bougainvillea • *n* bougainvillea
bour • *n* aurochs
bovid • *n* bovid
bovideu • *n* bovid
bovin • *n* bovine
bovine • *n* cattle

bowling • *n* bowling
box • *n* boxing
bractee • *n* bract
brad • *n* fir
brahial • *adj* brachial
brându • *n* crocus
branhie • *n* gill
bran • *n* branch
brânz • *n* cheese
bras • *n* breaststroke
braserie • *n* tavern
bra • *n* arm, fathom
brar • *n* bracelet
brâu • *n* belt
brav • *adj* brave
bravo • *n* bravo • *interj* bravo
bravur • *n* bravery, gallantry
brzda • *v* furrow
brazd • *n* furrow
brzdar • *n* plowshare
breloc • *n* charm
breton • *n* bang, fringe
breviar • *n* breviary
briceag • *n* pocketknife
brichet • *n* lighter
brici • *n* razor
bridge • *n* bridge
brie • *n* brie
brilian • *n* brilliancy
briofit • *n* bryophyte
brio • *n* muffin
briz • *n* breeze
broasc • *n* frog, lock
broboad • *n* wimple
broccoli • *n* broccoli
brom • *n* bromine
bromur • *n* bromide
bronit • *n* bronchitis
bronz • *n* bronze, tan
bronza • *v* bronze, tan
bronzare • *n* tan
bronzat • *adj* bronze, tan
brour • *n* booklet
brotac • *n* frog
bruia • *v* jam
bruma • *v* frost
brum • *n* frost, rime
brumriu • *adj* gray
brun • *n* brown • *adj* brown
brunch • *n* brunch
brunet • *adj* brunette
brusc • *adj* sudden • *adv* suddenly
brusture • *n* burdock
brut • *adj* gross
brutal • *adj* brutal
brutal • *adj* brutal
brutar • *n* baker
brutarie • *n* bakery
buberic • *n* figwort
buboi • *n* boil
bubon • *n* bubo
bubuit • *n* boom
buc • *n* buttock, cheek
bucat • *n* bit, cake, fragment, item, piece, portion
buctar • *n* cook
buctrie • *n* kitchen
buchet • *n* bouquet, nose
buci • *n* buttock
bucl • *n* lock
bucura • *v* rejoice
bucurie • *n* happiness, joy
bucuros • *adj* glad, happy
bufni • *n* owl
bufon • *n* clown, fool
bufonerie • *n* tomfoolery
buhai • *n* twayblade
buhai-de-balt • *n* bittern
building • *n* skyscraper
bujor • *n* peony
bul • *n* bubble
bulangiu • *n* fag
bulb • *n* bulb
bulboan • *n* eddy, vortex
bulbuc • *n* globeflower
buldozer • *n* bulldozer
bulgre • *n* clod
bum • *interj* boom
bumbac • *n* cotton
bumerang • *n* boomerang
bun • *adj* good, hot, kind • *n* good
bun • *adj* good • *interj* hello, hi
bun-cuviin • *n* urbanity
bunstare • *n* well-being
buntate • *n* clemency, generosity, goodness, humanity, kindness
bunvoin • *n* benevolence, condescension, goodwill, kindness
bunic • *n* grandfather
bunic • *n* grandmother
bura • *v* drizzle
burete • *n* eraser, sponge
burghezie • *n* bourgeoisie
burghiu • *n* bit, drill
buric • *n* navel
burlac • *adj* unmarried
burni • *n* drizzle
bursuc • *n* badger
burt • *n* abdomen, belly
buruian • *n* weed
busculad • *n* stampede
bui • *v* thrust
businessman • *n* businessman
busol • *n* compass

butean • *n* log
busuioc • *n* basil
butan • *n* butane
bute • *n* barrel, cask
butelie • *n* container
butil • *n* butyl
butoi • *n* barrel, cask
buton • *n* button
butuc • *n* stocks
butucnos • *adj* clumsy
buz • *n* lip
buzdugan • *n* mace
buze • *n* lip, lips
buzunar • *n* pocket

C

c • *conj* that
ca • *conj* as • *prep* as, than
cabalin • *n* horse
caban • *n* box, hut, lodge
cabin • *n* car, lodge
cablare • *v* cable
cablu • *n* cable, cord
cabluri • *n* cable
cca • *v* shit
câca • *v* defecate
cacadu • *n* cockatoo
cacao • *n* cacao, cocoa
ccat • *n* bullshit, crap, shit
cache • *n* cache
cci • *conj* for
cacofonia • *n* cacophony
cactus • *n* cactus
cad • *n* bath, bathtub
cadavru • *n* cadaver, carcass, corpse
cdea • *v* fall
caden • *n* cadence
cdere • *n* collapse, decency, decorum, drop, fall
cadmiu • *n* cadmium
cadou • *n* gift
cadrilater • *n* quadrilateral
cadru • *n* frame
cafea • *n* coffee
cafein • *n* caffeine
cafeniu • *n* coffee, fawn • *adj* fawn, tan
câh • *interj* ugh
câine • *n* dog
câini • *n* dog
câinos • *adj* evil
cin • *n* atonement
cais • *n* apricot
cais • *n* apricot
cior • *n* tit
cal • *n* horse, knight
cal-putere • *n* horsepower
cal • *n* hold
calambur • *n* pun
calamitate • *n* calamity
calamiti • *n* calamity
calao • *n* hornbill
clre • *n* horseman, rider
cltor • *n* passenger
cltori • *v* fare, journey, travel, trip
cltorie • *n* journey, travel, trip, voyage
clu • *n* executioner, hangman
clca • *v* iron, tread
clcâi • *n* heel
calcar • *n* limestone
calcaros • *adj* calciferous
calciu • *n* calcium
calcul • *n* calculation, calculus
calcula • *v* calculate
calculabil • *adj* calculable
calculare • *n* calculation
calculatoare • *n* calculator
calculator • *n* calculator, computer
cald • *adj* hot, warm
cald • *adj* warm
caldarâm • *n* pavement
cldare • *n* bucket
cldru • *n* columbine
cldur • *n* heat, warmth
cale • *n* avenue, road, way
calendar • *n* calendar
cli • *v* temper
caliciu • *n* calyx, chalice
clifar • *n* shelduck
calificare • *n* qualification
calificat • *adj* qualified
californiu • *n* californium
caligrafic • *adj* calligraphic
calitate • *n* quality
calitativ • *adj* qualitative
calm • *adj* calm, composed • *adv* calmly • *n* calmness, composure
calma • *v* alleviate, calm, still
calmar • *n* squid
calorie • *n* calorie
calorifer • *n* radiator
calorimetrie • *n* calorimetry
cluna • *n* nasturtium
clunul-doamnei • *n* avens
clugr • *n* monk

clugrie • *n* cloister
clugri • *n* mantis, nun, sister
clu • *n* horse, tit
calvar • *n* ordeal
cam • *adv* about, pretty
cam • *n* cam
cmar • *n* pantry
camarad • *n* associate, comrade
cma • *n* shirt
cameleon • *n* chameleon
camelie • *n* camellia
camer • *n* house, room
camfor • *n* camphor
cmil • *n* camel
cmin • *n* chimney, fireplace
camion • *n* truck
câmp • *n* field
câmpenesc • *adj* rural
câmpie • *n* plain
campioan • *n* champion, championship
campion • *n* champion, championship
campionat • *n* championship
campus • *n* campus
cana • *n* henna
can • *n* mug
canal • *n* canal, channel
canapea • *n* sofa
canapele • *n* sofa
canar • *n* canary
canava • *n* canvas
cancelar • *n* chancellor
cancelar • *n* chancellor
cancer • *n* cancer
cancerigen • *adj* carcinogenic
canceros • *adj* cancerous
canci • *n* zilch
când • *conj* as, when • *adv* when • *pron* when
candelabru • *n* chandelier
cândva • *adv* sometime
cânep • *n* cannabis, hemp
cangren • *n* gangrene
cangur • *n* kangaroo
cangur • *n* kangaroo
canibal • *n* cannibal
canibal • *n* cannibal
canibalic • *adj* cannibalistic
canibalism • *n* cannibalism
canibalistic • *adj* cannibalistic
canion • *n* canyon
canistr • *n* canister
canoe • *n* canoe
canoniza • *v* canonize
canonizat • *adj* canonized
canonizat • *adj* canonized
cant • *n* border, line
cânt • *n* canto
cânta • *v* play, sing
cantalup • *n* cantaloupe
cântar • *n* scale
cântare • *n* singing, song
cântrea • *n* singer
cântre • *n* singer
cântri • *v* weigh
cantat • *n* cantata
cântec • *n* song
cantin • *n* canteen
cantitate • *n* amount, magnitude, number, quantity
cantusul • *n* canthus
cap • *n* cape, head, nut
cap • *n* cape
capabil • *adj* able, capable
capabilitate • *n* capability
capac • *n* lid
capacitate • *n* ability, capacity, cunning, faculty
cpstru • *n* halter
capt • *n* end, extremity
cpcun • *n* ogre
capel • *n* chapel
caper • *n* caper
caper • *n* caper
cpetenie • *n* chief, head
capibara • *n* capybara
capilaritate • *n* capillarity
capîntortur • *n* wryneck
cpi • *n* stack
capital • *n* capital
capitalism • *n* capitalism
capitalist • *n* capitalist
capitat • *adj* capitate
capitol • *n* chapter
capitonare • *n* upholstery
capitula • *v* capitulate
capodoper • *n* masterpiece
capotare • *n* upset
capr • *n* goat, horse, leapfrog, sawhorse
capr-de-munte • *n* chamois
capr-neagr • *n* chamois
capricios • *adj* capricious
capriciu • *n* caprice, whim
caprifoi • *n* honeysuckle
caprimulg • *n* whippoorwill
cprioar • *n* deer, doe
cprior • *n* rafter, roebuck
cpriu • *adj* hazel
cprui • *adj* hazel
capsa • *v* staple
caps • *n* staple
capsul • *v* pod
cpun • *n* strawberry
cpun • *n* strawberry
captiva • *v* beguile

captivat • *adj* absorbed
cpu • *n* tick
car • *n* cart, wagon
cra • *v* bear, carry, convey, transport
carabin • *n* carbine
crbu • *n* cockchafer
caracara • *n* caracara
caracati • *n* octopus
caracter • *n* letter, property, temper
caracteristic • *adj* characteristic, particular
caracteristic • *n* characteristic, feature, idiosyncrasy
caracteriza • *v* characterize
caracud • *n* fry
caraghios • *adj* funny
caraghioslâc • *n* tomfoolery
caramea • *n* chew
caramel • *n* caramel
caramel • *n* caramel
crmid • *n* brick
carapace • *n* carapace, shell
crare • *n* footpath, parting, path
carate • *n* karate
carbohidrat • *n* carbohydrate
carbon • *n* carbon
carbonat • *n* carbonate
carbonic • *adj* carbonic
crbune • *n* carbon, charcoal, coal
carburant • *n* fuel
carburator • *n* carburetor
carcas • *n* carcass
carcinogen • *adj* carcinogenic
cârcium • *n* pub
card • *n* card
cârd • *n* herd, wedge
carda • *v* card
cardama • *n* watercress
cardamom • *n* cardamom
cardiac • *adj* cardiac
cardinal • *n* cardinal • *adj* cardinal
cardiolog • *n* cardiologist
cardiologie • *n* cardiology
cardon • *n* cardoon
care • *conj* lest • *pron* what, which, who
caren • *n* hull
caribu • *n* caribou
caricatur • *n* cartoon
carier • *n* quarry
carilon • *n* carillon
carism • *n* charisma
carismatic • *adj* charismatic, charming
cârj • *n* crutch
cârlig • *n* hook
carling • *n* cockpit
cârm • *n* helm, rudder, run
cârmâz • *n* carmine
cârmâziu • *adj* carmine
carmin • *n* carmine, crimson • *adj* carmine, crimson
cârmui • *v* govern
cârmuibil • *adj* steerable
cârnat • *n* sausage
carne • *n* flesh, meat
carnivor • *adj* carnivorous
carnivor • *adj* carnivorous
crnos • *adj* fleshy
carot • *n* carrot
cârp • *n* cloth, rag
carpel • *n* carpel
carpen • *n* hornbeam
cârpitur • *n* rag
carte • *n* book, card
crticic • *n* booklet
cartilaginos • *adj* cartilaginous
cartilaj • *n* cartilage
cârti • *n* mole
cartof • *n* potato
cartografie • *n* cartography
carton • *n* cardboard
cartu • *n* cartridge
crucior • *n* trolley
cru • *n* cart, wagon
ca • *n* cheese
cas • *n* home, house
cstori • *v* marry, wed
cstorie • *n* marriage
csca • *v* yawn
casc • *n* helmet
casca • *v* yawn
cascad • *n* cascade, waterfall
cacaval • *n* cheese
casnic • *n* housewife
csnicie • *n* marriage
cast • *adj* chaste, pure
castan • *n* chestnut
castaniete • *n* castanet
castaniu • *adj* hazel
castel • *n* castle
câtig • *n* profit
câtiga • *v* earn, gain, net
câtigtoare • *n* winner
câtigtor • *n* winner
castitate • *n* modesty
castor • *n* beaver
castra • *v* castrate
castravete • *n* cucumber
castron • *n* bowl, jar
cât • *adv* how
cat • *n* level
cataclism • *n* cataclysm
catacomb • *n* catacomb
catalitic • *adj* catalytic
cataliz • *n* catalysis

catalizator • *n* catalyst
catâr • *n* mule
cataract • *n* cataract
ctare • *n* aim
catarg • *n* mast
catastrof • *n* catastrophe, disaster
catastrofal • *adj* catastrophic
catastrofic • *adj* catastrophic
catastrofic • *adj* catastrophic
cea • *n* bitch, slut
catedral • *n* cathedral
categorie • *n* category
categorii • *n* category
categorisi • *v* label
categorisire • *n* categorization
categoriza • *v* assign
catehism • *n* catechism
cel • *n* clove, pup, puppy, whelp
celu • *n* pup, puppy
câteodat • *adv* occasionally, sometimes
catgut • *n* catgut
catifea • *n* velvet
catifelat • *adj* velvety
ctin • *n* tamarisk
cation • *n* cation
ctre • *prep* to
ctu • *n* handcuff
ctue • *n* handcuffs, manacle
ctunic • *n* catnip
cauciuc • *n* caoutchouc, rubber, tyre
cauciucuri • *n* rubber
caudal • *adj* caudal
caustic • *adj* acrid • *n* caustic
cuta • *v* search, seek
cauz • *n* cause, lawsuit, matter, purpose
cauza • *v* cause
cavaler • *n* horse, horseman, knight
cavalerie • *n* cavalry, chivalry
cavalerism • *n* chivalry
cavern • *n* cave
caviar • *n* caviar
caz • *n* case, incident, instance, occurrence
cazanie • *n* sermon
cazarm • *n* base
cazma • *n* spade
cazuistic • *n* casuistry
cazuri • *n* case
czut • *adj* down
ce • *adv* how • *pron* what, which
cea • *art* the
ceaf • *n* nape
ceai • *n* tea
ceainic • *n* teakettle, teapot
ceap • *n* onion
cear • *n* wax • *adj* wax
ceart • *n* argument, brawl, conflict, disagreement, quarrel
ceas • *n* clock, hour, time, watch
ceac • *n* cup
ceasornicar • *n* watchmaker
cea • *n* fog, mist
cec • *n* caecum, cheque, draft
cecidie • *n* gall
cecum • *n* caecum
cedru • *n* cedar
cel • *art* the
cele • *art* the
celebra • *v* celebrate
celebrant • *adj* celebratory
celebrare • *n* celebration
celebru • *adj* famous
celest • *n* celesta
celibatar • *adj* single
celul • *n* cell
celular • *n* cell • *adj* cellular
cent • *n* centime
centenar • *n* centennial
centiped • *n* centipede
centra • *v* center
central • *adj* central
central • *n* headquarters
centralizare • *n* centralization
centrist • *n* moderate • *adj* moderate
centrist • *n* moderate
centru • *n* center, downtown, heart
centur • *n* belt
centurie • *n* century
cenu • *n* ash
cenuiu • *adj* ashen, cinereous, gray, neutral
cenzor • *n* censor
cenzura • *v* censor
cer • *n* heaven, sky
cera • *v* wax
ceramic • *adj* ceramic
ceramic • *n* ceramic
cerb • *n* deer, stag
cerbice • *n* nape
cerc • *n* circle, hoop
cercel • *n* earring
cercelu • *n* fuchsia
cerceta • *v* scan
cercetare • *n* reconnaissance, research
cercui • *v* circulate
cere • *v* ask, demand, request
cereal • *n* cereal, corn
cereasc • *adj* celestial
cerebel • *n* cerebellum
cerebral • *adj* cerebral
ceremonie • *n* ceremony
ceremonios • *adv* ceremonially
cerenel • *n* avens
cerere • *n* demand, request

ceresc • *adj* celestial
cerin • *n* need, requirement
ceriu • *n* cerium
cerne • *v* sieve, sift
cerneal • *n* ink
ceretor • *n* beggar
ceri • *v* beg
cert • *adj* certain, sure
certa • *v* argue, chide, quarrel, rebuke, reprove, row, scold, squabble
certare • *v* berate
certre • *adj* belligerent
certifica • *v* certify
certificare • *n* validation
certitudine • *n* certainty, certitude
cetaceu • *n* cetacean
cetate • *n* citadel, city, fortress
cetean • *n* citizen
cetenie • *n* citizenship
ceva • *n* anything • *pron* something
charism • *n* charisma
cheag • *n* clot, rennet
chedi • *n* stupa
chef • *n* banquet
chei • *n* platform, quay, wharf
cheie • *n* clef, key
chel • *adj* bald
chelner • *n* waiter
chelneri • *n* waitress
cheltui • *v* spend
chema • *v* call
chemare • *n* call, vocation
chestie • *n* thing
chestiune • *n* matter
cheza • *n* guarantee
chiar • *adv* even
chibrit • *n* match
chibzui • *v* contemplate, weigh
chibzuire • *n* reflecting
chibzuit • *adj* sensible
chica-voinicului • *n* love-in-a-mist, nigella
• *n* sky
chifl • *n* bun
chiftea • *n* meatball
chihlimbar • *n* amber
chilie • *n* cell
chilipir • *n* steal
chiloi • *n* underpants, underwear
chimen • *n* caraway
chimic • *adj* chemical
chimie • *n* chemistry
chimion • *n* cumin
chimist • *n* chemist
chimist • *n* chemist
chin • *n* anguish, ordeal, pain, torment, torture
ching • *n* cinch
chinovar • *n* cinnabar
chinui • *v* anguish, torment, torture
chior • *adj* one-eyed
chioc • *n* kiosk
chiparos • *n* cypress
chipe • *adj* handsome
chirie • *n* rent
chiropractician • *n* chiropractor
chirpici • *n* adobe
chirurg • *n* surgeon
chirurgie • *n* surgery
chicar • *n* lamprey
chitan • *n* acknowledgement
chitar • *n* guitar
chican • *n* shrew
chitr • *n* citron
chitru • *n* citron
chiuretaj • *n* curettage
chiuretare • *n* curettage
chiuvet • *n* basin, sink, washbasin
cianura • *n* cyanide
cicad • *n* cicada
cicli • *v* nag
cicatrice • *n* scar
ciclam • *n* cyclamen
ciclism • *n* cycling
ciclist • *n* cyclist
cicloid • *n* cycloid
ciclon • *n* cyclone
ciclostom • *n* cyclostome
ciclu • *n* circuit, cycle
cicoare • *n* chicory, cicada
cifr • *n* digit
cîine • *n* dog
cilindric • *adj* cylindrical
cilindric • *adj* cylindrical
cilindru • *n* cylinder
cimbru • *n* savory, thyme
ciment • *n* cement
cimiir • *n* box
cimpanzeu • *n* chimpanzee
cimpoaie • *n* bagpipes
cimpoi • *n* bagpipes
cina • *v* dine, supper
cin • *n* dinner, dinnertime, supper
cinabru • *n* cinnabar, vermilion
cincea • *adj* fifth
cinci • *n* five
cincila • *n* chinchilla
cincilea • *adj* fifth
cine • *pron* who
cinematic • *n* kinematics
cinematografie • *n* cinema
cinetic • *adj* kinetic
cineva • *n* anything • *pron* somebody
cinic • *adj* cynical

cinism • *n* cynicism
cinste • *n* honor, treat
cinsti • *v* honor
cinstit • *adj* honest
cintez • *n* chaffinch, finch
cioar • *n* crow, nigger
cioban • *n* shepherd
cioc • *n* beak, bill, nose
cioc-întors • *n* avocet
ciocan • *n* hammer, malleus
ciocni • *v* knock
ciocnitoare • *n* woodpecker
ciocârlie • *n* lark, skylark
ciocnire • *n* collision
ciocolat • *n* chocolate
ciocolatiu • *adj* chocolate
ciolan • *n* limb
ciomag • *n* bat
ciopli • *v* hew
ciorap • *n* sock
ciordi • *v* filch
ciorna • *n* draft
cioroi • *n* blackamoor, spade
ciot • *n* stump
cip • *n* chip
circ • *n* circus
circuit • *n* circuit
circuit-cascad • *n* cascade
circular • *adj* circular
circumcide • *v* circumcise
circumcizie • *n* circumcision
circumferin • *n* circumference
circumscrie • *v* circumscribe
circumstan • *n* circumstance, instance
cirea • *n* cherry
cire • *n* cherry
cirear • *n* hawfinch
ciripitor • *n* ear
cistein • *n* cysteine
cistern • *n* cistern
citadel • *n* citadel
citare • *n* citation
citat • *n* citation, quotation
cite • *adj* legible
citi • *v* read
citire • *n* read
citologie • *n* cytology
citoplasm • *n* cytoplasm
citrice • *n* citrus
ciuboica-cucului • *n* cowslip, oxlip, primrose
ciud • *n* spite
ciudat • *adj* curious, strange, unusual, weird • *adv* strangely, unusually
ciufut • *adj* miserly, stingy
ciuin • *n* soapwort
ciulin • *n* thistle
cium • *n* pestilence, plague
ciuperc • *n* fungus, mushroom
ciupi • *v* pinch, pluck
ciut • *n* deer, doe
civilitate • *n* civility, civilization, politeness
civilizare • *n* civilization
civilizat • *adj* civilized
civilizat • *adj* civilized
civilizaie • *n* civilization
cizm • *n* boot
cldi • *v* build
cldire • *n* building, construction
cldit • *v* built
clamoare • *n* uproar
clandestin • *adj* clandestine
clan • *n* lock
clap • *n* key
clapon • *n* capon
clar • *adj* apparent, bright, clear, cloudless, obvious, transparent, unambiguous
clarifica • *v* clarify, spell
clarificare • *n* clarification
clarinet • *n* clarinet
clarinet • *n* clarinet
clarinetist • *n* clarinetist
claritate • *n* clarity
clarviziune • *n* clairvoyance
clas • *n* class, classroom
clasic • *adj* classical
clasic • *adj* classical
clasici • *adj* classical
clasifica • *v* classify, distribute, sort
clasificabil • *adj* classifiable
clasificare • *n* classification
clasificaie • *n* classification
cltit • *n* pancake
claun • *n* clown
claustra • *v* cloister
claustru • *n* cloister
clauz • *n* term
clavecin • *n* harpsichord
claviatur • *n* keyboard
clavicul • *n* clavicle
claxon • *n* horn
clei • *n* glue
cleios • *adj* viscous
clematit • *n* clematis
clemen • *n* clemency
clepsidr • *n* hourglass
cleptomanie • *n* kleptomania
cleric • *n* clergyman
clete • *n* claw, pincers, pliers
clic • *n* click
clica • *v* click
clicare • *n* click
client • *n* buyer, client

clim • *n* climate
climat • *n* environment
climatologie • *n* climatology
clinic • *n* clinic
clip • *n* blink, flicker, moment, wink
clipi • *v* blink
clipire • *n* blink
clipit • *n* blink
clipit • *n* blink
clitoris • *n* clitoris
cloci • *v* brood, hatch
clopot • *n* bell
clor • *n* chlorine
closet • *n* bathroom, lavatory, toilet
clovn • *n* clown
coace • *v* bake, ripen
coad • *n* line, ponytail, queue, stem, tail
coada-calului • *n* horsetail
coada-mielului • *n* mullein
coada-vulpii • *n* foxtail
coafor • *n* hairdresser
coafur • *n* haircut
coagulabil • *adj* coagulable
coagulare • *n* coagulation
coaie • *n* balls
coaliie • *n* league
coam • *n* mane
coaps • *n* thigh
coard • *n* chord, cord, rope, string
coarda • *n* slut
coarne • *n* antler, horn
coas • *n* scythe
coase • *v* sew
coast • *n* coast, rib, shore
coati • *n* coati
cobalt • *n* cobalt
coborâtoare • *adj* downward
coborâtor • *adj* downward
coborî • *v* descend
coc • *n* hull
coca • *n* coca
cocain • *n* cocaine
cochilie • *n* shell
cocin • *n* pigsty, sty
cocioab • *n* hovel, hut
cocktail • *n* cocktail
cocoa • *n* hump
cocoloi • *v* crumple
cocor • *n* crane
coco • *n* cock, rooster
coco-de-munte • *n* grouse
coco-slbatic • *n* grouse
cocoei • *n* popcorn
cocoel • *n* cockerel
cocs • *n* coke
cocteil • *n* cocktail
cod • *n* cod, code
codare-decodare • *n* coding
codi • *v* hesitate
codificare • *n* codification
codificare-decodificare • *n* coding
codire • *n* reluctance
codobatur • *n* wagtail
codru • *n* forest
coeficient • *n* coefficient
coercitare • *n* coercion
coerciie • *n* coercion
coercitiv • *adj* compulsive
coerent • *adj* cohesive
coeziv • *adj* cohesive
cofein • *n* caffeine
cofetrie • *n* cafeteria
cognitiv • *adj* cognitive
coi • *n* ball, nut
coif • *n* helmet
coiot • *n* coyote
cola • *n* cola
colaborare • *n* collaboration
colaborri • *n* collaboration
colaj • *n* collage
colan • *n* necklace
colaps • *n* collapse
colastr • *n* colostrum
colb • *n* dust
colecta • *v* gather
colectare • *n* collection
colecie • *n* collection, set
colecionar • *n* collector
colectivism • *n* collectivism
colectivizare • *n* collectivization
colector • *n* commutator
coleg • *n* associate, colleague
coleg • *n* colleague
colegiu • *n* college, school
colet • *n* bundle, parcel
colhoz • *n* kolkhoz
colib • *n* hut, lodge
colibri • *n* hummingbird
colier • *n* necklace
colin • *n* hill
coliziune • *n* collision, wreck
colo • *adv* there
coloan • *n* column
colocvial • *adj* colloquial
colocviul • *n* colloquy
coloid • *n* colloid
colonel • *n* colonel
colonial • *adj* colonial
colonialism • *n* colonialism
colonie • *n* colony, establishment
colonist • *n* colonist
colonist • *n* colonist
colora • *v* color
colorat • *adj* colored

colosal • *adj* colossal, monstrous
col • *n* angle, nook
colii-babei • *n* caltrop
column • *n* column
com • *n* coma
comanda • *v* command, control, order
comand • *n* control, order
comandament • *n* commandment
comandare • *n* conduct
combatant • *n* fighter
combatant • *n* fighter
combate • *v* combat, fight
combativ • *adj* combative
combina • *v* combine
combinare • *n* combination
combinat • *n* combine
combinaie • *n* combination
combustibil • *n* fuel
combustie • *n* combustion
combustii • *n* combustion
comedie • *n* comedy
comentariu • *n* note
comerciabil • *adj* marketable
comercial • *adj* commercial
comercial • *adj* commercial
comerciant • *n* merchant
comestibil • *adj* consumable, edible
comestibil • *adj* edible
comite • *v* commit, perpetrate
comizeraie • *n* commiseration
comoar • *n* treasure
comod • *adj* comfortable
compact • *adj* compact, solid
companie • *n* company
compara • *v* compare
comparabil • *adj* comparable
comparativ • *adj* comparative
compartiment • *n* compartment
compartimente • *n* compartment
compas • *n* compass
compasiune • *n* commiseration, compassion, mercy, pity, rue, sympathy
comptimire • *n* commiseration, condolence, mercy, pity, sympathy
comptimitor • *adj* commiserative
compatriot • *n* compatriot
compendiu • *n* compendium
compensa • *v* compensate
compensabil • *adj* compensable
compensare • *n* compensation
compensaie • *n* compensation, remuneration
competent • *adj* able, qualified
competiie • *n* competition, contest
competitiv • *adj* competitive
competitivitate • *n* competitiveness
compila • *v* compile
compilator • *n* compiler
complementar • *adj* complementary
complementaritate • *n* complementarity
complet • *adj* complete, completed, full, sound • *adv* completely, outright
complet • *adv* completely
completa • *v* complete
complex • *adj* complex
complexitate • *n* complexity
complica • *v* complicate
complicat • *adj* complicated, difficult, sophisticated, uneasy
complicaie • *n* entanglement
compliment • *n* compliment
complot • *n* plot
component • *n* constituent
component • *n* component, device
comporta • *v* behave
comportament • *n* behavior, conduct, manner
comportare • *n* address
compoziie • *n* composite, composition, mixture
compozitor • *n* composer
comprehensibilitate • *n* comprehensibility
comprimat • *adj* compressed
compromis • *n* compromise
compromite • *v* endanger
compunciune • *n* compunction, qualm
compune • *v* compose
compunere • *n* composition
compus • *n* composite, mixture • *adj* composite
computer • *n* calculator, computer
computere • *n* calculator
computero-lingvistic • *adj* linguistic
comun • *adj* common, general, pedestrian, vulgar
comun • *n* parish
comunica • *v* speak
comunicare • *n* communication
comunicaie • *n* communication
comunism • *n* communism
comunist • *n* communist • *adj* communist
comunist • *n* communist
comunitar • *adj* communal
comunitate • *n* community
comuta • *v* switch
comutabil • *adj* commutable
comutator • *n* switch
con • *n* cone
conac • *n* mansion
concasor • *n* breaker
concavitate • *n* concavity
concediere • *n* termination

concentra • *v* center
concentrare • *n* concentration, mind
concentrat • *n* abstract • *adj* concentrated
concentraie • *n* concentration
concepere • *n* conception
concept • *n* concept, conception, draft
concepie • *n* apprehension, conception
concepii • *n* conception
conceptor • *n* developer
concern • *n* concern
concert • *n* concert
concesie • *n* concession
concesiere • *n* concession
concesiune • *n* concession
conchide • *v* conclude, gather, infer, resolve
concilia • *v* conciliate
concluziona • *v* conclude, infer
concorda • *v* conform
concordan • *n* concordance
concret • *adj* concrete
concupiscen • *n* lust
concura • *v* run
concuren • *n* competition
concurs • *n* competition
condamnabil • *adj* blameworthy
condamnare • *n* condemnation
condensa • *v* precipitate
condensare • *n* condensation
condescenden • *n* condescension
condiment • *n* spice
condimenta • *v* season
condiie • *n* condition, requirement, term
condiiona • *v* condition
condiional • *adj* conditional
condoleane • *n* condolence
conductor • *n* driver, leader
conduce • *v* drive, govern, lead, master, run
conducere • *n* conduct, ruling
conduct • *n* drain
conductan • *n* conductance
conductor • *n* cable, conductor
conduit • *n* manner
conecta • *v* bind, connect
conectare • *n* connection
conectat • *adj* connected
conectiv • *n* connective
conector-fi • *n* jack
conector-pin • *n* jack
conexiune • *n* connection
confederaie • *n* confederacy, confederation
conferi • *v* confer
confesiune • *n* confession
confiden • *n* confidence
confidenial • *adj* confidential
confidenial • *adj* confidential
configuraie • *n* configuration
confirma • *v* attest, confirm
confirmare • *n* attestation, confirmation, validation
confisca • *v* confiscate
confiscare • *n* seizure
conflagraie • *n* conflagration
conflict • *n* conflict
confluen • *n* confluence
conform • *adj* agreeable, conformable
conforma • *v* conform
conformare • *n* tolerance
conformist • *n* conformist
conformist • *n* conformist
conformitate • *n* conformity
confort • *n* comfort, ease
confortabil • *adj* comfortable
confrunta • *v* cope, face
confunda • *v* mistake, obfuscate
confuz • *adj* baffled, confused, confusing
confuzie • *n* confusion
congela • *v* freeze, ice
congregaie • *n* congregation
congres • *n* congress
conic • *adj* conical
conidie • *n* conidium
conifer • *n* conifer
conifere • *n* conifer
conjuga • *v* conjugate
conjugare • *n* conjugation
conjunctare • *n* conjunction
conjuncie • *n* conjunction
conjuncionalizare • *n* conjunction
conjura • *v* treat
conopid • *n* cauliflower
conoscut • *adj* recognized
conotaie • *n* connotation
conotativ • *adj* connotative
consecutiv • *adj* consecutive
consecven • *n* consequence
consens • *n* concord
conserva • *v* husband
conservant • *n* preservative
conservare • *n* conservation
conservatoare • *n* conservative
conservator • *n* conservative
consftui • *v* deliberate
considera • *v* think
considerabil • *adj* sensible
considerare • *n* consideration
consideraie • *n* attentiveness, consideration
considerent • *n* consideration
consilia • *v* counsel
consiliu • *n* council
consista • *v* consist

consistent • *adj* consistent
consoan • *n* consonant
consolare • *n* comfort, condolence, consolation, solace
consolidare • *n* consolidation
consolidat • *adj* consolidated
conspect • *n* abstract
consta • *v* consist
constant • *adj* constant, invariant • *adv* constantly
constant • *adj* constant
constelaie • *n* constellation
consternare • *n* bewilderment, consternation
consternaie • *n* consternation
contient • *adj* conscious, sensible
contiinciozitate • *n* conscientiousness
contiin • *n* conscience, consciousness
constipa • *v* constipate
constipaie • *n* constipation
constituent • *n* constituent
constituionalitate • *n* constitutionality
constrângtor • *adj* compulsive
constrângere • *n* compulsion, constraint, duress
construcie • *n* construction
construcional • *adj* constructive
constructiv • *adj* constructive
constructivism • *n* constructivism
construi • *v* built, construct, craft
construire • *n* building, construction
construit • *v* built
consul • *n* consul
consulat • *n* consulate
consultan • *n* counsel
consultare • *n* consultation
consultaie • *n* consultation, counsel
consum • *n* consumption
consuma • *v* consume
consumabil • *n* consumable • *adj* consumable
consumator • *n* user
cont • *n* account, slate
contabil • *n* accountant, bookkeeper
contabilitate • *n* accountancy, accounting
contact • *n* contact, contingence
contact-pin • *n* pin
contacta • *v* contact
contagios • *adj* contagious
contagiune • *n* contagion
container • *n* container
contamina • *v* infect
contaminare • *n* contamination
conte • *n* count, earl
contempla • *v* contemplate
contemporan • *adj* contemporary
contemporan • *adj* contemporary
contemporani • *adj* contemporary
contes • *n* countess
contestabil • *adj* contestable
contestare • *n* contestation
contiguitate • *n* contiguity
conine • *v* contain, hold
continent • *n* mainland
continental • *adj* landlocked
continuare • *n* continuation
continuri • *n* continuation
continuitate • *n* continuity, continuousness
coninut • *n* content
continuu • *adj* continuous, ongoing • *adv* continuously, everlasting
contor • *n* counter, meter
contra • *prep* against
contraargumentare • *n* argument
contraceptiv • *adj* contraceptive
contract • *n* contract
contracie • *n* contracture
contracurent • *n* countercurrent, eddy
contradicie • *n* contradiction, contradictory, variance
contradictoriu • *adj* contradictory
contraexemplu • *n* counterexample
contrafcut • *adj* false
contrar • *adj* contradictory, contrarious, contrary, opposed
contrariu • *n* reverse
contrasemna • *v* countersign
contrast • *n* contrast
contraveni • *v* contravene
contrazice • *v* controvert, oppose
contrazicere • *n* contradiction, contradictory
contribuire • *n* contribution
contribuie • *n* contribution
control • *n* check, control
controla • *v* command, control, master
controlabil • *adj* controllable
controlare • *n* inspection
controlat • *adj* controlled
controlor • *adj* controlling
controvers • *n* contest, controversy, debate
controversabil • *adj* controversial, controvertible
controversat • *adj* controversial
conturna • *v* circumvent
convenabil • *adj* suitable
convenie • *n* convention
convenional • *adj* conventional
convergent • *adj* convergent
convergen • *n* convergence
conversaie • *n* conversation, dialogue, discourse

conversaional • *adj* conversational
conversie • *n* conversion
conversiune • *n* conversion
converti • *v* convert
convertibil • *adj* convertible
convertit • *n* convert
convertit • *n* convert
conviciune • *n* belief
convingtor • *adj* convincing
convinge • *v* convince, decide, persuade
convingere • *n* belief, certitude, conviction
convoi • *n* convoy
convorbire • *n* conversation
coolitate • *n* coolness
coopera • *v* cooperate
cooperant • *adj* compliant
cooperare • *n* cooperation
coordona • *v* coordinate
coordonare • *n* coordination
coordonat • *n* coordinate
coordonate • *n* coordinate
copac • *n* tree
copeic • *n* kopek
copia • *v* copy
copiator • *n* duplicator
copie • *n* copy, duplicate, replica
copiere • *n* replication
copieri • *n* replication
copii • *n* replica
copil • *n* baby, brat, child
copil • *n* child, girl
copilrie • *n* childhood
copilului • *adj* baby
copist • *n* scribe
copit • *n* hoof
coplei • *v* avalanche
copleit • *adj* awestruck
copleitor • *adj* crushing, overwhelming
copt • *adj* cooked, ripe
cor • *n* choir, chorale
corabie • *n* ship
corai • *n* coral • *adj* coral
coral • *adj* choral • *n* chorale, coral
coraliu • *n* coral • *adj* coral
corasl • *n* colostrum
corb • *n* raven
corbiu • *adj* raven
corcitur • *n* mongrel
corcituri • *n* bastard
corcodel • *n* diver, grebe
cord • *n* heart
cordial • *adj* affable
cordialitate • *n* affability
cordon • *n* belt, cord, cordon
corect • *adj* correct • *adv* correctly
corecta • *v* correct, rectify
corectare • *n* edit
corectitudine • *n* correctness, propriety, truth • *adj* right
corelaie • *n* correlation
corespondent • *adj* corresponding
coresponden • *n* connection
corespunztor • *adj* corresponding
coriandru • *n* coriander
corid • *n* bullfighting
coridor • *n* corridor
corigibil • *adj* correctable
corimb • *n* corymb
corl • *n* curlew
cormoran • *n* cormorant
corn • *n* antler, dogwood, horn
cornee • *n* cornea
cornion • *n* gherkin
cornuri • *n* horn
cornut • *adj* horned
coroan • *n* crown, wreath
corobora • *v* corroborate
corolar • *n* corollary
corp • *n* body
corporal • *adj* bodily, corporeal, physical
corporaie • *n* corporation
corpuscul • *n* corpuscle
corpuscular • *adj* corpuscular
cort • *n* tent
cortin • *n* curtain
corupe • *v* corrupt
corupt • *adj* corrupt
corupt • *adj* corrupt
corupie • *n* corruption, depravity
corvad • *n* fatigue
co • *n* basket, chimney, hoop, pimple
cos • *n* chimney
cociug • *n* coffin
cosecant • *n* cosecant
coenil • *n* carmine
cosinus • *n* cosine
cositor • *n* tin
comar • *n* nightmare
cosmetician • *n* cosmetician
cosmetician • *n* cosmetician
cosmic • *adj* cosmic
cosmogonie • *n* cosmogony
cosmologie • *n* cosmology
cosmos • *n* cosmos
cosor • *n* bill
cost • *n* cost
costa • *v* cost
costisitor • *adj* expensive
costum • *n* outfit, suit
cot • *n* elbow
cot-parte • *n* portion
cotangent • *n* cotangent
cotidian • *adj* daily, everyday, quotidian

• *adv* daily • *n* quotidian
cotiledon • *n* cotyledon
cotire • *n* angle
cotitur • *n* angle, wimple
coofan • *n* magpie
cotoi • *n* cat, tom
cotoroan • *n* hag
cotractare • *n* contracture
coulomb • *n* coulomb
covâritor • *adj* overwhelming
covor • *n* carpet
covrig • *n* bagel • *v* pretzel
covrigel • *v* pretzel
crab • *n* crab
crcnat • *adj* bandy
crai • *n* womanizer
cri • *n* marigold
crampon • *n* cleat
crâng • *n* copse, grove, thicket
cranial • *adj* cranial
cranian • *adj* cranial
craniu • *n* skull
crap • *n* carp
crpa • *v* crack
crptur • *n* crack, crevasse
cras • *adj* crass
crati • *n* saucepan
crava • *n* crop
cravat • *n* necktie
crea • *v* author, create, generate
creang • *n* bough, branch, stick
creare • *n* creation
creast • *n* crest, ridge
creaie • *n* creation, work
creaionism • *n* creationism
creativ • *adj* creative
creativitate • *n* creativity
creator • *adj* creative • *n* developer
creatur • *n* being, creature
crede • *v* believe, creed, think
credibil • *adj* credible
credibilitate • *n* credibility
credin • *n* belief, conviction, creed, faith
credit • *n* credit, trust
creier • *n* brain
creiera • *n* cerebellum
creion • *n* pencil
crem • *n* cream
crematoriu • *n* crematorium
cremene • *n* flint
crepuscul • *n* dusk, sunset, twilight
cre • *n* nursery
creson • *n* watercress
cresta • *v* dimple
crete • *v* expand, grow, increase
cretere • *n* increase, nurture
cret • *n* chalk
cretin • *n* clown, cretin
cretin • *n* cretin
cretinism • *n* cretinism
crevas • *n* crevasse
crevet • *n* prawn, shrimp
crichet • *n* cricket
crim • *n* crime, murder
criminal • *n* murderer
criminalitate • *n* crime
crin • *n* lily
crinolin • *n* pannier
cristal • *n* crystal
cristalin • *n* lens
cristalizare • *n* crystallization
cristalizaie • *n* crystallization
cristei • *n* corncrake, crake
criteriu • *n* criterion
critic • *n* critic • *adv* critically
critic • *n* criticism
critica • *v* criticise
criz • *n* crisis
crizantem • *n* chrysanthemum
crocodil • *n* crocodile
croi • *v* tailor
croitor • *n* dressmaker, tailor
croitoreas • *n* dressmaker, tailor
crom • *n* chromium
cromozom • *n* chromosome
cronic • *n* chronicle
cronograf • *n* timer
cronologic • *adj* chronological
cronologie • *n* chronology
cronometraj • *n* timekeeping
cronometrare • *n* timekeeping
cronometru • *n* timer
cruce • *n* cross
crucea-voinicului • *n* hepatica, liverwort
cruci • *v* cross
cruciad • *n* crusade
crucial • *adj* crucial
crucifica • *v* crucify
crucifix • *n* crucifix
cruciform • *adj* crucial
crud • *adj* cruel, raw, stark
crunt • *adj* bloody, cruel
crustaceu • *n* crustacean
cruzime • *n* cruelty, mercilessness
cu • *prep* by, to, with
cuantifica • *v* quantify
cuar • *n* quartz
cub • *n* cube
cubeb • *n* cubeb
cubism • *n* cubism
cuc • *n* cuckoo
cuceri • *v* conquer, subdue
cucurig • *n* hellebore
cucurigu • *interj* cock-a-doodle-doo

cucut • *n* hemlock
cufundar • *n* diver, grebe
cufundtur • *n* dimple
cuget • *n* thought
cugeta • *v* contemplate, think
cugetare • *n* thought
cugetat • *adj* thoughtful
cui • *n* nail
cuib • *n* nest
cuier • *n* hanger
cuioare • *n* clove
culca • *v* lay
culege • *v* collect, crop, gather, harvest
culegere • *n* selection
cules • *n* harvest
culis • *n* coulisse
culise • *n* scenery
culme • *n* apex, climax, height, peak, summit, top
culoar • *n* corridor
culoare • *n* color, paint
culp • *n* fault
culpabil • *adj* culpable
cult • *n* cult
cultiva • *v* crop, culture
cultivare • *n* cultivation, nurture
cultivaie • *n* cultivation
cultivator • *n* cultivator
cultur • *n* civilization, crop, cultivation, culture
cultural • *adj* cultural
cum • *conj* as • *adv* how
cumineca • *v* communicate
cumnat • *n* brother-in-law
cumnat • *n* sister-in-law
cumpni • *v* weigh
cumpra • *v* buy, purchase
cumprtoare • *n* buyer
cumprtor • *n* buyer
cumprturi • *n* shopping
cumpt • *n* balance
cumptare • *n* frugality, moderation, parsimony, sobriety, temperance, thrift
cumplit • *adj* cruel, monstrous
cumulonimbus • *n* cumulonimbus
cumva • *adv* somehow
cunoate • *v* know
cunoatere • *n* knowledge
cunoscut • *n* acquaintance
cunoscut • *n* acquaintance
cunotin • *n* acquaintance
cunotine • *n* knowledge
cununa • *v* marry, wed
cunun • *n* crown, wreath
cununie • *n* marriage
cup • *n* cup, goblet, heart, hearts, scoop
cupiditate • *n* cupidity
cupla • *v* bind, couple
cuplu • *n* couple
cuprinde • *v* comprehend
cuprinztor • *adj* comprehensive
cupru • *n* copper
cuptor • *n* oven
cur • *n* ass, asshole, bottom, butt
curaj • *n* bravery, courage, fearlessness, gallantry, nerve, sand
curajos • *adj* brave, courageous, valiant
curând • *adv* soon
curat • *adj* blank, clean, clear, pure
cur • *v* prune
cura • *v* clean
curire • *n* purification
curb • *n* curve
curba • *v* bend
curbat • *adj* curved
curbe • *n* curve
curbur • *n* curvature, wimple
curc • *n* turkey
curcan • *n* turkey
curcubeu • *n* rainbow
curea • *n* belt, bracelet
curent • *n* current, stream
curge • *v* flow
curgere • *n* flow
curios • *adj* curious
curiozitate • *n* curiosity
curiu • *n* curium
curling • *n* curling
curmal • *n* date
curry • *n* curry
curs • *n* course, current, path
curs • *n* race, racing, snare
cursiv • *adj* cursive
cursor • *n* cursor
curta • *v* woo
curte • *n* court, courtship, courtyard, garden, mansion, yard
curtenie • *n* civility, courtliness
curtoazie • *n* courtliness, gallantry
curv • *n* prostitute, whore
cuc • *n* cage
cuer • *adj* kosher
cusurgiu • *adj* fastidious
cuta • *v* wrinkle
cute • *n* whetstone
cuteza • *v* dare
cutezan • *n* fearlessness, gallantry
cutie • *n* box, container
cuit • *n* cutter, knife
cutremur • *n* earthquake
cuvânt • *n* term, word
cuvântare • *n* speech
cuviincios • *adj* decorous
cuviin • *n* decency, decorum, propriety

cuvinte • *n* voice
cvadrat • *n* square
cvadratur • *n* quadrature
cvadridimensional • *adj* four-dimensional
cvadrilateral • *adj* quadrilateral
cvadriplegic • *n* quadriplegic
cvadriplegie • *n* quadriplegia
cvadruplu • *adj* quadruple
cvartet • *n* quartet
cvas • *n* kvass
cvintet • *n* quintet
cvorum • *n* quorum
cyborg • *n* cyborg

D

da • *v* give
dac • *conj* if, whether
dacea • *n* dacha
dafin • *n* laurel
dal • *n* flag
dalie • *n* dahlia
dalt • *n* chisel
dam • *n* queen
daman • *n* hyrax
damasc • *n* damask
dame • *n* draughts, lady
damigian • *n* demijohn
dans • *n* dance
dansa • *v* dance, shake
dansatoare • *n* dancer
dansator • *n* dancer
dantel • *n* lace
dar • *conj* albeit, but • *n* gift
drci • *v* card
drâma • *v* demolish, tear
drâmtur • *n* wreck
drpna • *v* wreck
dare • *n* tax
darnic • *adj* generous
drui • *v* gift
data • *v* date
dat • *n* date, time
dttor • *n* giver
date • *n* data
datin • *n* tradition
dator • *adj* indebted
datorie • *n* debt, duty
datorit • *conj* because
daun • *n* damage, prejudice
duna • *v* harm, prejudice
dunat • *adj* prejudiced
duntor • *adj* derogatory, detrimental, injurious, noisome, pernicious
daune • *n* damage
de • *prep* by, from, of
deal • *n* hill
deasemenea • *adv* too
deasupra • *adv* above • *prep* above, on, over
debandad • *n* rowdiness
debil • *adj* feeble, weak
debilita • *v* flag
debilitate • *n* infirmity
debloca • *v* unlock
debut • *n* beginning
debutant • *n* novice
decad • *n* decade
decdea • *v* waste
decdere • *n* waste
decapita • *v* behead, decapitate
decar • *n* ten
decât • *prep* than
decatlon • *n* decathlon
deczut • *adj* evil
deceniu • *n* decade
decen • *n* decency, decorum, propriety, urbanity
decepie • *n* disappointment
deci • *conj* so • *adv* therefore, thus
decibel • *n* decibel
decibeli • *n* decibel
decide • *v* decide
decisiv • *adj* crucial
decizie • *n* award, decision, resoluteness
declara • *v* bear, declare, state, testify
declarare • *n* declaration
declaraie • *n* declaration, proposition, statement, testimony
declin • *n* sunset
declinare • *n* declension
declinaie • *n* declension
decolare • *n* takeoff
decor • *n* backdrop, scenery
decora • *v* adorn, decorate
decorare • *n* decoration
decoraie • *n* decoration
decoratoare • *n* decorator
decorator • *n* decorator
decoros • *adj* decorous
decret • *n* decree
decupa • *v* crop
decupare • *n* cutting
dedesubt • *prep* below, beneath

dedicare • *n* devotion
dedicaie • *n* dedication
deduce • *v* infer
defima • *v* defame, libel, slander
defavorabil • *adj* derogatory
defeca • *v* defecate
defect • *adj* defective • *n* failing
defecta • *v* damage
defectiv • *adj* defective
defectuos • *adj* defective
deferen • *n* deference
deficient • *adj* deficient
deficien • *n* deficiency
deficit • *n* deficit
defileu • *n* canyon
definire • *n* definition
definit • *adj* defined
definit • *adj* defined
definiie • *n* definition
deflagraie • *n* deflagration
deflora • *v* deflower
defrauda • *v* defraud
degajare • *n* insouciance
degenera • *v* degenerate
degenerare • *n* degeneration
degenerri • *n* degeneration
degenerat • *adj* degenerate
degertur • *n* chilblain
deget • *n* digit, finger, toe
degetar • *n* foxglove, thimble
degetari • *n* foxglove
degeel • *n* foxglove
deghiza • *v* disguise, mask
deghizare • *n* disguise
degrada • *v* debase, degenerate
degradare • *n* abasement, degeneration, degradation
degradat • *adj* degenerate
dehiscent • *adj* dehiscent
dehiscen • *n* dehiscence
deism • *n* deism
deja • *adv* already
delsare • *n* negligence
delator • *n* betrayer
delectare • *n* enchantment
deleter • *adj* deleterious
delfin • *n* dauphin, dolphin
delibera • *v* deliberate
deliberare • *n* deliberation
deliberat • *adj* premeditated
delicat • *adj* delicate
delicatee • *n* refinement
delicios • *adj* delicious, delightful, lush
deliciu • *n* delight
delicven • *n* crime
delimitare • *n* determination
delir • *n* delirium
delirant • *adj* insane
delta • *n* delta
delt • *n* delta
deluit • *adj* legible
deluzoriu • *adj* delusive
demagog • *n* demagogue
demagog • *n* demagogue
demagogie • *n* demagogy
demaror • *n* starter
demen • *n* insanity
demenial • *adj* insane
demiurg • *n* demiurge
demn • *adj* worthy
demnitate • *n* dignity, honor
democratic • *adj* democratic
democraie • *n* democracy
demodat • *adj* antic, old-fashioned, unfashionable
demodat • *adj* old-fashioned
demola • *v* tear
demon • *n* demon
demonic • *adj* fiendish
demonie • *n* possession
demonism • *n* possession
demonstra • *v* show
demonstrabil • *adj* demonstrable
demonstrare • *n* demonstration
demonstraie • *n* demonstration, show
demonstrativ • *adj* demonstrative
demontare • *n* decomposition
denatura • *v* falsify
denigrator • *adj* derogatory
denivelat • *adj* uneven
densitate • *n* density
dentist • *n* dentist
denumrare • *n* countdown
denumi • *v* designate
denuna • *v* divulge
denuntor • *n* betrayer, telltale
deoarece • *conj* as, because
deodat • *adv* abruptly, suddenly
deodorant • *n* deodorant
deosebire • *n* distinction
deosebit • *adj* different
departament • *n* office, section
departe • *adv* away, far • *adj* distant, far
depi • *v* exceed, overtake, surpass
dependent • *adj* addictive, dependent
dependen • *n* dependence
deplânge • *v* bemoan, bewail
deplasament • *n* displacement
deplintate • *n* wholeness
deplorabil • *adj* deplorable
deportare • *n* deportation
depozit • *n* deposit, storage, store, warehouse
depozita • *v* warehouse

depozitare • *n* storage
depoziie • *n* testimony
depravare • *n* depravity
depravat • *adj* evil
depravaiune • *n* depravity
depreciere • *n* depreciation
depresionat • *adj* depressed
depresiune • *n* depression
deprimant • *adj* dismal
deprimare • *n* depression
deprimat • *adj* blue, depressed, down
depune • *v* depose, deposit
depunere • *n* deposit
deranj • *n* bother, disturbance, harassment, inconvenience
deranja • *v* bother, distress, disturb, gall, inconvenience, upset
deranjament • *n* complaint, disturbance, incident
deranjare • *n* disturbance, upset
deranjat • *adj* upset
dereglare • *n* complaint, deregulation
deriva • *v* derive
derivare • *n* derivation
derivat • *n* derivative • *adj* derived
derivat • *n* derivative • *adj* derived
derogatoriu • *adj* derogatory
derula • *v* scroll
dervi • *n* dervish
des • *adv* often
desvârire • *n* performance
desvârit • *adv* outright
descânta • *v* charm
descântare • *n* incantation
descânttur • *n* spell
descântec • *n* incantation, spell
descrca • *v* discharge, disembark, empty, unload
descrna • *v* waste
descendent • *n* descendant • *adj* downward
descenden • *n* parentage
deschide • *v* yawn
deschis • *adv* outright
deschiztur • *n* aperture, mouth
deschizatura • *n* sluice
descifrabil • *adj* legible
descinde • *v* descend
descompune • *v* decompose, rot
descompunere • *n* decomposition
desconsidera • *v* disregard
desconsiderare • *n* disdain, disregard
descoperi • *v* betray, discover
descoperire • *n* find
descrete • *v* decrease
descrie • *v* depict, describe, set
descriere • *n* description
descripie • *n* description
descriptiv • *adj* descriptive
descuia • *v* unlock
descul • *adv* barefoot
descuraja • *v* discourage
descurcre • *adj* dexterous, smart
desear • *adv* tonight
desemna • *v* designate
desemnare • *n* election
desen • *n* cartoon, drawing
desena • *v* draw
deseori • *adv* frequently
desert • *n* dessert
deert • *n* desert, waste • *adj* deserted, desolate, empty, waste
deerta • *v* empty
deeu • *n* trash, waste
desface • *v* loosen, relax, undo, untie
desfura • *v* unfold, unfurl
desftare • *n* delight, enchantment, treat
desfigura • *v* mangle
desfrânare • *n* depravity, lust
desfrânat • *adj* abandoned, evil, scarlet
desfrâu • *n* dissipation, lechery
deshidratare • *n* dehydration
deshidratat • *adj* dry
desi • *conj* though
dei • *conj* although, while
designa • *v* designate
desigur • *adv* certainly, naturally
desime • *n* frequency
deira • *v* unravel, unwind
desi • *n* thicket
despgubire • *n* remuneration
despri • *v* divide, divorce, separate
desprire • *n* detachment, divorce, valediction
despritur • *n* section
despera • *v* despair
desperare • *n* despair, desperation, dismay, hopelessness
desperaie • *n* hopelessness
despica • *v* split
despotic • *adj* despotic, tyrannical
despotism • *n* despotism
despre • *prep* about
desprindere • *n* detachment
despuia • *v* despoil, plunder, strip
detept • *adj* bright, clever, intelligent, smart
detepta • *v* awake, awaken
destin • *n* destiny, fate
destina • *v* assign, slate
destinde • *v* relax
destrblare • *n* debauch, depravity
destul • *adv* enough, sufficiently
detalia • *v* itemize

detaa • *v* detach, tear
detaament • *n* detachment
detaare • *n* detachment
detector • *n* detector
detergent • *n* detergent • *adj* detergent
deteriora • *v* damage
deteriorare • *n* degradation, deterioration
determinare • *n* determination, purpose
detesta • *v* abhor
detestabil • *adj* abominable, loathsome
deine • *v* arrest, own, possess
deinere • *n* arrest
detona • *v* detonate
detonare • *n* detonation
detonaie • *n* detonation
detonator • *n* detonator
detronare • *v* depose
detuntur • *n* boom, explosion
devasta • *v* devastate, mutilate, waste
devastare • *n* devastation, ravage
developator • *n* developer
deveni • *v* become
devia • *v* deviate, digress
deviaie • *n* aberration, bypass
deviere • *n* aberration
deviz • *n* motto
devora • *v* devour
devotament • *n* devotion
devotare • *n* devotion
devoiune • *n* devotion, praise
devreme • *adj* early • *adv* early
dexteritate • *n* address, adroitness, dexterity, ease
dezacord • *n* disagreement, friction
dezactivat • *adj* disabled
dezagreabil • *adj* disagreeable, distasteful, obnoxious
dezagrega • *v* disintegrate
dezamgire • *n* disappointment
dezamgit • *adj* disappointed
dezaprobare • *n* disapprobation, disapproval, displeasure
dezasamblare • *n* decomposition
dezastru • *n* catastrophe, disaster
dezastruoas • *adj* catastrophic
dezastruos • *adj* catastrophic
dezavantaj • *n* disadvantage
dezavantajos • *adj* disadvantageous
dezbatere • *n* contest, debate, discussion
dezbinare • *n* faction
dezbrca • *v* disarray, disrobe, strip
dezbrcat • *adj* naked, unclothed
dezechilibrare • *n* disequilibrium
dezechilibru • *n* disequilibrium, imbalance
dezertare • *n* desertion
dezertor • *n* deserter
dezgolire • *n* exposure
dezgust • *n* disgust, repulsion
dezgusta • *v* disgust
dezgusttor • *adj* disgusting, distasteful, gross, loathsome, noisome
dezice • *v* retract
deziderat • *n* desire
dezintegra • *v* disintegrate
dezintegrare • *n* disintegration
dezinteres • *n* disinterest
dezinteresat • *adj* tepid, uninterested
dezintoxicare • *n* detoxification
dezinvoltur • *n* insouciance
dezlnui • *v* unchain
dezlega • *v* loose, unbind, untie
dezlipi • *v* detach
dezlocuire • *n* displacement
dezm • *n* dissipation
dezmat • *adj* scarlet
dezmierda • *v* caress, fondle
dezmierdare • *n* endearment
deznodmânt • *n* catastrophe
dezobedient • *adj* disobedient
dezolant • *adj* stark
dezordine • *n* disarray
dezorganiza • *v* disarray
dezorganizare • *n* disorganization
dezorganizat • *adj* disorganized
dezoxiriboz • *n* deoxyribose
dezrdcina • *v* eradicate, extirpate
dezrobi • *v* emancipate
dezvolta • *v* develop
dezvoltare • *n* development
dezvoltator • *n* developer
diabet • *n* diabetes
diabetic • *adj* diabetic
diabolic • *adj* satanic
diacon • *n* deacon
diafragm • *n* diaphragm
diagonal • *n* diagonal
diagram • *n* diagram
dialect • *n* dialect
dialectal • *adj* dialectal
dialog • *n* dialogue
diamant • *n* diamond
diametral • *adj* diametral, diametric
diametric • *adj* diametral
diametru • *n* diameter
diapazon • *n* compass
diapozitiv • *n* slide
diaree • *n* diarrhea
diastol • *n* diastole
diatez • *n* voice
diatriba • *n* diatribe
diavol • *n* devil
diavolesc • *adj* satanic

dibcie • *n* ability, dexterity, hand
dicotiledonat • *adj* dicotyledonous
dicta • *v* impose
dictator • *n* dictator
dictatori • *n* dictator
dictatur • *n* dictatorship
dicionar • *n* dictionary
diez • *adj* sharp
diferen • *n* difference, distinction, variance
difereniere • *n* differentiation, discrimination
diferit • *adj* different
difícil • *adj* difficult
dificil • *adj* uneasy
dificultate • *n* difficulty, hardship
difiden • *n* distrust, mistrust
diftong • *n* diphthong
difuza • *v* broadcast
difuzare • *n* broadcast
difuzie • *n* diffusion
difuzor • *n* loudspeaker
dig • *n* dike
digera • *v* digest
digerabil • *adj* digestible
digestibil • *adj* digestible
digestie • *n* digestion
digital • *adj* digital
digital • *adj* digital
digitigrad • *n* digitigrade • *adj* digitigrade
digresiune • *n* digression
dihor • *n* polecat
dildo • *n* dildo
dilem • *n* dilemma
diletant • *n* dilettante
diligent • *adj* hardworking
diligen • *n* diligence
diluat • *adj* diluted
dimensiona • *v* dimension
dimensional • *adj* dimensional
dimensiune • *n* dimension
dimensiuni • *n* dimension
diminea • *n* morning
diminua • *v* cut, reduce
diminuabil • *adj* reducible
diminuare • *n* attenuation, diminution
diminuat • *adj* impaired
diminutiv • *n* diminutive • *adj* diminutive
diminutiv • *adj* diminutive
diminutive • *n* diminutive
din • *prep* from
dinainte • *prep* before
dinamit • *n* dynamite
dinastie • *n* dynasty, house
dincolo • *adv* across
dineu • *n* dinner
dingo • *n* dingo
dinozaur • *n* dinosaur
dinte • *n* tooth
diocez • *n* diocese
dionisiac • *n* bacchanal
dioram • *n* diorama
diplomaie • *n* diplomacy
direct • *adj* direct
direcie • *n* direction, line
direcionare • *n* guidance
director • *n* chairman, director, folder, headmaster, manager, principal
directori • *n* director
dirija • *v* govern
dirijabil • *adj* steerable
dirijare • *n* conduct
dirijoare • *n* conductor
dirijor • *n* conductor
disc • *n* disk, record
disc-audio • *n* record
disc-video • *n* record
discernmânt • *n* discernment, perception
discerne • *v* discern
discernere • *n* discernment, perception
disciplin • *n* discipline, subject
discomfort • *n* upset
disconfort • *n* discomfort
discordie • *n* discord
discredita • *v* discredit
discreditare • *n* disregard
discrepan • *n* variance
discret • *adj* discreet
discreie • *n* discretion
discriminare • *n* discrimination
discuri • *n* record
discurs • *n* address, discourse, speech
discuta • *v* argue, speak
discutabil • *adj* controversial, controvertible
discutare • *n* discussion
discuie • *n* controversy, debate, disagreement, discussion
disear • *adv* tonight
diseca • *v* dissect
disensiune • *n* dissension
disforie • *n* dysphoria
disipare • *n* dissipation
disipaie • *n* dissipation
disloca • *v* dislocate
dislocare • *n* displacement
disociere • *n* dissociation
disocieri • *n* dissociation
disprea • *v* disappear, flee, go
dispariie • *n* disappearance
dispensa • *v* exempt
dispensare • *n* exempt

dispensat • *adj* exempt
disperare • *n* despondency
disperat • *adj* pathetic
dispersare • *n* dispersion
dispersie • *n* dissipation
displcea • *v* dislike
disponibil • *adj* available
disponibilizare • *n* termination
dispoziie • *n* disposition, temper
dispozitiv • *n* device, disposition
dispre • *n* disdain, disregard, scorn, spite
dispreui • *v* disrespect, scorn
dispreuibil • *adj* contemptible, despicable
disprosiu • *n* dysprosium
dispunere • *n* configuration
disput • *n* argument, contest, dispute
distant • *adv* aloof • *adj* far-flung
distana • *v* distance
distan • *n* aloofness, distance, interval, measure
distilare • *n* distillation
distilerie • *n* distillery
distinct • *adj* distinct, distinguished
distincie • *n* badge, distinction
distinctiv • *adj* distinctive
distinge • *v* distinguish
distingere • *n* distinction
distingibil • *adj* distinguishable
distingibilitate • *n* distinction
distracie • *n* entertainment, fun
distractiv • *adj* fun
distrat • *adj* absent
distribui • *v* apportion, distribute, share
distribuire • *n* distribution
distribuit • *adj* shared
distribuie • *n* distribution
distributiv • *adj* distributive
district • *n* district
distructibil • *adj* destructible
distructiv • *adj* destructive
distrugtor • *adj* destructive
distruge • *v* abolish, destroy, go, waste, wreck
distrugere • *n* destruction, harassment
distrus • *adj* blasted, kaput
divergen • *n* divergence, friction
divers • *adj* miscellaneous
divertisment • *n* entertainment, fun
divide • *v* divide
divin • *adj* godlike
divinitate • *n* deity
divinizare • *n* praise
diviza • *v* divide, split
divizare • *n* bifurcation, division
divizibil • *adj* divisible
divizie • *n* division
diviziune • *n* division
divizor • *n* divisor
divor • *n* divorce, separation
divora • *v* divorce
divorare • *n* separation
divulga • *v* divulge
dizgraia • *v* disgrace
dizgraie • *n* disgrace
dizolvabil • *adj* solvable
dizolvabil • *adj* solvable
dizolvare • *n* dissolution
doag • *n* stave
doamn • *n* lady, woman
doar • *adv* just, merely
dobând • *n* interest
dobra • *n* dobra
docil • *adj* docile, obedient, submissive
docilitate • *n* docility
doctor • *n* doctor
doctori • *n* doctor
doctrin • *n* doctrine, dogma
doctrinal • *adj* doctrinal
document • *n* document, paper
documenta • *v* document
documentar • *n* documentary • *adj* documentary
documentaie • *n* documentation
dodecagon • *n* dodecagon
dogar • *n* cooper
doge • *n* doge
dogm • *n* dogma
dogmatic • *adj* dogmatic • *n* pedagogue
dohotar • *n* shepherd
doi • *n* deuce, two
doic • *n* babysitter
dolar • *n* dollar
doliu • *n* lamentation
domeniu • *n* domain, field
domestici • *v* domesticate
domesticire • *n* domestication
domiciliu • *n* domicile
domina • *v* dominate
dominant • *adj* dominant, domineering
dominan • *n* dominance
dominant • *adj* dominant
dominaie • *n* dominion
dominator • *adj* domineering
domn • *n* gentleman, mister, sir, sire
domni • *n* gentleman • *v* reign, rule
domnie • *n* dominance
domnilor! • *n* gentleman
domnule • *n* sir
domoli • *v* soothe
donaie • *n* contribution, donation
donaii • *n* donation
donator • *n* donor
dor • *n* longing, pine, yearning

dori • *v* desire, long, pine, wish
dorin • *n* desire, itch, wish
dorit • *adj* desirable
doritor • *adj* anxious, eager
dormi • *v* sleep
dormita • *v* doze, nap, nod, slumber, snooze
dormitoare • *n* bedroom
dormitor • *n* bedroom
dornic • *adj* eager
dos • *n* back, bottom, reverse
dosar • *n* folder
dospi • *v* ferment
dovad • *n* proof, testimonial
dovedi • *v* prove
dovleac • *n* pumpkin
dovlecel • *n* marrow
drac • *n* demon, devil
drcesc • *adj* satanic
dracil • *n* barberry
drag • *n* beloved, darling, honey, sweetheart • *adj* darling, dear, loved
drag • *n* beloved, darling, honey, sweetheart • *adj* dear
drgla • *adj* cute
dragon • *n* dragon, dragoon
dragoste • *n* love
drgu • *adj* cute, darling, pretty, sweet
drgu • *n* baby, sweetheart • *adj* pretty
drajeu • *n* drop
• *n* demon
dram • *n* drama
dramaturg • *n* playwright
dramaturgic • *adj* dramaturgic
drapel • *n* banner, flag
draperie • *n* curtain
drastic • *adj* stark
dreapta • *n* right • *adj* right
dreapt • *n* line
drege • *v* mend
drepnea • *n* swift
drept • *n* law, privilege, right • *adj* right, stand-up, straight
dreptaci • *n* right-handed
dreptate • *n* justice
drepi • *n* attention
dreptunghi • *n* rectangle
dres • *n* blush
dric • *n* zenith
drob • *n* broom
drobuor • *n* woad
drog • *n* substance
drogat • *adj* high
droguri • *n* substance
drojdie • *n* yeast
dromader • *n* dromedary
dront • *n* dodo
dropie • *n* bustard
drum • *n* path, road, track, way
dubios • *adj* dubious, suspicious
dubiu • *n* doubt
dubla • *v* double, duplicate
dublare • *n* duplicate
dublat • *adj* double
dublu • *adj* double
dublur • *n* stand-in
ducat • *n* duchy
duce • *v* bear, carry, go, lead • *n* duke
dud • *n* mulberry
dud • *n* mulberry
dugong • *n* dugong
duh • *n* spirit
dulap • *n* cupboard
dulce • *n* sweet • *adj* sweet, tender • *adv* sweet
dulceag • *adj* sweetish
dulcea • *n* sweetness
dulcior • *adj* sweetish
dulciu • *adj* sweetish
dulciuri • *n* sweets
dulgher • *n* carpenter
dulie • *n* socket
duma • *n* duma
dumbrav • *n* copse, grove
dumneaei • *pron* she
dumnealor • *pron* they
dumnealui • *pron* he
dumneata • *pron* you
dumneavoastr • *pron* you
dumnezeiesc • *adj* godlike
dumnezeu • *n* deity, god
dumping • *n* dumping
dun • *n* dune
dung • *n* stripe
dup • *adv* after • *prep* after, behind
dup-amiaz • *n* afternoon
duplica • *v* duplicate
duplicare • *n* replication, reproduction
duplicat • *n* copy, duplicate, reproduction
duplicator • *n* duplicator
dur • *adj* hard, rough, stark, stern
dur • *adj* hard
dura • *v* last
durabil • *adj* durable
durat • *n* duration, life
durativ • *adj* durative
durdliu • *adj* buxom
durea • *v* ache, hurt, pain
durere • *n* ache, pain, sorrow, woe
du • *n* shower
duman • *n* enemy
dumnie • *n* enmity, hostility
dumnos • *adj* vindictive

duz • *n* jet
duzin • *n* dozen

E

e • *v* is
ea • *pron* she
ebulment • *n* avalanche
echer • *n* square
echidn • *n* echidna
echidneu • *n* echidna
echilibrat • *adj* balanced
echilibru • *n* balance, equilibrium
echinociu • *n* equinox
echinox • *n* equinox
echip • *n* team
echipament • *n* apparatus, equipment, hardware
echipare • *n* equipment
echitabil • *adj* equitable
echitate • *n* equity, rectitude
echivalent • *adj* equivalent
echivalent • *adj* equivalent
echivoc • *adj* equivocal
eclips • *n* eclipse
eclipsa • *v* eclipse, steal
ecluza • *n* sluice
ecolocaie • *n* echolocation
ecologic • *adj* ecological
ecologie • *n* ecology
econometric • *adj* econometric
econometrician • *n* econometrician
econometrie • *n* econometrics
econometrist • *n* econometrician
economie • *n* economics, economy, saving
economisire • *n* saving
ecosistem • *n* ecosystem, environment
ecou • *n* echo
ecran • *n* screen
ecstasy • *n* ecstasy
ecuaie • *n* equation
ecuator • *n* equator, line
edelvais • *n* edelweiss
edentat • *adj* toothless
edentate • *n* edentate
edificare • *n* building, edification
edificiu • *n* building, edifice
edita • *v* edit
ediie • *n* edition
editor • *n* editor
educa • *v* educate, school
educare • *n* education, nurture
educaie • *n* education, schooling
efect • *n* effect
efectent • *adj* effective
efectiv • *adj* effective, factual
efemer • *adj* fugacious, transient, volatile
eficace • *adj* effective
eficacitate • *n* effectiveness, efficacy
eficient • *adj* effective
eficien • *n* effectiveness
efigie • *n* brand
eflorescen • *n* efflorescence
efort • *n* effort, work
efuziv • *adj* effusive
efuziv • *adj* effusive
egal • *adj* equal, even • *adv* equally • *n* match
egala • *v* be
egal • *n* match
egalitate • *n* draw, equality
eglefin • *n* haddock
egoist • *adj* selfish
egret • *n* egret
ei • *pron* they
eider • *n* eider
einsteiniu • *n* einsteinium
ejaculare • *n* ejaculation
ejaculaie • *n* ejaculate, ejaculation
ejaculator • *adj* ejaculatory
el • *pron* he
elan • *n* moose
elastic • *adj* elastic
elasticitate • *n* elasticity
ele • *pron* they
elebor • *n* hellebore
electorat • *n* electorate
electric • *adj* electric, electrical
electricitate • *n* electricity, power
electrobiologie • *n* electrobiology
electrocardiogram • *n* electrocardiogram
electrocutare • *n* electrocution
electrodinamometru • *n* electrodynamometer
electroliz • *n* electrolysis
electromagnetic • *adj* electromagnetic
electromagnetism • *n* electromagnetism
electromecanic • *adj* electromechanical
electron • *n* electron
electronic • *adj* electric, electronic
electronic • *n* electronics
electrostatic • *adj* electrostatic
elefant • *n* elephant
elefantin • *adj* elephantine

elefantin • *adj* elephantine
elefantini • *adj* elephantine
elegant • *adj* sophisticated
elegan • *n* elegance, grace
element • *n* device, element
elementar • *adj* elementary
elementar • *adj* elementary
elemente • *n* element
eleron • *n* aileron
elev • *n* pupil, schoolboy
eleva • *n* pupil
elibera • *v* emancipate, free
elice • *n* propeller, screw
elicopter • *n* helicopter
eligibil • *adj* eligible
eligibilitate • *n* eligibility
elimina • *v* eradicate
eliminare • *n* elimination, exclusion
elips • *n* ellipse
elipsoid • *n* ellipsoid
elit • *n* elite
elogiabil • *adj* commendable
elogiere • *n* commendation
elogiu • *n* eulogy, praise
eluda • *v* elude, escape
emacia • *v* waste
emailat • *n* glaze
emancipa • *v* emancipate
emancipare • *n* emancipation
embrion • *n* abortion, embryo
emi- • *adj* half
emigrant • *n* emigrant
emigrant • *n* emigrant
emigrare • *n* emigration
emigraie • *n* emigration
emisfer • *n* hemisphere
emisie • *n* emission
emisiune • *n* broadcast, emission, issue, show
emitan • *n* radiance
emitor • *n* sender
emite • *v* broadcast, emit, mint
emonda • *v* prune
emoie • *n* emotion
emoiona • *v* move, touch
emoionabil • *adj* emotional
emoional • *adj* emotional
emoionant • *adj* moving, pathetic
emoionant • *adj* moving
emoionat • *adj* excited, nervous
empatie • *n* empathy, sympathy
empiric • *adj* empirical
empirism • *n* empiricism
empirist • *n* empiricist
emu • *n* emu
emulgator • *n* emulsifier
emulsie • *n* emulsion
emulsificator • *n* emulsifier
enciclopedie • *n* encyclopedia
endemic • *adj* endemic
endoderm • *n* endoderm
endogen • *adj* endogenous
endosperm • *n* endosperm
energetic • *adj* energetic
energic • *adj* quick
energie • *n* energy
enerva • *v* gall, irritate, roil
enervant • *adj* irksome
enervare • *n* anger, annoyance
english • *n* english
enigmatic • *adj* enigmatic
enorie • *n* parish
enorm • *adj* enormous, huge, monstrous, prodigious
enormitate • *n* enormity
enteric • *adj* enteric
enterit • *n* enteritis
entomologie • *n* entomology
entropie • *n* entropy
entuziasm • *n* enthusiasm, fuss
entuziasmat • *adj* excited
entuziast • *n* enthusiast
enzim • *n* ferment
epav • *n* wreck
epicicloid • *n* epicycloid
epidemic • *adj* epidemic
epidemie • *n* epidemic
epidemii • *n* epidemic
epidemiolog • *n* epidemiologist
epidemiologie • *n* epidemiology
epiderm • *n* epidermis
epifanie • *n* epiphany
epigraf • *n* epigraph
episcop • *n* bishop
episod • *n* incident
epistol • *n* epistle
epistole • *n* epistle
epoc • *n* age, epoch, era, time
epocal • *adj* epochal
epopee • *n* epopee
epuiza • *v* jade
epuizare • *n* exhaustion
epuizat • *adj* depleted, emaciated, exhausted, haggard, jaded
er • *n* age, epoch, era, time
eradica • *v* eradicate
erbacee • *adj* herbaceous
erbaceu • *adj* herbaceous
erbiu • *n* erbium
erbivor • *n* herbivore • *adj* herbivorous
erecie • *n* boner, erection
ereditar • *adj* hereditary
ereditate • *n* heredity
erete • *n* harrier, kite

ergonomic • *adj* ergonomic
ergonomic • *adj* ergonomic
eroare • *n* mistake
erogen • *adj* erogenous
eroic • *adj* heroic
eroin • *n* hero, heroine
erotic • *adj* erotic
erou • *n* hero
eroziune • *n* erosion
erudit • *n* brain • *adj* learned
erudiie • *n* erudition
erupere • *n* eruption
erupie • *n* eruption
eafod • *n* scaffold
eafodaj • *n* scaffolding
earf • *n* scarf
esc • *n* escape
escalada • *v* escalade
escava • *v* dig
eec • *n* failure
eseist • *n* essayist
esen • *n* abstract, core, hypostasis
esenial • *adj* essential • *adv* essentially
esenial • *adj* essential
esenialitate • *n* essentiality
est • *n* east
este • *v* is
estetic • *n* aesthetics
estic • *adj* eastern
estimare • *n* estimation
estrad • *n* platform
etaj • *n* level
etaje • *n* level
etan • *n* ethane
etanamid • *n* acetamide
etap • *n* situation
etate • *n* age
eter • *n* air
eteric • *adj* ethereal
etern • *adv* everlasting
eternitate • *n* eternity, lifetime
eterogen • *adj* heterogeneous
eterogen • *adj* heterogeneous
etic • *adj* ethical
etichet • *n* tag
eticheta • *v* label
etimologic • *adj* etymological
etimologie • *n* etymology
etnografie • *n* ethnography
etos • *n* ethos
eucalipt • *n* eucalyptus
eufemism • *n* euphemism
euforie • *n* bliss, euphoria
euristic • *adj* heuristic
europiu • *n* europium
eutanasie • *n* euthanasia
ev • *n* age
evada • *v* flee, shun
evadat • *n* fugitive
evalua • *v* amount, weigh
evaluare • *n* appraisal, assessment
evanghelie • *n* gospel
evapora • *v* evaporate
evaziv • *adj* elusive
eveniment • *n* epoch, event, occurrence
eventualitate • *n* eventuality
evident • *adj* apparent, evident, obvious, transparent
evinge • *v* evict
evita • *v* avoid, eschew, shun
evlavie • *n* piety
evolua • *v* evolve
evoluial • *adj* evolutionary
evoluie • *n* evolution
evoluional • *adj* evolutionary
evoluionar • *adj* evolutionary
évrica • *interj* eureka
ex- • *adj* sometime
exact • *adv* accurately, even
exactitate • *n* accuracy, precision
exagera • *v* exaggerate
exagerare • *n* exaggeration, excess
exagerat • *adj* exaggerated
exaltat • *adj* excited
examen • *n* examination, test
examinare • *n* examination
exaspera • *v* gall
exasperare • *n* exasperation, gall
exasperat • *adj* exasperated
excela • *v* master
excelent • *adj* excellent
excelent • *adj* excellent
excentricitate • *n* eccentricity
excepional • *adj* superb
excepional • *adj* superb
exces • *n* excess
excesiv • *adj* excessive
excesiv • *adj* excessive
excita • *v* titillate, wet
excitare • *n* excitation, excitement
excitat • *adj* excited, horny
excitaie • *n* excitement
exclamare • *n* exclamation
exclamaie • *n* exclamation
excludere • *n* exclusion
excrement • *n* excrement, shit, waste
excroc • *n* hustler
excursie • *n* trip
execrabil • *adj* execrable
executa • *v* execute
execuie • *n* execution
executor • *n* executor
exemplar • *n* item, specimen
exemplu • *n* example, instance

exercita • *v* exert
exerciiu • *n* exercise
exhibiionist • *n* exhibitionist
exil • *n* exile
exila • *v* exile
exilare • *n* exile
exilat • *n* exile
exista • *v* be, exist
existent • *adj* extant
existen • *n* being
exod • *n* exodus
exoftalmie • *n* exophthalmos
exogamie • *n* exogamy
expanda • *v* expand
expectativ • *n* expectation
expedia • *v* send
expeditiv • *adj* expedient
expeditiv • *adj* expedient
expeditive • *adj* expedient
expeditivi • *adj* expedient
expeditoare • *n* sender
expeditor • *n* sender
expeditori • *n* sender
experienta • *n* experience
experien • *n* experience
experimental • *adj* experimental
experimentare • *n* try
experimentat • *adj* experienced
expert • *n* expert • *adj* expert
expertiz • *n* counsel
expiaie • *n* atonement
expiere • *n* atonement
explica • *v* explain
explicabil • *adj* explicable
explicabil • *adj* explicable
explicabile • *adj* explicable
explicabili • *adj* explicable
explicare • *n* explanation, explication
explicaie • *n* explanation
explicit • *adj* explicit
exploata • *v* exploit
exploatator • *n* user
exploda • *v* detonate
explodare • *n* detonation
explora • *v* scan
explozie • *n* blast, detonation, explosion
exponeniere • *n* exponentiation
export • *n* export
exportare • *n* export
exportator • *n* exporter
expoza • *v* exhibit
expoziie • *n* exhibition, exposition, show
expres • *n* express
exprese • *n* express
expresie • *n* expression, phrase, term, voice
expresionism • *n* expressionism
expresiv • *adj* expressive
exprimabil • *adj* expressible
exprimare • *n* voice
expropriere • *n* expropriation
expulza • *v* evict
expune • *v* expose
expunere • *n* exposition, exposure
expurga • *v* expurgate
extaz • *n* bliss, ecstasy
extensibil • *adj* extendible
extensie • *n* extension
extenua • *v* fatigue, jade
extenuare • *n* exhaustion, fatigue
extenuat • *adj* fatigued
exterior • *n* outside
exterminare • *v* exterminate • *n* holocaust
extern • *adj* external
externizare • *n* externalization
extinde • *v* reach
extindere • *n* extension
extins • *adj* widespread
extirpa • *v* eradicate
extrabursier • *adj* over-the-counter
extract • *n* abstract, extract
extragalactic • *adj* extragalactic
extraordinar • *adj* amazing, extraordinary, fabulous, lush
extraordinare • *adj* outstanding
extrapolare • *n* extrapolation
extras • *n* abstract, extract
extraterestru • *n* alien, extraterrestrial • *adj* extraterrestrial
extravagan • *n* extravagance, profusion
extrem • *adv* exceedingly • *adj* far
extremism • *n* extremism
extremitate • *n* appendage, extremity
ezita • *v* hesitate
ezitare • *n* reluctance
ezoteric • *adj* esoteric

F

fabrica • *v* manufacture
fabric • *n* factory
fabricant • *n* maker, manufacturer
fabricare • *n* fabrication, manufacture
fabuloas • *adj* mythological
fabulos • *adj* fabulous, mythological
fctor • *n* maker
face • *v* do, make, produce, strip, work
fachie • *n* torch
facibil • *adj* feasible
facibilitate • *n* feasibility
facilita • *v* facilitate
facilitare • *n* facilitation
facilitate • *n* ease, facility
fclie • *n* torch
facocer • *n* warthog
factiune • *n* splinter
faciune • *n* faction
factoriza • *v* expand
factur • *n* bill, check, invoice
facturi • *n* invoice
facultate • *n* college, faculty, school
facultativ • *adv* optionally
fad • *adj* insipid
fag • *n* beech
fagot • *n* bassoon
fagure • *n* honeycomb
faian • *n* faience
faim • *n* fame, name, renown, reputation
faimos • *adj* fabled, famous, renowned
fin • *n* flour, meal
finos • *adj* floury, mealy
falc • *n* jaw
falez • *n* cliff
falic • *adj* phallic
faliment • *n* bankruptcy
falnic • *adj* imposing
fals • *adj* artificial, false, fraudulent, untruthful
falsifica • *v* falsify
falsitate • *n* falsehood, falsity, mendacity
falus • *n* phallus
familiar • *adj* colloquial • *n* family
familiaritate • *n* familiarity
familie • *n* family
fân • *n* hay
fânea • *n* hayfield
fanfaronad • *n* swagger
fanion • *n* pennant
fântân • *n* fountain, source, well
fantastic • *adj* fantastic
fantezie • *n* imagination
fantom • *n* phantom
fapt • *n* fact
fapt • *n* action, deed, fact
fpta • *n* perpetrator
faptic • *adj* factual
fptuitor • *n* perpetrator
fptur • *n* being, creature
far • *n* headlight, light, lighthouse
fr • *adj* carefree • *prep* without
faraon • *n* pharaoh
fra • *n* dustpan
fard • *n* blush
farda • *v* rouge
farfurie • *n* plate
farmacie • *n* pharmacy
farmacist • *n* pharmacist
farmacolog • *n* pharmacologist
farmacologie • *n* pharmacology
farmec • *n* charm, enchantment, spell
fa • *n* band, bandage
fâs • *n* pipit
fascicul • *n* bundle, sheaf
fascina • *v* bewitch, charm
fascinat • *adj* rapt
fascism • *n* fascism
fasole • *n* bean
fastidios • *adj* boring, irksome
fasung • *n* socket
ft • *n* fetus
fta • *v* farrow, foal, litter, whelp
fa • *n* face, side
fat • *n* girl
fatalism • *n* fatalism
fatalmente • *adv* deadly
fathom • *n* fathom
fatidic • *adj* ominous
faun • *n* fauna
furar • *n* smith
furi • *v* forge
favoare • *n* favor
favorabil • *adj* golden
favorabil • *n* occasion
favorit • *adj* favorite
favorit • *adj* favorite
fax • *n* fax
faz • *n* phase
fazan • *n* pheasant
faze • *n* phase
febr • *n* fever, temperature
febril • *adj* hot
fecale • *n* excrement
fecioar • *n* damsel, virgin
fecior • *n* damsel
feciorelnic • *adj* virgin
fecioresc • *adj* virgin
feciorie • *n* virginity
fecundare • *n* fertilization
fecunditate • *n* fruitfulness
federal • *adj* federal
federalism • *n* federalism
federalizare • *n* federalization
federaie • *n* federation

fel • *n* kind, manner, sort, style, type, variety, way
felaie • *n* fellatio
felicita • *v* congratulate
felicitri • *interj* congratulations
felie • *n* wedge
felin • *adj* feline
felin • *n* cat • *adj* feline
felinar • *n* lantern, streetlight
femei • *n* lady
femeie • *n* woman
femeiesc • *adj* feminine, womanly
femel • *n* cow
feminin • *adj* feminine, womanly
feminitate • *n* femininity
fenicul • *n* fennel
fenilalanin • *n* phenylalanine
fenix • *n* phoenix
fenomen • *n* phenomenon
fenotip • *n* phenotype
fent • *n* balk
fenugrec • *n* fenugreek
ferstru • *n* saw
ferbinte • *adj* burning
ferbineal • *n* ardor
fereastr • *n* window
fereca • *v* handcuff, hoop
feri • *v* guard
ferici • *v* congratulate
fericire • *n* felicity, happiness, joy
fericit • *adj* happy
ferig • *n* fern
ferm • *adj* immovable, implacable
ferm • *n* farm
fermeca • *v* beguile, bewitch, charm
fermector • *adj* charming, magic, magical
ferment • *n* ferment, yeast
fermenta • *v* ferment, work
fermentare • *n* fermentation
fermentaie • *n* fermentation
fermier • *n* farmer
fermitate • *n* decision, determination, resoluteness
fermiu • *n* fermium
fermoar • *n* fly
fernambuc • *n* brazilwood
feroce • *adj* fierce
ferocitate • *n* ferocity, mercilessness
feros • *adj* irony
fertil • *adj* fruitful, productive
fertilitate • *n* fruitfulness
fertiliza • *v* fertilize
fertilizant • *n* fertilizer
fertilizare • *n* fertilization
fertilizator • *n* fertilizer
fervoare • *n* fervor
festin • *n* banquet, feast
festiv • *adj* festive
festivitate • *n* celebration
fetic • *n* tit
fetid • *adj* fetid
fetiism • *n* fetishism
fetioar • *n* tit
feti • *n* tit
feud • *n* feud
feudalism • *n* feudalism
fezabil • *adj* feasible
fezabilitate • *n* feasibility
fi • *v* be • *n* phi
fiabil • *adj* dependable, reliable
fiabilitate • *n* reliability
fiar • *n* animal, beast
ficat • *n* liver
fictiv • *adj* fictitious
fidel • *adj* true
fidelitate • *n* fidelity, steadfastness
fiecare • *pron* everyone
fiecine • *pron* everybody
fief • *n* fief
fier • *n* iron • *adj* iron
fierar • *n* blacksmith, smith
fierbe • *v* boil
fierbinte • *adj* hot
fiere • *n* bile, bitterness, venom
fierea-pământului • *n* centaury
figur • *n* figure
figurativ • *adj* figurative
figurin • *n* figurine
fiic • *n* child, daughter
fiindc • *conj* as
fiin • *n* being, creature
filamentos • *adj* filamentous
filantropic • *adj* philanthropic
filantropie • *n* philanthropy
filde • *n* ivory
file • *n* fillet
filial • *n* branch
filigran • *n* filigree
filimic • *n* marigold
film • *n* movie
filma • *v* lens
filodendron • *n* monstera
filologie • *n* philology
filoxer • *n* phylloxera
filozof • *n* philosopher
filozofic • *adj* philosophical
filozofie • *n* philosophy
filtra • *v* filter
fin • *n* godson
fin • *n* goddaughter
final • *n* completion, ending, finish
financiar • *adj* financial
finee • *n* elegance, refinement
finic • *n* date

finisa • *v* close
finit • *adj* finite
finitate • *n* finiteness
fiol • *n* vial
fior • *n* shudder, thrill, wince
fiord • *n* fjord
fiori • *n* shudder
fioros • *adj* fierce
fir • *n* thread, whisker, wire, yarn
fire • *n* temper
firete • *adv* naturally
firm • *n* company
fi • *n* plug
fiier • *n* file
fisionabil • *adj* fissionable
fisiune • *n* fission
fisur • *n* crack, cranny, fissure
fisur • *n* crevice
fitil • *n* wick
fiu • *n* boy, child, son
fix • *adj* immovable • *adv* sharp
fixa • *v* fasten, set
fixat • *adj* set
fizic • *adj* physical
fizic • *adj* physical
fizician • *n* physicist
fiziognomonie • *n* physiognomy
fiziolog • *n* physiologist
fiziologic • *adj* physical, physiological
fiziologic • *adj* physical
fiziologie • *n* physiology
flacr • *n* flame
flcu • *n* bachelor
flag • *n* flag
flagel • *n* calamity, scourge
flmând • *adj* hungry
flmânzi • *v* starve
flamboiant • *adj* flamboyant
flamur • *n* banner, flag
flanc • *n* flank
flata • *v* fawn
flatulen • *n* fart
flaut • *n* flute
flautist • *n* flautist
flautist • *n* flautist
fleac • *pron* nothing
flecar • *adj* garrulous, loquacious, talkative
flecial • *n* sleet
flexibil • *adj* flexible
flexibilitate • *n* flexibility
flint • *n* rifle
floare • *n* flower
floare-de-col • *n* edelweiss
floc • *n* flock, tuft
flor • *n* flora
florar • *n* florist
flot • *n* navy
flotant • *adj* floating
flox • *n* phlox
fluen • *n* fluency
fluid • *n* fluid • *adj* fluid
fluiditate • *n* fluency
fluier • *n* whistle
fluiera • *v* blow, whistle
fluierar • *n* piper, plover
fluierar-cu-picioare-roii • *n* redshank
fluierat • *n* whistle
fluor • *n* fluorine
fluorit • *n* fluorite
flutura • *v* brandish
flutura • *n* payslip
fluture • *n* butterfly
fluturei • *n* gaillardia
fluvial • *adj* fluvial
fluviu • *n* river
flux • *n* current, flow, run, stream
foaie • *n* leaf, sheet
foaie-gras • *n* butterwort
foale • *n* bellows
foame • *n* hunger
foamete • *n* famine, starvation
foarfec • *n* scissors
foarfece • *n* scissors, shears
foarte • *adv* very, well
fobie • *n* fear, phobia
foc • *n* fire
foc • *n* seal
focar • *n* fireplace
focos • *adj* fiery
foileton • *n* feature
folder • *n* folder
folie • *n* leaf
folos • *n* utility
folosi • *v* use, work
folosibil • *adj* practicable
folosin • *n* use
folosire • *n* use
folosit • *adj* used
folositor • *adj* useful
fond • *n* foundation, matter
fondare • *n* foundation
fondator • *n* founder
fonem • *n* phoneme
fonetic • *adj* phonetic
font • *n* font
forfecu • *n* crossbill
forint • *n* forint
forja • *v* forge
forj • *n* forge
forma • *v* form
form • *n* form, shape
formal • *adj* formal
formalism • *n* formalism

formalist • *adj* formalist
format • *n* format, template
formaie • *n* band
formidabil • *adj* formidable
formul • *n* formula
formular • *n* form
formulare • *n* formulation
forsiia • *n* forsythia
for • *n* force, power
fora • *v* exert, force
fortrea • *n* fortification, fortress
forat • *adj* contrived
fortificare • *n* fortification
fortificaie • *n* citadel, fortification
fortuit • *adj* fortuitous
fosfat • *n* phosphate
fosfata • *v* phosphate
fosfor • *n* phosphorus
fosil • *n* fossil
fosilizare • *n* fossilization
fosilizaie • *n* fossilization
fost • *adj* old, sometime
fostul • *n* ex
fotbal • *n* football, soccer
foto • *n* photo
fotografia • *v* photograph • *n* photography
fotografie • *n* photo, photograph, photography, picture
fotoliu • *n* armchair
fotomontaj • *n* photomontage
foton • *n* photon
fotosensibilitate • *n* speed
fotovoltaic • *adj* photovoltaic
fracie • *n* fraction
fracional • *adj* fractional
fracionar • *adj* fractional
fraciune • *n* faction, fraction
fractur • *n* fracture
fractura • *v* fracture
fracturare • *n* fracture
frag-ttreasc • *n* goosefoot
fragment • *n* chip, fragment, portion
fragmenta • *v* fragment
fraier • *n* sucker
fraieri • *v* sucker
frmânta • *v* knead
frmântare • *n* concern, disquietude, fuss
frân • *n* brake
frâna • *v* brake
franc • *n* franc
franciu • *n* francium
frânghie • *n* cable, ligature, line, rope
frânt • *adj* broken, fractured
frate • *n* brother
fratern • *adj* brotherly, fraternal
fraternitate • *n* brotherhood, fraternity
fraterniza • *v* brother, fraternize
fresc • *adj* brotherly, fraternal
frie • *n* brotherhood, fraternity
frâu • *n* bit, bridle
frauda • *v* defraud
fraudulos • *adj* fraudulent
fraz • *n* phrase
freamt • *n* bustle, commotion, flurry, fuss, murmur, rustle, tumult, uproar
freca • *v* rub
frecare • *n* friction
frecvent • *adj* frequent • *adv* frequently
frecven • *n* frequency
fredona • *v* hum
frenezie • *n* frenzy
fresc • *n* fresco
frez • *n* haircut
frezie • *n* freesia
fric • *n* dread, fear
fricos • *adj* cowardly
friciune • *n* friction
frig • *n* cold, coldness
frigare • *n* skewer, spit
frige • *v* fry, grill, roast
frigider • *n* refrigerator
friguros • *adj* cool
fringilid • *n* finch
fringilid • *n* finch
friptur • *n* roast
frizer • *n* barber, hairdresser
frizur • *n* haircut
frontier • *n* border, boundary
frontispiciu • *n* frontispiece
frotiu • *n* smear
fruct • *n* fruit
fructoz • *n* fructose
fructuos • *adj* fruitful
frugalitate • *n* frugality
frumoas • *adj* beautiful
frumoaso • *n* baby
frumos • *adj* beautiful, handsome
frumusee • *n* beauty
frunte • *n* forehead
frunz • *n* leaf
frunzos • *adj* leafy
frustrare • *n* frustration
frustraie • *n* frustration
fucsie • *n* fuchsia
fug • *n* escape, run
fugaci • *adj* fleeting • *n* sandpiper, stint
fugar • *n* fugitive, outlaw • *adj* fugitive
fugi • *v* flee, run
fugitiv • *adj* fleeting, fugitive
fulg • *n* feather, plume
fulger • *n* lightning, thunderbolt
fum • *n* smoke
fuma • *v* smoke

fumar • *n* chimney
fumric • *n* fumitory
fumri • *n* fumitory
fumtoare • *n* smoking
fumtor • *n* smoker, smoking
fumtori • *n* smoking
fumega • *v* fume, smoke
fumegar • *n* smoke
fumigen • *adj* smoking
fumigen • *adj* smoking
fumuriu • *n* smoke • *adj* smoke
funcie • *n* function, office, position, procedure, use
funciona • *v* function, work
funcionabil • *adj* practicable
funcional • *adj* practicable
funcionar • *n* clerk, officer
funciune • *n* procedure
fund • *n* ass, backside, bottom, butt
fund • *n* ribbon
fundal • *n* backdrop
fundament • *n* base, foundation
fundamental • *adj* basal, cardinal, elementary, essential, fundamental
fundamentalism • *n* fundamentalism
fundamentare • *n* foundation
funda • *n* defender
fundaie • *n* foundation
funerar • *adj* funeral, funerary
fungibil • *adj* fungible
funicular • *n* funicular
funie • *n* ligature, line, rope
funigel • *n* gossamer
funingine • *n* soot
fura • *v* filch, rob, steal
furaj • *n* fodder
furat • *n* steal
furtur • *n* steal
furc • *n* cradle, fork, pitchfork
furculi • *n* fork
furgonet • *n* van
furie • *n* anger, choler, fury, ire, outrage, rage, wrath
furios • *adj* furious
furia • *v* steal
furnic • *n* ant
furnicar • *n* anteater, anthill
furt • *n* larceny, steal, theft
furtun • *n* blow, storm, tempest, thunderstorm
furtunar • *n* puffin
furtunos • *adj* stormy
furuncul • *n* boil
fus • *n* spindle
fust • *n* skirt
fute • *n* lance
futai • *n* ass, fuck
fute • *v* fuck
futere • *n* fuck, fucking
futurism • *n* futurism

G

gabardin • *n* worsted
gâde • *n* hangman
gâdila • *v* tickle, titillate
gadoliniu • *n* gadolinium
gaf • *n* gaffe
gagat • *n* jet
gaid • *n* bagpipes
gaie • *n* kite
gin • *n* chicken, hen
ginu • *n* moorhen
ginu-de-balt • *n* curlew, moorhen
gai • *n* jay
gal • *n* gall
glgie • *n* fuss, noise, uproar
glgios • *adj* loud
galant • *adj* gallant
galanterie • *n* chivalry, gallantry
galaxie • *n* galaxy
galaxii • *n* galaxy
galben • *n* yellow • *adj* yellow
galben-verziu • *adj* lemon
galben • *n* yellow
glbenare • *n* jaundice
glbenea • *n* buttercup
glbenele • *n* marigold
glbenu • *n* yolk
glbinare • *n* jaundice, paleness, pallor
gâlci • *n* quinsy
gleat • *n* bucket
galion • *n* galleon
galiu • *n* gallium
gâlm • *n* wart
galon • *n* facing
galop • *n* gallop
galopa • *v* gallop
galvanometru • *n* galvanometer
gam • *n* gamut
gamb • *n* calf, leg
gând • *n* thought
gândac • *n* beetle, bug, cockroach
gândi • *v* mean, think
gândibil • *adj* thinkable

gândire • *n* thought
gânganie • *n* bug
ganglion • *n* ganglion
gânsac • *n* gander, goose
goaz • *n* asshole
gar • *n* station, terminal
garaj • *n* garage
garant • *n* guarantee, guarantor
garanta • *v* guarantee, pledge
garantat • *adj* warranted
garanie • *n* guarantee, warranty
gârbov • *adj* bent
gard • *n* fence
gard • *n* guard, soldier, vigil, watch
gardenie • *n* gardenia
garderoba • *n* cloakroom
gardian • *n* guard
grgun • *n* hornet
gargui • *n* gargoyle
garnizoan • *n* garrison
garoaf • *n* carnation, pink
gâsc • *n* goose
gâscan • *n* gander
gasconad • *n* swagger
gsi • *v* find
gastric • *adj* gastric
gastrointestinal • *adj* gastrointestinal
gastronomie • *n* gastronomy
gastrulaie • *n* gastrulation
gât • *n* neck, throat
gata • *adj* set
gti • *v* cook
gaur • *n* gaur
gaur • *n* hole
gauri • *v* drill
gaurii • *v* bore
gaz • *n* gas
gazd • *n* host, landlord
gzduire • *n* lodging
gaze • *n* gas
gazel • *n* gazelle
gazetar • *n* journalist
gazifica • *v* gasify
gazometru • *n* gasometer
gazon • *n* sward
gazos • *adj* gaseous
gealat • *n* hangman
geam • *n* windowpane
geamn • *n* twin
geamandur • *n* buoy
geamt • *n* moan, sigh
gean • *n* eyelash
gelos • *adj* jealous
gelozie • *n* jealousy
gem • *n* jam
gem • *n* gem
geme • *v* groan, moan
gen • *n* gender, kind, sort, style, type
genealogie • *n* genealogy
genera • *v* generate
general • *n* general • *adj* general
generare • *n* generation
generaie • *n* age, generation
generator • *n* generator
generos • *adj* altruistic, generous
generozitate • *n* altruism, generosity
genet • *n* genet
genetic • *adj* genetic
genetic • *n* genetics
genetician • *n* geneticist
genial • *adj* ingenious
genialitate • *n* brilliance, genius
genitiv • *n* genitive
geniu • *n* genius
genocid • *n* genocide, holocaust
genom • *n* genome
genotip • *n* genotype
genian • *n* gentian
gentil • *adj* bland, tender
gentilee • *n* gentleness
gentlemen • *n* gentleman
genuflexare • *n* genuflection
genuflexiune • *n* genuflection
genunchi • *n* knee
genune • *n* precipice
geocentric • *adj* geocentric
geochimie • *n* geochemistry
geofizic • *n* geophysics
geografic • *adj* geographic
geografie • *n* geography
geolog • *n* geologist
geometrie • *n* geometry
ger • *n* frost
geraniu • *n* cranesbill, geranium
gerbil • *n* gerbil
germaniu • *n* germanium
germen • *n* abortion
germina • *v* germinate
gest • *n* gesture
gesticulaie • *n* gesticulation
ghear • *n* claw
ghea • *n* ice
gheat • *n* shoe
gheizer • *n* geyser
ghem • *n* ball
ghemui • *v* duck
ghepard • *n* cheetah
gheret • *n* lodge
gherghin • *n* may
gherghin • *n* dahlia
gheril • *n* guerrilla
ghear • *n* glacier
ghetou • *n* ghetto
ghid • *n* guide

ghida • *v* drive
ghidare • *n* guidance
ghidon • *n* handlebar
ghilotin • *n* guillotine
ghilotina • *v* guillotine
ghimber • *n* ginger
ghimpe • *n* thorn
ghind • *n* acorn
ghinion • *n* misfortune
ghintuit • *n* rifle
ghionoaie • *n* woodpecker
ghiozdan • *n* satchel
ghitar • *n* guitar
• *n* mouth
gibon • *n* gibbon
gigant • *adj* enormous • *n* giant
gigant • *n* giantess
gigantic • *adj* gigantic, huge, prodigious
gigantism • *n* gigantism
gigolo • *n* gigolo
gimnast • *n* gymnast
gimnast • *n* gymnast
gimnastic • *adj* gymnastic
gimnastic • *n* gymnastics
gimnaziu • *n* gymnasium, school
ginecologic • *adj* gynecological
ginere • *n* son-in-law
ginet • *n* genet
gingie • *n* gum
gingivit • *n* gingivitis
ginkgo • *n* ginkgo
ginseng • *n* ginseng
giraf • *n* giraffe
giuvaergiu • *n* jeweler
giuvaeruri • *n* jewel
giuvaier • *n* gem
gladiol • *n* gladiolus
gland • *n* gland
glas • *n* voice
glasa • *v* ice
glasuri • *n* voice
glauc • *adj* glaucous
glaucom • *n* glaucoma
glazur • *n* icing
glazurat • *n* glaze
glezn • *n* ankle
glicin • *n* glycine, wisteria
gloat • *n* crowd
glob • *n* globe
glockenspiel • *n* glockenspiel
glon • *n* bullet
glonte • *n* bullet
glorie • *n* glory
glorifica • *v* glorify
glorificare • *n* praise
glorios • *adj* glorious
glosar • *n* vocabulary
glucide • *n* sugar
glucoz • *n* glucose
glucozid • *n* glucoside
glum • *n* glume, joke
glume • *adj* jocose
glutamin • *n* glutamine
gluton • *n* wolverine
gnu • *n* gnu
goal • *adj* unclothed
goelet • *n* schooner
gogoa • *n* doughnut
gol • *adj* empty, naked, nude, unclothed, vacant • *n* goal
goldan • *n* damson
goldan • *n* damson
golf • *n* bay, cove, gulf, run
goli • *v* drain, empty
goliciune • *n* inanition
golire • *n* vacation
golit • *adj* devoid, empty
gondol • *n* gondola
gondolier • *n* gondolier
goniometru • *n* goniometer
goral • *n* goral
goril • *n* gorilla
gospodin • *n* housewife
grbi • *v* precipitate
grbit • *adj* fast
grad • *n* degree, level
grade • *n* degree, level
grdin • *n* garden
grdinar • *n* gardener, horticulturist
grdinar • *n* gardener
grdinreas • *n* gardener
grdinri • *v* garden
grdinrit • *n* gardening
grdini • *n* kindergarten
grafic • *n* graph
grafic • *n* graphic
grafit • *n* graphite
grajd • *n* stable
gram • *n* gram
grmad • *n* crowd, mountain
gramatic • *n* grammar
gramatical • *adj* grammatical
gramofon • *n* gramophone
grânar • *n* granary
granat • *n* garnet
grandoare • *n* brilliance, greatness
grandomanie • *n* megalomania
grâne • *n* wheat
grani • *n* border, boundary, limit
grap • *n* harrow
gras • *adj* fat
grsime • *n* fat, grease
graie • *n* charm, elegance, grace
gratis • *adv* gratis

gratitudine • *n* gratefulness, gratitude
gratuit • *adj* complimentary, free
grâu • *n* wheat
grunte • *n* grain
graur • *n* starling
grava • *v* brand
gravid • *adj* pregnant
graviditate • *n* pregnancy
gravitaie • *n* gravitation
gravitaional • *adj* gravitational
gravur • *n* gravure
grea • *adj* heavy
grea • *n* nausea, qualm, sickness, upset
grebl • *n* rake
grefon • *n* graft
gregar • *adj* gregarious
greier • *n* cricket
grenad • *n* grenade
greoi • *adj* clumsy
greeal • *n* fault, mistake
grei • *v* err, mistake, transgress
gresie • *n* sandstone, whetstone
greit • *adj* wrong
greos • *adj* obnoxious, upset
greu • *adj* difficult, hard, heavy, weighty
greutate • *n* hardship, weight
grev • *v* strike • *n* strike
gri • *n* gray
grifon • *n* griffin
grij • *n* care, tenderness, worry
grimas • *n* grimace
grind • *n* balk, beam, girder
grindin • *n* hail
grindina • *v* hail
grip • *n* cold, flu, influenza
gri • *n* semolina
groap • *n* pit
groaz • *n* horrible
groaznic • *adj* fearful, formidable, ghastly, horrible, monstrous, terrible
groparul • *n* gravedigger
gropi • *n* dimple
gros • *adj* fat, thick
grosier • *adj* coarse, crass
grosolan • *adj* clumsy, crass, vulgar
grot • *n* cave
grotesc • *adj* grotesque
grozav • *adj* copacetic, lush
grumaz • *n* nape
grup • *n* group, set
grupa • *v* group
guaiac • *n* guaiacum
guanaco • *n* guanaco
gudron • *n* tar
gudura • *v* fawn
guler • *n* neck
gulie • *n* kohlrabi
gunoi • *n* dung, garbage, trash, waste
gur • *n* draught, mouth, mouthful
gura-leului • *n* snapdragon
gura-lupului • *n* skullcap
guraliv • *adj* garrulous, loquacious, talkative • *n* telltale
gure • *adj* garrulous, loquacious, talkative
gu • *n* crop
gu-albastr • *n* bluethroat
gu-roie • *n* robin
gust • *n* taste
gusta • *v* taste, try
gustos • *adj* delicious
gut • *n* gout
gutui • *n* quince
gutuie • *n* quince
guvern • *n* government
guverna • *v* govern
guvernamental • *adj* governmental

H

habitat • *n* habitat
habitudine • *n* habit
hafniu • *n* hafnium
haimana • *n* bastard
haimanale • *n* bastard
hain • *adj* evil, wicked
hain • *n* clothing, dress, garment
haine • *n* clothes, wear
hait • *n* pack
halebard • *n* bill
halebardier • *n* bill
halen • *n* breath
halíce • *n* bullet
haló • *interj* hello
halogen • *n* halogen
halter • *n* weight
haltere • *n* weight
halterofilie • *n* weightlifting
halucinogen • *adj* hallucinogenic
ham • *n* harness
ham-ham • *n* woof
hamac • *n* hammock
hambar • *n* barn, hold
hamei • *n* hop
hmesit • *adj* famished
hamsie • *n* anchovy

hamster • *n* hamster
han • *n* inn, khan
handbal • *n* handball
handicapat • *adj* lame
hangar • *n* hangar
haos • *n* bedlam, chaos, pandemonium
haotic • *adj* chaotic, confused, confusing
har • *n* grace
hârciog • *n* hamster
hardware • *n* hardware
harf • *n* harp
harnaament • *n* harness
harnic • *adj* assiduous, busy, diligent, hardworking, industrious
hrnicie • *n* diligence
harp • *n* harp
harpie • *n* harpy
harpist • *n* harpist
harpon • *n* harpoon
hart • *n* map
hârtie • *n* paper • *adj* paper
hai • *n* hashish
ham • *n* shallot
hasmauchi • *n* chervil
hat • *n* balk
hatman • *n* hetman
hu • *n* abyss
hazard • *n* hazard, occasion
hectar • *n* hectare
hedonism • *n* hedonism
hei • *interj* hey
heliocentric • *adj* heliocentric
heliometru • *n* heliometer
heliotrop • *n* heliotrope
heliu • *n* helium
hemoroid • *n* hemorrhoid
henna • *n* henna
hen • *n* handball
hepatic • *adj* hepatic
hepatit • *n* hepatitis
heptagon • *n* heptagon
herald • *n* herald
heraldic • *n* heraldry
hering • *n* herring
hermafrodit • *n* hermaphrodite • *adj* hermaphrodite
hermelin • *n* ermine
hermeneutic • *n* hermeneutics
hermin • *n* ermine
herminat • *n* ermine
heterosexual • *n* heterosexual • *adj* heterosexual
heterosexual • *n* heterosexual
heterosexualitate • *n* heterosexuality
hib • *n* fault
hibiscus • *n* hibiscus
hibrid • *n* bastard
hibrizi • *n* bastard
hicori • *n* hickory
hidos • *adj* monstrous
hidr • *n* hydra
hidrargir • *n* hydrargyrum, mercury, quicksilver
hidrat • *n* hydrate
hidrocarbur • *n* hydrocarbon
hidrocarburi • *n* hydrocarbon
hidrogen • *n* hydrogen
hidromel • *n* mead
hidroxid • *n* hydroxide
hien • *n* hyena
hiene • *n* hyena
higrometru • *n* hygrometer
higroscopic • *adj* hygroscopic
hil • *n* hilum
himer • *n* smoke
himeric • *adj* insane
hiperglicemia • *n* hyperglycemia
hipermetrop • *adj* farsighted
hipersomnie • *n* hypersomnia
hipertrofia • *v* hypertrophy
hipertrofie • *n* hypertrophy
hiponim • *n* hyponym
hipopotam • *n* hippopotamus
hipostaz • *n* hypostasis
histidin • *n* histidine
hlei • *n* clay
hoa • *n* thief
hochei • *n* hockey
hoinri • *v* roam
hoit • *n* carcass
holba • *v* goggle, ogle
holmiu • *n* holmium
holocaust • *n* holocaust
holografie • *n* holography
homar • *n* lobster
homeopatic • *adj* homeopathic
homeopatie • *n* homeopathy
hominid • *n* hominid
homo • *n* gay
homofobie • *n* homophobia
homosexual • *n* gay, homosexual • *adj* homosexual
homosexualitate • *n* homosexuality
hop • *interj* hey
hor • *n* hora
horn • *n* chimney
hortensie • *n* hydrangea
horticol • *adj* horticultural
horticultoare • *n* horticulturist
horticultor • *n* horticulturist
horticultur • *n* horticulture
ho • *n* highwayman, thief
hotar • *n* balk, coast
hotrâre • *n* decision, resoluteness

hotrât • *adj* set
hotrî • *v* elect, resolve
hotel • *n* hotel
hran • *n* food
hrni • *v* feed
hrean • *n* horseradish
hric • *n* buckwheat
huligan • *n* hooligan
humus • *n* humus
huo • *interj* boo
hurmuz • *n* snowberry
hybris • *n* hubris
hyperlink • *n* link

I

i • *n* i
iac • *n* yak
iacint • *n* hyacinth
iap • *n* mare
iari • *adv* again
iarb • *n* garden, grass, sward, weed
iarb-gras • *n* purslane
iarb-mare • *n* elecampane
iarba-mâei • *n* catnip
iarb-neagr • *n* figwort
iarn • *n* winter
iasc • *n* tinder
iasomie • *n* jasmine
iaurt • *n* yogurt
iazm • *n* goblin
ibex • *n* ibex
ibis • *n* ibis
ibric • *n* teakettle
ibuprofen • *n* ibuprofen
ici-colo • *adv* around
icoan • *n* icon
iconi • *n* icon
icre • *n* roe, spawn
icter • *n* jaundice
ideal • *adv* ideally
idealism • *n* idealism
idealiza • *v* idealize
idealizare • *n* idealization
idee • *n* apprehension, conception, idea
îdemânare • *n* address
identificabil • *adj* identifiable
identitate • *n* identity, sameness
ideogram • *n* ideogram
ideolog • *n* ideologist
ideologi • *n* ideologist
ideologic • *adj* ideological
ideologie • *n* ideology
ideologii • *n* ideology
ideologist • *n* ideologist
ideologiste • *n* ideologist
idioat • *n* idiot
idioate • *n* idiot
idiolect • *n* idiolect
idiom • *n* idiom
idiomatic • *adj* idiomatic
idiosincrasie • *n* idiosyncrasy
idiosincratic • *adj* idiosyncratic
idiosincrazic • *adj* idiosyncratic
idiosincrazie • *n* idiosyncrasy
idiot • *n* ass, idiot
idioi • *n* idiot
idol • *n* god, idol
ied • *n* fawn, kid
ieder • *n* ivy
ienibahar • *n* allspice
ienicer • *n* janissary
ienupr • *n* juniper
iepura • *n* bunny, leveret
iepure • *n* rabbit
iepure-de-câmp • *n* hare
ierarhic • *adj* hierarchical
ierarhie • *n* hierarchy
ierbivor • *n* vegetarian
ierbos • *adj* grassy, herbaceous
ieri • *n* yesterday • *adv* yesterday
ierna • *v* winter
ierta • *v* forgive
iertare • *n* forgiveness, mercy
iei • *v* exit
ieire • *n* exit
igien • *n* hygiene
igienic • *adj* hygienic
ignam • *n* yam
ignifug • *adj* fireproof
ignominie • *n* ignominy
ignora • *v* disregard
ignorant • *adj* ignorant
ignoran • *n* ignorance
ignorant • *adj* ignorant
ihneumon • *n* ichneumon
ihtiozaur • *n* ichthyosaur
ilar • *adj* hilarious
ilariant • *adj* hilarious
ilaritate • *n* hilarity
ilu • *n* anvil
ilegal • *adj* illegal • *adv* illegally
ilegitim • *adj* illegitimate
ilice • *n* holly
ilogic • *adj* illogical
ilumina • *v* illuminate, light, radiate

iluminaie • *n* illumination
ilustra • *v* depict, illustrate
ilustru • *adj* shining
iluzie • *n* illusion, smoke
iluzionare • *n* imagination
iluzoriu • *adj* illusory
imaculat • *adj* immaculate
imaculat • *adj* immaculate
imagina • *v* dream, imagine
imaginabil • *adj* thinkable
imaginare • *n* imagination
imaginaie • *n* imagination
imagine • *n* conception, image, imagination, picture
imam • *n* imam
imatur • *n* baby
imaturitate • *n* immaturity
îmbrbta • *v* encourage
îmbarcare • *n* boarding
îmbtat • *adj* drunk, drunken, intoxicated
îmbtrâni • *v* age
imbecil • *n* clown, imbecile
îmbiba • *v* imbibe
îmbina • *v* combine, connect
îmbinare • *n* connection
îmbrca • *v* address, clothe, dress
îmbrcabil • *adj* wearable
îmbrcminte • *n* clothes, clothing, wear
imbracat • *n* dressing
îmbria • *v* embrace, fathom, hug
îmbriare • *n* cuddle, embrace, hug
îmbuca • *v* lap
îmbufnat • *v* sulk
îmbuiba • *v* stuff
îmbujora • *v* blush
îmbujorare • *n* blush
îmbuna • *v* conciliate
îmbunti • *v* better, improve
îmbuntire • *n* amelioration, improvement
îmbuntit • *adj* improved
imediat • *adj* immediate • *adv* immediately
imens • *adj* huge, immense
imensitate • *n* enormity
imi • *pron* me
imigrant • *n* immigrant
imigrare • *n* immigration
imigraie • *n* immigration
iminent • *adj* imminent
imita • *v* ape, copy
imitare • *n* imitation
imitaie • *n* imitation
imn • *n* anthem, hymn
imobil • *n* immovable • *adj* immovable, implacable
imobilizat • *n* standstill
imoportunare • *n* harassment
imoral • *adj* abandoned, immoral, obscene, unclean
imoralitate • *n* immorality
imortal • *adj* immortal
împca • *v* cope, reconcile
împcare • *n* reconciliation
împacheta • *v* wrap
impacien • *n* impatience
împduri • *v* forest
impala • *n* impala
impar • *adj* odd
împrat • *n* emperor
împrteas • *n* empress
împrie • *n* empire
împrti • *v* share
împri • *v* assign, distribute, divide, impart, share, sort
imparial • *adj* impartial, neutral
imparialitate • *n* detachment, equity, impartiality
împrire • *n* distribution, division
impartire • *n* division
împrit • *adj* shared
impasibil • *adj* pococurante
impasibilitate • *n* insouciance
impasiv • *adj* immovable
impediment • *n* hindrance, impediment
impenetrabil • *adj* impenetrable, impervious, impregnable
împerechea • *v* couple
imperfect • *adj* imperfect
imperfeciune • *n* imperfection
imperial • *adj* imperial
imperialism • *n* imperialism
imperiozitate • *n* imperiousness
imperiu • *n* empire
impermeabil • *adj* impervious • *n* raincoat
impermeabil • *adj* impervious
impertinen • *n* familiarity, gall, impertinence
imperturbabilitate • *n* imperturbability
împiedica • *v* hinder, obstruct, restrain, trip
împiedicare • *n* obstruction, trip
împietri • *v* petrify
împinge • *v* push, shun, thrust
implacabil • *adj* implacable
implant • *n* implant
implanta • *v* implant
implantare • *n* implantation
implantri • *n* implantation
implantat • *n* implant
implantaie • *n* implantation
implanturi • *n* implant
împleti • *v* plait

împletitur • *n* braid
implica • *v* connote
implicit • *adj* implicit
împlini • *v* fill, fulfill
implora • *v* beseech, plead, treat
împodobi • *v* adorn, grace
împodobire • *n* decoration
impolitee • *n* impoliteness
împopoonat • *adj* ostentatious
important • *adj* essential, important, significant, weighty
important • *adj* essential
importan • *n* importance, significance
importuna • *v* inconvenience
imposibil • *n* impossibility • *adj* impossible, unthinkable
imposibilitate • *n* impossibility
impostur • *n* imposture
impoten • *n* impotence
împotrivire • *n* opposition
impozant • *adj* imposing
impozit • *n* duty, impost, tax
impozita • *v* levy
impozitare • *n* levy
impractibilitate • *n* impracticability
impracticabil • *adj* impracticable
împrtia • *v* strew
împrejurare • *n* circumstance
împrejurul • *prep* around
impresar • *n* manager
impresie • *n* impression
impresionabil • *adj* sensitive
impresionant • *adj* awful, impressive, terrible
impresionism • *n* impressionism
împresura • *v* beleaguer, beset, besiege
împreuna • *v* couple, join
împreun • *adv* along, jointly, together
imprevizibil • *adj* uncertain
imprevizibili • *adj* uncertain
Imprima • *v* print
imprimant • *n* printer
imprimare • *n* impression
imprimator • *n* printer
imprimerie • *n* printing
improbabil • *adj* improbable, unlikely
improbabil • *adj* unlikely
improbabilitate • *n* unlikelihood
impropriu • *adj* improper, inappropriate
împrospta • *v* freshen, refresh
improviza • *v* contrive
improvizare • *n* improvisation
împrumut • *n* loan, loanword
împrumuta • *v* borrow, lend, loan
impuden • *n* impudence
impudoare • *n* impudence
impuls • *n* impulse
impulsivitate • *n* caprice
impuntor • *adj* imposing
impune • *v* impose
împunge • *v* sting, thrust
impur • *adj* mixed
impuritate • *n* impurity
împurpura • *v* blush
împurpurare • *n* blush
impus • *adj* incumbent
imputa • *v* impute, reproach
împuternicire • *n* authorization
împuit • *adj* stinking
imuabil • *adj* immutable
imunologie • *n* immunology
in • *n* flax, linen
în • *n* holocaust • *prep* in
inacceptabil • *adj* unacceptable
inacceptabilitate • *n* unacceptability
inaccesibil • *adj* inaccessible
inactiv • *adj* dormant
inadecvat • *adj* inadequate, inappropriate
inadecvat • *adj* inadequate
inadmisibil • *adj* inadmissible
inadmisibil • *adj* inadmissible
înaintat • *adj* progressive
înainte • *adv* ahead, along, before • *prep* before • *adj* forward
inalienabil • *adv* inherently
înalt • *adj* high, tall
înalt • *adj* high
înla • *v* ascend
înlat • *adj* high
înlime • *n* altitude, height, pitch
inamic • *n* enemy
îndrăgostit • *adj* amorous, enamored
inanitie • *n* inanition
înapoi • *adv* back • *adj* backward
înapoia • *v* return
înapoiere • *n* return
inri • *n* redpoll
înarmai • *adj* embattled
inatacabil • *adj* unexceptionable
inaugural • *adj* maiden
înuntru • *adv* inside
inauzibil • *adj* inaudible
înc • *adv* also, still, yet
încadra • *v* frame
încierare • *n* brawl
înclca • *v* infringe, violate
înclcare • *n* infringement
încâlci • *v* muddle
încleca • *v* mount
înclminte • *n* footwear, shoe
înclzi • *v* sun, warm
incandescent • *adj* fiery
incandescent • *adj* fiery

încânta • *v* beguile, charm
încântant • *adj* enchanting
încântare • *n* enchantment, treat
incantaie • *n* incantation
încânttoare • *adj* enchanting
încânttor • *adj* charming, darling, enchanting, enticing, magical
incapabil • *adj* incapable, unable
incapabilitate • *n* inability
incapacitate • *n* inability
încpânare • *n* obstinacy, stubbornness
încpânat • *adj* obstinate
încpea • *v* fit
încpere • *n* room
încrca • *v* charge, load
încrcat • *adj* loaded
încrctur • *n* charge
încarcera • *v* imprison
încarcerare • *n* imprisonment
înctua • *v* handcuff, manacle
incendiu • *n* conflagration, fire
începtoare • *n* beginner
începtor • *n* beginner, colt, novice
începe • *v* begin, commence, start
începere • *n* beginning
început • *n* beginning, birth, start
încerca • *v* try
încercare • *n* try
încercat • *adj* experienced
incert • *adj* uncertain
incertitudine • *n* uncertainty
incest • *n* incest
încet • *adj* quiet, slow, soft • *adv* slowly
înceat • *adj* foggy
înceoa • *v* fog
înceoat • *v* fog
închega • *v* clot, curdle
încheia • *v* conclude
încheiere • *n* ending, termination
închide • *v* close, plug
închidere • *n* closure
închina • *v* bow, cross, pray, subdue, submit, worship, yield
închipui • *v* imagine
închipuire • *n* imagination, representation
închiria • *v* rent
închis • *adj* closed, dark
închisoare • *n* prison
incident • *n* incident, instance • *adj* incident
incidental • *adj* incident
incint • *n* precinct
incisiv • *n* incisor
incizie • *n* cut, incision, section
inclina • *v* lean
inclinare • *n* pitch
înclinare • *n* inclination
înclinaie • *n* disposition, inclination, notion, tendency
încoace • *adv* here, hither
încolo • *adv* away, thither
încoli • *v* germinate
incomestibil • *adj* inedible
incomoda • *v* bother, gall, inconvenience
încomodare • *n* disturbance
incomodare • *n* bother, inconvenience
incomparabil • *adj* incomparable
incompatibilitate • *n* incompatibility
incompetent • *adj* unable, unqualified
incomplet • *adj* incomplete
înconjura • *v* circumvent, surround
inconsistent • *adj* inconsistent
inconsisten • *n* inconsistency
inconstant • *adj* uncertain, unstable, versatile
incontient • *adj* unconscious
incontestabil • *adj* unexceptionable
încontinuu • *adv* continuously
incontrolabil • *adj* uncontrollable
inconvenabil • *adj* unsuitable
inconvenien • *n* inconvenience
încordare • *n* stress, tension
incorect • *adj* incorrect, wrong • *adv* incorrectly
încornorat • *n* cuckold
încorona • *v* crown
încotomna • *v* bundle
încotro • *conj* where • *adv* whither
încrede • *v* trust
încredere • *n* trust
incredibil • *adj* fabulous, incredible, unthinkable
încredina • *v* address
incredulitate • *n* incredulity
încrengtur • *n* phylum
încrei • *v* wrinkle
încrunta • *v* frown, scowl
încruntare • *n* frown
incub • *n* incubus
incubaie • *n* incubation
incubatoare • *n* incubator
incubator • *n* incubator
încuia • *v* lock
încuietoare • *n* lock
inculca • *v* inculcate
inculpa • *v* blame
inculpare • *n* charge
incult • *n* boor
încumeta • *v* dare
încununa • *v* crown
încuraja • *v* encourage
încurajare • *n* encouragement, facilitation

încurca • *v* confound, confuse, encumber, entangle, muddle, obfuscate
încurcat • *adj* confused
încurctor • *adj* confusing
încurctur • *n* entanglement
încuviinare • *n* concession
îndrt • *adj* backward • *adv* behind
îndatorat • *adj* indebted, obliged
indecent • *adj* indecent, lewd
indecent • *adj* indecent
indecis • *adj* irresolute, uncertain
indecis • *adj* irresolute
îndeletnicire • *n* work
îndelungat • *adj* prolonged
îndemânare • *n* ability, dexterity, hand
îndemânatic • *adj* handy
îndemna • *v* goad, incite, spur
îndeosebi • *adv* chiefly, mainly
îndeprta • *v* remove
îndeprtare • *n* recession
îndeprtat • *adj* far
independent • *adj* independent
independen • *n* independence
îndeplinire • *n* fulfillment, performance
îndesa • *v* cram, stuff
îndesat • *adj* stocky
indescriptibil • *adj* indescribable
indestructibil • *adj* indestructible
index • *n* index
indica • *v* designate, mean, spell
indicaie • *n* instruction
indicator • *n* indicator, shield
indiciu • *n* vestige
indiferent • *adj* impervious, indifferent, pococurante, uninterested, unresponsive
indiferen • *n* detachment, disregard, indifference, insouciance
indigen • *adj* indigenous • *n* native
indigenitate • *n* indigenousness
indigent • *adj* destitute
indigestie • *n* indigestion
indignare • *n* indignation
indigo • *adj* indigo
indiscreie • *n* indiscretion
indispensabili • *n* underwear
indisponibil • *adj* away, unavailable
indispoziie • *n* ailment, complaint, displeasure, fuss, malaise
indisputabil • *adj* indisputable
indistingibil • *adj* indistinguishable
indiu • *n* indium
individ • *n* individual
individual • *adj* individual, single
individual • *adj* individual
individuali • *adj* individual
individualism • *n* individualism
individualist • *adj* maverick
îndoctrina • *v* indoctrinate
îndoctrinare • *n* indoctrination
îndoi • *v* bend, double, fold
îndoial • *n* doubt
îndoielnic • *adj* unassured, untrustworthy
îndoit • *adj* bent
indolent • *adj* lazy
îndopa • *v* stuff
îndrgire • *n* endearment
îndrgostit • *adj* enamored
îndrzneal • *n* audacity
îndrzni • *v* dare
îndrepta • *v* address, straighten
îndrumare • *n* instruction
inductan • *n* inductance
inducie • *n* influence
îndulci • *v* sugar, sweeten
îndulcit • *adj* sweet
indulgent • *adj* gracious, indulgent, lenient, uncritical
indulgen • *n* indulgence, leniency, mercy
indulgent • *adj* indulgent
îndura • *v* endure
îndurare • *n* clemency, mercy
îndurera • *v* pain
industrial • *adj* industrial
industrializat • *adj* industrial
industrie • *n* industry
industrios • *adj* industrious
îneca • *v* drown
inecuaie • *n* inequality
inefabil • *adj* ineffable
inegal • *adj* unequal
inegalitate • *n* inequality
inel • *n* annulus, ring
inerent • *adj* implicit • *adv* inherently
inevitabil • *adj* inevitable, unavoidable • *adv* inevitably
inevitabilitate • *n* inevitability
inexistent • *adj* absent, nonexistent
inexistent • *adj* absent
inexplicabil • *adj* inexplicable
inexplicabil • *adj* inexplicable
inexpresiv • *adj* blank
inexprimabil • *adj* indescribable, inexpressible
inexpugnabil • *adj* impregnable
infam • *adj* infamous
infamie • *n* vileness
infanterie • *n* infantry
infanterist • *n* infantryman
înfa • *v* swaddle
înfura • *v* wrap
înfurtoare • *n* envelope
înfia • *v* depict
înfiare • *n* appearance, exposure, repre-

sentation
infecta • *v* infect
infectare • *n* infection
infecie • *n* infection
infecios • *adj* infectious
infera • *v* infer
inferior • *adj* inferior
infertil • *adj* infertile
infestaie • *n* infestation
infidelitate • *n* infidelity
înfiera • *v* brand
înfige • *v* stick
înfiinare • *n* foundation
infinit • *adj* infinite • *n* infinity
infinitate • *n* infinity
infinitiv • *n* infinitive
înfiora • *v* horrify
înfiorare • *n* horrible
înfiortor • *adj* awful
infirm • *adj* crippled, infirm
infirm • *adj* infirm
infirmier • *n* nurse
infirmitate • *n* infirmity
înflcra • *v* flame
înflcrare • *n* ardor
înflcrat • *adj* excited, passionate
inflamabil • *adj* inflammable
inflamare • *n* inflammation
inflaie • *n* inflation
inflaionabil • *adj* inflatable
inflexibil • *adj* inflexible
inflorescen • *n* inflorescence
înflori • *v* blossom, burgeon, flower
influen • *n* influence
influena • *v* influence
influenare • *n* influence
influentor • *n* influence
înfocat • *adj* quick
înfofoli • *v* bundle
înfometa • *v* starve
înfometat • *adj* famished
înfometat • *adj* famished
înfometate • *adj* famished
înfometai • *adj* famished
informaie • *n* information
informator • *n* betrayer, ear
infracional • *adj* criminal
infraciune • *n* crime, infringement, transgression
infractoare • *n* criminal
infractor • *n* criminal
înfrâna • *v* bridle, restrain
înfrânge • *v* defeat
infraroie • *adj* infrared
infraroii • *adj* infrared
infrarou • *adj* infrared
infrasonic • *adj* infrasonic
infrastructur • *n* infrastructure
înfri • *v* brother, fraternize
înfricoare • *n* horrible
înfrigurare • *n* restlessness
înfrigurat • *adj* cold
infructuos • *adj* unfruitful
înfrumusea • *v* adorn, ornament
înfrumuseare • *n* decoration
înfrunta • *v* beard, cope, face
înfuleca • *v* gorge
înfumurat • *adj* conceited
înfunda • *v* clog, obstruct, stuff
ínfuria • *v* enrage
înfuria • *v* ire
infuzare • *n* infusion
infuzie • *n* infusion
îngdui • *v* allow
îngduin • *n* leniency
îngduire • *n* indulgence
îngduitor • *adj* gracious, lenient
înglbeni • *v* yellow
îngâmfare • *n* pride, vanity
îngândurat • *adj* absorbed
ingenios • *n* engineer • *adj* ingenious
îngenunchea • *v* kneel
înger • *n* angel
îngeresc • *adj* angelic
înghesui • *v* cram, stuff
înghea • *v* freeze, ice
îngheat • *adj* frozen
îngheat • *n* ice
înghii • *v* swallow
înghiitur • *n* bite, draught
inginer • *n* engineer
inginer • *n* engineer
inginerie • *n* engineering
îngrdi • *v* restrain
îngra • *v* fatten
îngrmânt • *n* fertilizer
îngrtoare • *n* butterwort
ingredient • *n* ingredient
îngreoa • *v* disgust
îngreuna • *v* weight
îngriji • *v* care, treat
îngrijora • *v* concern, eat
îngrijorare • *n* bother, concern
îngrijorat • *adj* anxious, concerned, worried
îngropa • *v* bury
îngropare • *n* burial, funeral
îngrozi • *v* horrify
îngrozit • *adj* aghast
îngrozitor • *adj* awful, horrible, terrible
îngust • *adj* narrow
îngusta • *v* narrow
inhala • *v* inhale
inhalare • *n* inhalation

inhiba • *v* inhibit
inhibare • *n* inhibition
inhibiie • *n* inhibition
inhibitor • *n* inhibitor
înhumare • *n* burial, funeral, interment
inim • *n* guts, heart
inimaginabil • *adj* unimaginable, unthinkable
inimiciie • *n* enmity
iniiativ • *n* initiative
iniiator • *n* originator
iniiere • *n* beginning
injectabil • *n* injectable
înjosire • *n* abasement, degradation, humiliation
înjuga • *v* yoke
înjunghia • *v* stab
înjura • *v* curse, swear
înjurtur • *n* profanity
injurie • *n* insult
injust • *adj* unrighteous
înlcrimat • *adj* tearful
înlocui • *v* change, replace, spell, substitute
înlocuitor • *n* substitute
înmagazina • *v* warehouse
înmagazinare • *n* storage
înmatriculare • *n* matriculation
înmiresmat • *adj* sweet
înmormântare • *n* burial, funeral, interment
înmuguri • *v* burgeon
înmuia • *v* soften
înmuli • *v* multiply
înmulire • *n* multiplication
înmulit • *n* multiplicand, multiplier
înnmoli • *v* mud
înnebunit • *adj* crazy
înnebunitor • *adj* insane
înnegri • *v* blacken
înnegura • *v* cloud, fog
înnoda • *v* knot
înnoi • *v* renew
înnoptare • *n* nightfall
înnora • *v* cloud
înnorat • *adj* cloudy
inocent • *adj* blameless, innocent
inocent • *adj* blameless
inoportun • *adj* inappropriate, inopportune
înot • *n* swimming
înota • *v* swim
înrdcina • *v* inculcate
înrma • *v* frame
înrâuri • *v* influence
înrautit • *adj* impaired
înregistra • *v* register
înregistrare • *n* logging, register
înregistrat • *adj* registered
înrobi • *v* enslave
înrolare • *n* draft
înroi • *v* blush
înroire • *n* blush
înrudire • *n* connection, kinship, relationship
insa • *conj* although
insalubru • *adj* noisome
însmâna • *v* fertilize
însmânare • *n* insemination
însângera • *v* blood
însrcinare • *n* mission
însrcinat • *adj* pregnant
insatisfacie • *n* dissatisfaction
înscenare • *n* production
inscrutabil • *adj* inscrutable
insect • *n* insect
insecticid • *n* insecticide
insectivor • *adj* insectivorous
înela • *v* beguile, deceive, delude, gull, swindle, trick
însemna • *v* brand, mean
însemntate • *n* importance
insensibil • *adj* hardhearted, impervious, pococurante
însera • *v* dusk
înserare • *n* night, nightfall
insidios • *adj* insidious
insign • *n* badge
insipid • *adj* insipid
insolen • *n* effrontery, insolence, nerve
insolit • *adj* unusual
insomnie • *n* insomnia
însori • *v* sun
însorit • *adj* sunny
însoi • *v* accompany
înspimânta • *v* frighten, terrify
înspimânttor • *adj* terrible
inspectare • *n* inspection
inspecie • *n* check
inspecionare • *n* inspection
inspira • *v* inhale, inspire
inspiraie • *n* aspiration, inspiration
înspre • *prep* at
instabil • *adj* infirm, uncertain, unstable
instabili • *adj* uncertain
instabilitate • *n* disequilibrium
instalare • *n* establishment, installation
instalaie • *n* installation
instant • *n* instant
instan • *n* instance
instantaneu • *adj* instantaneous • *adv* suddenly
înstelat • *adj* starry
întiinare • *n* notice

instituire • *n* establishment
institut • *n* college, institute
instituie • *n* establishment, institution
instruciune • *n* instruction, statement
instruciuni • *n* statement
instructor • *n* instructor
instrui • *v* educate, school, teach
instruire • *n* cultivation, instruction, learning, literacy, schooling
instrument • *n* instrument, tool
instrumental • *adj* instrumental
insuficient • *adj* insufficient
insuficien • *n* deficiency
însuflei • *v* animate, encourage, move
însufleire • *n* animation, liveliness
insul • *n* island
insulin • *n* insulin
insulta • *v* insult
insult • *n* insult
insulttor • *adj* insulting
insuportabil • *adj* insufferable, obnoxious, unbearable
însura • *v* marry, wed
insurmontabil • *adj* insurmountable
înuruba • *v* screw
înurubare • *n* screw
însui • *v* steal
însuire • *n* property
intact • *adj* sound
întâlni • *v* encounter, meet
întâlnire • *n* date, match
întâmpina • *v* greet, welcome
întâmpla • *v* happen
întâmplare • *n* chance, hazard, instance, occasion, occurrence
întâmpltor • *adj* accidental, fortuitous
intangibil • *adj* intangible
întri • *v* enforce, set, stiffen
întârzia • *v* delay, obstruct, stay
întârziat • *adj* deferred
întârziat • *adj* deferred
întârziere • *n* delay, lateness
integra • *v* integrate
integral • *adj* integral
integral • *n* integral
integrare • *n* integration
integrat • *adj* integrated
integritate • *n* integrity
intelect • *n* brain, intellect
intelectual • *n* intellect, intellectual, thinker • *adj* intellectual
intelectual • *n* intellect, intellectual
înelege • *v* comprehend, fathom, perceive, understand
înelegere • *n* accord, apprehension
înelepciune • *n* wisdom
înelept • *adj* sage, wise
inteligent • *adj* intelligent, sensible
inteligen • *n* intelligence
inteligibil • *adj* intelligible
întemeiere • *n* foundation
întemeietor • *n* founder
întemnia • *v* imprison
întemniare • *n* imprisonment
intemperii • *n* weather
intens • *adj* intense
intensitate • *n* intensity
intenie • *n* aim, intention
intenionat • *adv* intentionally
înepa • *v* bite, sting
interacionare • *n* interaction
interaciune • *n* interaction
interastral • *adj* interstellar
intercalare • *n* intercalation
interconectare • *n* interconnection
interconexiune • *n* interconnection
interdisciplinar • *adj* interdisciplinary
interes • *n* interest
interesa • *v* interest
interesant • *adj* interesting
interesat • *adj* interested
intergalactic • *adj* intergalactic
intergalactic • *adj* intergalactic
interior • *adj* interior
intermediar • *n* intermediary
interminabil • *adj* endless, interminable • *adv* everlasting
intermolecular • *adj* intermolecular
intern • *adj* interior
internaional • *adj* international
interplanetar • *adj* interplanetary
interpret • *n* interpreter, player, translator
interpret • *n* interpreter
interpretare • *n* interpretation
interpretor • *n* interpreter
intersectare • *n* intersection
intersecie • *n* crossroads, intersection
interstelar • *adj* interstellar
interval • *n* interval, spell, window
intervertebral • *adj* intervertebral
intervieva • *v* interview
interviu • *n* interview
interviuri • *n* interview
interzice • *v* ban, forbid, prohibit, proscribe
interzis • *adj* forbidden
înesat • *adj* crowded
intestin • *n* intestine
intestinal • *adj* enteric
intestine • *n* intestine
intim • *adj* intimate
intimida • *v* bully
intimitate • *n* familiarity, intimacy

întinde • *v* reach, spread, stretch
întindere • *n* extension, extent
întipri • *v* brand
întoarce • *v* flip, return, reverse
întocmai • *adv* just
intoleran • *n* intolerance
intonare • *n* read
intonaie • *n* accent
întortochea • *v* twist
întotdeauna • *adv* always
intoxica • *v* intoxicate, poison
intoxicat • *adj* intoxicated
intoxicaie • *n* intoxication
într-adevr • *adv* indeed
intra • *v* enter
intracranial • *adj* intracranial
intransitiv • *adj* intransitive
intrare • *n* entrance
între • *prep* among, between, betwixt
întreba • *v* ask, question
întrebare • *n* question
întrebuinare • *n* use
întrebuinat • *adj* used
întrece • *v* overtake, surpass
întrecere • *n* contest
întreg • *adj* entire, full, single, whole • *n* integer, whole
întreprinde • *v* undertake
întreprindere • *n* business, company, concern, establishment
întreprinztor • *n* entrepreneur
întreruptor • *n* switch
întrerupe • *v* interrupt, suspend
întrerupere • *n* interruption
întreine • *v* preserve
întrista • *v* sadden
întristare • *n* darkness, grief, sorrow
introduce • *v* enter, set
introducere • *n* introduction
introductiv • *adj* preliminary
întrucâtva • *adv* somewhat
întrunire • *n* convention
întuneca • *v* cloud, darken, obfuscate, obscure
întunecat • *adj* dark, tenebrous
întunecime • *n* darkness
întunecos • *adj* obscure
întuneric • *n* dark, darkness, night
inunda • *v* flood
inundare • *n* inundation
inundaie • *n* flood, inundation
inutil • *adj* unnecessary, useless, waste
invadator • *n* invader
invalidare • *n* annulment
învlmeal • *n* stampede
învpiat • *adj* quick
invariabil • *adj* invariable, invariant
invariabil • *adj* invariable
invariant • *n* invariant
învârti • *v* brandish, spin, turn, twist
învârtire • *n* crank
înva • *v* learn, school, study, teach
învcel • *n* learner
învmânt • *n* education, instruction
învare • *n* instruction, learning
învat • *adj* learned
învtor • *n* pedagogue, teacher
învtur • *n* instruction, learning, schooling
învechit • *adj* antic, archaic, old-fashioned, ossified
înveli • *n* envelope, integument
învelitur • *n* envelope
învenina • *v* poison
inventa • *v* contrive, invent
inventar • *n* bill
invenial • *adj* inventive
invenie • *n* invention
invenii • *n* invention
inventiv • *adj* creative, inventive
inventivitate • *n* inventiveness
invers • *adj* reciprocal, reverse
invers • *adj* reverse
inversa • *v* reverse
invertor • *n* inverter
investigator • *n* investigator
invidia • *v* envy
invidie • *n* envy
invidios • *adj* envious
înviere • *n* resurrection
învingtoare • *n* victor
învingtor • *n* victor
învingtori • *n* victor
învinge • *v* conquer, defeat, triumph
învinovi • *v* blame
învinui • *v* blame
înviora • *v* enliven
invita • *v* ask, invite
invizibil • *adj* invisible
invizibilitate • *n* invisibility
involucru • *n* involucre
înzpezit • *adj* snowy
iobag • *n* serf, villain
ioc • *n* zilch
iod • *n* iodine
ionizare • *n* ionization
ionizaie • *n* ionization
ionosfer • *n* ionosphere
iota • *n* iota
iot • *n* ace, whit
ipocrit • *n* hypocrite • *adj* hypocritical
ipocrit • *n* hypocrite
ipocrizie • *n* hypocrisy
ipotec • *n* mortgage
ipotenuz • *n* hypotenuse

ipotetic • *adj* hypothetical
ipotez • *n* conjecture, hypothesis
iradia • *v* glow, radiate
iradiere • *n* radiance
irascibil • *adj* irascible
irascibilitate • *n* bile
iraional • *adj* absurd, irrational
irealist • *adj* unrealistic
iredent • *adj* irredentist
iredentist • *n* irredentist • *adj* irredentist
iredentist • *n* irredentist
iregular • *adj* irregular
iregularitate • *n* irregularity
irelevant • *adj* irrelevant
irelevan • *n* impertinence, irrelevance
iremediabil • *adj* irredeemable
ireproabil • *adj* irreproachable
irezistibil • *adj* irresistible
iridiu • *n* iridium
iriga • *v* water
iris • *n* flag, iris
irita • *v* irritate, roil
iritabil • *adj* cantankerous, irritable, prickly
iritare • *n* irritation
iritaie • *n* irritation
ironic • *adj* ironic
ironie • *n* irony
irosi • *v* waste
irosire • *n* waste
iscusin • *n* ability, dexterity
iscusit • *adj* ingenious
isop • *n* hyssop
ispire • *n* atonement
ispiti • *v* tempt
isterie • *n* hysteria
iste • *adj* smart
istm • *n* isthmus
istoric • *adj* historic, historical
istoric • *adj* historical
istoricete • *adv* historically
istorici • *adj* historical
istorie • *n* history, story
istovit • *adj* emaciated, exhausted, haggard
iubire • *n* baby, love
iubit • *n* beloved, darling, flame, friend, honey, love, lover, sweetheart • *adj* beloved, darling, loved, tender
iubit • *n* beloved, darling, flame, honey, love, lover, sweetheart • *adj* beloved
iubito • *n* baby
iubitul • *n* beau
iubitule • *n* baby
iud • *n* betrayer
iut • *n* jute
iute • *adj* fast, hot, quick
iueal • *n* speed
iuitor • *n* accelerator
ivire • *n* apparition, appearance
ivoriu • *n* ivory
izbitura • *n* butt
izmene • *n* underwear
izola • *v* isolate
izolare • *n* insulation, separation
izolat • *adj* isolated
izolaie • *n* insulation
izolator • *n* insulator
izoleucin • *n* isoleucine
izotop • *n* isotope
izvor • *n* source, spring

J

jad • *n* jade
jaguar • *n* jaguar
jais • *n* jet
jale • *n* sage
jalnic • *adj* lame
jandarm • *n* gendarme
jandarmi • *n* gendarme
jargon • *n* jargon, language, slang
jasmin • *n* jasmine
jasp • *n* jasper
jder • *n* marten
jder-pescresc • *n* fisher
jecmni • *v* pluck
jefui • *v* pluck
jeleu • *n* jelly
jelui • *v* bemoan, bewail
jen • *n* abashment, discomfiture, displeasure, embarrassment
jerboa • *n* jerboa
jertf • *n* sacrifice, victim
jertfi • *v* sacrifice
jet • *n* jet
jgheab • *n* gutter
jiclor • *n* jet
jidan • *n* kike
jidov • *n* kike
jigni • *v* humiliate, insult
jignire • *n* insult
jigodie • *n* mange
jihad • *n* jihad
jiletc • *n* waistcoat
jivin • *n* animal

jneapn • *n* juniper
joc • *n* game, match, play
jocheu • *n* jockey
jonciune • *n* connection, junction
jos • *adv* down • *adj* low
josnicie • *n* vileness
joule • *n* joule
jovialitate • *n* joy
jubila • *v* gloat
juca • *v* dance, play
jucrie • *n* toy
juctoare • *n* player
juctor • *n* player
juctori • *n* player
judeca • *v* judge, think, try
judecare • *n* judgment
judecat • *n* intelligence, judgment, mind, trial, wisdom
judector • *n* judge, justice
judet • *n* shire
jude • *n* county, district
judo • *n* judo
jug • *n* yoke
juisare • *n* delight
julitur • *n* bruise
jumtate • *n* half
jumuli • *v* pluck
jumulire • *n* pluck
junc • *n* bullock
junc • *n* heifer
june • *adj* young
jungher • *n* dagger
jungl • *n* jungle
junimea • *n* youth
juninc • *n* heifer
jupân • *n* master
jupui • *v* strip
jur • *n* surroundings
jura • *v* swear
jurmânt • *n* oath, profession, vow
juridic • *adj* juridical, legal
jurisdicie • *n* jurisdiction
juriu • *n* jury
jurnalism • *n* journalism
justee • *n* justice
justificare • *n* justification
justificaie • *n* justification
justiie • *n* justice

K

kaki • *n* khaki • *adj* khaki
kaliu • *n* potassium
karibu • *n* caribou
kava • *n* kava
kelvin • *n* kelvin
kilobyte • *n* kilobyte
kilogram • *n* kilogram
kilogram-metru • *n* kilogram-meter
kilooctet • *n* kilobyte
kinkaju • *n* kinkajou
kiwi • *n* kiwi
koala • *n* koala
kob • *n* kob
kompot • *n* compote
kripton • *n* krypton
kudu • *n* kudu
kumquat • *n* kumquat

L

la • *prep* at, to
lab • *n* paw
labie • *n* labium
labirint • *n* labyrinth
laborator • *n* laboratory
laborios • *adj* hardworking, industrious
lac • *n* finish, lacquer, lake
lact • *n* lock, padlock
lacom • *adj* edacious
lcomie • *n* avidity, gluttony, greed
laconic • *adj* laconic
lacrim • *n* tear, teardrop
lcrima • *v* tear, weep
lcrimos • *adj* lachrymose
lactate • *n* dairy
lcust • *n* grasshopper, locust
lad • *n* case
lady • *n* lady
lalea • *n* tulip
lama • *n* lama
lam • *n* blade, llama, slide
lmâi • *n* lemon
lmâie • *n* lemon
lmâioar • *n* thyme
lamantin • *n* manatee
lamenta • *v* lament

lamentabil • *adj* deplorable, ghastly
lamentare • *n* lamentation
lamentaie • *n* lamentation
lamin • *n* lamina
laminaria • *n* kelp
lamp • *n* lamp
lmpi • *n* lamp
lmuri • *v* enlighten, solve
lân • *n* fleece, wool
lance • *n* lance, spear
lânced • *adj* feeble, languid, weak
lncier • *n* lance
lâng • *prep* about, beside, by
langoare • *n* languor
lânos • *adj* woolly
lan • *n* chain, stream
lantan • *n* lanthanum
lantern • *n* flashlight, lantern, torch
laolalt • *adv* together
lapovi • *n* sleet
lapovia • *v* sleet
lptar • *n* milkman
laptop • *n* laptop
lptos • *adj* milky
lptuc • *n* lettuce
lard • *n* bacon
larg • *adj* wide
lrgi • *v* widen
lrgime • *n* width
larice • *n* larch
laringe • *n* larynx
larm • *n* noise, uproar
larv • *n* larva, maggot
la • *n* coward • *adj* cowardly, yellow • *adv* cowardly
la • *n* coward
lsa • *v* allow, forsake, let
lasciv • *adj* lascivious, lewd, prurient
lascivitate • *n* prurience
laser • *n* laser
laitate • *n* cowardice
lsnicior • *n* bittersweet
lstun • *n* martin, swallow
la • *n* noose, snare
lat • *adj* wide
laten • *n* latency
latex • *n* latex
latice • *n* lattice
lime • *n* width
latitudine • *n* latitude, line
ltra • *v* bark, woof
ltrat • *n* bark
latrin • *n* latrine
latur • *n* flank, hand, side
laud • *n* praise
luda • *v* laud, praise
ludabil • *adj* commendable
ludare • *n* commendation
ludroenie • *n* swagger
laudativ • *adj* complimentary
laur • *n* holly, laurel
lut • *n* lute
lav • *n* lava
lavand • *n* lavender
lawrenciu • *n* lawrencium
leaf • *n* wage
leagn • *n* cradle
leandru • *n* oleander
leapa • *n* tag
lebd • *n* swan
lectic • *n* litter
lecie • *n* lesson
lectura • *v* read
lecturare • *n* read
lega • *v* bind, connect, tie
legal • *adj* lawful, legal • *adv* legally
legalitate • *n* legality
legmânt • *n* covenant, oath, pledge, profession, promise
legna • *v* dangle, rock, swing
legare • *n* binding, conjunction, connection, ligature
legat • *adj* connected
legatura • *n* bund
legtur • *n* bond, bundle, communication, connection, contact, ligature, link, relation, relationship, sheaf
lege • *n* law
legend • *n* key, legend, myth
legendar • *adj* fabled, fabulous, legendary, mythological
legendar • *adj* legendary, mythological
leghe • *n* league
legislativ • *adj* legislative
legislator • *n* legislator
legitimitate • *n* legitimacy
legiuitor • *n* legislator
legiune • *n* legion
legum • *n* cabbage, vegetable
legume • *n* vegetable
leguminoas • *n* legume • *adj* leguminous
leming • *n* lemming
lemn-câinesc • *n* privet
lemnar • *n* carpenter
lemnos • *adj* wooden
lemnul-Domnului • *n* southernwood
lemur • *n* lemur
lene • *n* sloth
lene • *adj* lazy • *n* player, sloth
lenevi • *v* linger
lenjerie • *n* linen
lentil • *n* lens
lentoare • *n* slowness
leoaic • *n* lioness

leopard • *n* leopard
lepda • *v* abandon, forsake, renounce
lesbi • *n* lesbian
lesbian • *n* lesbian
leie • *n* lye
lespede • *n* flag
lest • *n* ballast
letal • *adj* deadly
letargic • *adj* supine
letargie • *n* lethargy
leu • *n* leu, lion
leucemie • *n* leukemia
leucin • *n* leucine
leutean • *n* lovage
levnic • *n* lavender
levur • *n* yeast
lexem • *n* lexeme
lexic • *n* vocabulary
lexicon • *n* lexicon
leziune • *n* lesion, wound
lian • *n* liana
libarc • *n* cockroach
libelul • *n* dragonfly
liber • *adj* clear, free, independent • *v* empty
liberal • *adj* liberal
libertate • *n* freedom, liberty
libidinos • *adj* libidinous, prurient
librar • *n* bookseller
librrie • *n* bookshop
licr • *n* flicker
licri • *v* flicker
licrire • *n* flicker
lichen • *n* lichen
lichid • *n* liquid • *adj* liquid
lichid • *adj* liquid
lichiditate • *n* liquidity
lichior • *n* liquor
lichioruri • *n* liquor
licurici • *n* firefly, glowworm
lider • *n* head, leader
lie-de-vin • *adj* damask
lift • *n* lift
lig • *n* league
ligament • *n* tendon
ligatur • *n* ligature
lila • *adj* lilac
liliac • *n* bat, lilac
liliachiu • *adj* lavender, lilac, mauve
lilie • *n* lily
liman • *n* coast
limax • *n* slug
limb • *n* clapper, hand, language, tongue
limba-cucului • *n* cowslip, moonwort
limb-de-mare • *n* sole
limba-mielului • *n* borage
limbaj • *n* language
limbut • *adj* garrulous, loquacious, talkative • *n* telltale
limet • *n* lime
limfocit • *n* lymphocyte
limfocit • *n* lymphocyte
limit • *n* boundary, coast, limit, term
limita • *v* limit
limitat • *adj* finite, limited
limpede • *adj* clear, cloudless, limpid, obvious, transparent
limuzin • *n* limousine
lin • *adj* smooth
linari • *n* toadflax
lindic • *n* clitoris
lindin • *n* nit
linge • *v* lick
lingou • *n* ingot
lingur • *n* spoon
linguri • *n* teaspoon
lingui • *v* fawn
lingvistic • *adj* linguistic
lingvistic • *n* linguistics
linie • *n* line, measure, row, ruler
linite • *n* calm, calmness, ease, equanimity, peace, silence
linite! • *interj* silence
liniti • *v* calm, ease, soothe, still
linitit • *adj* calm, composed
linititor • *adj* bland
liniu • *n* hyphen
linte • *n* lens, lentil
linti • *n* duckweed
linx • *n* lynx
lipi • *v* paste, stick
lipici • *n* glue
lipicios • *adj* gluey, sticky
lipitoare • *n* leech
lips • *n* deficiency, lack, want
lipsit • *adj* destitute
lir • *n* pound
lis • *adj* smooth
lii • *n* coot, teal
list • *n* list
litera • *v* spell
liter • *n* letter
literal • *adj* literal
literally • *adj* literal
literalmente • *adv* literally
literar • *adj* literary
literar • *adj* literary
literari • *adj* literary
literatur • *n* literature
litier • *n* litter
litiu • *n* lithium
litorin • *n* periwinkle
liturghie • *n* liturgy
livad • *n* meadow, orchard

livr • *n* pound
livra • *v* deliver, distribute
livrare • *n* delivery
livrea • *n* livery
lizibil • *adj* legible
lizin • *n* lysine
lob • *n* lobe
loba • *v* lob
lobelie • *n* lobelia
loc • *n* locus, place, room
local • *adj* local
local • *adj* local
localitate • *n* locus
localizare • *n* localization, situation
localnic • *adj* native
localnic • *adj* native
locaiune • *n* rent
locomotiv • *n* engine
lociitor • *n* substitute
locui • *v* live
locuibil • *adj* habitable
locuitoare • *n* inhabitant
locuitor • *n* inhabitant
locuri • *n* locus
logaritm • *n* logarithm
logaritm • *n* logarithm
logic • *adj* logical, sensible
logic • *n* logic • *adj* logical
logistica • *n* logistics
logodi • *v* betroth
logodire • *n* engagement
logodn • *n* betrothal, engagement
logogram • *n* logogram
logogrif • *n* logogriph
loial • *adj* true
loialitate • *n* loyalty
loj • *n* box, lodge
longitudine • *n* line, longitude
lonjeron • *n* balk
lopat • *n* shovel, spade
lot • *n* parcel
loterie • *n* lottery
loiune • *n* lotion
lotus • *n* lotus
lovi • *v* hit, kick
lovitur • *n* blow, hit
lua • *v* take
lubeni • *n* watermelon
lubrifia • *v* lubricate
lubrifiant • *n* lubricant
lucarn • *n* skylight
luceafr • *n* paragon
lucern • *n* alfalfa
luci • *v* shine
luciditate • *n* lucidity
lucios • *adj* shining
lucire • *n* radiance
lucitor • *adj* ablaze
luciu • *n* shine
lucra • *v* net, work
lucrare • *n* work
lucrativ • *adj* lucrative
lucrtoare • *n* worker
lucrtor • *n* worker
lucru • *n* object, thing
lufar • *n* tailor
lufta • *v* scuff
lugubru • *adj* lugubrious
lumânare • *n* candle
lumânric • *n* mullein
lume • *n* people, world
lumina • *v* illuminate, light, shine
lumin • *n* light
luminiscen • *n* luminescence
luminos • *adj* bright, luminous
luminozitate • *n* luminosity
lun • *n* month, moon
lunar • *adj* lunar • *adv* monthly
lunar • *adj* lunar
lunet • *n* telescope
lung • *adj* long
lungi • *v* elongate, lengthen, prolong, reach
lungime • *n* length
luntre • *n* boat
lup • *n* wolf
lupan • *n* whelp
lupanar • *n* brothel
lupesc • *adj* lupine
lupoaic • *n* bitch
lupt • *n* combat, fight, wrestling
lupta • *v* fight, struggle
lupttoare • *n* fighter
lupttor • *n* fighter, warrior, wrestler
lupus • *n* lupus
lustru • *n* luster, shine
lustrui • *v* shine
lut • *n* clay
luteiu • *n* lutetium
lutr • *n* otter
luxur • *n* lust
luxuriant • *adj* lush, verdant
luxurios • *adj* luxurious

M

m • *pron* me
mac • *n* poppy, quack
mac-mac • *n* quack
macac • *n* macaque
mci • *v* quack
mcit • *n* quack
mcitur • *n* quack
mcleandru • *n* robin
mcnit • *n* quack
macara • *n* crane
mcel • *n* slaughter
mcelar • *n* butcher
mcelri • *v* butcher, slaughter
mcelrie • *n* abattoir
machiaj • *n* makeup
mcina • *v* crush, grind, mill
mciuc • *n* bat
mcri • *n* sorrel
macrocosm • *n* macrocosm
macrocosmos • *n* macrocosm
macromolecul • *n* macromolecule
macromolecular • *adj* macromolecular
macroscopic • *adj* macroscopic
macrospor • *n* megaspore
macrou • *n* mackerel
mdular • *n* limb, member
mduv • *n* marrow
maestru • *n* master
mag • *n* wizard
mgar • *n* ass, donkey
magazie • *n* storage, store, warehouse
magazin • *n* shop
magic • *adj* magic, magical
magician • *n* magician, wizard
magie • *n* enchantment, magic
magistral • *n* bus
magnet • *n* magnet
magnetic • *adj* magnetic
magnetism • *n* magnetism
magnetizare • *n* magnetization
magnetizaie • *n* magnetization
magneziu • *n* magnesium
magnific • *adj* gorgeous
magnificen • *n* brilliance
magnitudine • *n* magnitude
magnolie • *n* magnolia
mguli • *v* fawn
mgulitor • *adj* complimentary
mahmureal • *n* hangover
mâhni • *v* sadden
mâhnire • *n* despondency, grief, sorrow, woe
mahon • *n* mahogany
mahon • *n* barge
mai • *n* liver, mallet
maic • *n* mother
micu • *n* mum, mummy
maiestate • *n* majesty
maimu • *n* ape, monkey
maimuri • *v* ape
mâine • *n* tomorrow • *adv* tomorrow
maionez • *n* mayonnaise
maior • *n* major
maiori • *n* major
maiou • *n* singlet
majorat • *n* age, majority
majoreta • *n* cheerleader
majoritate • *n* majority
mal • *n* coast, shore
mala • *n* hawk
maladie • *n* disease, sickness
malahian • *n* masturbator
malahist • *n* masturbator
malahit • *n* malachite
mlai • *n* dough
malaxor • *n* blender
maldr • *n* crowd
maleabil • *adj* compliant, malleable
maleabilitate • *n* malleability
maledicie • *n* curse
maliie • *n* malice
malitios • *adj* malicious, spiteful
maliiozitate • *n* malice
maltrata • *v* spite
mam • *n* mother, mummy
mamaie • *n* grandmother
mamalogie • *n* mammalogy
mamelon • *n* tit
mmic • *n* mum, mummy
mamifer • *n* mammal
mamut • *n* mammoth
man • *n* manna
mâna • *v* drive
mân • *n* hand
mnstire • *n* cloister, monastery
mânstire • *n* monastery
mânca • *v* eat
mâncabil • *adj* consumable, edible
mâncare • *n* food
mâncrime • *n* itch
mânctor • *n* eater
mandarin • *n* mandarin
mandibul • *n* jaw
mandibule • *n* jaw
mandol • *n* mandola
mandolin • *n* mandolin
mandragor • *n* mandrake
mândrie • *n* arrogance, greatness, pride, vanity
mandril • *n* mandrill
mandrin • *n* chuck
mândru • *adj* haughty
mânec • *n* sleeve
manechin • *n* mannequin

mâner • *n* handlebar
manevra • *v* maneuver
manevrabil • *adj* maneuverable
mângâia • *v* caress, fondle, pet, stroke
mangl • *n* mangle
manglui • *v* mangle
mangan • *n* manganese
mango • *n* mango
mangold • *n* chard
mangust • *n* mongoose
mangustan • *n* mangosteen
mânia • *v* ire
maniabil • *adj* manageable
maniac • *n* crank
mânie • *n* anger, choler, fury, ire, mania, outrage, rage, wrath
manier • *n* current, manner
manierat • *adj* well-behaved
manifest • *adj* apparent
manifesta • *v* work
manifestare • *n* manifestation
manifestaie • *n* manifestation
mânios • *adj* angry
manipula • *v* manipulate, massage
manipulator • *n* key • *adj* manipulative
manivel • *n* crank
mânji • *v* sully, taint
mansard • *n* attic
manta • *n* mantle
mantie • *n* mantle
manual • *n* manual, textbook • *adj* manual
mânuibil • *adj* manageable
mnunchi • *n* bunch, bundle, handful, sheaf
mnu • *n* glove
manuscris • *n* manuscript
mânz • *n* colt, foal
mânz • *n* filly, foal
mr • *n* apple
marabu • *n* marabou
mrcinar • *n* stonechat
mrcine • *n* briar
maranta • *n* arrowroot
mrar • *n* dill
maraton • *n* marathon
maratonist • *n* marathoner
marc • *n* brand, mark, trademark
marca • *v* brand, flag
marcaj • *n* note
mare • *adj* bulky, great, high, large, sensible • *n* sea
maree • *n* tide
mre • *adj* imposing
mreie • *n* brilliance, greatness, majesty
marf • *n* commodity, goods, merchandise
margaret • *n* daisy
margarin • *n* margarine
mrgritar • *n* pearl
margine • *n* border, edge, limit
mrginit • *adj* limited
mri • *v* expand, increase, magnify
marijuana • *n* marijuana
marimba • *n* marimba
mrime • *n* extent, greatness, magnitude, measurement
marin • *adj* marine, navy
marin • *n* navy
marinar • *n* sailor, seaman
mrinimos • *adj* generous
marionet • *n* marionette, puppet
mrire • *n* greatness, increase, power
mrita • *v* marry, wed
mrit-m-mam • *n* coneflower
maritim • *adj* marine, navy
mritor • *adj* augmentative
marmelad • *n* jam, jelly, marmalade
marmot • *n* marmot
marmur • *n* marble
maro • *n* brown, maroon • *adj* brown, maroon
mrlui • *v* march
mrui • *v* march
marsuin • *n* porpoise
marsupial • *n* marsupial • *adj* marsupial
maripan • *n* marzipan
martir • *n* martyr
martiriza • *v* martyr
martor • *n* witness
mrturie • *n* testimony
mrturisi • *v* avow, confess, depose
mrturisire • *n* confession
mrunt • *adj* minute, petty, trifling
mruntaie • *n* guts, pluck
mas • *n* aggregate, banquet, holocaust, mass, meal, table, weight
masa • *n* bulk • *v* massage
masaj • *n* massage
masare • *n* massage
masc • *n* mask
masca • *v* disguise, mask
mascara • *n* mascara
mascare • *n* disguise
mascul • *n* male, tom • *adj* male
masculin • *adj* male, manly, masculine
masculinitate • *n* masculinity
masculinizare • *n* masculinization
mascur • *n* boar
mselari • *n* henbane
maseur • *n* masseur
maseuz • *n* masseur
main • *n* automobile, car, machine
mainist • *n* machinist
masiv • *adj* bulk, solid

mslin • *n* olive
mater • *n* stepmother
mastodont • *n* mastodon
masturbare • *n* masturbation
masturbaie • *n* masturbation
masturbator • *n* masturbator
msura • *v* fathom, measure
msur • *n* amount, measure, measurement, scoop
msurabil • *adj* measurable
msurare • *n* measure, measurement
msurtoare • *n* measurement
ma • *n* intestine
mâ • *n* cat
mthlos • *adj* bulky
mtnii • *n* rosary
mtase • *n* silk
matc • *n* womb
mae • *n* entrails, guts
matelot • *n* sailor
matematic • *adj* mathematical
matematic • *adj* mathematical • *n* mathematics
material • *n* material, matter • *adj* material, physical
material • *adj* material
materialism • *n* materialism
materialist • *n* materialist • *adj* materialistic
materialist • *n* materialist
materie • *n* material, matter, science, subject
matern • *adj* maternal, native
matinal • *adj* matutinal
mâior • *n* catkin
mtrea • *n* dandruff
matrice • *n* matrix
matricid • *n* matricide
matroz • *n* sailor
matur • *adj* mature, ripe
mtura • *v* brush, sweep
mtur • *n* broom
maturitate • *n* discretion, maturity
mtu • *n* aunt
maus • *n* mouse
mausoleu • *n* mausoleum
maxilar • *n* jaw
maxim • *n* maxim
maximal • *adj* maximal
maxime • *n* maxim
maximum • *n* maximum
mazre • *n* pea
mzriche • *n* vetch
meandr • *n* wimple
mecanic • *n* engineer, mechanic • *adj* mechanical
mecanism • *n* mechanism
meci • *n* match
medalie • *n* award, medal
medalion • *n* medallion
media • *v* mediate
mediator • *n* mediator
medic • *n* doctor
medicament • *n* medicine
medicaie • *n* medication
medicin • *n* medicine
medicinal • *adj* medicinal
medie • *n* average, mean
mediere • *n* mediation
mediocr • *adj* mediocre, moderate
mediocru • *adj* mediocre, moderate
mediu • *adj* average, mean, medium, middle, moderate • *n* environment, mean, medium, society
medium • *n* medium
meduz • *n* jellyfish
mefia • *v* distrust
megabyte • *n* megabyte
megaloman • *adj* megalomaniacal
megalomanie • *n* megalomania
megaoctet • *n* megabyte
megaspor • *n* megaspore
meger • *n* shrew
mei • *n* millet
melancolic • *adj* melancholy
melancolie • *n* despondency, melancholy
melanj • *n* melange
melc • *n* slug, snail
meleu • *n* scrum
melodic • *adj* melodic
melodie • *n* melody, music
melodios • *adj* melodic, melodious, sweet
melodram • *n* melodrama
melodramatic • *adj* melodramatic
mem • *n* meme
membran • *n* diaphragm, membrane
membrane • *n* membrane
membru • *n* appendage, limb, member
memorabil • *adj* eventful, memorable
memorare • *n* retention, storage
memorie • *n* memory, mind, remembrance, retention
memoriza • *v* memorize
menajerie • *n* menagerie
mendeleviu • *n* mendelevium
menestrel • *n* minstrel
menhir • *n* menhir
meniu • *n* menu
mensual • *adv* monthly
ment • *n* mint
mental • *adj* mental
menuet • *n* minuet
mercur • *n* mercury, quicksilver
mereu • *adv* always

merge • *v* go, walk
meridian • *n* meridian
meridional • *adj* meridional
merior • *n* cranberry, lingonberry
merita • *v* deserve, pay
mers • *n* current, path
mersi • *interj* cheers, thanks
mesager • *n* herald
mesaj • *n* communication
meserie • *n* handicraft, profession, trade
mesteacn • *n* birch
mesteca • *v* chew, mix
meteugar • *n* craftsman
metabolism • *n* metabolism
metafor • *n* metaphor
metal • *n* metal
metaloid • *n* metalloid
metamorfoz • *n* metamorphosis
metan • *n* methane
metanfetamin • *n* methamphetamine
metanol • *n* methanol
meteor • *n* meteor
meteoric • *adj* meteoric
meticulos • *adj* meticulous, pedantic
meticulozitate • *n* meticulousness, thoroughness
metil • *n* methyl
metionin • *n* methionine
metis • *n* metis
metod • *n* method
metodic • *adj* methodical
metodologic • *adj* methodological
metodologie • *n* methodology
metonimia • *n* metonymy
metric • *adj* metric
metric • *n* prosody
metropol • *n* metropolis
metropolitan • *n* metro
metrou • *n* metro, subway
metru • *n* meter
mezin • *n* baby
mezina • *n* baby
mezofit • *n* mesophyte
mia • *n* lamb
miau • *interj* meow
mic • *adj* baby, little, small
mic • *adj* little
miceliu • *n* mycelium
mici • *adj* small
micime • *n* smallness
microb • *n* microbe
microcosm • *n* microcosm
microcosmos • *n* microcosm
microfon • *n* bug, microphone
micrometru • *n* micrometer
microorganism • *n* microorganism
microprocesor • *n* microprocessor
microscop • *n* microscope
microscopic • *adj* microscopic
microunde • *n* microwave
micsandr-de-munte • *n* wallflower
micsandr-slbatic • *n* wallflower
micora • *v* ease, reduce, shrink
micorabil • *adj* reducible
micorare • *n* diminution
micorat • *adj* reduced
micu • *adj* tiny
mied • *n* mead
miel • *n* dick, lamb
mieluel • *n* lamb
miere • *n* honey
mieriu • *n* honey • *adj* honey
mierl • *n* blackbird, redwing
mierla-neagr • *n* blackbird
mieros • *adj* sugary
mieuna • *v* meow
miez • *n* core, crumb, middle, nucleus
migdal • *n* almond
migdal • *n* almond
migdal-de-pmânt • *n* chufa
migrare • *n* migration
migraie • *n* migration
mijloc • *n* center, heart, mean, middle, milieu, waist
mijlocie • *adj* moderate
mijlociu • *adj* moderate
mil • *n* mercy, mile, pity
milan • *n* kite
mileniu • *n* millennium
miligram • *n* milligram
milisecund • *n* millisecond
militar • *adj* military • *n* soldier
miliia • *n* militia
mimoz • *n* mimosa
min • *n* mine
mina • *v* mine
mincinoas • *n* liar
mincinos • *n* liar • *adj* mendacious, untruthful
minciun • *n* lie
mine • *pron* me
miner • *n* miner
mineral • *n* mineral
minerale • *n* mineral
mineralog • *n* mineralogist
mineralogie • *n* mineralogy
minereu • *n* ore
minge • *n* ball
mîngîia • *v* grope
minimal • *adj* minimal
minimiza • *v* dwarf
minimum • *n* minimum
minister • *n* ministry, office
ministr • *n* minister

ministru • *n* minister
minoritate • *n* minority
mintal • *adj* mental • *adv* mentally
minte • *n* mind
mini • *v* lie
mînui • *v* grope
minuna • *v* amaze
minunat • *adj* great, lush, magic, swell
minunie • *n* miracle
minune • *n* miracle, wonder
minuscul • *adj* dwarf, minute, tiny
minut • *n* minute
minuios • *adj* fastidious, minute
mioar • *n* lamb
miocard • *n* myocardium
miopie • *n* myopia
miorli • *v* meow
miozotis • *n* forget-me-not
mira • *v* wonder
miracol • *n* miracle
miraculos • *adj* miraculous
miraj • *n* mirage
mirare • *n* wonder
mire • *n* bridegroom
mireas • *n* bride
miriapod • *n* millipede
miros • *n* smell
mirosi • *v* nose, smell
mirt • *n* myrtle
mica • *v* move
micabil • *adj* movable
micare • *n* motion, move, movement
mictor • *adj* impressive, moving
miel • *adj* cowardly • *n* rascal, scoundrel, villain
mielie • *n* vileness
misionar • *n* missionary
misiune • *n* commission, mission
misiuni • *n* mission
misoginie • *n* misogyny
mister • *n* mystery
misterios • *adj* mysterious
mito • *adj* lush, sweet
mistrie • *n* trowel
mistui • *v* digest
mit • *n* legend, myth
mit • *n* bribe
mitic • *adj* fabulous, legendary, mythological
mitolog • *n* mythologist
mitolog • *n* mythologist
mitologic • *adj* mythological
mitologic • *adj* mythological
mitologie • *n* mythology
mitologist • *n* mythologist
mitropolit • *n* archbishop, metropolitan
mixt • *adj* mixed
mixtur • *n* mix, mixture
miz • *n* ante
mizantropie • *n* misanthropy
mizer • *adj* poor
mizericordie • *n* mercy
mizerie • *n* dirt, gall, misery, poverty
mlatin • *n* morass, swamp
moale • *adj* soft
moar • *n* mill
moarte • *n* death
moartea • *n* death
moa • *n* midwife
moate • *n* relic
mobil • *n* cell • *adj* mobile, movable
mobil • *n* furniture
mobilizare • *n* mobilization
moca • *n* mocha
mod • *n* manner, way
modalitate • *n* modality
model • *n* pattern, template
modela • *v* shape
modem • *n* modem
modera • *v* moderate, temper
moderare • *n* moderation
moderat • *adj* moderate
moderat • *adj* moderate
moderaie • *n* moderation
moderatoare • *n* host
moderator • *n* host
modest • *adj* modest
modestie • *n* modesty
modifica • *v* change, edit, modify
modificabil • *adj* changeable
modificare • *n* change, edit, modification
modificat • *adj* modified
modulaie • *n* modulation
mofturos • *adj* fastidious
mojar • *n* mortar
mojic • *n* boor, yokel
molaritate • *n* molarity
molecul • *n* molecule
molecular • *adj* molecular
moleeal • *n* languor
molesta • *v* gall, molest
molibden • *n* molybdenum
moliciune • *n* softness
molid • *n* spruce
molie • *n* moth
molipsitor • *adj* contagious
momâie • *n* scarecrow
momeal • *n* bait, fly
moment • *n* moment
momentan • *adj* instantaneous
momite • *n* sweetbread
monah • *n* monk
monarh • *n* monarch
monarhie • *n* monarchy, royalty

monarhist • *n* monarchist
moned • *n* coin
monetar • *adj* monetary, pecuniary
monetria • *n* mint
monetarism • *n* monetarism
monism • *n* monism
monitor • *n* monitor
monoclu • *n* monocle
monocrom • *adj* monochrome
monogamie • *n* monogamy
monografie • *n* monograph
monolit • *n* monolith
monomer • *n* monomer
monopol • *n* monopoly
monoteism • *n* monotheism
monoton • *adj* flat, monotone
monoton • *adj* flat
monotonie • *n* monotony, sameness
monotrem • *n* monotreme
monotrem • *n* monotreme
monoxid • *n* monoxide
monstru • *n* monster
monstruos • *adj* monstrous
monstruozitate • *n* monstrosity
monta • *v* mount
monteuz • *n* editor
monument • *n* monument
moped • *n* moped
moralitate • *n* morality
morar • *n* miller
morcov • *n* carrot
moren • *n* moraine
morfem • *n* morpheme
morfologie • *n* morphology
morg • *n* morgue
mormânt • *n* grave, tomb
mormântal • *adj* funeral
mormântare • *n* funeral
mormoloc • *n* tadpole
morocnos • *adj* morose
moros • *adj* morose
mors • *n* walrus
mort • *adj* blasted, dead
mortal • *adj* deadly, mortal • *adv* deadly
mortar • *n* mortar
mortier • *n* mortar
mosc • *n* musk
moschee • *n* mosque
moier • *n* squire
moteni • *v* inherit
motenire • *n* inheritance, legacy
motenitor • *n* scion
mostr • *n* sample
motan • *n* cat, tom
motiv • *n* consideration, motive, purpose, stimulus
motiva • *v* infer
motivare • *n* motivation
motivaie • *n* motivation
motociclet • *n* motorcycle
motor • *n* engine, motor
motorin • *n* diesel
mov • *adj* mauve
movil • *n* mound
mozaic • *n* mosaic
mrean • *n* barbel
mu • *interj* moo
muabil • *adj* mutable
muc • *n* booger, wick
mucava • *n* cardboard
muced • *adj* fusty, musty
mucegai • *n* mildew, mold
mucenic • *n* martyr
muchie • *n* line
muci • *n* mucus, snivel, snot
mucos • *n* greenhorn • *adj* mucous
mucus • *n* mucus
muflon • *n* mouflon
muget • *n* moo
mugi • *v* bellow, moo, roar
mugur • *n* bud
mugure • *n* bud
muia • *v* douse, soak, soften
muieratic • *n* womanizer
muiere • *n* wife, woman
muist • *n* cocksucker
muist • *n* cocksucker
mul • *n* mule
mult • *adv* much
multicolor • *adj* rainbow
multicultural • *adj* multicultural
multidimensional • *adj* multidimensional
multilateral • *adj* comprehensive, versatile
mulime • *n* army, crowd, forest, quantity, set • *pron* many
multimedia • *n* multimedia • *adj* multimedia
multiplexor • *n* multiplexer
multiplica • *v* multiply
multiplicare • *n* multiplication
multiplicat • *n* multiplicand
multiplicator • *n* multiplier
multiplu • *adj* composite • *n* multiple
multitudine • *n* army, rainbow
mulumesc • *interj* thanks
mulumi • *v* content
mulumire • *n* contentment
mulumit • *adj* content, happy, satisfied
mulumitor • *adj* thankful
mumie • *n* mummy
munc • *n* work
munci • *v* work

muncitoare • *n* worker
muncitor • *adj* hardworking • *n* worker
municipalitate • *n* municipality
muniie • *n* ammunition
munte • *n* mount, mountain
mur • *n* blackberry, bramble
mur • *n* blackberry
mura • *v* pickle
murdar • *adj* dirty, squalid, unclean
murdri • *v* dirty
murdrie • *n* dirt, filth
murg • *adj* dark
muri • *v* die
muribund • *adj* dying
muritor • *adj* mortal
musaca • *n* moussaka
musafir • *n* guest
musc • *n* fly
muca • *v* bite
mucat • *n* geranium, pelargonium
muctur • *n* bite
muschet • *n* musket
muschet • *n* musket
muchi • *n* moss, muscle
muchiular • *adj* muscular
muchiulos • *adj* muscular
muscular • *adj* muscular
musculos • *adj* muscular
must • *n* must
mutar • *n* mustard
musta • *n* moustache, whisker
mustra • *v* chide, rebuke, reprimand, reprove, twit
muuroi • *n* anthill
mut • *adj* mute, voiceless
muta • *v* move
mutantului • *n* mutant
mutare • *n* move, transformation
mutaie • *n* transformation
muenie • *n* muteness
mutila • *v* maim, mangle, mutilate
mutual • *adj* mutual
muzeu • *n* museum
muzic • *n* music
muzician • *n* musician, player
muzician • *n* musician

N

nad • *n* bait
ndjdui • *v* hope
ndejde • *n* hope
nfram • *n* handkerchief
nagâ • *n* lapwing
nalb • *n* hollyhock, mallow, marshmallow
nalb-de-grdin • *n* hollyhock
nandu • *n* rhea
naos • *n* nave
nap • *n* beet, swede, turnip
npârc • *n* viper
nar • *n* nostril
narare • *n* relation
narcis • *n* daffodil, narcissus
narcolepsie • *n* narcolepsy
narcoman • *n* user
narcotic • *adj* narcotic • *n* substance
narcotic • *n* narcotic
narghilea • *n* hookah
narval • *n* narwhal
na • *n* godfather
nas • *n* nose
na • *n* godmother
nscoci • *v* invent
nscocit • *adj* fictitious
nscut • *adj* born
natere • *n* being, birth, nativity
nasture • *n* button
nsturel • *n* watercress
natal • *adj* natal
natalitate • *n* nativity
naional • *adj* national
naionalism • *n* nationalism
naionalitate • *n* nationality
naiune • *n* country, nation, people
nativ • *adj* native
natr • *n* warp
natriu • *n* sodium
natur • *n* nature
natural • *adj* natural • *adv* naturally
natural • *adj* natural
naturalee • *n* naturalness
naturalism • *n* naturalism
naturalitate • *n* naturalness
naturaliza • *v* naturalize
naufragiat • *n* maroon
nausea • *n* nausea
nut • *n* chickpea
nav • *n* nave, ship
navet • *n* turnip
naviga • *v* sail
navigaie • *n* navigation
nzuin • *n* yearning
ne • *pron* us
nea • *n* snow

neacceptabil • *adj* unacceptable
neacceptabilitate • *n* unacceptability
neaccesibil • *adj* inaccessible
neachitat • *adj* unpaid
neacvatic • *adj* terrestrial
neadaptabil • *adj* ossified
neadecvat • *adj* antic, inadequate, unsuitable
neadecvat • *adj* inadequate
neadevr • *adj* false • *n* falsity
neadmisibil • *adj* inadmissible
neagr • *n* black, sable
neagreabil • *adj* disagreeable
neagreabilitate • *n* unpleasantness
neagreat • *adj* unpleasant
neajutorat • *adj* helpless
neam • *n* people, race
neambiguu • *adj* unambiguous
neamestecabil • *adj* immiscible
neanchetabil • *adj* inscrutable
neanticipabil • *adj* unpredictable
neanticipabilitate • *n* unpredictability
neanticipat • *adj* unanticipated, unexpected
neaprabil • *adj* indefensible
neasculttor • *adj* disobedient, unruly
neascutit • *adj* blunt
neasigurat • *adj* unassured
neastâmpr • *n* restlessness
neateptat • *adj* sudden, unanticipated, unexpected
neatent • *adj* absent
neatenie • *n* absence
neatingibil • *adj* inaccessible
neautorizat • *adj* unauthorized
neauzibil • *adj* inaudible
nebuloas • *n* nebula
nebulozitate • *n* nebulosity
nebun • *n* bishop, crazy, mind, nut • *adj* crazy, insane
nebun • *n* crazy • *adj* insane
nebunesc • *adj* insane
nebunie • *n* insanity
necji • *v* bother, molest, upset
necalificat • *adj* unqualified
necstorit • *adj* single
necaz • *n* pain, trouble
necercetabil • *adj* inscrutable
necercetat • *adj* unqualified
necerut • *adj* unrequested
necesar • *adj* essential, necessary
necesitate • *n* necessity, need
nechezat • *n* neigh
necinste • *n* falsity
necinstit • *adj* dishonest, disingenuous, unrighteous
necioplit • *n* boor
neclar • *adj* unclear, unobvious
neclintire • *n* steadfastness
neclintit • *adj* immovable
necomestibil • *adj* inedible
necomparabil • *adj* incomparable
necompetent • *adj* unqualified
necompletat • *adj* blank
necomplicat • *adj* simple
necomun • *adj* uncommon
neconcepibil • *adj* unthinkable
neconceptibil • *adj* inconceivable
neconform • *adj* atypical
neconsistent • *adj* inconsistent
neconstructiv • *adj* unconstructive
necontaminat • *adj* uncontaminated
necontenit • *adj* ongoing
necontrolabil • *adj* uncontrollable
necontrolat • *adj* crazy
necontroversat • *adj* uncontroversial
neconvenabil • *adj* unsuitable
neconvenional • *adj* unconventional, unorthodox
necorespunztor • *adj* inappropriate
necredincios • *n* infidel
necredin • *n* disbelief, incredulity
necritic • *adj* uncritical
necrolog • *n* obituary
necromania • *n* necromancy
necropol • *n* necropolis
necrotic • *adj* necrotic
necroz • *n* necrosis
nectarin • *n* nectarine
necunoscut • *adj* unknown
necurat • *adj* unclean
necurenie • *n* impurity
nedecis • *adj* uncertain
nedefinit • *adj* undefined
nedefinitiv • *adj* defeasible
nedemn • *adj* contemptible
nediluat • *adj* concentrated
nedistingibil • *adj* indistinguishable
nedivizat • *adj* single
nedomesticit • *adj* haggard
nedorit • *adj* undesirable, unpleasant, unwanted
nedrept • *adj* unrighteous
nedureros • *adj* painless
neechivoc • *adj* unambiguous • *adv* unequivocally
neelastic • *adj* inelastic
neesenial • *adj* inessential
neevident • *adj* unobvious
neexaminabil • *adj* inscrutable
neexistent • *adj* absent, nonexistent
neexplicabil • *adj* inexplicable
neexpresiv • *adj* blank
neexprimabil • *adj* inexpressible

nefavorabil • *adj* adverse, unfavorable
nefavorabil • *adj* unfavorable
nefericire • *n* sorrow, unhappiness
nefericit • *adj* depressed • *n* wretch
nefertil • *adj* barren
neflexibil • *adj* inflexible
nefolosit • *adj* unused
nefolositor • *adj* useless
nefrancat • *adj* unpaid
nefructuos • *adj* fruitless, unproductive
nefundamentat • *adj* indefensible
neg • *n* wart
nega • *v* controvert, deny
negândibil • *adj* unthinkable
negare • *n* negation
negaie • *n* negation
neghiob • *n* clown
neglija • *v* neglect, omit
neglijent • *adj* careless
neglijen • *n* negligence, recklessness
negocia • *v* treat
negramatical • *adj* ungrammatical
negreal • *n* darkness
negres • *n* black
negrilic • *n* nigella
negru • *n* black • *adj* black, sable
negru-abanos • *n* ebony • *adj* ebony
negruc • *n* nigella
negur • *n* cloud, fog, mist
negustor • *n* grocer, merchant
negustoreas • *n* grocer
negua • *v* haggle
nehotrât • *adj* irresolute
neimaginabil • *adj* unimaginable, unthinkable
neîmblânzit • *adj* haggard
neîmbrcat • *adj* unclothed
neîmpiedicat • *adj* free, unimpeded
neimportant • *adj* inessential, insignificant, peripheral, unimportant
neimportan • *n* insignificance
neîmputernicit • *adj* unauthorized
neînchipuibil • *adj* unimaginable
neîncredere • *n* disbelief, distrust, mistrust
neîndemânatic • *adj* awkward, clumsy
neîndestultor • *adj* insufficient
neinformat • *adj* uninformed
neînfricare • *n* fearlessness
neinspirat • *adj* pedestrian
neînelegere • *n* friction
neinteligibil • *adj* unintelligible
neinteresat • *adj* uninterested
neîntrebuinat • *adj* unused
neîntrerupt • *adj* continuous, ongoing, uninterrupted • *adv* continuously
neîntrerupt • *adj* uninterrupted
nejustificabil • *adj* indefensible
nelegal • *adj* illegal, illegitimate • *adv* illegally
nelegat • *adj* free
nelimitat • *adj* infinite, unlimited
nelimitat • *adj* unlimited
neliniar • *adj* nonlinear
neliniar • *adj* nonlinear
nelinite • *n* restlessness, uneasiness
nelinitit • *adj* anxious, restless
nelogic • *adj* illogical
nemagnetic • *adj* nonmagnetic
nemrginit • *adj* unlimited
nemsurabil • *adj* immeasurable
nemilos • *adj* hardhearted
nemicabil • *adj* immovable, implacable
nemicare • *n* stagnation
nemicat • *adj* immovable, implacable
nemior • *n* delphinium, larkspur
nemulumire • *n* complaint, displeasure, dissatisfaction
nemulumit • *adj* discontented, dissatisfied
nemuritor • *adj* deathless, immortal • *adv* everlasting
nenatural • *adj* artificial, strange, unnatural
nenecesar • *adj* unnecessary
nenimerit • *adj* unsuitable
nenormal • *adj* abnormal
nenormalitate • *n* abnormity
nenorocire • *n* disaster
nenorocit • *adj* deplorable, miserable, wretched • *n* wretch
nenorocos • *adj* unlucky
nenumrabil • *adj* countless, unnumbered
nenumrat • *adj* unnumbered
neobedient • *adj* disobedient
neobiectiv • *adj* partial
neobinuit • *adj* curious, extraordinary, prodigious, singular, strange, unusual
neobstrucionat • *adj* unimpeded
neoclasicism • *n* neoclassicism
neocolibil • *adj* inevitable
neocolonialism • *n* neocolonialism
neocupat • *adj* free
neodim • *n* neodymium
neoficial • *adj* unofficial
neologism • *n* neologism
neomenie • *n* inhumanity
neon • *n* neon
neonatal • *adj* neonatal
neoportun • *adj* inopportune
neopribil • *adj* unstoppable
neorganizat • *adj* disorganized
neortodox • *adj* unorthodox
nepalpabil • *adj* intangible

neprtinire • *n* equity
neprtinitate • *n* impartiality
neprtinitor • *adj* impartial
nepsare • *n* disregard, insouciance
nepstor • *adj* careless, heedless, pococurante
neperiat • *adj* unbrushed
neplcere • *n* dissatisfaction, inconvenience
neplcut • *adj* distasteful, obnoxious, unpleasant
nepltit • *adj* unpaid
nepoat • *n* granddaughter, niece
nepoluat • *adj* uncontaminated
nepopular • *adj* unpopular
nepopularitate • *n* unpopularity
nepot • *n* grandson, nephew
nepotism • *n* nepotism
nepotrivit • *adj* inadequate, inappropriate, unsuitable
nepracticabil • *adj* impracticable
neprevzut • *adj* sudden, unanticipated, unexpected
neprevenit • *adj* unaware
neprevizibil • *adj* unpredictable
neprevizibil • *adj* unpredictable
neprevizibili • *adj* unpredictable
neprevizibilitate • *n* unpredictability
neprezent • *adj* absent
nepriceput • *adj* unskillful
neprietenos • *adj* unfriendly
neprihnit • *adj* blameless
neproductiv • *adj* fruitless, unproductive
neprofesional • *adj* amateur
neprotejat • *adj* unprotected
neptuniu • *n* neptunium
neputincios • *adj* unable
neputin • *n* inability
nerbdabil • *adj* insufferable
nerbdare • *n* impatience, restlessness
nerbdtor • *adj* anxious, eager, nervous
nerspundent • *adj* unresponsive
neraional • *adj* irrational
nereacionant • *adj* unresponsive
nereactiv • *adj* unresponsive
nereal • *adj* unreal
nerealist • *adj* unrealistic
nerecunoscut • *adj* unacknowledged
nereglementar • *adj* irregular
neregularitate • *n* irregularity
neregulat • *adj* irregular, uncertain
nerelevant • *adj* irrelevant
nereproabil • *adj* unexceptionable
nerestaurabil • *adj* irredeemable
nerestricionat • *adj* unrestricted
neretribuit • *adj* unpaid
nerezonabil • *adj* unreasonable
neroditor • *adj* unfruitful
nerodnic • *adj* unfruitful
nerodnicie • *n* unfruitfulness
nerozie • *n* nonsense
nerozii • *n* nonsense
neruinare • *n* effrontery, nerve
neruinat • *adj* abandoned, infamous
nerv • *n* nerve
nervi • *n* nerve
nervos • *adj* nervous
nervozitate • *n* nervousness
nervur • *n* nerve
nesntos • *adj* noisome, noxious
neans • *n* misfortune
nesatisfctor • *adj* unacceptable
nesatisfcut • *adj* discontented, dissatisfied
neschimbabil • *adj* invariable
neschimbat • *adj* constant
nescris • *adj* blank
nesemnificant • *adj* insignificant
nesemnifican • *n* insignificance
nesemnificant • *adj* insignificant
nesemnificativ • *adj* insignificant
nesensibil • *adj* insipid, unresponsive
nesfânt • *adj* unholy
nesfârit • *adj* infinite • *n* infinity
nesfîrit. • *adj* endless
nesigur • *adj* unassured, uncertain, unsafe, untrustworthy
nesiguran • *n* uncertainty
nesiguri • *adj* uncertain
nesimetric • *adj* asymmetrical
nesimitor • *adj* insipid
nesincer • *adj* insincere
nesinceritate • *n* insincerity
nesistematic • *adj* unsystematic
nesolicitat • *adj* unrequested
neovin • *n* resoluteness
nespiritual • *adj* insipid
nestabil • *adj* uncertain
nestatornic • *adj* uncertain
nestemat • *n* gem, jewel
nestemate • *n* jewel
netiut • *adj* unknown
netiutor • *adj* unaware
nestopabil • *adj* unstoppable
nestructural • *adj* nonstructural
nestudiat • *adj* unqualified
nesubstanial • *adj* insubstantial
nesuferibil • *adj* insufferable
nesuferit • *adj* obnoxious
nesuficient • *adj* insufficient
nesuportabil • *adj* insufferable, unbearable
nesupus • *adj* disobedient, unruly
net • *n* net

net • *n* net
neted • *adj* flat, smooth
netezi • *v* flatten
netimbrat • *adj* unpaid
netipic • *adj* atypical
netraductibil • *adj* untranslatable
netransparent • *adj* opaque
netrasabil • *adj* untraceable
netrebuibil • *adj* unnecessary
netrebuincios • *adj* useless
netulburat • *adj* composed, immovable
neuitabil • *adj* unforgettable
neumanitate • *n* inhumanity
neuniform • *adj* heterogeneous
neurolog • *n* neurologist
neurologic • *adj* neurological
neurologic • *adj* neurological
neurologie • *n* neurology
neurosarcom • *n* neurosarcoma
neurotiin • *n* neuroscience
neutilizabil • *adj* unavailable
neutilizat • *adj* unused
neutrino • *n* neutrino
neutron • *n* neutron
neutru • *adj* neutral
neuzual • *adj* unusual
nevdit • *adj* unobvious
nevariabil • *adj* invariable
nevast • *n* bride, wife
nevstuic • *n* ferret, weasel
nevtmat • *adj* sound
neveridic • *adj* untruthful
neveridicitate • *n* untruthfulness
neverosimil • *adj* inconceivable
neverosimilitate • *n* unlikelihood
nevertebrat • *n* invertebrate • *adj* invertebrate
nevertebrat • *n* invertebrate
nevinovat • *adj* blameless, innocent
nevoia • *adj* destitute, poor
nevoiai • *n* poor
nevoie • *n* need
nevoit • *adj* unwanted
newton • *n* newton
nezgomotos • *adj* noiseless
nicieri • *adv* nowhere
nichel • *n* nickel
nichela • *v* nickel
nici • *adv* either, neither • *conj* nor
nicicând • *adv* never
niciodat • *adv* never
niciunde • *adv* nowhere
nicotin • *n* nicotine
nicoval • *n* anvil, incus
nigelu • *n* love-in-a-mist
nihilism • *n* nihilism
nihilist • *n* anarchist
nimb • *n* aureole, halo
nimeni • *n* insect, nobody • *pron* none
nimeri • *v* reach
nimerit • *adj* suitable
nimf • *n* nymph
nimic • *pron* anything, nothing
nimici • *v* destroy
nimicibil • *adj* destructible
ninge • *v* snow
ninsoare • *n* snow
niobiu • *n* niobium
ni • *n* niche
nisip • *n* sand
nisipi • *v* sand
nisipiu • *adj* sand, sandy
nisipos • *adj* sandy
nivel • *n* level
nivela • *v* flatten
nivelat • *adj* level
nivele • *n* level
noapte • *n* night
nobeliu • *n* nobelium
nobil • *n* noble
nobilime • *n* nobility
noblee • *n* generosity, nobility
nociv • *adj* deleterious, noxious
noctambulism • *n* somnambulism
nod • *n* knot, node
nodos • *adj* knotty
nodul • *n* nodule
noi • *pron* we
noian • *n* mountain
nomenclatur • *n* nomenclature
nominal • *adj* nominal
nominativ • *adj* nominative
nonconformist • *n* nonconformist
nonconformist • *n* nonconformist
nonexistent • *adj* nonexistent
nonalan • *n* insouciance, nonchalance
nonsens • *n* nonsense
nor • *n* cloud
nor • *n* daughter-in-law
nord • *n* north
nord-vest • *n* northwest
nord-vestic • *adj* northeast
nordestic • *adj* northeast
nordic • *adj* northern
nordvestic • *adj* northwest
norm • *n* norm
normal • *adj* normal, ordinary
normalitate • *n* normality
normativ • *adj* normative
noroc • *n* fortune, luck • *interj* hello
norocos • *adj* golden, happy, lucky
noroi • *v* mud • *n* mud
not • *n* bill, mark, note
nota • *v* note

notabil • *adj* remarkable
notti • *n* phalarope
notebook • *n* laptop
notificare • *n* notice, notification
noti • *n* note
noiune • *n* notion
nou • *adj* new, novel
nou-nscut • *n* newborn • *adj* newborn
nou-nscut • *n* newborn • *adj* newborn
nou • *pron* us
nousprezecelea • *n* nineteenth
nouzecilea • *adj* ninetieth
noutate • *n* newness, news, novelty
nov • *n* nova
novice • *n* colt, fledgling, pup
nu • *n* no • *adv* not
nu-m-uita • *n* forget-me-not
nuan • *n* nuance
nuane • *n* nuance
nuc • *n* walnut
nuc • *n* nut, walnut
nucel • *n* nucellus
nuclear • *adj* nuclear
nucleon • *n* nucleon
nucleotide • *n* nucleotide
nucleu • *n* nucleus
nucoar • *n* nutmeg
nucor • *n* nutmeg
nud • *adj* nude
nud • *adj* nude
nudism • *n* nudism
nudist • *adj* nudist
nuditate • *n* nudity
nuia • *n* rod, stick, twig
nuizibil • *adj* noisome
nul • *adj* void
numai • *adv* just, only
numaidecât • *adv* immediately
numr • *n* number
numra • *v* count, number
numrabil • *adj* countable
numrare • *n* count
numrtoare • *n* count, counter
numrtor • *n* counter, numerator
nume • *n* name, noun
numerar • *n* cash
numeric • *adj* digital, numeric
numeric • *adj* numeric
numeriza • *v* scan
numerizare • *n* scan
numerizor • *n* scanner
numeros • *adj* numerous
numerota • *v* number
numi • *v* call, designate
numitor • *n* denominator
nun • *n* godfather
nun • *n* godmother
nunt • *n* bridal, marriage, wedding
nupial • *adj* nuptial
nupial • *adj* nuptial
nurc • *n* mink
nutre • *n* dinner, feed, fodder
nutri • *v* nourish
nutrire • *n* nutrition
nutriie • *n* food, nutrition

O

o • *art* an
oaie • *n* ewe, mutton
oal • *n* pot, saucepan
oameni • *n* people
oar • *n* time
oaspete • *n* guest
oaste • *n* army
oaz • *n* oasis
obedient • *adj* obedient
obez • *adj* obese
obezitate • *n* obesity
obicei • *n* custom, habit, wont
obiect • *n* object, thing
obiecta • *v* object
obiectare • *n* objection
obiecie • *n* objection
obiectiv • *n* aim, goal, objective, purpose, vision • *adj* objective
obiectivitate • *n* detachment, impartiality, objectivity
obinuin • *n* custom
obinuit • *adj* common, normal, quotidian, usual
oblic • *adj* lopsided
obliga • *v* enforce
obligare • *n* obligation
obligat • *adj* bound, obliged
obligaie • *n* constraint, obligation
obligator • *adj* compulsory
obligatoriu • *adj* incumbent
obligean • *n* calamus
oboi • *n* oboe
oboseal • *n* fatigue
obosi • *v* jade
obosit • *adj* exhausted, fatigued, haggard, tired
obosit • *adj* tired
obraz • *n* cheek

obraznic • *adj* mischievous
obrznicie • *n* impudence, insolence
obscen • *adj* obscene, vulgar
obscur • *adj* obscure, unknown
obscura • *v* obscure
obscurantism • *n* obscurantism
obscuritate • *n* obscurity
obsecvios • *adj* obsequious
observa • *v* descry, observe
observabil • *adj* sensible
observare • *n* notice, observation, vigil
observaie • *n* observation, remark
observator • *adj* observant • *n* observatory
obsesie • *n* obsession
obsidian • *n* obsidian
obstacol • *n* balk, difficulty, hindrance, hurdle, impediment, obstacle
obstetric • *adj* obstetric
obstetric • *n* obstetrics
obstinat • *adj* obstinate
obstinaie • *n* obstinacy
obstrucionare • *n* obstruction
obine • *v* obtain
obtura • *v* obstruct
obtuzitate • *n* dullness
ocar • *n* disgrace
ocazie • *n* chance, instance, occasion
ocazional • *adj* occasional • *adv* occasionally, sometimes
occidental • *adj* western
ocean • *n* ocean
oceanografie • *n* oceanography
oceanologie • *n* oceanography
ocelot • *n* ocelot
ochead • *n* gander
ochelari • *n* spectacles
ochi • *n* eye, optic • *v* target
ochire • *n* gander
oclusiv • *n* plosive
ocoli • *v* avoid, circumvent, eschew
ocolire • *n* bypass
ocroti • *v* protect
ocrotire • *n* protection
ocular • *adj* ocular
oculta • *v* obscure
ocupare • *n* tenure
ocupaie • *n* vocation, work
od • *n* ode
odagaci • *n* soapwort
odaie • *n* room
odat • *adv* once
odihn • *n* rest
odihni • *v* rest
odios • *adj* loathsome
odolean • *n* valerian
odrasl • *n* brat
ofens • *n* offense
ofensa • *v* digress, pique, spite
ofensant • *adj* offensive
ofensant • *adj* offensive
ofensator • *adj* distasteful, insulting
ofensiv • *n* offense, offensive
oferi • *v* offer
oficial • *adj* formal, official
oficiu • *n* office
ofili • *v* wither
ofilit • *adj* withered
ofier • *n* officer
oftalmolog • *n* ophthalmologist
oftalmolog • *n* ophthalmologist
oftat • *n* sigh
oglind • *n* mirror
oier • *n* shepherd
oierie • *n* sheepfold
oi • *n* ewe
okapi • *n* okapi
olan • *n* tile
olar • *n* potter
olrie • *n* pottery
olrit • *n* pottery
oleandru • *n* oleander
oligozaharid • *n* oligosaccharide
oliv • *n* olive
olivin • *n* peridot
olog • *adj* lame
om • *n* human, man • *adj* human
omag • *n* aconite
omagiu • *n* homage
omt • *n* snow
omega • *n* omega
omenesc • *adj* human
omenete • *adj* human • *adv* humanly
omenie • *n* humaneness
omenire • *n* humanity, mankind
omid • *n* caterpillar
omite • *v* omit
omnipotent • *adj* almighty, omnipotent
omniprezent • *adj* omnipresent, ubiquitous
omniprezent • *adj* ubiquitous
omniprezen • *n* omnipresence
omniscient • *adj* all-knowing, omniscient
omogen • *adj* homogeneous
omogen • *adj* homogeneous
omolog • *adj* homologous
omologie • *n* homology
omonim • *n* homonym
omorî • *v* butcher, slaughter, waste
onanist • *n* masturbator
onest • *adj* honest, stand-up, straightforward
onestitate • *n* honesty
onix • *n* onyx

onoare • *n* honor
onomatopee • *n* onomatopoeia
onomatopeic • *adj* onomatopoeic
onora • *v* grace, honor
onorabil • *adj* honorable
ontologic • *adj* ontological
ontologie • *n* ontology
opac • *adj* opaque
opera • *v* work
oper • *n* construction, opera, work
operabil • *adj* operable
operand • *n* operand
operare • *n* operation
operaie • *n* operation
operaional • *adj* operational
operaiune • *n* operation
operatoare • *n* operator
operator • *n* operator
opinie • *n* apprehension, notion, opinion, sentence
opiu • *n* opium
oponent • *n* antagonist, opponent, opposition
oportun • *adj* opportune
oportunitate • *n* opportunity
oposum • *n* opossum
opozant • *adj* opposed
opoziie • *n* opposition
opresiv • *adj* tyrannical
opri • *v* arrest, restrain, stop
oprit • *n* standstill
opta • *v* opt
optic • *adj* optic
opional • *adv* optionally
opulen • *n* opulence
opune • *v* object, oppose
opunere • *n* opposition, resistance
opunia • *n* opuntia
opus • *adj* adverse, contrary, opposite
opus • *adj* adverse, opposite
or • *n* hour, time
oral • *adj* verbal
oranj • *n* orange • *adj* orange
ora • *n* city, town
orae • *n* town
oratoare • *n* orator
orator • *n* orator
orb • *adj* blind
orbit • *n* orbit
orbital • *adj* orbital
orbital • *adj* orbital
orc • *n* orc
orchestral • *adj* orchestral
ordalie • *n* ordeal
ordin • *n* order
ordinar • *adj* ordinary, vulgar
ordine • *n* order
ordona • *v* arrange, command, order
ordonan • *n* ordinance
oregano • *n* oregano
orez • *n* rice
orfan • *n* orphan
orfan • *n* orphan
org • *n* organ
organ • *n* organ
organism • *n* organism
organiza • *v* organize
organizare • *n* organization
organizaie • *n* organization
orgasm • *n* orgasm
orgie • *n* orgy
orgoliu • *n* pride
orhidee • *n* orchid
ori • *conj* or
oribil • *adj* awful, ghastly, horrible, monstrous
oricare • *pron* any
orice • *pron* anything
oricine • *pron* everybody, everyone
oricum • *adv* however
oriental • *adj* eastern
orientalist • *n* orientalist
orificiu • *n* mouth
origin • *n* origin
original • *n* master • *adj* novel
originalitate • *n* originality
originar • *adj* native
originar • *adj* native
origine • *n* birth, origin
oripila • *v* horrify
oriunde • *adv* anywhere
orizont • *n* horizon
orizontal • *adv* across, horizontally • *adj* horizontal
orizontal • *n* horizontal
orizonturi • *n* horizon
orna • *v* adorn, decorate
ornament • *n* decoration, ornament
ornamenta • *v* adorn, ornament
ornamental • *adj* ornamental
ornamentare • *n* ornamentation
ornamentaie • *n* decoration, ornamentation
ornitin • *n* ornithine
ornitorinc • *n* platypus
ortoepie • *n* orthoepy
ortogonalitate • *n* orthogonality
ortografic • *adj* orthographic
ortografie • *n* orthography
ortolan • *n* ortolan
ortoz • *n* orthoclase
oryx • *n* oryx
orz • *n* barley
os • *n* bone

osatur • *n* frame
oscila • *v* hover, oscillate
oscilare • *n* oscillation
oscilator • *n* oscillator
osie • *n* axle
osifica • *v* ossify
osmiu • *n* osmium
osos • *adj* bony, osseous
osp • *n* banquet, feast
ospta • *v* regale, treat
osptar • *n* waiter
osptar • *n* stewardess
osptri • *n* waitress
osta • *n* soldier
ostatic • *n* hostage
ostatic • *n* hostage
ostentaie • *n* ostentation
ostentaios • *adj* ostentatious
ostentativ • *adj* ostentatious
ostil • *adj* adverse, hostile, unfriendly
ostilitate • *n* hostility, malevolence
ostracism • *n* ostracism
ostrigar • *n* oystercatcher
osuar • *n* ossuary
oel • *n* steel
oet • *n* vinegar
oetar • *n* cruet
otrav • *n* poison
otrvi • *v* poison
otrvit • *adj* intoxicated
otrvitor • *adj* poisonous
ou • *n* egg
oua • *v* lay
ou • *n* balls, plum
oval • *n* oval
ovar • *n* ovary
ovz • *n* oat, oats
ovul • *n* egg, ovum
oxid • *n* oxide
oxida • *v* rust
oxidare • *n* combustion
oxigen • *n* oxygen
oximoron • *n* oxymoron
ozon • *n* ozone

P

pa • *interj* bye, cheers, goodbye
pcleal • *adj* sham
pcli • *v* fool, gull, screw, sham, trick
pcat • *n* guilt, pity, sin
pctui • *v* sin
pace • *n* ease, peace, rest
pachet • *n* bundle, package, packet, parcel
pachete • *n* packet
pcur • *n* oil
pcurar • *n* shepherd
pducel • *n* hawthorn, may
pduche • *n* louse
pduchios • *adj* lousy
pdure • *n* forest
pdurice • *n* grove, thicket
pgân • *adj* gentile, heathen, pagan • *n* heathen, pagan
pgântate • *n* paganism
pgânism • *n* paganism
pagin • *n* page
pagod • *n* pagoda
pagub • *n* damage
pagube • *n* damage
pgubitor • *adj* injurious
pahar • *n* glass
pai • *n* straw
pianjen • *n* spider
paia • *n* clown
paie • *n* straw
pâinar • *n* baker
pâine • *n* bread, loaf
pajite • *n* lea, sward
pajur • *n* eagle
pal • *adj* pale
paladiu • *n* palladium
plmid • *n* bonito
palanchin • *n* palanquin
plrie • *n* hat
palat • *n* mansion, palace, palate
paleontolog • *n* paleontologist
paleontologic • *adj* paleontological
paleontologie • *n* paleontology
palet • *n* gamut
paliditate • *n* paleness, pallor
palimpsest • *n* palimpsest
plinc • *n* slivovitz
palm • *n* palm
pâlnie • *n* funnel
palpabil • *adj* tangible
pâlpâi • *v* flicker
paltin • *n* maple
Pmânt • *n* globe
pmânt • *n* country, dirt, earth, ground, land, world
pan • *n* feather, plume, wedge
pana-zburtorului • *n* honesty
pancreas • *n* pancreas

pandalie • *n* tantrum
pandantiv • *n* pendant
pandemoniu • *n* pandemonium
panicat • *adj* panicky
panou • *n* panel
pansament • *n* bandage
pansea • *n* pansy
panselu • *n* pansy
pant • *n* cliff, inclination, slope
pantalon • *n* pants
pântec • *n* bowel
pântece • *n* belly, bowel
panteon • *n* pantheon
panter • *n* panther
pantof • *n* shoe
pantofar • *n* shoemaker
pânz • *n* cloth, material, sail
pap • *n* pope
ppdie • *n* dandelion
papagal • *n* goon, parrot
papagaliza • *v* parrot
papaia • *n* papaya
papric • *n* paprika
papuc • *n* slipper
papur • *n* bulrush, cattail, rush
papus • *n* pappus
ppu • *n* doll, puppet
par • *adj* even • *n* stake
pr • *n* hair, pear
par • *adj* even • *n* flame, pear
paracliser • *n* sexton
parad • *n* parade
parada • *v* flaunt
paradis • *n* paradise
paradox • *n* paradox
parafina • *v* paraffin
parafraza • *v* paraphrase
prgini • *v* wreck
paragraf • *n* paragraph
paralax • *n* parallax
paralel • *adj* parallel
paralelism • *n* parallelism
paralelitate • *n* parallelism
paralitic • *n* paralytic • *adj* paralytic
paralitic • *n* paralytic
paralizie • *n* paralysis
prlu • *n* daisy
parametric • *adj* parametric
parametru • *n* parameter, variable
paramilitar • *n* paramilitary • *adj* paramilitary
paraplegic • *adj* paraplegic
prsi • *v* abandon, forsake
prsit • *adj* abandoned
paraut • *n* parachute
pârâu • *n* brook, stream
parazit • *n* parasite
parazit • *n* parasite
parazitar • *adj* parasitic
parazitar • *adj* parasitic
parbriz • *n* windshield
parc • *n* garden, park
parca • *v* park • *conj* though
parcel • *n* parcel
parchet • *n* parquet
parcheta • *v* parquet
parcimonie • *n* parsimony, stinginess
pardesiu • *n* overcoat
pardon • *n* forgiveness • *interj* pardon
prea • *v* appear, look, seem
parenchim • *n* parenchyma
prere • *n* apprehension, idea, opinion
parfumat • *adj* sweet
printe • *n* parent
prini • *n* parentage
parlament • *n* parliament
parlamentar • *n* parliamentarian • *adj* parliamentary
parmezan • *n* parmesan
paroh • *n* rector
parohial • *adj* parochial
parohie • *n* parish
parol • *n* password
pros • *adj* hairy
pâr • *n* fart
pârâi • *v* fart
partaja • *v* share
parte • *n* division, hand, part, party, section, share, side
partener • *n* associate, partner
partener • *n* partner
pri • *n* share
parial • *adj* partial
prticic • *n* element
participa • *v* partake, participate
participant • *n* party
participant • *n* party
particul • *n* corpuscle, element, particle
particular • *adj* particular
particularitate • *n* feature, idiosyncrasy, particularity, quirk
partid • *n* congress, party
partid • *n* match
partinic • *adj* one-sided
prtinitor • *adj* partial
partitur • *n* music
partizan • *n* supporter
ps • *n* care, suffering
pas • *n* gait, pace, pitch, run, step
psa • *v* mind
pasa • *v* set
pasager • *n* passenger
pasaj • *n* arcade
paaport • *n* passport

pasre • *n* bird
pasre-cu-cioc-încruciat • *n* crossbill
psrea • *n* fledgling
psric • *n* beaver, fledgling, pussy
psat • *n* porridge
pi • *v* step
pai • *n* step, traveling
pasibil • *adj* liable
pasiune • *n* ardor, passion
pasiv • *n* bottom • *adj* passive, supine
panic • *adj* peaceful
pstaie • *n* bean, pod
pstârnac • *n* parsnip
pate • *v* graze, pasture
pasteuriza • *v* pasteurize
pasti • *n* pastiche
pstor • *n* shepherd
pstori • *v* graze, pasture
pstra • *v* husband, keep
pastram • *n* pastrami
pstrv • *n* trout
puna • *v* pasture
pune • *n* lea, pasture
pat • *n* bed
pta • *v* blot • *n* stain
pat • *n* mark, spot
panie • *n* misfortune
peal • *n* misfortune
pateri • *n* crosier
patern • *adj* paternal
patetic • *adj* pathetic
pi • *v* experience
patimi • *n* passion
patin • *n* patina
ptlagin • *n* plantain
patologic • *adj* pathological
patologie • *n* pathology
patra • *adj* fourth
ptrar • *n* quarter
ptrat • *n* place, square • *adj* square
patrie • *n* country, fatherland
ptrime • *n* quarter
patriot • *n* patriot
patriotism • *n* patriotism
patron • *n* master
patronim • *n* surname
patrulare • *n* patrol
patrulater • *n* quadrilateral
patrulea • *adj* fourth
ptrunde • *v* fathom, penetrate, pervade
ptrunjel • *n* parsley
patruzecilea • *adj* fortieth
ptur • *n* blanket
pun • *n* peacock, peafowl
pauper • *adj* poor
pauperiza • *v* impoverish
paupertate • *n* poverty
pauz • *n* pause, recess
pava • *v* flag
pavz • *n* shield
paz • *n* guard, soldier
• *n* page
pzi • *v* guard, watch
pzitor • *n* guard
paznic • *n* guard
pe • *prep* on
pecari • *n* peccary
pectin • *n* pectin
pectoral • *adj* pectoral
pedagog • *n* pedagogue
pedagog • *n* pedagogue
pedant • *n* pedagogue • *adj* pedantic
pedeaps • *n* penalty, punishment
pedepsi • *v* punish
pedepsibil • *adj* punishable
pedepsire • *n* punishment
pederast • *n* pederast
pederastic • *adj* pederastic
pederastie • *n* pederasty
pedestru • *n* pedestrian • *adj* pedestrian
peduncul • *n* stem
peisaj • *n* landscape, scenery
pelargonie • *n* geranium, pelargonium
pelerin • *n* pilgrim
pelican • *n* pelican
pelin • *n* absinthe, wormwood
peluz • *n* lawn
penalizabil • *adj* punishable
penalizabil • *adj* punishable
penalizare • *n* penalty, punishment
pendul • *n* pendulum
penetra • *v* penetrate
penetrabil • *adj* penetrable
peni • *v* pluck
penicilin • *n* penicillin
peninsul • *n* peninsula
penis • *n* penis
pensul • *n* brush, paintbrush
pentru • *prep* for
penultim • *adj* penultimate
pepene • *n* melon, watermelon
peptid • *n* peptide
peramel • *n* bandicoot
percepe • *v* discern
percepere • *n* notice, perception
perceptibil • *adj* sensible
percepie • *n* perception
perceptiv • *adj* perceptive
perdea • *n* curtain
perdele • *n* curtain
pereche • *n* couple, pair
perete • *n* wall
perfect • *adj* perfect
perfecta • *v* perfect

perfectibilitate • *n* perfectibility
perfeciune • *n* perfection
performan • *n* performance
pergament • *n* parchment
peria • *v* brush
periat • *n* brush
pericard • *n* pericardium
pericardit • *n* pericarditis
pericarp • *n* pericarp
periclita • *v* endanger
pericol • *n* danger, distress
periculos • *adj* dangerous
perie • *n* brush
periferic • *adj* peripheral
periferie • *n* periphery
perifraza • *v* paraphrase
perigeu • *n* perigee
perin • *n* pillow
perineal • *adj* perineal
perineu • *n* perineum
perioad • *n* age, era
periodic • *n* periodical
peristaltic • *adj* peristaltic
peristaltic • *n* peristalsis
peristaltism • *n* peristalsis
perl • *n* pearl
permanganat • *n* permanganate
permeabilitate • *n* permeability
permis • *n* permit
permite • *v* allow
pern • *n* cushion, pillow
pernambuc • *n* brazilwood
pernicios • *adj* pernicious
peron • *n* platform
perpendicular • *adj* stand-up
perpetuu • *adv* continuously, everlasting
perplexitate • *n* perplexity
persecutare • *n* persecution
persevera • *v* persevere
perseverent • *adj* sedulous
perseveren • *n* perseverance, pluck
persistent • *adj* obstinate
persisten • *n* persistence
persoan • *n* person
personaj • *n* actor, character
personal • *n* personnel, staff
personalitate • *n* personality
perspectiv • *n* outlook, vista
perspicace • *adj* perceptive, perspicacious
perspicacitate • *n* perspicacity
pertinent • *adj* relevant
pertinen • *n* relevance
perturba • *v* upset
perturbare • *n* disturbance
perturbaie • *n* disturbance, noise
peruc • *n* wig
peru • *n* parakeet
peruzea • *n* turquoise
pervers • *adj* perverse
perversitate • *n* perversity, wickedness
pervinc • *n* periwinkle
pescaj • *n* draft
pescar • *n* fisher, fisherman, fishmonger
pescari • *n* fisher
pescru • *n* gull
pescui • *v* angle, fish
pescuire • *n* fish, fishing
pescuit • *n* fish
pest • *n* plague
peste • *prep* across, after, over
pete • *n* fish, fishmonger, pimp
peter • *n* cave, den
pestifer • *adj* pestiferous
pestilenial • *adj* pestiferous
petior • *n* fishy, fry
petal • *n* petal
petard • *n* firecracker
pei • *v* propose
petiie • *n* claim, petition
petrece • *v* happen, party
petrecere • *n* celebration, entertainment, party
petrifica • *v* petrify
petrochimic • *adj* petrochemical
petrochimic • *adj* petrochemical
petrol • *n* oil
petunie • *n* petunia
pfund • *n* pound
pi • *n* pi
pian • *n* piano
pianist • *n* pianist
pianist • *n* pianist
pia • *n* market, place, plaza, square
piatr • *n* calculus, stone
piaz • *n* augury, foreboding
pic • *n* grudge, pique, rancor, spade
pica • *v* drip
picant • *adj* hot, piquant
pictur • *n* drop
pichet • *n* picket
picior • *n* foot, leg, stem
piciorong • *n* stilt
piciorul-cocoului • *n* buttercup
picolo • *n* busboy
picta • *v* brush, depict, paint
pictare • *n* painting
pictor • *n* painter
pictori • *n* painter
pictur • *n* painting
piedestal • *n* pedestal
piedic • *n* balk, difficulty, hindrance, impediment, obstacle, trip
pielar • *n* tanner
piele • *n* leather, skin

piept • *n* breast, chest
pieptna • *v* comb
pieptar • *n* breastplate, shirtfront
pierde • *v* lose, waste
pierdere • *n* leakage, waste
pierdut • *adj* lost
pieri • *v* perish
pieritor • *adj* mortal
piersic • *n* peach
piersic • *n* peach
piersiciu • *n* peach
pies • *n* device, element
pietate • *n* piety
piee • *n* square
pietist • *n* pietist
pietri • *n* pebble
piftie • *n* aspic
pigmentare • *n* pigmentation
pigmeu • *n* pygmy
pijama • *n* pajamas
pil • *n* file
pilaf • *n* pilaf
pilar • *n* column
pild • *n* paragon
pileal • *n* booze
pilot • *n* pilot
pilotabil • *adj* steerable
pin • *n* pin, pine, plug
pingea • *n* sole
pingeli • *v* sole
pinguin • *n* penguin
pion • *n* pawn
pionier • *n* pioneer
piper • *n* pepper
pipera • *v* pepper
pipi • *n* pee
pipirig • *n* rush
pipota • *n* gizzard
piramid • *n* pyramid
pirania • *n* piranha
pirat • *n* pirate
pirit • *n* pyrite
piron • *n* spike
pisa • *v* grind, pound
pia • *v* pee, piss
pislog • *n* pain • *adj* pestiferous
pica • *v* pinch, sting
pictor • *adj* biting
picot • *n* ladyfinger
pisic • *n* cat, pussy
pisicu • *n* kitten
pisoi • *n* kitten
pistil • *n* pestle
pistol • *n* gun, pistol
piston • *n* piston
pistrui • *n* freckle
pitic • *n* dwarf, pygmy
piigoi • *n* chickadee
piton • *n* python
pitoresc • *adj* picturesque
pitulice • *n* wren
piu • *n* mortar
piuli • *n* mortar, nut
pivni • *n* cellar
pivot • *n* pivot
pivotant • *adj* versatile
pivotare • *n* pivot
pivotri • *n* pivot
pizd • *n* cunt, pussy
pizm • *n* grudge, malevolence
pizma • *adj* envious
pizza • *n* pizza
plac • *n* plate
placard • *n* bill
plcea • *v* like, please
placent • *n* placenta
placentar • *n* placental • *adj* placental
plcere • *n* delight, fun, pleasure
plachet • *n* booklet
plcint • *n* pie
plcut • *adj* agreeable, fun, pleasant
plcut • *adj* pleasant
plafon • *n* ceiling
plag • *n* sore, wound
plagia • *v* plagiarize
plaj • *n* beach, sand, strand
plmân • *n* lung
plmâni • *n* lung
plan • *n* blueprint, draft, layout • *adj* flat, level
planar • *adj* planar
planet • *n* planet
planetar • *adj* planetary
planetariu • *n* planetarium
planetoid • *n* planetoid
plânge • *v* complain, cry, deplore, weep
plângere • *n* bill, complaint
planifica • *v* slate
planor • *n* glider
plânset • *n* cry
planeu • *n* floor
plant • *n* plant
planta • *v* plant
plpând • *adj* feeble
plas • *n* net
plasm • *n* plasma
plat • *adj* even, flat, level, shallow
plat • *n* payment, remuneration, wage
platan • *n* plane, sycamore
plti • *v* pay
pltibil • *adj* solvable
pltic • *n* bream
platin • *n* platinum
pltire • *n* payment

platou • *n* plate, plateau, set
plauzibil • *adj* credible, plausible
plauzibilitate • *n* plausibility
pleav • *n* chaff
plebe • *n* plebeian
pleca • *v* depart
plecare • *n* departure
pleda • *v* argue, plead
plenar • *adj* plenary
plenipoteniar • *n* plenipotentiary
plenitudine • *n* wholeness
pleoap • *n* eyelid
pleonasm • *n* tautology
pleuv • *adj* bald
pletoric • *adj* plethoric
plia • *v* fold
pliabil • *adj* pliable
pliabilitate • *n* pliability
pliant • *adj* pliable
plic • *n* envelope
plicticos • *adj* boring
plictiseal • *n* boredom, dullness, tedium
plictisi • *v* bore
plictisit • *adj* bored
plictisitor • *adj* boring, irksome, lame, pestiferous
plimba • *v* stroll, wander
plin • *adj* full, lousy, saturated, solid
plisa • *v* pleat, wrinkle
plisc • *n* bill
ploaie • *n* rain
plod • *n* brat
ploier • *n* plover
ploier-de-munte • *n* dotterel
ploios • *adj* rainy, wet
plomb • *n* filling
plomba • *v* fill
plonjare • *n* dive
plop • *n* poplar
ploni • *n* bedbug
ploua • *v* rain
plug • *n* plough
plumb • *n* lead
plural • *n* plural • *adj* plural
pluralism • *n* pluralism
pluralist • *n* pluralist
pluralitate • *n* plurality
plut • *n* float, raft
pluta • *n* raftsman
pluti • *v* float, hover
plutitor • *n* float • *adj* floating
plutocratic • *adj* plutocratic
plutoniu • *n* plutonium
pneu • *n* tyre
poam • *n* fruit
poarc • *n* sow
poart • *n* gate, goal
poate • *adv* maybe, perhaps
pocin • *n* penance
pocnitoare • *n* firecracker
pod • *n* attic, bridge
podagr • *n* gout
podbeal • *n* coltsfoot
podea • *n* floor
podi • *n* plateau
podium • *n* platform
poem • *n* poem
poet • *n* poet
poet • *n* poet, poetess
poetic • *adj* poetic
poezie • *n* poetry
poft • *n* appetite, craving
poftim • *interj* pardon
pogrom • *n* pogrom
poian • *n* glade
poker • *n* poker
pol • *n* pole
polc • *n* polka
polemic • *n* debate
polemizabil • *adj* controvertible
polemizat • *adj* controversial
polen • *n* pollen
polenizare • *n* pollination
polenizaie • *n* pollination
policar • *n* thumb
policrom • *adj* polychrome, rainbow
policromatic • *adj* polychromatic
poliedre • *n* polyhedron
poliedru • *n* polyhedron
polietilen • *n* polyethylene
polifosfat • *n* polyphosphate
poligal • *n* milkwort
poligamie • *n* polygamy
poligon • *n* polygon
polimer • *n* polymer
polimerizare • *n* polymerization
polinom • *n* polynomial
polinomial • *adj* polynomial
polinomic • *adj* polynomial
poli • *n* shelf
politeism • *n* polytheism
politee • *n* civility, politeness
politic • *adj* political
politic • *adj* political • *n* politics
politician • *n* politician
politico • *adj* polite
poliie • *n* police
poliist • *n* policeman
polonic • *n* ladle
poloniu • *n* polonium
poltronerie • *n* cowardice
pom • *n* tree
pomelo • *n* pomelo
pomet • *n* orchard

pomp • *n* pomp, pump
pompa • *v* pump
pompare • *n* pump
pompos • *adj* highfalutin, pompous
pondera • *v* weight
ponderaie • *n* equilibrium
ponei • *n* pony
pontif • *n* pontiff
ponton • *n* pontoon
pop-corn • *n* popcorn
pop • *n* king
popându • *n* suslik
popicar • *n* bowler
popice • *n* bowling
poponar • *n* fag, gay
popor • *n* people
popou • *n* ass
popular • *adj* popular
popular • *adj* popular
popularitate • *n* popularity
populaie • *n* population
porc • *n* pig
porc-ghimpos • *n* porcupine
porcar • *n* swineherd
porcrie • *n* crap
porecl • *n* nickname
porecli • *v* nickname
porni • *v* start
pornire • *v* bootstrap
pornograf • *n* pornographer
pornografic • *adj* pornographic
pornografie • *n* pornography
port • *n* port
portabilitate • *n* portability
portaltoi • *n* rootstock
portar • *n* doorkeeper, goalkeeper
portri • *n* goalkeeper
portativ • *n* staff
portbagaj • *n* trunk
porelan • *n* porcelain
porie • *n* portion
poriune • *n* portion
portmoneu • *n* wallet
portocal • *n* orange
portocal • *n* orange
portocaliu • *n* orange • *adj* orange, tangerine
portofel • *n* wallet
portret • *n* portrait
portulac • *n* purslane
porumb • *n* pigeon
porumbar • *n* dovecote
porumbrie • *n* dovecote
porumbel • *n* dove, pigeon
porunc • *n* order
porunci • *v* command, order
poseda • *v* possess
posesie • *n* possession, property, tenure
posesiune • *n* ownership, possession, property
posibil • *n* possibility • *adj* possible, thinkable
posibilitate • *n* possibility
post • *n* situation
potalion • *n* diligence
pota • *n* mailman
poster • *n* bill, poster
posteritate • *n* posterity
posti • *v* fast
postmodernism • *n* postmodernism
postscriptum • *n* postscript
postur • *n* attitude, posture
posturi • *n* situation
potabil • *adj* drinkable, potable
potârniche • *n* partridge
potasiu • *n* potassium
potcoav • *n* horseshoe
potcovar • *n* blacksmith
potec • *n* footpath, path
poten • *n* potency, power
potenial • *n* potential
poticneal • *n* trip
poiune • *n* potion
potoli • *v* ease, soothe
potpuriu • *n* medley
potrivi • *v* adjust, set
potrivire • *n* concordance, suitability
potrivit • *adj* agreeable, applicable, apt, opportune, suitable
potrivnic • *adj* contrarious
povârni • *n* inclination
pova • *n* counsel
povui • *v* counsel
poveste • *n* fable, story, tale, yarn
povestire • *n* history, relation
poz • *n* image, photo, photograph
poziie • *n* attitude, exposure, position, situation, status
poziiona • *v* position
poziional • *adj* positional
pozitiv • *adj* positive
pozitivism • *n* positivism
pozitron • *n* positron
prbui • *v* collapse
prbuire • *v* collapse • *n* drop
practic • *adj* practical, sensible
practic • *n* practice
practicabil • *adj* practicable
practicabilitate • *n* practicability
prad • *n* booty, loot, plunder, prey, raven, spoil
prda • *v* loot, pillage, pluck, plunder, ransack, ravage, sack
prdui • *v* strip

praf • *n* dust
prag • *n* threshold
pragmatic • *adj* pragmatic
pragmatic • *adj* pragmatic
pragmatism • *n* pragmatism
prji • *v* fry
prjitur • *n* cake
pralin • *n* chocolate, praline
prânz • *n* dinner, lunch
prânzi • *v* lunch
prpstie • *n* precipice
prpastie • *n* abyss
praseodim • *n* praseodymium
pri • *v* hoe
pratie • *n* sling
praz • *n* leek
praznic • *n* banquet
prea • *adj* real • *adv* too
precaut • *adj* careful, vigilant • *adv* cautiously
preceda • *v* precede
precedent • *n* precedent
preceden • *n* precedence
preceptor • *n* tutor
precipita • *v* precipitate
precipitaie • *n* precipitation
precis • *adv* accurately • *adj* unambiguous
precizie • *n* accuracy, precision
precum • *conj* as
precursor • *n* progenitor
predecesor • *n* ascendant, progenitor
predic • *n* sermon
predicat • *n* predicate
predicator • *n* preacher
predictibil • *adj* predictable
predicie • *n* prediction
predilecie • *n* predilection
predispoziie • *n* predisposition, vocation
predominant • *adj* dominant
preface • *v* pretend
prefacere • *n* conversion
prefectur • *n* prefecture
prefera • *v* choose, prefer
preferat • *n* preference
preferin • *n* like, preference
prefix • *n* prefix
pregti • *v* address, prepare, set
pregtire • *n* preparation
pregtit • *adj* set
pregtitor • *adj* preliminary, preparatory
pregeta • *v* hesitate
pregnant • *adj* pregnant
preîntâmpinare • *n* prevention
preistoric • *adj* prehistoric
prejudecat • *n* prejudice
prejudicia • *v* prejudice
prejudiciat • *adj* prejudiced
prejudiciator • *adj* derogatory
prejudicios • *adj* injurious
prejudiciu • *n* prejudice
preleva • *v* withdraw
preliminar • *adj* preliminary, preparatory
prelucrare • *n* processing
preludiu • *n* foreplay
prelung • *adj* oblong, prolonged
prelungi • *v* elongate, prolong, reach
prelungire • *n* overtime
premeditat • *adv* intentionally • *adj* premeditated
premis • *n* premise
premiu • *n* prize
prenatal • *adj* prenatal
prenupial • *adj* prenuptial
preocupa • *v* concern
preocupare • *n* concern, interest
preocupat • *adj* concerned
preot • *n* priest
prepara • *v* address, prepare
preparare • *n* preparation
preparat • *n* preparation
preparator • *adj* preparatory
prepelia • *n* quail
preponderent • *adj* dominant, prevalent
preponderen • *n* preponderance
prepoziie • *n* preposition
prepune • *v* assume
prepu • *n* prepuce
precolar • *adj* preschool
precolar • *adj* preschool
prescrie • *v* prescribe
prescripie • *n* prescription
prescriptiv • *adj* prescriptive
prescurtare • *n* abbreviation, shortcut
prescurtat • *adj* abbreviated
preedint • *n* chair
preedinte • *n* chair, president
preedini • *n* chair
presiune • *n* pressure
prestaie • *n* performance
presupune • *v* assume, guess, presume, suppose
presupunere • *n* conjecture, presumption
presur • *n* bunting
pre • *n* cost, price
pretenie • *n* claim, pretension
pretenios • *adj* pretentious
preteniozitate • *n* pretension
pretinde • *v* pretend
preios • *adj* precious, valuable
preui • *v* cost, treasure
prevalent • *adj* prevalent
prevztor • *adv* cautiously • *adj* reluctant
prevedea • *v* anticipate

prevenire • *n* prevention
prevenitor • *adj* bland
prevestire • *n* prediction
prevestitor • *adj* ominous
previzibil • *adj* predictable
previzibilitate • *n* predictability
previziune • *n* prediction
prezent • *adj* present
prezenta • *v* broadcast
prezen • *n* presence
prezentare • *n* appearance, exposure, introduction, pitch, presentation
prezentator • *n* host
prezervativ • *n* condom
prezice • *v* predict, prophesy
prezida • *v* preside
prezidare • *n* moderation
preziu • *n* eve
prezumie • *n* hypothesis, presumption
pricepe • *v* perceive, understand
pricepere • *n* apprehension, skill
priceput • *adj* cunning, happy, skillful
prichindel • *n* dwarf
pricinui • *v* cause
pricolici • *n* werewolf
prieten • *n* boyfriend, friend
prieten • *n* friend, girlfriend
prietenete • *adv* friendly
prietenie • *n* closeness, friendliness, friendship
prietenos • *adj* bland, friendly
prim • *adj* first
prim-model • *n* prototype
prim • *adj* first
prima • *adj* first
primar • *n* mayor
primri • *n* mayoress
primvar • *n* spring
primejdie • *n* danger, distress
primejdui • *v* endanger
primi • *v* gain, get, receive
primire • *n* acceptance
primitiv • *adj* primitive
primitivism • *n* primitivism
primitivitate • *n* primitivism
primitor • *adj* receptive
primul • *n* first • *adj* first
primul • *n* primrose
prin • *prep* across, through, via
principal • *adj* principal
principat • *n* principality
prinde • *v* catch
prin • *n* prince
prines • *n* princess
printre • *prep* among
priorat • *n* priory
prioritate • *n* priority
prism • *n* prism
prismatoid • *n* prismatoid
prisme • *n* prism
prisos • *n* excess • *adj* waste
pritenos • *adj* bland
privat • *adj* closed
privat • *n* latrine, toilet
priveghi • *n* wake
privelite • *n* sight
privi • *v* look, watch
privighetoare • *n* nightingale
privilegiu • *n* honor, privilege
privire • *n* gander
privitor • *n* spectator
priz • *n* socket
proaspt • *adj* fresh, sweet, verdant
prob • *n* proof, test, try
proba • *v* prove, try
probabil • *adj* probable • *adv* probably
probabilitate • *n* chance, likelihood, probability
probare • *n* try
problem • *n* issue, matter, problem
proceda • *v* proceed
procedeu • *n* procedure
procedur • *n* procedure
proces • *n* lawsuit, process, trial
procesare • *n* processing
procese • *n* process
procesor • *n* processor
procrastina • *v* procrastinate
procrea • *v* father, generate, procreate
procreare • *v* father
procurabil • *adj* available
prodigios • *adj* prodigious
productor • *n* manufacturer
produce • *v* generate, manufacture, produce, work
producere • *n* production
producie • *n* output, product, production
productiv • *adj* productive
produs • *n* product
proeminent • *adj* prognathous, prominent, salient
proeminen • *n* prominence
profesie • *n* profession
profesional • *n* professional • *adj* professional • *adv* professionally
profesionalism • *n* professionalism
profesionist • *adj* professional
profesiune • *n* profession
profesoar • *n* professor, teacher
profesor • *n* professor, teacher
profesoral • *adj* professorial
profei • *v* prophesy
profetiza • *v* prophesy
profit • *v* profit • *n* profit

profita • *v* profit
profituri • *v* profit
profund • *adj* deep, profound • *adv* deeply
profunzime • *n* depth
profuziune • *n* profusion
program • *n* calendar, program, show
programa • *v* slate
programare • *n* programming
programatoare • *n* programmer
programator • *n* programmer
progresa • *v* progress
progresist • *adj* progressive
progresist • *adj* progressive
progresiv • *adv* gradually • *adj* progressive
proiect • *n* project
proiectare • *n* projection
proiecie • *n* projection
proiectil • *n* missile, projectile
proiectile • *n* missile
prolin • *n* proline
promeiu • *n* promethium
promisiune • *n* pledge, promise
promite • *v* pledge, promise
promontoriu • *n* cape
promotor • *n* originator, promoter
promovare • *n* facilitation
prompt • *adv* hastily • *adj* prompt
promulga • *v* promulgate
promulgare • *n* promulgation
pronume • *n* pronoun
pronuna • *v* pronounce
pronunare • *n* pronunciation
pronunie • *n* pronunciation
proporie • *n* degree
proporii • *n* degree
proporional • *adj* proportional
proporional • *adj* proportional
propovedanie • *n* sermon
propoziie • *n* sentence
proprietar • *n* master, proprietor • *adj* proprietary
proprietate • *n* feature, ownership, possession, property
proprieti • *n* ownership
propriu • *adj* proper
propti • *v* support
propulsare • *n* propulsion
propulsie • *n* propulsion
propune • *v* move, propose
propunere • *n* proposal, proposition, suggestion
pror • *n* prow
proroc • *n* prophet
prosodie • *n* prosody
prosop • *n* towel
prosper • *adj* golden
prosperitate • *n* boom, prosperity, well-being
prost • *n* fool • *adj* poor, stupid
prostat • *n* prostate
prosti • *v* fool
prostie • *n* nonsense
prostime • *n* crowd
prostitua • *v* prostitute
prostituat • *n* prostitute, whore
prostituie • *n* demimonde
protactiniu • *n* protactinium
protecie • *n* guard, protection
protectoare • *n* protector, shield
protector • *n* protective, protector, shield
protectori • *n* shield
protein • *n* protein
proteja • *v* guard, preserve
protejare • *n* protection
protejat • *adj* protected, secure
protest • *n* objection
protesta • *v* protest
protez • *n* prosthesis
proteze • *n* prosthesis
protocol • *n* protocol
proton • *n* proton
prototip • *n* prototype
prov • *n* prow
proveni • *v* descend
proverb • *n* proverb, saying
proverbe • *n* proverb
provincie • *n* province
provizie • *n* provision, supply
provoca • *v* challenge, wreak
provocare • *n* challenge
provocator • *adj* ostentatious
proxenet • *n* pimp
proximitate • *n* proximity
prozaic • *adj* pedestrian
prudent • *adj* careful • *adv* cautiously
pruden • *n* prudence, tenderness
prun • *n* plum
prun • *n* plum • *adj* plum
pruncie • *n* babyhood
prundra-de-munte • *n* dotterel
prunda • *n* wagtail
prundí • *n* pebble
psalm • *n* psalm
psihedelic • *adj* psychedelic
psihiatrie • *n* psychiatry
psihiatru • *n* psychiatrist
psihoanaliz • *n* psychoanalysis
psihologic • *adj* psychological
psihologie • *n* psychology
psihometrie • *n* psychometry
psihoz • *n* psychosis
ptarmigan • *n* ptarmigan

ptomain • *n* ptomaine
public • *adj* communal
publicare • *n* publication
publicaie • *n* publication
publicitate • *n* advertising
pucioas • *n* brimstone
pudel • *n* poodle
pudic • *n* prude
pudr • *n* powder
pufuli • *n* willowherb
puhoi • *n* torrent
pui • *n* baby, calf, chick, chicken, cub, litter, young
puic • *n* pullet
puku • *n* puku
pula • *adv* fucking • *n* prick
pul • *n* dick, penis
pulbere • *n* dust, powder
pulmon • *n* lung
pulos • *adj* hung
pulp • *n* calf, pulp
pulsa • *v* pulsate, throb
pulsar • *n* pulsar
pulveriza • *v* crush
pum • *n* cougar, puma
pumn • *n* fist
pumnal • *n* dagger
punct • *n* point, stop, switch
punctual • *adj* prompt
punctualitate • *n* punctuality
punctuaie • *n* punctuation
pune • *v* place, put, set
pung • *n* bag, envelope
punitiv • *adj* punitive
punte • *n* bridge, footbridge
pup • *n* pupa
pupa • *v* kiss
pupz • *n* hoopoe
pupic • *n* kiss
pupil • *n* pupil
pur • *adj* pure
purcea • *n* sow
purcel • *n* piglet
purgatoriu • *n* purgatory
purice • *n* flea
purificare • *n* purification
puritate • *n* modesty, purity
puroi • *n* pus
puroia • *v* fester
purpuriu • *adj* amethyst, purpure
purta • *v* bear, behave, carry, wear
purtabil • *adj* wearable
purtare • *n* manner
purtat • *v* worn
purulent • *adj* pussy
puc • *n* gun, rifle
pucria • *n* prisoner
pucrie • *n* prison
puti • *n* brat
pustietate • *n* waste
pustiire • *n* harassment
pustiu • *n* desert • *adj* waste
pustul • *n* pustule
pu • *n* well
putea • *v* can, may
putere • *n* nerve, potency, power
puternic • *adj* robust, stark, strong
pui • *v* stink
puin • *adv* little
putin • *n* ability, faculty
putoare • *n* stink
putred • *adj* putrid, rotten
putrezi • *v* rot
puturos • *adj* lazy
puzderie • *n* army

R

rabat • *n* discount
rbda • *v* endure
rbdare • *n* nerve, patience
rabie • *n* rabies
rabin • *n* rabbi
rabota • *v* plane
rac • *n* crayfish
rceal • *n* aloofness, cold, coldness
racem • *n* raceme
rachet • *n* missile, racket, rocket
rachiu • *n* brandy
rci • *v* ice
raclaj • *n* curettage
racola • *v* tout
rcoritoare • *n* soda
rad • *n* roadstead
rdcin • *n* root
rdcinal • *adj* radical
radar • *n* radar
râde • *v* laugh
rade • *v* shave
radial • *adj* radial
radian • *n* radiance
radiaie • *n* radiation
radiator • *n* radiator
radicchio • *n* radicchio
radier • *n* eraser
radio • *n* radio

radio-goniometru • *n* goniometer
radioactiv • *adj* radioactive
radioactiv • *adj* radioactive
radioactivitate • *n* radioactivity
radioreceptor • *n* radio
radiu • *n* radium
radon • *n* radon
rafinaj • *n* refinement
rafinament • *n* refinement
rafinare • *n* refinement
rafinat • *adj* sophisticated
râgâi • *v* belch, burp
rgaz • *n* leisure
rage • *v* bellow, howl, roar
rgueal • *n* hoarseness
rguit • *adj* hoarse
rahat • *n* bullshit, crap, shit
rahis • *n* rachis
rahitism • *n* rickets
rai • *n* heaven, paradise
râie • *n* mange, scabies
raion • *n* district
ralid • *n* crake
ram • *n* branch
ram • *n* frame, framework, oar
râm • *n* earthworm
rmâne • *v* linger, remain, stay
rmas • *v* left
rmi • *n* vestige
rmie • *n* trash
rambursa • *v* reimburse
rambursabil • *adj* redeemable
rambursare • *n* refund, reimbursement, remuneration
ramia • *n* ramie
ramie • *n* ramie
ramifica • *v* branch
ramificare • *n* branch
ramificat • *adj* branched
ramificat • *adj* branched
ramur • *n* branch, offshoot
rmurea • *n* twig
rmuric • *n* twig
rmuros • *adj* branchy
ran • *n* injury, wound
rânced • *adj* rancid, rank
râncheza • *v* neigh
ranchiun • *n* grudge, rancor, umbrage
ranchiunos • *adj* spiteful, vindictive
rancoare • *n* rancor
rând • *n* row
randament • *n* performance, power
rânduial • *n* order
rândunea • *n* swallow
rândunic • *n* swallow
rândunic-de-mare • *n* gurnard, tern
rni • *v* hurt, wound
râp • *n* precipice, ravine
rapacitate • *n* rapacity, raven
rpi • *v* abduct, rape, usurp
rapid • *adj* fast, prompt, quick, rapid • *adv* quickly
rapiditate • *n* speed
rpire • *n* rape
rpirea • *n* rapture
rpitor • *n* abductor
raport • *n* relationship
rar • *adv* infrequently, rarely, seldom • *adj* rare, uncommon
rarefiat • *adj* rare
rareori • *adv* rarely, seldom
raritate • *n* oddity, rareness, rarity
rariti • *n* rarity
râs • *n* laugh, laughter, lynx
ras • *n* breed, race
rsad • *n* seedling
rsri • *v* rise
rsrit • *n* dawn, sun
rachet • *n* scraper
rscruce • *n* crossroads
rscumprare • *n* atonement
râset • *n* laugh, laughter
râsete • *n* hilarity
rsfa • *v* fawn, pamper, spoil
rsfat • *n* minion
rsfoi • *v* skim
rin • *n* pitch, resin
rinos • *adj* resinous
rasism • *n* racism
rasist • *n* racist
rasist • *n* racist
rspândi • *v* strew
rspândit • *adj* widespread
rspunde • *v* answer, reply, respond
rspundent • *adj* responsive
rspuns • *n* answer
rspunztor • *adj* liable
rsturna • *v* flip, reverse, upset • *n* snooker
rsturnat • *adj* reverse
rsuci • *v* twist
rsucire • *n* wrench
rsuflare • *n* blow
rsuna • *v* echo, resonate, resound
rsunet • *n* noise
rat • *n* snout
ra • *n* duck
raional • *adj* rational, sensible
raionalism • *n* rationalism
rioar • *n* duckling
raiune • *n* motive, reason, reasonableness
roi • *n* drake, duck
raton • *n* puppy, raccoon
ruc • *n* duckling
ruc • *n* duckling

râu • *n* river
ru • *adj* bad, evil, fiendish, mischievous, unholy, wicked • *adv* badly • *n* evil
rufctor • *n* malefactor, villain
rutcios • *adj* evil, mischievous, wicked
rutate • *n* badness, evil, spite, wickedness
ruvoitor • *adj* mischievous
ravagiu • *n* ravage
raven • *n* ravine
râvn • *n* appetite, craving
raz • *n* ray
rzbel • *n* war
rzboi • *n* war
rzbuna • *v* avenge, revenge
rzbunare • *n* retribution, revenge, vengeance, wrath
rzbuntor • *adj* vindictive
rzuitoare • *n* scraper
rea • *adj* unholy
reavoin • *n* malevolence
reactant • *n* reactant
reactan • *n* reactance
reactani • *n* reactant
reacia • *n* reaction
reacie • *n* feedback, reaction
reactiv • *n* reactant
real • *adj* real
realism • *n* realism
realist • *adj* realistic
realitate • *n* reality
realiza • *v* perceive, realize
realizare • *n* performance, sunrise
realizri • *n* performance
reamintire • *n* recollection, remembrance, reminiscence
reanima • *v* resuscitate
reanimare • *n* resuscitation
rearanjare • *n* rearrangement
reazem • *n* support
rebut • *n* trash
recapitula • *v* recapitulate
rece • *adj* cold
recent • *adj* recent • *adv* recently, ultimately
recenzent • *n* reviewer
recepiona • *v* receive
recepionabil • *adj* receivable
receptiv • *adj* receptive, sensitive
receptor • *n* set
recesie • *n* recession
recesiune • *n* recession
rechin • *n* shark
reciclare • *n* recycling
recidiva • *v* relapse
recif • *n* reef
recipient • *n* container, tank, vessel
recipis • *n* acknowledgement
reciproc • *adj* mutual, reciprocal
reciproc • *adj* reciprocal
reciprocitate • *n* reciprocity
recldit • *adj* reconstructed
reclam • *n* advertisement, advertising
reclamaie • *n* claim, complaint
recolta • *v* crop, harvest
recolt • *n* crop, harvest
recomanda • *v* advise, counsel, move
recomandabil • *adj* commendable
recomandare • *n* commendation, prescription
recompens • *n* consideration
reconcilia • *v* reconcile
reconciliere • *n* atonement, reconciliation
reconfortare • *n* solace
reconstituire • *n* reconstruction
reconstrucie • *n* reconstruction
reconstrui • *v* reconstruct
reconstruire • *n* reconstruction
reconstruit • *adj* reconstructed
record • *n* record
recorduri • *n* record
recrea • *v* recreate
recruta • *v* levy
recrutare • *n* draft
rectifica • *v* rectify
rectitudine • *n* rectitude
rector • *n* rector
recul • *n* repulsion
recunoate • *v* acknowledge, distinguish, recognize
recunoatere • *n* acknowledgement, confession, recognition, reconnaissance
recunosctor • *v* appreciate • *adj* grateful, thankful
recunoscut • *adj* acknowledged
recunoscut • *adj* acknowledged
recunotin • *n* acknowledgement, gratefulness, recognition, thankfulness
recupera • *v* recover
recuperare • *n* recovery
recurent • *adj* recurrent
recurs • *n* appeal
redactare • *n* edit
redresa • *v* redress
redresor • *n* rectifier
reduce • *v* cut, ease, reduce
reductibil • *adj* reducible
redus • *adj* reduced, scanty
redut • *n* redoubt
referi • *v* allude
referin • *n* reference, testimonial
reflectare • *n* reflecting, reflection
reflecie • *n* reflection
reflectiv • *adj* reflective
reflector • *n* reflector • *adj* shining

reflexie • *n* reflection
reflexiv • *adj* reflexive
reflux • *n* ebb
reform • *n* reform
reformabil • *adj* redeemable
reformabili • *adj* redeemable
refracie • *n* refraction
refractometru • *n* refractometer
refrigera • *v* refrigerate
refugiu • *n* sanctuary
refuta • *v* refute
refuza • *v* reject, scorn
regal • *adj* regal, royal
regal • *adj* regal, royal
regalitate • *n* royalty
regat • *n* kingdom
rege • *n* king
regent • *n* regent
regicid • *n* regicide
regiment • *n* regiment
regin • *n* queen
registru • *n* register
regiune • *n* district, region
regizor • *n* director
regizori • *n* director
regla • *v* adjust, govern, set
reglare • *n* regulation
reglementa • *v* govern
reglementare • *n* regulation
regn • *n* kingdom
regresa • *v* regress
regresiv • *adj* backward
regret • *n* compunction, regret, remorse, rue
regula • *v* temper
regul • *n* norm, regulation, rule
regulament • *n* regulation
regulare • *n* moderation
regulariza • *v* govern
regulat • *adv* habitually
regulator • *n* governor
reîncepere • *n* recurrence
reînceput • *adj* recurrent
reînnoi • *v* renew
reinstala • *v* reinstall
reîntoarcere • *n* recurrence, return
reînvia • *v* resuscitate
reînviere • *n* resurrection, resuscitation
relatare • *n* relation
relaie • *n* connection, relation, relationship
relaionat • *adj* related
relativ • *adj* relative
relativism • *n* relativism
relativitate • *n* relativity
relaxa • *v* relax
relaxare • *n* relaxation
relaxat • *adj* relaxed
releu • *n* relay
relevant • *adj* relevant
relevan • *n* relevance
relicv • *n* relic
relicvariu • *n* reliquary
relief • *n* relief
religie • *n* religion
relua • *v* rerun
reluctan • *n* reluctance
remarc • *n* remark, statement
remarcabil • *adj* remarkable
reminiscen • *n* reminiscence
remocher • *n* tugboat
remodela • *v* remodel
remuneraie • *n* remuneration
remucare • *n* atonement, compunction, remorse
ren • *n* reindeer
renate • *v* resuscitate
renglot • *n* damson
renglot • *n* damson
reniu • *n* rhenium
renova • *v* renew
rent • *n* rent
renume • *n* name, renown
renumit • *adj* renowned
renuna • *v* abandon, forsake, renounce
renunare • *n* abandonment
repara • *v* mend, repair
reparare • *n* reparation
reparaie • *n* reparation
repartiza • *v* allot, apportion, distribute, split
repatriere • *n* repatriation
repaus • *n* ease, relaxation, repose, rest
repauza • *v* rest
repede • *adj* fast, quick, rapid • *adv* fast, quickly
reperabil • *adj* traceable
repetare • *n* recurrence, repetition
repetat • *adj* recurrent
repetiie • *n* repetition
repezitor • *n* accelerator
replic • *n* replica
replicare • *n* replication
reporta • *v* report
reportaj • *n* feature
reprezenta • *v* depict, represent
reprezentabil • *adj* representable
reprezentare • *n* depiction, production, representation
reprezentativ • *adj* representative
reproba • *v* reprobate
reproduce • *v* generate, reproduce
reproducere • *n* replica, replication, reproduction

reproducie • *n* reproduction
reproductiv • *adj* reproductive
reproductor • *adj* reproductive
repro • *n* reproach
reproa • *v* reproach
reptil • *n* reptile
republic • *n* republic
republican • *adj* republican
republican • *adj* republican
republicanism • *n* republicanism
repugnant • *adj* repugnant
repugnan • *n* abhorrence
repulsie • *n* reluctance, repulsion
repulsiv • *adj* repellent
reputabil • *adj* reputable
reputat • *adj* shining
reputaie • *n* name
reedin • *n* residence
resentiment • *n* resentment
resorbi • *v* resorb
reou • *n* stove
respect • *n* consideration, honor, respect
respecta • *v* respect
respectabil • *adj* respectable
respectabilitate • *n* respectability
respectos • *adj* respectful
respingtor • *adj* disgusting, noisome, obnoxious, repellent
respinge • *v* reject, scorn
respingere • *n* repulsion
respira • *v* breathe
respiraie • *n* breath
responsabil • *adj* liable, responsible
responsabilitate • *n* accountability, liability, responsibility
rest • *n* rest, waste
restaura • *v* reconstruct
restaurant • *n* restaurant
restaurare • *n* reconstruction
restauraie • *n* reconstruction
restitui • *v* return
restituibil • *adj* redeemable
restrânge • *v* limit, restrain
restricie • *n* restriction
restricionat • *adj* restricted
restrictiv • *adj* restrictive
resurs • *n* resource
resurse • *n* resource
resuscita • *v* resuscitate
resuscitare • *n* resuscitation
reea • *n* lattice, net, network
reele • *n* network
retenie • *n* retention
reet • *n* prescription, recipe
retin • *n* retina
reine • *v* hinder, restrain, retain
reinere • *n* retention
retort • *n* retort
retracta • *v* retract
retrage • *v* recede, retract, withdraw
retragere • *n* recession
retras • *adj* obscure
retribuie • *n* remuneration
retrogradare • *n* degradation
retrospectiv • *adj* retrospective
returna • *v* return
reui • *v* obtain, succeed
revrsa • *v* flood
revrsare • *n* overflow
revelare • *n* revelation
revelaie • *n* revelation
revelator • *n* developer
revendica • *v* claim
revendicare • *n* claim
reveni • *v* temper
revenire • *n* return, temper
revent • *n* rhubarb
revers • *n* reverse
revigora • *v* reinvigorate
revist • *n* magazine, publication
revoca • *v* annul, reverse
revocabil • *adj* defeasible
revocare • *n* revocation
revolta • *v* revolt
revolt • *n* revolt
revoluie • *n* revolution
revoluionar • *n* revolutionary • *adj* revolutionary
revolver • *n* gun
revolverul • *n* revolver
rezed • *n* mignonette
rezema • *v* lean
rezerv • *n* aloofness, discretion, modesty, stockpile, supply
rezerva • *v* book
rezervaie • *n* sanctuary
rezervor • *n* storage, tank
rezident • *n* resident
reziden • *n* residence
reziduu • *n* trash
rezista • *v* resist
rezistare • *n* resistance
rezistent • *adj* resistant
rezisten • *n* nerve, resistance, tolerance
rezistent • *adj* resistant
rezistibil • *adj* resistible
rezolva • *v* resolve, solve
rezolvare • *n* answer, solution
rezonabil • *adj* logical, sensible
rezonabili • *adj* logical
rezonan • *n* resonance
rezultant • *adj* resultant
rezultat • *n* result, solution
rezumat • *n* abstract

rictus • *n* rictus
rid • *n* furrow
rida • *v* wrinkle
ridica • *v* arise, heft, lift, stand
ridicat • *adj* high
ridiche • *n* radish
ridicol • *adj* ludicrous, ridiculous
rigid • *adj* inflexible, rigid, stark
rigl • *n* measure, ruler
rigoare • *n* rectitude
rima • *v* rhyme
rim • *n* rhyme
rindea • *n* plane
rinichi • *n* kidney
rinit • *n* rhinitis
rinocer • *n* rhinoceros
risc • *n* risk
risca • *v* chance, endanger, risk
risip • *n* extravagance
risipi • *v* waste
rit • *n* rite
ritm • *n* cadence, meter, pace, rhythm
ritual • *n* rite
rival • *n* rival
rivalitate • *n* faction
rizoto • *n* risotto
roab • *n* wheelbarrow
roade • *v* eat, gall, gnaw
roat • *n* wheel
rob • *n* slave
robi • *v* enslave
robie • *n* slavery
robotica • *n* robotics
robust • *adj* bouncing, robust, sound
robust • *adj* robust
robustee • *n* robustness, soundness
roc • *n* rock
rochie • *n* dress
rochii • *n* dress
rod • *n* fruit, harvest
rodie • *n* pomegranate
rodier • *n* pomegranate
roditor • *adj* fruitful
rodiu • *n* pomegranate, rhodium
rodnic • *adj* fruitful, productive
rodnicie • *n* fruitfulness
rododendron • *n* rhododendron
rogojin • *n* mat
rogoz • *n* sedge
roi • *n* swarm
roib • *adj* chestnut, sorrel
rom • *n* rum
roman • *n* novel
romantic • *adj* sentimental
romantism • *n* romanticism
romb • *n* rhombus
rostur • *n* gall
rocat • *adj* reddish, ruddy, rusty
rocat-cafeniu • *adj* auburn
rocov • *n* carob
rocov • *n* carob
roea • *n* blush
roi • *v* blush
roie • *n* tomato
rost • *n* purpose
rosti • *v* spell
rostogolire • *n* somersault
rou • *n* gules, red • *adj* gules, red
rotaie • *n* cycle
roti • *v* rotate
rotire • *n* crank
rotor • *n* rotor
rotund • *adj* round
rou • *n* dew
roua-cerului • *n* sundew
roua-soarelui • *n* sundew
roz • *adj* carnation, pink, rose • *n* pink
roz • *n* rose
rozacee • *n* rose
roztor • *n* rodent
rozet • *n* mignonette
rozmarin • *n* rosemary
rubarb • *n* rhubarb
rubidiu • *n* rubidium
rubin • *n* ruby
rubiniu • *adj* ruby
rubl • *n* ruble
• *n* ruble
ruchet • *n* rocket
rucol • *n* rocket
rucsac • *n* backpack
rudenie • *n* kinship, relationship
rufe • *n* clothes, garment, laundry
rug • *n* bonfire, bramble, pyre
ruga • *v* ask, beg, pray, request
rugciune • *n* prayer
rugin • *n* rust
rugini • *v* rust
ruginit • *adj* rusty
ruginiu • *n* rust
ruina • *v* spoil, wreck
ruin • *n* ruin, wreck
ruj • *n* lipstick
rujeol • *n* measles
ruliu • *n* roll
rumega • *v* ruminate • *n* rumination
rumegtoare • *n* ruminant
rumegu • *n* sawdust
rupe • *v* tear
rupere • *n* fracture, tear
rupt • *adj* broken
ruptur • *n* rupture, tear
rural • *adj* country, rural
ruinare • *n* abashment

ruinat • *adj* ashamed
ruine • *n* abashment, disgrace, humiliation, shame
rut • *n* heat
rut • *n* rue, run
ruteniu • *n* ruthenium
rutherfordiu • *n* rutherfordium
rutin • *n* routine

S

s • *v* may
a • *n* saddle
sabie • *n* sword
sabla • *v* sand, sandblast
ablon • *n* pattern, template
sabotaj • *n* sabotage
sabotare • *n* sabotage
sac • *n* bag, envelope, sack
sâcâi • *v* gall, irritate
sâcâitor • *adj* pestiferous
acal • *n* jackal
sacrifica • *v* sacrifice
sacrificiu • *n* sacrifice
sacrosanct • *adj* sacrosanct
sacru • *adj* sacred
sadea • *adj* sheer
sadic • *adj* sadistic
sadism • *n* sadism
safir • *n* sapphire
safterea • *n* fumitory
sgeat • *n* arrow
sgeata-apei • *n* arrowhead
sgeata-apelor • *n* arrowhead
sgettor • *n* archer
sagitar • *n* archer
ah • *n* check, chess, shah
ah-mat • *n* checkmate
aib • *n* washer
saiga • *n* saiga
aizecilea • *adj* sixtieth
al • *n* scarf, shawl, wrap
salam • *n* salami
salamandr • *n* salamander
salariat • *n* breadwinner
salariu • *n* remuneration, salary, wage
salat • *n* lettuce, salad
salb • *n* necklace
salb-moale • *n* spindle
slbatic • *adj* animal, haggard, wild
slbie • *n* darnel
salcie • *n* willow
saliva • *v* slobber
saliv • *n* saliva
salt • *n* caper, hop, leap
slta • *v* jump, leap
sltare • *n* leap
saltea • *n* mattress
salut • *interj* hello, hi • *n* salutation, salute
saluta • *v* greet, hail
salutare • *n* salute
salv • *n* salvo
salva • *v* save
salvare • *n* salvation
salvgarda • *v* safeguard
salvie • *n* sage
amanism • *n* shamanism
smân • *n* seed
samariu • *n* samarium
sâmbovin • *n* hackberry
sâmbure • *n* pit
amoa • *n* chamois
samovar • *n* samovar
ampanie • *n* champagne
ampon • *n* shampoo
amponare • *n* shampoo
samur • *n* sable
samurai • *n* samurai
sân • *n* bowel, breast, tit
sntate • *n* health, well-being
sntate! • *interj* cheers
sntos • *adj* healthy, right, sane, sound
sanctuar • *n* asylum, sanctuary
sandvi • *n* sandwich
sânge • *n* blood
sânger • *n* dogwood
sângera • *v* bleed
sângeros • *adj* bloody, sanguinary
sanguinar • *adj* sanguinary
sangvin • *adj* sanguinary
sanie • *n* sledge
snioar • *n* sanicle
ans • *n* chance, luck
ans • *n* fortune
anse • *n* chance
an • *n* ditch, moat
sânt • *n* saint
sânt • *n* saint
antaj • *n* blackmail
antaja • *v* blackmail
santal • *n* sandalwood
sap • *n* hoe
spa • *v* dig, hoe, undermine
sapien • *n* wisdom
sptmân • *n* week

sptmânal • *adj* weekly
apte • *n* seven
spun • *n* soap
spunari • *n* soapwort
spuni • *v* soap
sra • *v* salt
srac • *adj* destitute, poor
sraci • *n* poor
srci • *v* impoverish
srcie • *n* poverty
saramur • *n* brine
srbtoare • *n* celebration, holiday
srbtori • *v* celebrate
srbtorire • *n* celebration
sarcasm • *n* sarcasm
sarcin • *n* burden, charge, duty, load, pack
sarcofag • *n* sarcophagus
sardele • *n* anchovy
sardin • *n* sardine
sare • *n* salt
aret • *n* cart
sârguincios • *adj* hardworking
sârguin • *n* appetite, diligence
sri • *v* branch, caper, dive, jump, leap
sarig • *n* opossum
sritur • *n* caper
arj • *n* batch
arm • *n* charm
sârm • *n* wire
srman • *adj* poor
armant • *adj* charming
arnier • *n* hinge
arpe • *n* serpent, snake, worm
sarsel • *n* teal
srut • *n* kiss
sruta • *v* kiss
sâsâit • *n* hiss
saschiu • *n* periwinkle
ase • *n* six
asea • *adj* sixth
aselea • *adj* sixth
sat • *n* country, countryside, village
satan • *n* devil
satanic • *adj* satanic
satelit • *n* satellite
saietate • *n* satiety
satir • *n* satire
satiric • *adj* satirical
satisfctor • *adj* satisfactory
satisface • *v* fulfill
satisfacere • *n* fulfillment, satisfaction
satisfacie • *n* contentment, fulfillment, satisfaction
satisfcut • *adj* happy, satisfied
stul • *adj* full
satura • *v* saturate
stura • *v* cloy, sate, satiate
sturat • *adj* full
saturat • *adj* saturated
sau • *conj* or
saun • *n* sauna
savant • *n* scientist
savura • *v* enjoy
savurabil • *adj* pleasant
savurabilitate • *n* pleasantness
savuros • *adj* lush
saxifrag • *n* saxifrage
saxofonist • *n* saxophonist
scabie • *n* mange, scabies
scdea • *v* decrease, subtract
scdere • *n* diminution, subtraction
scafandrier • *n* diver
scafandru • *n* diver
scai • *n* leatherette
scaiete • *n* thistle
scalar • *adj* scalar
scalpa • *v* scalp
scam • *n* flock, fluff, lint
scamonee • *n* scammony
scana • *v* scan
scanare • *n* scan
scanat • *n* scan
scandiu • *n* scandium
scândur • *n* board, plank
scaner • *n* scanner
scaneriza • *v* scan
scanerizare • *n* scan
scanerizor • *n* scanner
scânteia • *v* glimmer, sparkle
scânteie • *n* glint, spark, sparkle
scânteiere • *n* flicker
scânteind • *adj* ablaze
scap • *n* scape
scpa • *v* drop, escape, flee, shake
scpare • *n* escape
scpta • *v* set
scar • *n* ladder, stair, staircase, stairs, stirrup
scarabeu • *n* scarab
scârbi • *v* disgust
scârbos • *adj* disgusting, gross, noisome
scri • *n* stapes
scrmna • *v* card, pluck
scrpina • *v* scratch
scatiu • *n* serin
scaun • *n* chair, seat, stool, throne
scaune • *n* chair
scen • *n* platform
scepticism • *n* incredulity, skepticism
schelet • *n* frame, framework, skeleton
schepsis • *n* wit
scherzo • *n* scherzo
schi • *n* ski, skiing

schia • *v* ski
schilod • *adj* crippled
schilodi • *v* mutilate
schimb • *n* change, exchange
schimba • *v* change, edit, exchange, switch
schimbabil • *adj* changeable, variable
schimbare • *n* alteration, change
schinduf • *n* fenugreek
chiop • *adj* lame
chiopta • *v* limp
schiopatand • *adj* lame
schisma • *n* splinter
schi • *n* blueprint, draft, sketch
schizofrenie • *n* schizophrenia
scila • *n* squill
scinda • *v* split
sclav • *n* slave
sclavie • *n* slavery
sclipire • *n* flicker
coal • *n* school
scoar • *n* bark
scoate • *v* pluck, remove, tear
scobitoare • *n* toothpick
scobitur • *n* dimple
scoic • *n* seashell, shell
scoicar • *n* oystercatcher
colariza • *v* school
colarizare • *n* schooling
colire • *n* literacy
scop • *n* aim, goal, purpose
scor • *n* mark, score
scorni • *v* invent
scorpie • *n* shrew
scorpion • *n* scorpion
scorar • *n* nuthatch
scorioar • *n* cinnamon
scorior • *n* cinnamon
scoru-de-munte • *n* rowan
scoru-psresc • *n* rowan
scrâni • *v* grit
scrib • *n* scribe
scrie • *v* author, write
scriere • *n* writing
scriitoare • *n* writer
scriitor • *n* writer
scrima • *v* fence
scrim • *n* fencing
scripete • *n* pulley
scris • *n* writing • *adj* written
scris • *adj* written
scrisoare • *n* letter
scroaf • *n* sow
scrofulare • *n* figwort
scrot • *n* scrotum
scrotal • *adj* scrotal
scrum • *n* ash
scrumier • *n* ashtray
scrupul • *n* qualm
scrupulos • *adv* scrupulously
scruta • *v* scan
scufunda • *v* immerse, sink
scufundare • *n* dive
scufundtor • *n* diver
scufundtur • *n* dimple
scuipa • *v* spit
scuipat • *n* spit, spittle
scula • *v* arise, awake, awaken
scul • *n* tool
sculpta • *v* hew, sculpture
sculptor • *n* sculptor
sculptori • *n* sculptor
sculptur • *n* sculpture
scump • *adj* darling, dear, expensive, loved
scund • *adj* short
scurge • *v* drain
scurt • *adj* brief, short
scurta • *v* abbreviate, shorten • *n* cutoff
scurtare • *n* shortcut
scurttur • *n* shortcut
scut • *n* shield
scutec • *n* diaper
scuter • *n* scooter
scuti • *v* exempt
scutire • *n* exempt
scutit • *adj* exempt
scutura • *v* dust
scuturare • *n* shake
scuza • *v* excuse
scuz • *n* forgiveness • *interj* sorry
scuz-m • *interj* sorry
scuzai • *interj* sorry
scuzai-m • *interj* sorry
se • *pron* herself, himself
sear • *n* evening
searbd • *adj* insipid
sec • *adj* dry
seca • *v* strip
secant • *n* secant
secar • *n* rye
sectuit • *adj* emaciated, exhausted, haggard
secera • *v* harvest, reap, sickle
secer • *n* sickle
seceri • *n* harvest
secet • *n* drought
sechestra • *v* sequester
sechestru • *n* distraint
secol • *n* century
secret • *n* secret • *adj* secret
secret • *adj* secret
secretar • *n* clerk, secretary
secretar • *n* secretary

secretare • *n* secretion
secretee • *n* secrecy
secreie • *n* secretion
secreiere • *n* secretion
secreionare • *n* secretion
secretism • *n* secrecy
secretos • *adj* secretive
secie • *n* section
secionare • *n* section
seciune • *n* section
sector • *n* section, sector
secund • *adj* second
secunda • *v* second
secund • *n* second
secundar • *adj* peripheral, secondary
securitate • *n* safety, security
secven • *n* sequence
edea • *v* sit
sedentar • *adj* sedentary
sedil • *n* cedilla
edin • *n* meeting
sediu • *n* headquarters
seductor • *adj* enticing
seduce • *v* seduce
ef • *n* boss, chief, head, manager
segment • *n* section, segment
segmenta • *v* segment
eic • *n* sheik
sejur • *n* sojourn
selectare • *n* selection
selecie • *n* election, selection
selectiv • *adj* selective
selector • *n* switch
seleniu • *n* selenium
selianism • *n* somnambulism
semna • *v* resemble, sow
semestru • *n* semester
semi- • *adj* half
semicerc • *n* semicircle
semicercuri • *n* semicircle
semicircular • *adj* semicircular
semiconductor • *n* semiconductor
semilun • *n* crescent, half-moon
seminar • *n* academy
emineu • *n* fireplace
semiton • *n* undertone
semivocal • *n* semivowel
semn • *n* augury, mark, note, sign
semna • *v* sign
semnal • *n* signal
semnala • *v* flag
semnaliza • *v* flag
semnalizator • *n* indicator, signal
semntur • *n* signature
semnificant • *adj* significant
semnifican • *n* significance
semnificativ • *adj* significant
semnificativitate • *n* significance
enil • *n* caterpillar
senilitate • *n* senility
senin • *adj* clear, cloudless, serene
senintate • *n* serenity
sens • *n* sense
sensibil • *adj* responsive, sensible, sensitive
sensibilitate • *n* sensitivity, tenderness
sensibilizare • *n* sensitization
sentiment • *n* feeling, sentiment
sentimental • *adj* feeling, sentimental
sentimentalitate • *n* sentimentality
sentimente • *n* feeling
sentin • *n* decision, sentence
senzaional • *adj* swell
senzualitate • *n* sensuality
separa • *v* separate, split
separare • *n* detachment, insulation, separation
separat • *adj* separate, single
separat • *adj* separate
sepia • *n* sepia • *adj* sepia
sepie • *n* cuttlefish, sepia
sepulcral • *adj* funeral
sequoia • *n* sequoia
ser • *n* greenhouse
erb • *n* serf, villain
serbare • *n* celebration
serenad • *n* serenade
serendipitate • *n* serendipity
sergent • *n* sergeant
serial • *adj* serial
serie • *n* series, string
erif • *n* sheriff
serin • *n* serine
sering • *n* syringe
serios • *adj* serious, solemn, weighty
seriozitate • *n* seriousness
serotonin • *n* serotonin
sertar • *n* drawer
serv • *n* slave
erveel • *n* napkin, tissue
servi • *v* serve
serviciu • *n* service, work
servil • *adj* obsequious, servile
servilism • *n* servility
servilitate • *n* servility
servitor • *n* servant
servus • *interj* hello
es • *adj* flat, level • *n* lowland, plain
sesam • *n* sesame
esime • *n* sixth
sesizabil • *adj* sensible
sesizare • *n* perception
set • *n* set
set • *n* seta

sete • *n* craving, thirst
setos • *adj* thirsty
evalet • *n* easel
sever • *adj* hard, harsh, relentless, stern
severitate • *n* severity
sex • *n* gender, sex
sexism • *n* sexism
sexos • *adj* sexy
sextant • *n* sextant
sextet • *n* sextet
sexual • *adj* sexual
sexual • *adj* sexual
sexy • *adj* lush, sexy
sezon • *n* season
ezut • *n* bottom
sfânt • *adj* holy • *n* saint
sfânt • *adj* holy • *n* saint
sfârc • *n* nipple, teat, tit
sfâri • *v* end
sfârire • *n* termination
sfârit • *n* back, end, ending, finish
sfârtica • *v* mangle
sfâia • *v* tear
sfat • *n* advice, counsel
sftui • *v* advise, counsel
sftuire • *n* counsel
sfecl • *n* beet
sfer • *n* field, sphere
sferic • *adj* spherical
sferoid • *n* spheroid
sfert • *n* quarter
sfenic • *n* candlestick
sfida • *v* beard, defy
sfinenie • *n* sainthood
sfinx • *n* sphinx
sfoar • *n* ligature, line
sfori • *v* snore
sforial • *n* snore
sforit • *n* snore
sforitur • *n* snore
sfredel • *n* drill
sfruntare • *n* effrontery
i • *adv* also, even, still, too • *conj* and
siaj • *n* wake
sicomor • *n* sycamore
sicriu • *n* coffin
siena • *adj* sienna
sifilis • *n* syphilis
sigur • *adj* certain, reliable, secure, sound, sure, trustworthy • *adv* confidently • *interj* sure
siguran • *n* certainty, certitude, confidence, safety, security
sihstrie • *n* cloister
silab • *n* syllable
silenios • *adj* noiseless
silex • *n* flint
siliciu • *n* silicon
silicon • *n* silicone
silicul • *n* silicle
silicv • *n* silique
iling • *n* shilling
silogism • *n* syllogism
siloz • *n* silo
siluet • *n* silhouette
silur • *n* catfish
silv • *n* forest
silvie • *n* warbler
simbol • *n* symbol
simbolic • *adj* symbolic • *adv* symbolically
simboliza • *v* symbolize
simetric • *adj* symmetrical
simetrie • *n* symmetry
simian • *n* simian • *adj* simian
simie • *n* monkey
similar • *adj* similar
similaritate • *n* similarity
simonie • *n* simony
simpatic • *adj* sweet
simpatie • *n* sympathy
simpatizant • *adj* sympathizer
simpatizant • *adj* sympathizer
simpatizani • *adj* sympathizer
simpatizator • *adj* sympathizer
simplifica • *v* abbreviate, simplify
simplu • *adj* simple, straightforward
simpozion • *n* symposium
simptom • *n* symptom
simptomatic • *adj* symptomatic
sim • *n* sense
simi • *v* feel, sense, work
simitor • *adj* responsive, sensible, sensitive
simultan • *adv* simultaneously
simultaneitate • *n* simultaneity
in • *n* rail
sinagog • *n* synagogue
sincer • *adv* outright • *adj* sincere, straightforward, true
sinceritate • *n* sincerity, truth
sinclinal • *n* synclinal
sincron • *adj* synchronous
sincroniza • *v* synchronize
sincronizare • *n* synchronization
indril • *n* shingle
indrili • *v* shingle
sinecur • *n* sinecure
singular • *adj* single, singular
singularitate • *n* singularity
singur • *adv* alone • *adj* only, single, sole • *n* soul
singurtate • *n* aloneness, solitude
sinistru • *adj* fiendish, ominous, sinister

sinonim • *n* synonym
inil • *n* chinchilla
sintagm • *n* phrase
sintax • *n* syntax
sintetic • *adj* synthetic
sintetizator • *n* synthesizer
sintez • *n* synthesis
sinucidere • *n* suicide
sinuciga • *n* suicide
sinuciga • *n* suicide
sinus • *n* sine, sinus
sinuzit • *n* sinusitis
ir • *n* string, succession
siren • *n* mermaid
iret • *adj* cunning, vulpine • *n* lace, shoelace
iroi • *n* stream
sirop • *n* syrup
sistem • *n* system
sistematic • *adj* systematic
sistematiza • *v* systematize
sistematizare • *n* systematization
sistemic • *adj* systematic
sit • *n* sieve
sitar • *n* woodcock
situare • *n* situation
situaie • *n* occasion, situation, status
slab • *adj* feeble, lame, lean, poor, sickly, skinny, thin, weak
slbi • *v* flag, thin, waste, weaken
slbit • *adj* effete, impaired
lagr • *n* hit
slalom • *n* slalom
slang • *n* slang
slnin • *n* bacon
lap • *n* flip-flop
slav • *n* glory
libovi • *n* slivovitz
slobod • *adj* free • *n* freedom
sloboz • *n* cum
slobozi • *v* cum
slug • *n* servant
slujb • *n* church
slujitor • *n* servant
smahoz • *n* sperm
smântân • *n* cream
smaragd • *n* emerald
smarald • *n* emerald
smaraldiu • *n* emerald • *adj* emerald
smarand • *n* emerald
smârc • *n* swamp
smârcu • *n* sperm
smecleu • *n* sperm
smicea • *n* twig
smoal • *n* pitch
smoc • *n* tuft
smochin • *n* fig
smochin • *n* fig
smuci • *v* tug
smulge • *v* pluck, tear
smulgere • *n* pluck
niel • *n* cutlet
snob • *n* snob
snop • *n* bundle
nur • *n* ligature, line
soacr • *n* mother-in-law
oapt • *n* whisper
soare • *n* sun, sunshine
oarece • *n* mouse
oarece-de-câmp • *n* vole
soart • *n* destiny, fate, fortune, luck
sob • *n* fire, stove
sobol • *n* mole
sobrietate • *n* sobriety, temperance
soc • *n* elder, elderberry
oc • *n* choke
ocant • *v* shocking
sociabil • *adj* gregarious, sociable
social • *adj* social
socialism • *n* socialism
socialist • *adj* socialist
societate • *n* company, society
sociologie • *n* sociology
soclu • *n* socket
socoteal • *n* check
socoti • *v* calculate • *n* count
socru • *n* father-in-law
sodiu • *n* sodium
sodomie • *n* sodomy
ofer • *n* chauffeur, driver
sofisticat • *adj* sophisticated
ofran • *n* saffron
ofrna • *n* safflower
ofrnel • *n* safflower
ofrniu • *adj* saffron
software • *n* software
oim • *n* falcon
sol • *n* earth, ground, soil, sol
sol • *n* sole
old • *n* hip
soldat • *n* soldier
solemn • *adj* solemn
solemnitate • *n* solemnity
solicitare • *n* effort
solicitudine • *n* solicitude
solid • *adj* solid, sound
solidifica • *v* set, solidify
soliditate • *n* robustness, solidity, soundness
solist • *n* soloist
solist • *n* soloist
solo • *n* solo • *adj* solo
solstiiu • *n* solstice
solubil • *adj* solvable

soluie • *n* answer, solution
soluiona • *v* answer, solve
soluionare • *n* answer, solution
solvabil • *adj* solvable
solvabil • *adj* solvable
solz • *n* scale
omaj • *n* unemployment
omer • *adj* unemployed
somn • *n* catfish, sleep
somnambul • *n* somnambulist
somnambulism • *n* somnambulism
somnambulist • *n* somnambulist
somnior • *n* nap
somnola • *v* slumber
somnolent • *adj* sleepy
somnolen • *n* sleepiness
somnoros • *adj* sleepy
somnule • *n* nap
somon • *n* salmon
somptuos • *adj* sumptuous
sonat • *n* crazy
sonat • *n* crazy, sonata
sonda • *v* fathom, scan
sonerie • *n* doorbell
sonet • *n* sonnet
sonor • *n* voice
opârl • *n* lizard
sopran • *n* soprano
opron • *n* lean-to
opti • *v* whisper
sor • *n* sister
sorbi • *v* sip
sorg • *n* sorghum
sori • *v* sun
oricar • *n* buzzard
oricel • *n* mouse
ort • *n* shorts
sort • *n* apron, variety
sorta • *v* sort
sortiment • *n* variety
sos • *n* sauce
osea • *n* carriageway, highway
sosi • *v* arrive
sosire • *n* arrival
so • *n* husband
soie • *n* wife
ovi • *v* hesitate
ovitor • *adj* irresolute
sovârf • *n* oregano
soviet • *n* soviet
ovinism • *n* chauvinism
spad • *n* sword
spadice • *n* spadix
spadix • *n* spadix
spagatul • *n* split
spaim • *n* dismay, fear, fright, terror
spla • *v* wash
splcit • *adj* drab
splare • *n* ablution, laundry
splat • *n* laundry
spltorie • *n* laundry
spanac • *n* spinach
spânz • *n* hellebore
spânzura • *v* hang
spânzurtoare • *n* gallows
spânzurtoarea • *n* hangman
sparanghel • *n* asparagus
sparcet • *n* sainfoin
sprgtor • *n* burglar
sprtur • *n* crevice
spate • *n* back, behind, reverse
spaiu • *n* room, space
spaiu-timp • *n* spacetime
special • *adj* particular
specie • *n* species
specific • *adj* particular, specific
specifica • *v* itemize
specificitate • *n* specificity
specimen • *n* specimen
spectacol • *n* entertainment, show, sight, spectacle
spectacular • *adj* spectacular
spectaculos • *adj* spectacular
spectator • *n* spectator
spectral • *adj* spectral
spectru • *n* rainbow, spectrum
speculant • *n* bear
spera • *v* hope
speran • *n* hope, trust
sperare • *n* trust
speria • *v* frighten, scare
speriat • *adj* frightened
sperietoare • *n* dread, scarecrow
sperm • *n* semen, sperm
spermatozoid • *n* sperm, spermatozoon
spic • *n* ear, spike
spicul • *n* spicule
spin • *n* prickle, thorn
spinare • *n* back
spinet • *n* spinet
spinteca • *v* split
spioan • *n* spy
spion • *n* spy
spiona • *v* spy
spirit • *n* esprit, soul, spirit
spiritual • *adj* spiritual
spiritualism • *n* spiritualism
spiritualist • *n* spiritualist
spiritualitate • *n* spiritualism
spirt • *n* spirits
spirturi • *n* spirits
spi • *n* spoke
spital • *n* hospital
splendid • *adj* gorgeous

splendoare • *n* brilliance
splin • *n* goldenrod, spleen
splinu • *n* goldenrod
spongie • *n* sponge
sponsoriza • *v* sponsor
spontan • *adj* spontaneous
spontaneitate • *n* spontaneity
spor • *n* spore
spori • *v* increase • *n* spore
sporire • *n* increase
sport • *n* sport
spovedi • *v* confess
spovedire • *n* confession
sprâncean • *n* eyebrow
spre • *prep* at, to
spre-napoi • *adj* backward • *adv* behind
sprijin • *n* support
sprijini • *v* support
sprijinire • *n* support
sprint • *n* sprint
sprinta • *v* sprint
sprinten • *adj* quick
sprinter • *n* sprinter
sprinter • *n* sprinter
sprot • *n* sprat
spulbera • *v* dispel
spuma • *v* foam
spum • *n* foam
spum-de-mare • *n* meerschaum
spumega • *v* foam
spune • *v* say
spurca • *v* defile, desecrate, dirty, soil, sully, taint
sta • *v* linger, stand, stay
stabil • *adj* constant, secure, stable
stabili • *v* establish, prove, set
stabiliment • *n* establishment
stabilire • *n* establishment
stabilit • *adj* set
stabilitate • *n* equilibrium, stability
stacojiu • *adj* carmine, scarlet
stadion • *n* stadium
stadiu • *n* situation
tafet • *n* relay
stafid • *n* raisin
stagnare • *n* stagnation
stâlp • *n* column, pillar, post
stamin • *n* stamen
stan • *n* rock
stân • *n* sheepfold
stânc • *n* cliff, rock
stncu • *n* jackdaw
standard • *n* standard
standarde • *n* standard
stâng • *adj* left
stâng • *n* left
stângaci • *adj* awkward, clumsy • *n* left-handed
staniu • *n* tin
stânjen • *n* iris
stânjeneal • *n* discomfiture
stânjenel • *n* iris
stânjeni • *v* hinder
stan • *n* stanza
stpân • *n* master
stpâni • *v* command, master
stpânire • *n* possession
stârc • *n* heron
stare • *n* condition, shape, situation, state, status, temper
stârni • *v* titillate
stârpi • *v* eradicate
start • *n* beginning
struitor • *adj* assiduous, sedulous
stârv • *n* carcass
stat • *n* country, nation, state
static • *adj* static
staie • *n* station, terminal
statistic • *adj* statistical • *adv* statistically
statistic • *n* statistics
statornicie • *n* steadfastness
statuet • *n* figurine
statuie • *n* statue
statut • *n* status
staul • *n* stable, stall
stvilar • *n* lock
stea • *n* star
stea-de-mare • *n* starfish
steag • *n* banner, flag
tecr • *n* jack, plug
stejar • *n* oak
stel • *n* stele
stelar • *adj* astral, stellar
stelu • *n* asterisk, star
step • *n* steppe
terge • *v* brush, clean, wipe
steril • *adj* unfruitful
steril • *adj* barren
sterilitate • *n* unfruitfulness
sterilizare • *n* sterilization
sterilizaie • *n* sterilization
sterp • *adj* blasted, unfruitful, waste
terpeli • *v* filch
ters • *adj* neutral
sters • *adj* lame
stetoscop • *n* stethoscope
stewardes • *n* stewardess
ti • *v* know
stibiu • *n* antimony
sticl • *n* bottle, glass
sticlete • *n* goldfinch
stigmatism • *n* stigmatism
stigmatiza • *v* brand
tiin • *n* knowledge, science

tiinific • *adj* scientific
stil • *n* manner, style, stylus
stilet • *n* dagger
stilou • *n* pen
stim • *n* adoration, esteem
stima • *v* esteem
stimate • *adj* dear
stimul • *n* stimulus
stimula • *v* stimulate, titillate
stimulare • *n* encouragement
stimulator • *n* stimulant
stimulent • *n* stimulant
stindard • *n* banner, flag, standard
stinge • *v* extinguish
stinghereal • *n* discomfiture, displeasure, uneasiness
tire • *n* communication, knowledge, news
tiuc • *n* pike
tiulete • *n* corncob
stiv • *n* stack
stivui • *v* stack
stoarce • *v* fleece, squeeze, twist, wring
stoc • *n* store
stocare • *n* storage
stocastic • *adj* stochastic
stof • *n* cloth, material
stof-gabardin • *n* worsted
stoicism • *n* stoicism
stol • *n* flock
stomac • *n* stomach
stop • *n* stop
strbun • *n* grandfather, progenitor
strbunic • *n* grandfather
strad • *n* street
strdui • *v* try
strin • *n* alien, foreigner • *adj* foreign
strin • *n* alien
straj • *n* watch
strjer • *n* watch
strluci • *v* shine
strlucind • *adj* ablaze
strlucire • *n* brilliance, brilliancy, gleam, radiance, shine
stralucitor • *adj* shiny
strlucitor • *adj* bright, shining, stellar
strâmb • *adj* crooked, lopsided
strmo • *n* ancestor, ascendant, grandfather, progenitor
strmoi • *n* grandfather
strâmt • *adj* narrow
strâmtoare • *n* strait
strmurare • *n* goad
strânge • *v* harvest, squeeze, tighten
strangula • *v* neck
straniu • *adj* curious, eerie, strange, weird
strânsur • *n* feed, fodder, harvest
strnut • *n* sneeze
strnuta • *v* sneeze
strpunge • *v* pierce, stab
stranic • *n* spanking
strat • *n* coating, layer
strategie • *n* strategy
treang • *n* noose
streche • *n* botfly
strecura • *v* filter, steal, strain
strecurtoare • *n* colander
stres • *n* stress
strica • *v* damage, fuck, harm, mar, ruin, spoil
stricciune • *n* damage
stricare • *n* degradation
stricat • *adj* kaput, scarlet
strident • *adj* garish
striga • *v* call, scream, shout, shriek, yell
strigt • *n* cry, shriek
strigoaie • *n* vampire
strigoi • *n* vampire
strivire • *n* crushing
strof • *n* stanza
stroniu • *n* strontium
structur • *n* construction, fabric, frame, framework
structural • *adj* structural
structurat • *adj* structured
strudel • *n* strudel
strugure • *n* grape
strun • *n* string
strung • *n* lathe
strungrie • *n* turnery
stru • *n* ostrich
student • *n* student
student • *n* student
studia • *v* study
studiere • *n* study
studiu • *v* learn • *n* study
stuf • *n* reed, thatch
stup • *n* beehive
stup • *n* tow
stupefacie • *n* daze
stupefia • *v* daze
stupid • *adj* stupid
stupiditate • *n* stupidity
stupoare • *n* bewilderment, daze
sturion • *n* sturgeon
sturz • *n* thrush
sub • *prep* below, beneath, under • *adj* nether • *adv* underneath
sub-familie • *n* subfamily
subarboret • *n* copse, thicket
subatomic • *adj* subatomic
subcontient • *n* subconscious • *adj* subconscious
subcontiin • *n* subconscious

subcontinent • *n* subcontinent
subdiviza • *v* subdivide
subdiviziune • *n* section
subgrup • *n* subgroup
subiect • *n* matter, plot, purpose, subject
subiectiv • *adj* subjective
subiectivitate • *n* subjectivity
subit • *adj* sudden • *adv* suddenly
subjuga • *v* subdue, subjugate
subjugare • *n* dependence, subjugation
submarin • *n* submarine • *adj* submarine
submina • *v* undermine
subminare • *n* sabotage
subordonare • *n* dependence
subordonat • *adj* subordinate
subordonat • *adj* subordinate
subrutin • *n* procedure
subscrie • *v* subscribe
subsol • *n* basement
subsonic • *adj* subsonic
subsonic • *adj* subsonic
substan • *n* matter, substance
substanial • *adj* substantial
substanialitate • *n* substantiality
substantiv • *n* noun
substantiviza • *v* noun
substituent • *n* substitute
substitui • *v* replace, substitute
substituitor • *n* substitute
substitut • *n* substitute
substructur • *n* substructure
subsuoar • *n* armpit
subteran • *adj* nether
subia • *v* thin
subtire • *adj* slender
subire • *adj* lean, thin
subtropical • *adj* subtropical
suburban • *n* suburban
suburban • *n* suburban
suburbie • *n* suburb
subversiv • *adj* subversive
subzisten • *n* subsistence
suc • *n* juice
succeda • *v* succeed
succede • *v* succeed
succes • *n* success
succese • *n* success
succesiune • *n* succession
succesiv • *adj* consecutive
sucursal • *n* branch
sud • *n* south
sud-sudvest • *n* south-southwest
sud-vest • *n* southwest
sudestic • *adj* southeast
sudic • *adj* south, southern
sudoare • *n* sweat
sudvest • *n* southwest
sudvestic • *adj* southwest
suferi • *v* anguish, suffer
suferin • *n* agony, distress, pain, suffering, woe • *adj* suffering
suficient • *adv* enough, sufficiently
sufix • *n* suffix
sufla • *v* blow
suflare • *n* blast, blow, draft
suflet • *n* guts, heart, soul, spirit
sufletesc • *adj* animal, spiritual
sufletete • *adv* spiritually
suflu • *n* blast, breath
sugtor • *n* sucker
suge • *v* suck, suckle
sugera • *v* connote, suggest
sugestie • *n* proposition, suggestion
sugestiona • *v* propose
sugestionabil • *adj* suggestible
sugestionare • *n* suggestion
sughi • *n* hiccup
sughia • *v* hiccup
sugruma • *v* neck
sui • *v* ascend, climb
uiera • *v* blow, hiss, whistle
suit • *n* string
sul • *n* awl
sulf • *n* sulfur
sulfat • *n* sulfate
sulfur • *n* sulfide
sulfurare • *v* sulfur
sulfuri • *n* sulfur
suli • *n* javelin, lance, spear
sultan • *n* sultan
sultanat • *n* sultanate
sum • *n* amount, sum
suna • *v* call, ring, sound
unc • *n* ham
sunet • *n* noise, sound, voice
supa • *v* supper
sup • *n* broth
supra • *v* bother, pique, roil, upset
suprcios • *adj* cantankerous
suprare • *n* pain, sorrow, spite, umbrage, upset
suprat • *adj* upset
suprtor • *adj* irksome
super • *adj* real, swell
superb • *adj* gorgeous, great, superb
superb • *adj* superb
superflu • *adj* superfluous
superfluitate • *n* superfluity
superfluu • *adj* superfluous, waste
superioar • *n* superior
superior • *n* superior • *adj* superior
superioritate • *n* ascendancy
superlativ • *adj* superlative
supermagazin • *n* supermarket

supersonic • *adj* supersonic
superstiios • *adj* eerie
superviza • *v* supervise
supervizare • *n* supervision
supeu • *n* supper
suport • *n* support
suporta • *v* bear, tolerate
suporter • *n* supporter
suporturi • *n* support
supoziie • *n* conjecture
supraabundent • *adj* overabundant
supraevalua • *v* overvalue
suprafa • *n* area, surface
supraîncrca • *v* overload
supraînsrcina • *v* overload
suprainteligen • *n* brilliance
supranatural • *adj* supernatural
suprarealism • *n* surrealism
supraturare • *n* race
supraveghere • *n* check, supervision
supravieui • *v* live, survive
supravieuire • *n* survival
suprem • *adj* paramount, superlative, supreme
supremaie • *n* ascendancy, supremacy
supune • *v* force, subdue
supura • *v* fester
supurant • *adj* pussy
supus • *adj* obedient, submissive
sur • *adj* gray
surâde • *v* smile
surâs • *n* smile
surcea • *n* chip, sliver
surd • *adj* deaf
surori • *n* sister
surpa • *v* undermine
surprinde • *v* surprise
surprindere • *n* amazement, astonishment, disbelief, surprise
surpriz • *n* surprise, treat
surs • *n* source
urub • *n* screw
urubelni • *n* screwdriver
sus • *adv* up
susan • *n* sesame
susceptibil • *adj* cantankerous, sensitive, susceptible
susceptibilitate • *n* susceptibility
susceptivitate • *n* susceptibility
sushi • *n* sushi
suspect • *adj* suspicious
suspecta • *v* distrust
suspenda • *v* suspend
suspendare • *n* suspension
suspendat • *adj* dormant
suspensie • *n* suspension
suspicios • *adj* suspicious
suspin • *n* sigh, sob
suspina • *v* sigh
susine • *v* corroborate, second, support
sustrage • *v* subtract
susura • *v* whisper
suta • *adj* hundredth
sutlea • *n* hundredth • *adj* hundredth
sutien • *n* bra
sutime • *n* hundredth
suveran • *n* sovereign • *adj* sovereign
uvi • *n* wisp
uvie • *n* wisp
uvoi • *n* current, stream
svastic • *n* swastika

T

tabac • *n* tobacco
tbcar • *n* tanner
tbci • *v* tan
tabel • *n* table
tabel • *n* table
tabele • *n* calculator
tabl • *n* blackboard
table • *n* draughts
tblie • *n* panel
tbli • *n* slate
taburet • *n* stool
tcere • *n* silence
tcere! • *interj* silence
tachelaj • *n* rigging
tciune • *n* coal, ember, embers
tact • *n* cadence, measure
tactic • *n* tactic
tcut • *adj* quiet
tgdui • *v* controvert
tgduire • *n* contestation
tia • *v* butcher, crop, cut, slaughter
tiat • *adj* cut
tiere • *n* cut, section
tietor • *n* cutter
tietur • *n* cut, section, tear
taifun • *n* typhoon
taiga • *n* taiga
tain • *n* secret
tainic • *adj* secret
tainic • *adj* secret
tios • *adj* biting
ti • *n* edge

tiei • *n* noodle
talang • *n* cowbell
talent • *n* skill
talie • *n* waist
talisman • *n* charm, talisman
taliu • *n* thallium
taloner • *n* hooker
talp • *n* sole
talpa-gâtei • *n* motherwort
tmâie • *n* frankincense, incense
tamandua • *n* tamandua
tamarin • *n* tamarin, tamarind
tamarisc • *n* tamarisk
ambal • *n* dulcimer
tamburin • *n* tambourine
tâmpl • *n* temple
tâmplar • *n* carpenter
tânr • *adj* small, young • *n* youth
tanc • *n* tank
tandree • *n* tenderness
tangen • *n* contingence
tangent • *n* tangent
tangerin • *n* tangerine
tangibil • *adj* tangible
tanrec • *n* tenrec
tantal • *n* tantalum
ânar • *n* mosquito
ap • *n* goat
tapet • *n* wallpaper
tapir • *n* tapir
ar • *n* tsar
ara • *adj* country
ar • *n* country, land
trgna • *v* drawl, procrastinate
ârâi • *v* drizzle
ran • *n* boor, farmer, hick, peasant, yokel
rnesc • *adj* rural
rnoi • *n* hick
trâe • *n* bran
arc • *n* run, sheepfold
tare • *adj* hard, loud
târf • *n* prostitute, whore
târg • *n* bazaar, borough, market
tarhon • *n* tarragon
târî • *v* crawl
trie • *n* power, spirit
tarif • *n* fare
rm • *n* shore
târtan • *n* kike
tartan • *n* tartan
ru • *n* spike
târziu • *adv* afterwards, late • *adj* late
tast • *n* key
tastatur • *n* keyboard
tat • *n* dad, father
â • *n* teat, tit
tataie • *n* grandfather
tâân • *n* hinge
ttic • *n* daddy
tatu • *n* armadillo
tatua • *v* tattoo
tatuaj • *n* tattoo
tun • *n* horsefly
taur • *n* bull
tautologie • *n* tautology
tavan • *n* ceiling
tax • *n* duty, tax
taxa • *v* levy
taxare • *n* levy
taximetru • *n* taxi
taxonomic • *adj* taxonomic
taxonomie • *n* taxonomy
teac • *n* bean, scabbard, sheath
teafr • *adj* sound
team • *n* anxiety, dread, fear
eapn • *adj* rigid
east • *n* skull
teatral • *adj* theatrical
teatru • *n* theater
tec • *n* teak
techneiu • *n* technetium
tegument • *n* integument
tehnic • *adj* technical
tehnic • *adj* technical • *n* technique
tehnici • *adj* technical
tehnocraie • *n* technocracy
tehnologic • *adj* technological
tehnologie • *n* technology
tei • *n* basswood, linden
teism • *n* theism
el • *n* aim, purpose
telecomunicaii • *n* telecommunication
telefon • *n* phone, telephone
telefona • *v* call
telefonist • *n* operator
telegraf • *n* telegraph
telegram • *n* cable
telegrame • *n* cable
telemarketing • *n* telemarketing
telepatie • *n* telepathy
telescop • *n* telescope
telescopic • *adj* telescopic
televiziune • *n* television
televizor • *n* television
elin • *n* celery
elin-de-rdcin • *n* celeriac
telur • *n* tellurium
tem • *n* homework, purpose, subject, theme
temtor • *adj* frightened
teme • *v* dread
temei • *n* foundation
temeinic • *adj* solid
temelie • *n* foundation

temere • *n* dread
temeritate • *n* fearlessness, temerity
temni • *n* prison
tempera • *v* temper
temperament • *n* temper
temperamental • *adj* temperamental
temperatur • *n* fever, temperature
templu • *n* temple
tempo • *n* pace
temporal • *adj* temporal
temporar • *adj* temporal
ten • *n* complexion
tenace • *adj* feisty
tenacitate • *n* tenacity
tendin • *n* inclination, tendency
tendon • *n* tendon
tenebros • *adj* tenebrous
tenis • *n* tennis
tensioactiv • *adj* surface-active
tensional • *adj* tensional
tensiune • *n* stress, tension, voltage
tenta • *v* tempt
tentant • *adj* enticing, tempting
tentativ • *n* endeavor, go, try
teologic • *adj* theological
teologie • *n* theology
teorem • *n* conjecture
teorie • *n* theory
teorii • *n* theory
teozofie • *n* theosophy
terapeut • *n* therapist
terapeutic • *adj* therapeutic
terapie • *n* medicine
terasa • *v* terrace
teras • *n* terrace
terbiu • *n* terbium
terci • *n* porridge
terebentin • *n* turpentine
teren • *n* field, land, pitch, soil, terrain
terestru • *adj* terrestrial
teribil • *adj* awful, terrible
teritorial • *adj* territorial
teritoriu • *n* territory
termal • *adj* thermal
termen • *n* term
termic • *adj* thermal
termina • *v* close, complete, end, finish, stop
terminabil • *adj* terminable
terminal • *n* terminal
terminare • *n* termination
terminat • *adj* full
terminaie • *n* end
terminologie • *n* terminology
termistor • *n* thermistor
termit • *n* termite
termometru • *n* thermometer
termonuclear • *adj* thermonuclear
termosfer • *n* thermosphere
tern • *adj* dim
teroare • *n* terror
terorism • *n* terrorism
terorist • *n* terrorist • *adj* terrorist
terorist • *n* terrorist • *adj* terrorist
estur • *n* fabric, texture
ese • *v* weave
tesl • *n* adze
test • *n* test
testa • *v* try
testament • *n* testament, will
testicular • *adj* testicular
estoas • *n* tortoise
testosteron • *n* testosterone
esut • *n* tissue
tetin • *n* nipple
tetraplegic • *n* quadriplegic
tetraplegie • *n* quadriplegia
evrie • *n* plumbing
textile • *n* fabric
textur • *n* texture
tez • *n* thesis
tezaur • *n* treasury
tici • *v* tick
ticlos • *n* rascal, villain
ticloie • *n* vileness, wickedness
iclete • *n* nuthatch
icnit • *n* nut
ticsit • *adj* crowded
tifon • *n* gauze
tifos • *n* typhus
igan • *n* gypsy
iganc • *n* gypsy
igni • *v* haggle
igar • *n* cigarette, smoke
igaret • *n* cigarette
igl • *n* tile
tigroaic • *n* tigress
tigru • *n* tiger
tij • *n* cane
timiditate • *n* shyness
timoftic • *n* timothy
timon • *n* helm
timp • *n* time, weather
timpi • *n* time
timpizor • *n* timer
timpuri • *n* time
timpuriu • *adj* early
tinamu • *n* tinamou
tinctur • *n* tincture
ine • *v* hold, keep, lean
tineree • *n* youth
int • *n* aim, purpose
intar • *n* redpoll
intaur • *n* centaury

inti • *v* target
inut • *n* address, posture
tip • *n* bloke, boy, dude, guy
tip • *n* chick
ipa • *v* scream, shout, shriek, yell
ipar • *n* eel
tipar • *n* printing, typography
tiprit • *adj* typed
tipritur • *n* printing
ipt • *n* cry, shriek
iptor • *adj* garish, ostentatious
tipograf • *n* printer
tipografic • *adj* typographical
tipografie • *n* typography
tipografiere • *n* printing
tiraj • *n* draft, run
tiran • *n* bully
tiranic • *adj* tyrannical
tiranie • *n* tyranny
tiranozaur • *n* tyrannosaur
tirbuon • *n* corkscrew
tirozin • *n* tyrosine
tis • *n* yew
titan • *n* titanium
iei • *n* oil
iter • *n* zither
titlu • *n* headline, title
titular • *adj* incumbent
tiz • *n* namesake
toalet • *n* bathroom, toilet
toamn • *n* autumn
toan • *n* tantrum, whim
toarce • *v* purr, spin
toata • *adv* all
toate • *adv* all
tob • *n* drum
tobogan • *n* slide
toca • *v* mince
tocit • *adj* blunt
tocmai • *adv* just
tocsin • *n* curfew
toi • *n* crisis
ol • *n* inch
tolb • *n* quiver
tolera • *v* bear, tolerate
tolerabil • *adj* tolerable
tolerant • *adj* lenient
toleran • *n* leniency, tolerance
tolerant • *adj* lenient
tolerare • *n* indulgence
tolerna • *n* tolerance
tomat • *n* tomato
ton • *n* pitch, tuna, voice
opi • *v* caper
opit • *n* caper
topaz • *n* topaz
topi • *v* melt
topit • *adj* molten
topologie • *n* topology
topora • *n* viola
toporic • *n* hatchet
torace • *n* chest
torent • *n* stream, torrent
toriu • *n* thorium
tornad • *n* tornado
torpedo • *n* torpedo
torpil • *n* torpedo
tors • *n* body, purr
tort • *n* cake, thread
tor • *n* torch
tortura • *v* torment, torture
tortur • *n* torture
tot • *n* aggregate, all, whole • *adv* all, still • *pron* everything
total • *adj* full, stark • *adv* totally, whole • *n* whole
totalitate • *n* totality, whole
totdeauna • *adv* always
totem • *n* totem
totemism • *n* totemism
toi • *adv* all • *pron* everyone
totui • *conj* albeit, yet • *adv* however, nevertheless
tovar • *n* associate, companion, comrade
toxic • *adj* toxic
toxicologie • *n* toxicology
toxicoman • *n* user
trabuc • *n* cigar
tracasa • *v* gall
tractor • *n* tractor
trda • *v* betray
trdare • *n* treason
trdtor • *n* betrayer, traitor
tradescania • *n* spiderwort
tradiie • *n* custom, heritage, tradition
tradiional • *adj* traditional
traductor • *n* interpreter, translator
traduce • *v* translate
traducere • *n* translation
traductibil • *adj* translatable
trage • *v* pluck, pull, shoot, tug
tragedie • *n* tragedy
tragere • *n* draught, draw, drawing
trahee • *n* windpipe
tri • *v* dwell, live
traiectorie • *n* trajectory
trainic • *adj* durable • *v* endure
trainic • *v* endure
trainici • *v* endure
trinicie • *n* soundness
trambulin • *n* springboard, trampoline
tramvai • *n* tram
trandafir • *n* rose
trandafiriu • *adj* pink

trândvi • *v* loaf
trans- • *adv* across
transacie • *n* transaction
transatlantic • *adj* transatlantic
transatlantic • *adj* transatlantic
transbordare • *n* transshipment
transcendental • *adj* transcendental
transcrie • *v* transcribe
transcripie • *n* transliteration
transductor • *n* transducer
transfera • *v* convey, transfer
transforma • *v* change, convert, transform
transformare • *n* conversion, transformation
transformri • *n* transformation
transformator • *n* transformer
transgresiune • *n* transgression
translaie • *n* translation
translatoare • *n* interpreter
translator • *n* interpreter, translator
transliteraie • *n* transliteration
transmisie • *n* translation, transmission
transmisiune • *n* broadcast
transmiãtor • *n* transmitter
transmite • *v* air, convey, transmit
transmitere • *n* transmission
transparent • *adj* transparent
transparen • *n* transparency
transpira • *v* sweat
transpiraie • *n* sweat
transplantare • *n* transplant
transport • *n* transportation
transporta • *v* convey, transport
transportare • *n* transport, transportation
transsubstaniaie • *n* transubstantiation
transsubstaniere • *n* transubstantiation
transvazare • *n* transfusion
transversal • *adv* across
trântor • *n* drone
tranzient • *adj* transient
tranziional • *adj* transitional
tranzitiv • *adj* transitive
tranzitivitate • *n* transitivity
tranzitoriu • *adj* transient
trap • *n* run
tras • *n* draught
trasabil • *adj* traceable
trstur • *n* feature, idiosyncrasy
trstura • *n* complexion
trata • *n* traffic • *v* treat
tratament • *n* cure, medicine, treatment
tratat • *n* convention, treatise, treaty
trataie • *n* treat
traumatic • *adj* traumatic
travers • *n* sleeper, summer
treapt • *n* rung, stair, step
treaz • *adj* awake
trebui • *v* must, need
trebuincios • *adj* useful
trector • *adj* fugacious, fugitive, temporal, transient • *n* fugitive
trece • *v* occur, pass
trecut • *n* past • *adj* past
trecut • *adj* past
trei • *n* three
trei-ri • *n* hepatica
treiera • *v* thresh
treime • *n* third
tremolo • *n* quaver
tremur • *n* quaver, shudder
tremura • *v* shiver, shudder, tremble
tren • *n* train
trenci • *n* raincoat
trepidare • *n* trepidation
trepidaie • *n* trepidation
treptat • *adv* gradually
tres • *n* facing
tresri • *v* jump
trezi • *v* awake, awaken, wake
trezire • *n* sunrise
trezorerie • *n* treasury
trezorerii • *n* treasury
triad • *n* trinity
trib • *n* tribe
tribal • *adj* tribal
tribord • *n* starboard
tribunal • *n* courthouse
tributar • *n* tributary
triciclu • *n* tricycle
tridimensional • *adj* three-dimensional
tridimensional • *adj* three-dimensional
trifoi • *n* clover, shamrock, trefoil
trigonometrie • *n* trigonometry
trimestru • *n* quarter, term, trimester
trimis • *v* sent
trimite • *v* send, set
trinchet • *n* foremast
trinitarianism • *n* trinitarianism
triplu • *n* triple
triptofan • *n* tryptophan
trist • *adj* blue, sad
trist • *adj* sad
tristee • *n* darkness, grief, melancholy, sadness, sorrow
triton • *n* newt
triumf • *n* triumph
triumfa • *v* triumph
triumfant • *adj* triumphant
triumftor • *adj* triumphant
triunghi • *n* triangle
troc • *n* exchange
trofeu • *n* award, trophy
trol • *n* troll

• *n* troll
troll • *n* troll
trombon • *n* bullshit, trombone
tromboz • *n* thrombosis
trombus • *n* thrombus
trompet • *n* trumpet
tron • *n* throne
trop • *n* trope
tropical • *adj* tropical
tropical • *adj* tropical
troposfer • *n* troposphere
troscot • *n* knotgrass
trota • *v* trot
trotuar • *n* sidewalk
trubadur • *n* troubadour
truf • *n* truffle
trufie • *n* arrogance, conceit, greatness, pride
trunchi • *n* body, log, stem
trup • *n* body
trupesc • *adj* bodily
trus • *n* set
trust • *n* trust
tu • *pron* thou, you
tuberculoz • *n* tuberculosis
tucan • *n* toucan
tuf • *n* bush, shrub
tufi • *n* grove, thicket
uic • *n* slivovitz
tulbura • *v* upset
tulburare • *n* complaint, disturbance, turbulence, uneasiness
tulburat • *adj* crazy
tulbure • *adj* murky, thick, turbid
tulichin • *n* mezereon
tulip • *n* tulip
tuliu • *n* thulium
tulpin • *n* stalk, stem
tumb • *n* caper, somersault
tumul • *n* tumulus
tumult • *n* tumult, uproar
tumulte • *n* tumult
tun • *n* cannon, gun
tuna • *v* thunder
tunde • *v* crop, mow, shear
tundr • *n* tundra
tunel • *n* tunnel
tunet • *n* thunder, thunderclap
tungsten • *n* tungsten
tunic • *n* tunic
tunsoare • *n* haircut
tupeu • *n* brashness, gall, nerve
tur • *n* watch
turba • *v* rage
turbare • *n* rabies
turbat • *adj* rabid
turbulent • *adj* turbulent
turbulen • *n* turbulence
turcoaz • *n* turquoise • *adj* turquoise
turcoaz • *n* turquoise
turism • *n* tourism
turist • *n* tourist
turist • *n* tourist
turiti • *n* tourist
turl • *n* tower
turm • *n* flock, herd
turment • *n* torment
turn • *n* rook, tower
turna • *v* pour
turntor • *n* betrayer
turnichet • *n* turnstile
turnur • *n* bustle
turt • *n* cake
turtire • *n* crushing
urur • *n* icicle
tuse • *n* cough
tui • *v* cough
tutun • *n* tobacco

U

ubicuitate • *n* ubiquity
ubicuu • *adj* ubiquitous
ucenic • *n* apprentice
ucide • *v* waste
uciga • *n* killer
uciga • *n* killer
ucigtor • *adj* deadly
ud • *adj* wet
uda • *v* moisten, wet
uger • *n* udder
uimi • *v* amaze, astound
uimire • *n* amazement, astonishment, disbelief
uimitor • *adj* amazing
uita • *v* forget, look
uituc • *adj* forgetful
ulcer • *n* ulcer
ulei • *n* oil
uli • *n* lane
uliu • *n* goshawk
ulm • *n* elm
ultim • *adj* last, latest
ultragia • *v* outrage
ultraj • *n* outrage

ului • *v* astound, daze
uluire • *n* amazement, bewilderment, daze
uman • *adj* human
umanism • *n* humanism
umanitate • *n* humaneness, humanity
umr • *n* shoulder
umbel • *n* umbel
umbla • *v* pace, walk, wander
umbr • *n* shade, shadow, umbrage
umbrel • *n* umbrella
umbri • *v* obfuscate, shade, umbrage
umbros • *adj* shady
umed • *adj* damp, humid, moist, wet
umed • *adj* humid, moist
umezeal • *n* humidity, moisture
umezi • *v* moisten
umfla • *v* blow, inflate
umflabil • *adj* inflatable
umflat • *adj* inflated
umfltur • *n* swelling
umidiitate • *n* humidity
umil • *adj* humble, submissive
umili • *v* humiliate
umilin • *n* humility
umilire • *n* abasement, humiliation
umilitate • *n* humility
umple • *v* fill, full
un • *art* an
unchi • *n* uncle
unde • *adv* where • *conj* where
undeva • *adv* somewhere
undi • *n* rod
unealt • *n* tool
uneori • *adv* occasionally, sometimes
unge • *v* grease
ungher • *n* angle
unghi • *n* angle
unghie • *n* fingernail, nail
unghiular • *adj* angular
ungura • *n* horehound
uni • *v* join, unite
unic • *adj* only, singular, unique • *n* soul
unicameral • *adj* unicameral
unicorn • *n* unicorn
unificare • *n* unification
uniform • *n* uniform
uniformitate • *n* sameness
unilateral • *adj* one-sided, unilateral
unilateral • *adj* unilateral
unire • *n* conjunction, connection, union, unity
unit • *adj* connected, single, united
unit • *adj* united
unitar • *adj* single
unitarianism • *n* unitarianism
unitate • *n* device, oneness, union, unit, unity
uniune • *n* affiliation, bund, union
univers • *n* universe
universitar • *adj* academic
universitar • *adj* academic
universitate • *n* academy, school, university
univoc • *adj* unambiguous
unt • *n* butter
untrie • *n* dairy
untur • *n* lard
unu • *n* one
ura • *v* congratulate, wish
ur • *n* hatred
uragan • *n* hurricane
urangutan • *n* orangutan
uraniu • *n* uranium
urât • *n* tedium • *adj* ugly
urbanism • *n* urbanity
urbanitate • *n* urbanity
urbanizare • *n* urbanization
urbe • *n* city
urca • *v* ascend, climb, increase
urcior • *n* jug
urdinare • *n* diarrhea
urdoare • *n* blearedness, rheum
ureche • *n* ear
urechelni • *n* earwig
urgie • *n* wrath
urî • *v* hate, scorn, spite
uria • *adj* enormous, giant, gigantic, huge, immense • *n* giant
uria • *n* giantess
urina • *v* pee
urla • *v* howl, roar, scream, shout, shriek, yell
urlet • *n* cry, shriek, ululation, whoop
urma • *v* follow
urm • *n* behind, gleam, mark, trace, vestige
urmri • *v* follow, pursue, watch
urmrire • *n* chase
urma • *n* descendant
urmtor • *adj* next
urs • *n* bear
ursuz • *adj* churlish, morose
urzeal • *n* warp
urzi • *v* devise, hatch, plot
urzic • *n* nettle
u • *n* door
uscat • *adj* dry • *n* land
ui • *n* door
uor • *adj* easy, light, lightweight
usturoi • *n* garlic
uura • *v* alleviate, ease, facilitate, lighten
uurare • *n* ease, facilitation, relief
uurina • *n* ease

uter • *n* womb
util • *adj* helpful, useful
utilitate • *n* use, utility
utiliza • *v* use
utilizat • *adj* used
utilizatoare • *n* user
utilizator • *n* user
utopie • *n* utopia
uvul • *n* uvula
uz • *n* use
uzin • *n* factory
uzual • *adj* common, normal, ordinary, usual • *adv* habitually
uzur • *n* wear
uzurpa • *v* usurp
uzurpator • *n* usurper

V

vac • *n* cow
vacan • *n* recess, vacation
vcar • *n* cowboy, cowherd
vcri • *n* cowgirl
vacarm • *n* noise
vaccin • *n* vaccine
vad • *n* ford
vdit • *adj* apparent, obvious, transparent
vduv • *adj* widowed • *n* widower
vduv • *n* widow
vag • *adj* dim
vagabond • *adj* homeless • *n* vagabond
vagin • *n* vagina
vagon • *n* car, carriage
vai • *interj* alas, ouch
val • *n* swell
vl • *n* veil, wimple
valabilitate • *n* validity
vale • *n* valley
valen • *n* valence
valerian • *n* valerian
valid • *adj* valid
validare • *n* validation
validitate • *n* validity
valin • *n* valine
valoare • *n* amount, value
valoros • *adj* valuable
vâltoare • *n* vortex, whirlpool
valtrap • *n* blanket
valuri • *n* swell
valut • *n* currency
valv • *n* valve
vam • *n* custom, customs
vampir • *n* vampire
vampir • *n* vampire
vampiri • *n* vampire
vâna • *v* hunt
vân • *n* vein
vanadinit • *n* vanadinite
vanadiu • *n* vanadium
vânat • *n* quarry
vânt • *n* eggplant
vântoare • *n* hunt, pursuit
vântor • *n* hunter
vandabil • *adj* marketable
vandalism • *n* vandalism
vanilie • *n* vanilla
vanitate • *n* conceit, vanity
vânjos • *adj* robust
vânjoie • *n* robustness
vânt • *n* fart, wind
vântos • *adj* windy
vântura • *v* fan
vânturel • *n* kestrel
vânzare • *n* sale
vânztoare • *n* seller, vendor
vânztor • *n* betrayer, salesman, seller, vendor
vpaie • *n* flame
vapor • *n* boat
vr • *n* cousin
var • *n* lime
var • *n* cousin, summer
vra • *v* summer
vârcolac • *n* vampire
varec • *n* kelp
vârf • *n* nose, peak, top
varg • *n* rod, twig
varg-de-aur • *n* goldenrod
vrgat • *adj* variegated
variabil • *adj* uncertain, unstable, variable
variabil • *n* variable
variaie • *n* variance, variation
variere • *n* variance, variation
varietate • *n* rainbow, variety
variol • *n* smallpox
vrsa • *v* spill, vomit
vrsat • *n* smallpox
vârst • *n* age
vârstnici • *adj* elderly
vârtej • *n* eddy, vortex
vârtos • *adj* hard, strong
vrui • *v* lime
varus • *n* clubfoot
varz • *n* cabbage

vas • *n* jar, ship, vessel
vasal • *n* liege
vâsc • *n* mistletoe
vâscos • *adj* viscous
vasilisc • *n* basilisk
vâsl • *n* oar
vâsli • *v* row
vast • *adj* prodigious
vtma • *v* harm, hurt, wound
vtmtor • *adj* deleterious, detrimental, noisome, noxious, pernicious
vatr • *n* fireplace
vtrai • *n* poker
vz • *n* eyesight
vaz • *n* vase
vâzdoag • *n* marigold
vzduh • *n* air
veac • *n* century
vece • *n* toilet
vechi • *adj* old
vechi-modic • *adj* old-fashioned
vechitur • *n* rag
vecin • *n* villain
vecintate • *n* neighborhood, proximity, vicinity
vedea • *v* behold, descry, see
vedenie • *n* vision
vedere • *n* eyesight, outlook, sight, vision, vista
vegetal • *adj* vegetable
vegetal • *n* vegetable
vegetarial • *adj* vegetarian
vegetarian • *n* vegetarian
vegetarian • *n* vegetarian
vegetarianism • *n* vegetarianism
vegetaie • *n* vegetation
veghe • *n* vigil
veghea • *v* watch
vehemen • *n* vehemence
vehicul • *n* vehicle
vel • *n* sail
velociped • *n* velocipede
ven • *n* vein
venerare • *n* praise, veneration
veneraie • *n* veneration
veni • *v* come
venin • *n* poison, venom
veninos • *adj* poisonous, venomous
venire • *n* arrival
ventil • *n* valve
ventila • *v* air
ventilare • *n* airing
ventilator • *n* fan
ventral • *adj* ventral
verand • *n* veranda
verb • *n* verb
verbal • *adj* verbal
verbin • *n* verbena
verde • *n* green, vert • *adj* green, verdant
verdict • *n* decision, sentence
verg • *n* yard
vergea • *n* rod
veridicitate • *n* trust, truth, truthfulness
verifica • *v* verify
verificare • *n* check
verig • *n* link
verigar • *n* buckthorn
vermeil • *adj* vermilion
vermillon • *n* cinnabar, vermilion
verosimilitate • *n* likelihood, verisimilitude
verosimilitudine • *n* verisimilitude
vers • *n* rhyme, verse
versatil • *adj* versatile
verso • *n* reverse, verso
vertebr • *n* vertebra
vertebral • *adj* vertebral
vertebrat • *n* vertebrate
vertical • *adj* stand-up, vertical
verziu • *adj* greenish
verzui • *adj* greenish
verzuriu • *adj* greenish
vesel • *adj* fun, glad
veselie • *n* cheerfulness, joy
vemânt • *n* garment, wrap
venicie • *n* age, eternity
vest • *n* west
vest • *n* waistcoat
veste • *n* communication
veted • *adj* sere
veteji • *v* wither
vetejit • *adj* withered
vesti • *v* announce
vestibul • *n* vestibule
vestic • *adj* western
vestigial • *adj* vestigial
vestigiu • *n* vestige
vestimentar • *adj* sartorial
vestitor • *n* herald
veteran • *n* old-timer
vetrice • *n* tansy
veveri • *n* squirrel
vexa • *v* spite
vexare • *n* vexation
vexaiune • *n* spite, vexation
vezic • *n* bladder
vezír • *n* vizier
via • *prep* via
via • *n* age, life
vibrafon • *n* vibraphone
vibrare • *n* vibration
vibris • *n* whisker
vicios • *adj* abandoned
vicisitudine • *n* vicissitude

viciu • *n* vice
viclean • *adj* cunning • *n* villain
viclenie • *n* cunning
viconte • *n* viscount
vicontes • *n* viscountess
victim • *n* victim
victorie • *n* triumph, victory, win
victorios • *adj* triumphant, victorious
vid • *adj* empty • *n* vacuum, void
video • *n* video
videocaset • *n* videocassette
vidr • *n* otter
vie • *n* vineyard
vier • *n* boar
vierme • *n* maggot, worm
viespe • *n* wasp
viezure • *n* badger
vigilent • *adj* argus-eyed, vigilant, watchful
vigilen • *n* vigilance
viguroas • *adj* vigorous
viguros • *adj* bouncing, stark, vigorous
viitor • *n* future • *adj* future
vijelie • *n* blast, storm
vil • *n* villa
vilbrochen • *n* crankshaft
vin • *n* wine
vin • *n* fault, guilt
vinars • *n* brandy
vinde • *v* hawk, sell
vindeca • *v* heal
vindector • *adj* medicinal
vindere • *n* sale
vindereu • *n* kestrel
vindicativ • *adj* vindictive
vintre • *n* belly
vioaie • *adj* quick
vioar • *n* violin
vioi • *adj* quick
vioiciune • *n* liveliness
viol • *n* rape
viol • *n* viola
viola • *v* rape, violate
violaceu • *adj* lavender
violare • *n* infringement
violent • *adj* quick, stark, violent
violen • *n* abuse, violence
violenta • *v* force
violet • *adj* lilac, violet • *n* violet
violet • *n* violet
violoncel • *n* cello
violonist • *n* violinist
viorea • *n* squill, viola, violet
viper • *n* viper
vipuc • *n* facing
virgin • *adj* pristine, virgin • *n* virgin
virgin • *n* virgin • *adj* virgin
virginitate • *n* virginity
virgul • *n* comma
viril • *adj* manly, masculine, virile
virilitate • *n* manliness, virility
virnan • *n* rue
virtute • *n* virtue
virulent • *adj* virulent
virus • *n* virus
virusologie • *n* virology
vis • *n* dream
visa • *v* dream
vistoare • *n* dreamer
vistor • *n* dreamer
viscozimetru • *n* viscometer
viin • *n* cherry
viin • *n* cherry
vi • *n* vine
vit • *n* beef
vitalitate • *n* liveliness
vitamin • *n* vitamin
vite • *n* cattle
viea • *n* calf, heifer
viteaz • *adj* valiant
viel • *adj* bovine • *n* calf, veal
vitez • *n* speed, velocity
vitezometru • *n* speedometer
viticultur • *n* viticulture
vitrin • *n* showcase
viu • *adj* alive, live
vivacitate • *n* liveliness
viz • *n* visa
vizibil • *adj* visible
vizibilitate • *n* visibility
vizionar • *adj* visionary
vizit • *n* call, visit
vizita • *v* call, visit
viziune • *n* appearance, vision
vizuin • *n* burrow, lair, warren
vlguit • *adj* emaciated, exhausted
vlstar • *n* brat
voal • *n* gauze, veil
vocabular • *n* vocabulary
vocal • *n* vowel
vocaie • *n* vocation
voce • *n* voice
voci • *n* voice
vociferare • *n* vociferation
vodc • *n* vodka
vog • *n* vogue
voi • *pron* you
voiaj • *n* journey, travel, trip
voievod • *n* voivode
voin • *n* will
voioie • *n* joy
volatil • *adj* volatile
volbur • *n* bindweed, eddy, whirlpool
volei • *n* volleyball

volt • *n* volt

voltaic • *adj* voltaic

voltaj • *n* voltage

voltmetru • *n* voltmeter

volum • *n* extent, volume

voluminos • *adj* bulk, bulky, voluminous

voluntar • *n* volunteer

voluntar • *n* volunteer

vomita • *v* vomit

vopsea • *n* paint

vopsi • *v* brush, paint

voracitate • *n* gluttony

vorb • *n* word

vorbre • *adj* loquacious, talkative

vorbi • *v* speak, talk • *n* utterance

vorbire • *n* language, speech, utterance, voice

vorbitoare • *n* speaker

vorbitor • *n* speaker

voronic • *n* horehound

vot • *n* voice, vote

vota • *v* vote

vrabie • *n* sparrow

vrac • *n* bulk

vraj • *n* enchantment, spell

vrajb • *n* faction

vrjeal • *n* bullshit

vrji • *v* bewitch, charm

vrjitoare • *n* hag, witch

vrjitor • *n* magician, witch, wizard

vrjma • *n* enemy

vrea • *v* choose, mean, want

vreme • *n* time, weather, while

vuietoare • *n* crowberry

vulcan • *n* volcano

vulcanologie • *n* volcanology

vulgar • *adj* explicit, vulgar

vulnerabilitate • *n* vulnerability

vulpan • *n* cub

vulpe • *n* fox

vulpi • *n* vixen

vulpoaic • *n* bitch, vixen

vultur • *n* eagle, vulture

vultur-pescar • *n* osprey

vultura • *n* eaglet

vulturel • *n* eaglet

W

walkirie • *n* valkyrie

wapiti • *n* wapiti

WC • *n* lavatory

weekend • *n* weekend

whisky • *n* whiskey

wolfram • *n* tungsten

wolframit • *n* wolframite

wombat • *n* wombat

X

xenofobie • *n* xenophobia

xenon • *n* xenon

xilem • *n* xylem

Y

yterbiu • *n* ytterbium

ytriu • *n* yttrium

yucca • *n* yucca

Z

za • *n* link

zbav • *n* lateness

zbovi • *v* stay

zcmânt • *n* deposit

zcea • *v* lie

zad • *n* larch

zahr • *n* sugar

zaharuri • *n* sugar

zâmbet • *n* smile

zâmbi • *v* smile

zambil • *n* hyacinth
zmisli • *v* generate
zmislire • *n* conception
zân • *n* bottom, fairy
zpceal • *n* bedlam
zpci • *v* daze, disarray, entangle, obfuscate
zpcitor • *adj* confusing
zpad • *n* snow
zar • *n* die
zar • *n* buttermilk
zri • *v* descry
zvoare • *n* latch
zvor • *n* latch, lock
zbârci • *v* wrinkle
zbârciog • *n* morel
zbate • *v* struggle
zbiera • *v* roar
zbor • *n* flight
zbucium • *n* torment
zburare • *n* flight
zburda • *v* caper
zdravn • *adj* healthy, sound
zdrean • *n* rag, tatter
zdrobire • *n* crushing
zeam • *n* gravy
zebr • *n* zebra
zece • *n* ten
zecime • *n* tenth
zeciuial • *n* tithe
zei • *n* goddess
zel • *n* zeal
zer • *n* whey
zero • *n* insect, zero
zestre • *n* dowry
zeu • *n* god
zgârcenie • *n* stinginess
zgârci • *n* gristle
zgârcit • *n* miser
zgâria • *v* bruise, claw, gall, scrape, scratch, skin
zgârie-nori • *n* skyscraper
zgomot • *n* fuss, noise, uproar
zi • *n* day, daytime
ziar • *n* daily, journal, newspaper
ziare • *n* newspaper
ziarist • *n* journalist
zibelin • *n* sable
zibet • *n* civet
zical • *n* saying
zice • *v* say
zid • *n* wall
zidar • *n* mason
zidi • *v* mason
zile • *n* days
zilnic • *adj* daily • *adv* daily
zimbru • *n* bison, wisent
zinc • *n* zinc
zircon • *n* zircon
zirconiu • *n* zirconium
ziua • *adv* days
zmeoaic • *n* giantess
zmeoaie • *n* giantess
zmeu • *n* dragon, kite
zmeur • *n* raspberry
zmeur • *n* raspberry
zmeuriu • *n* raspberry • *adj* raspberry
zodiac • *n* zodiac
zombi • *n* zombie
zon • *n* area
zoo • *n* zoo
zoolog • *n* zoologist
zoolog • *n* zoologist
zoologie • *n* zoology
zooma • *v* zoom
zooparc • *n* zoo
zori • *n* dawn
zvânta • *v* air
zvon • *n* rumor

Made in the USA
Middletown, DE
05 January 2024

47271998R00128